The Hudson Valley Dutch
and Their Houses

D1714954

The Hudson Valley Dutch and Their Houses

Harrison Frederick Meeske

Purple Mountain Press
Fleischmanns, New York

Dedicated to Mother and Father

The Hudson Valley Dutch and Their Houses
by Harrison Frederick Meeske
First editon 1998, reprinted with minor changes 2001

Published by Purple Mountain Press, Ltd.
1060 Main Street, P.O. Box 309, Fleischmanns, NY 12430-0309
845-254-4062 • 845-254-4476 (fax) • purple@catskill.net
http://www.catskill.net/purple

Library of Congress Cataloging-in-Publication Data

Meeske, Harrison Frederick, 1941-
    The Hudson Valley Dutch and their houses / Harrison Frederick
Meeske. -- 1st ed.
        p. cm.
    Includes bibliographic references and index.
    ISBN 0-916346-64-1 (pbk : alk. paper)
    1. Architecture, Domestic--Hudson River Valley (N.Y. and N.J.) 2.
Architecture, Dutch--Hudson River Valley (N.Y. and N.J.) 3.
Architecture, Colonial--Hudson River Valley (N.Y. and N.J.) I.
Title.
    NA7235.N72 H846 1998   98-44141
    728'.37'097473--ddc21   CIP

9 8 7 6 5 4 3 2

Manufactured in the United States of America. Printed on acid-free paper.

Cover, back cover and half-title page: Lykus Van Alen House, 1737, Kinderhook, New York. Photographs by Geoffrey Gross.

Frontispiece and title page: The Van Bergen Overmantel, attributed to John Heaten (working about 1730-1745), the only known contemporary representation of a Dutch farm (the Marten Van Bergen farm near Leeds in present-day Greene County). Courtesy of the New York State Historical Association.

Table of Contents

Preface

FOR THREE GENERATIONS our understanding of Dutch houses has been through two pioneering books: Helen Reynolds' *Dutch Houses in the Hudson Valley before 1776* (1929), and Rosalie Fellows Bailey's *Pre-Revolutionary Dutch Houses and Families in Northern New Jersey and Southern New York* (1936). Prepared under the auspices of the Holland Society of New York (avid member Franklin Roosevelt wrote the introductions), they emphasized the surviving houses and their history of ownership, a reflection of the Society members' interests at that time. All of us with an interest in this subject have dogeared copies of both volumes, a testament to their continued usefulness, despite going out of print in recent years.

Now for the first time since the 1930s, we have a new book on the subject of the Dutch and their houses. It differs from the previous books in important ways. It contains extensive background material on Netherlands history, New Netherland settlement, immigrant origins, land tenure, title and valuation, and regional types of Dutch houses. It describes the fundamentals of construction and materials, delving into details of building and use not done in other sources. It illustrates and describes both urban and rural Dutch houses, those long gone and those extant. It traces the evolution of Dutch house design. It is not just about architecture—there are sections on landscaping and the uses and furnishing of rooms. A remarkable range of sources (personal, published, and unpublished, both American and Dutch) have been utilized and carefully cited. Throughout, the author has obtained photographs to illustrate all the major points, especially helpful in the sections with technical descriptions. For those who value access to original documents, they are quoted extensively from diaries, letters, building contracts, inventories, accounts, wills, and colonial documents. This is a big book, the product of an uncommon mind brought to bear on a complex subject which has daunted others.

I first met Hank Meeske one day in 1994 at my Dutch house in Kinderhook. He was enjoying the fun of exploring for a Dutch home for himself, as I had done 25 years before. Inadvertently my house had started me down an unplanned career road resulting in exhibitions and publications on Dutch culture in America. Hank's questions about Dutch houses were not casual, but penetrating, so I set him off on the road to see other houses and other people. When he came back, it was obvious he had the makings of a useful publication. I encouraged him to think about a book. Such advise goes wisely unheeded by most, but much to my surprise, within a year he had a manuscript well on its way.

Educated at Long Island University and NYU, Hank Meeske has been productive over the years, sharpening his writing skills with several fiction and non-fiction manuscripts, including the story of Freydis Erikdatter, daughter of the Erik the Red of Viking fame, based on the Icelandic sagas. He is employed by the *New York Times*.

This work will serve well a wide range of interests, including those of Dutch house owners, scholar historians, historic preservationists, New York and New Jersey armchair historians, persons curious about the old structures they have seen along the road for years, and teachers ready for a fresh perspective on our visible past. I have learned a lot from this book I did not know.

Roderic H. Blackburn, Kinderhook, New York

Introduction

GROWING UP at my family's summer place in Dutchess County, New York, I developed an appreciation for colonial homes as an integral part of the memories of a happy childhood. Therefore, my interest in early houses fondly lingered even after we had sold our small eyebrow saltbox. Eventually my thoughts turned to acquiring a rural retreat of my own and I began a random viewing of available colonial era properties that attracted my interest in real estate advertisements. Eventually I began to focus on the distinctive Dutch houses of the Hudson Valley, as they seemed to offer an intriguing variation on the traditional theme. Although at the start I had no especial familiarity with the subject, I eventually saw many examples of the style and came to recognize salient features identifying variations within the *genre*. To better familiarize myself with the subject I started to do some research in the available literature and discovered that there was a need for more specific material suitable for the history buff, home owner, and prospective restorer.

My growing interest in Dutch houses led to an introduction to Roderic Blackburn, who is widely recognized as an authority on the subject of Dutch colonial culture in New York and is the author of *Remembrance of Patria*, a social history of the Dutch in the Hudson Valley, and many other works in the field. He suggested that I delve deeper into the topic and consider writing the book that I had been seeking. Initially I took up the suggestion half seriously and then gradually became more committed to the project. As my knowledge increased, I pursued the topic in the less readily available archives and literature, contacted and met with various authorities, logged hours and miles in the field inspecting buildings, and traveled to the Netherlands to view the architectural heritage at its source.

As a tyro, I was obliged to seek out those people who have dedicated entire careers to the subject of Dutch colonial houses in academic research and physical restoration. Therefore, while having learned a lot, I still consider myself merely the Boswell to those professionals. I fully accept the onus for whatever may prove erroneous in the following material and the reader may rest assured that any brilliance contained herein must be attributed to those who were my sources. Therefore, I wish to acknowledge their expertise and express my thanks for their unstinting assistance.

First of all, I must thank Roderic Blackburn. Without his encouragment the book would never have been attempted and without his most generous contributions in time, introductions, technical assistance, and photographic material the manuscript probably would never have been completed. William McMillen of the Historic Richmond Town Restoration in Staten Island also gave unstintingly both time and expertise during the research phase of the project. Providing clear answers at every stage, he suffered through both initially halting questions and later more detailed demands. Donald Carpentier, who teaches restoration and has his own village of early buildings, provided insights into many specifically upper-valley Dutch regional building techniques. He highlighted the diversity within the Dutch colonial experience and he was one of the first to make me aware of the wider European cultural zone of heritage that influenced early New York home builders. Steve Levine, who collects early Dutch homes as others collect stamps, generously showed me through several of his houses and enabled me to gain access to many more houses I would otherwise have been unable to inspect. Greg Huber, researcher and author of several works on Dutch barns, showed me a number of interesting houses in New Jersey and noted the fundimental similarities in the practices of Dutch builders of both houses and barns in the colonial period.

When I traveled to the Netherlands seeking early prototypes in *patria* for colonial structures, J. Schipper, the former director of restoration at the Zaanse Schans Outdoor Museum, was most generous with his time and expertise; and E. van Olst, the Director of the Institute for Historic Farms Research, Arnhem, Netherlands, provided material from ongoing fieldwork conducted into early Dutch farmsteads. B. A. Beydals showed me through her seventeenth-century house in Amsterdam that has been restored by Henk J. Zantkuyl, Director of Municipal Restoration for the city of Amsterdam.

Robert Thill, at the Brooklyn Museum of Art, assisted me in reviewing material on Dutch culture related to the recreations of the Schenck houses displayed at the museum and generously provided materials from the Museum's Decorative Arts Department collection. Similarly, Alan Moscowitz researched and provided materials from the collections at Historic Hudson Valley as did Paul Dewe-Mathews at the DeWint House Museum in Tappan, and Dr. Mildred DeRiggi at the Hofstra University Research Library who made available information concerning the Dutch settlements on Long Island. In addition, I would like to thank the many other people not specifically named who were so helpful in the course of the project for providing materials or showing me to and through the many houses inspected in the course of this project.

Special thanks go to Geoffrey Gross for the cover picture and several others. I eagerly await his own book of photographs of American Dutch houses.

I urge anyone interested in the subject to contact and avail themselves of the collections of the Holland American Society Library in Manhattan. Similarly, extensive reference material on the subject that has become available resulting from the New Netherland Project of the New York State Library in Albany.

In the text some emphasis has been placed on the history and origins of the Dutch in the Hudson Valley as well as the relationship of the early buildings to the political and cultural environment from which they sprang because I believe it is essential that people and places be seen in context. The actual Dutch colonial period was limited to the years 1609 to 1673, however, the full blossoming of the Dutch culture in America occurred in the last quarter of the seventeenth century and first half of the eighteenth century. The Dutch heritage continued to be a significant factor in the upper Hudson Valley region through the end of the colonial period in 1776, and certainly the overwhelming majority of extant Dutch colonial structures and artifacts are from the eighteenth century. Nevertheless, the influence of the Dutch Reformed Church, the Dutch language and culture, and the distinctive Dutch architectural practices persisted in many areas well into the nineteenth century and contributed many of those elements that distinguish Hudson Valley culture to this day. Therefore, before the physical evidence has been further eroded, it is important that we record and acknowledge this unique and fundamental part of our regional and national heritage.

Chapter I

Historic Background

HENRY HUDSON sailed from the island of Texel, on the North Sea coast of the Netherlands, on April 16, 1609. His plan was to sail north and east of Norway and via Arctic waters around Siberia in search of a Northeast Passage to Japan and China. Hudson, an Englishman, had made his first voyage of exploration to the north in 1607 for the English Moscovy Company. He now sailed in the employ of the VOC, the *Vereenigde Oostindische Compagnie* (Dutch East India Company). Departing from the Netherlands, he sailed north to the Barents Sea, then made heading east and north for the island of Novaya Zemlya. West of Novaya Zemlya Hudson encountered impassable ice. Further progress blocked, he faced a choice, either return to report the failure or try an alternative route. He decided to turn his tiny vessel, *de Halve Maen*, a yacht only fifty-eight feet long and of eighty tons burden,[1] and sail west and south. In July 1609 *de Halve Maen* made landfall at Newfoundland. Hudson then coasted the Eastern Seaboard of North America in a southerly direction. On the third of September *de Halve Maen* hove to off Sandy Hook.

On September 12, 1609, Hudson passed between Staten Island and Long Island through the Narrows and entered a great bay. He landed on the small island known to the inhabitants as "Manahatin" and conducted some minor trading with the natives. After exploring the surrounding waters, he headed *de Halve Maen* north into the tidal surge that issued from towering highlands. He was still in hopes of discovering a passage to Asia through the North American landmass, as the waters of the passage were from seventy percent to ninety percent as salty as the sea. However, as he sailed north the waters began to freshen, and it soon became apparent that it was indeed a river and not a strait. Near the location of present day Newburgh, the waters no longer even tasted of salt; nevertheless, Henry Hudson continued exploring the valley and sounding the waters of the river that was to one day bear his name.

The imprint of Hudson, and subsequent Dutch navigators upon the river, can be recognized in the names given to sailing courses and reaches. The Long Reach, a ten-mile stretch from New Hamburgh north to Hyde Park, bears the Dutch name *Lange Rak*. *Kromme Elleboog* is today's Crum Elbow, or the Crooked Elbow, where the river bends. *Tappan Zee* is the broad point in the river between Westchester and Rockland Counties. On the west shore of the Hudson at Poughkeepsie is *Juffrouw's Hoeck* (the Madam's Point); and *de Dans Kammer* (the Dance Chamber) is located at New Hamburg.[2]

At a point generally identified as present-day Stuyvesant Landing, just below the city of Albany, where Hudson named a stream Kinderhook for the children swimming there, the waters became shallow, and he realized *de Halve Maen* was endangered by sandbars. He decided to sail no farther upstream and sent a small boat north to the Albany area or just beyond, before retracing the voyage downstream. During the voyage, Hudson conducted a brisk and profitable trade with the inhabitants: The Indians were offered unimagined, and immediately desired, European manufactures in the form of iron hatchets, knives, and cooking utensils, as well as the previously unknown luxury of woven duffel cloth. The Europeans received a bounty of rich furs in return. In the process the newcomers introduced the natives to two other previously unknown commodities—liquor and guns. The stage had been set for future contacts and a basis established for the profitable exchange of mutually desired goods.

On his return to Europe, Hudson landed at Dartmouth, England. *De Halve Maen* was detained and Hudson was arrested. The government of King James I looked upon Hudson's commission in the Dutch service as a violation of English national interests. In 1497 and 1498, John and Sebastian Cabot had sailed from England in the service of King Henry VII. They were the first Europeans to report sighting the North American mainland, and they claimed all the territory for England. Subsequently, the Italian explorer Giovanni da Verrazzano arrived on April 17, 1524, off the Hudson River estuary and anchored in the passage later known as the Narrows. Verrazzano sailed his hundred-ton caravel *Dauphine* into the upper bay, which he named Santa Margarita. Landing on Manhattan Island he claimed the land for the King of France. Verrazzano bestowed upon it the designation of "Angoulême" in honor of Marguerite Angoulême the sister of his sponsor Francis I.[3] The reports of the voyage were never followed up by the French, whose efforts were centered farther north. It could be said that the French actions were *de facto* recognition of the English title. Although a scattering of traders may have entered the bay, there was virtually no recorded exploratory activity in the immediate region between 1524 and 1609.

In established European legal terms Hudson had found a virgin territory unoccupied by the subjects of any Christian king. His claim in the name of the VOC was technically valid based upon a principle first set down in 1580 by England's Queen Elizabeth I asserting the right of "discovery and occupation," and specifically denied and rejected the generalized Spanish claims to all of North America based upon discovery alone. Her purpose was to assert the legitimacy of English settlement in Virginia and disallow the Spanish assertions to ownership to the entire Western Hemisphere by discovery alone. The Spanish pretension was based upon the actions of Pope Alexander VI. In 1493 Alexander saw fit to divide between Spain and Portugal and he most generously bestowed upon the two Catholic

monarchies hegemony over all non-Christian peoples of the world.
Two bulls entitled *Eximiae devotionis* and *Inter caetere* established a
Papal Line of Demarcation between the exploration claims of the two
Iberian kingdoms. The line was drawn from the North Pole to the
South Pole one hundred leagues west of the Azores and Cape Verde
Islands at longitude thirty-eight degrees west. The line was adjusted
and confirmed by the Treaty of Tordesillas in 1494, at longitude
forty-six degrees west. Therefore, even in terms of English legal
precedent, the Royal Charters of 1606, given to the London Company and to the Plymouth Company granting them overlapping
claims to all of the coastline from Chesapeake Bay to the Saint
Lawrence River, were excessive in their pretensions. Naturally, the
land ownership claims by the Native American inhabitants were
never seriously considered. The legal arguments concerning possession were to continue into the second half of the eighteenth century
and then were only to be resolved by force of arms.

The VOC protested and petitioned for the release of the ship,
crew, and captain. Henry Hudson never met his Dutch employers
again. The following year he was off on another voyage, once again
in the employ of the English. He died, cast away by members of his
own crew, in the area subsequently named Hudson's Bay. Although
Hudson never reported to the company in person, he sent a letter
outlining his discoveries. News of Hudson's voyage, the journals of
de Halve Maen's mate, Robert Juet, and the crew's word of mouth
recountings found an eager audience in the Netherlands. Johannes de
Laet, a widely read Dutch publicist, wrote an adventure travel series
entitled *Nieuwe Wereldt ofte beschrijvinghe van West-Indien* (*New
World or Descriptions of the West Indies*). De Laet popularized Hudson's voyage and extolled the wonders of the newly discovered lands
that soon came to be known as New Netherland.[4] The timing was
propitious.

The Dutch were triumphantly emerging from the long hard
struggle for independence from Spanish political and religious tyr-
anny. The signing of the Twelve Year's Truce in 1606 had suspended
the conflict with Spain. A glorious period, known as the Golden Age,
had begun. It was a time of military, financial, and cultural achievements that were to make the Netherlands a European world power

in the first half of the seventeenth century. The Dutch East India Company declared a dividend of 329 percent only months before Hudson's discoveries became known. The example set by the fabulous success of the VOC was an incentive to investors. However, it was only one part of a major rise in Dutch commercial activity at this time. A national effort enabled Dutch merchant seamen to dominate the lucrative carrying trade that transported goods by ship from port to port, encompassing coastal Europe from the Baltic to the Mediterranean, and the accumulated profits provided ready money for new investment. In addition, the carrying trade and a far-ranging fishing fleet contributed both experienced seamen and practical navigational skills that enabled the Dutch to implement bold plans for trade on a global scale.

When the directors of the Dutch East India Company hesitated to develop the new territory's potential, independent traders moved in to fill the vacuum. In 1611 Arnout Vogel, a south Netherlands Lutheran, joined in partnership with the brothers Leonard and Francoys Pelgrom, who were fellow congregants and refugees from Spanish oppression. They sent the ship *St. Peter* to the area of Hudson's discoveries. Several voyages followed. In 1612 Vogel sponsored the sailing of the ship *Fortune* captained by Adriaen Block. While Block was trading with the Indians, competition arrived from the Fatherland. The new ship was the *Jonge Tobias*, out of the port of Monnikendam, captained by Thijs Volckertsz Mossel. The newcomers were sponsored by a Dutch merchant named Hans Claesz. The Indians, who were sharp traders, quickly demanded more for their pelts. The competitive bidding by the Dutch immediately made the price of furs rise sharply at the source. With an increase in the number of traders importing furs to the Netherlands concern mounted that flooding the market would depress the price of the pelts and cut deeply into profits. On the vessels' return to the Netherlands, a legal dispute erupted between the principals.[5] The Vogle group sought to eliminate the intrusion of the independent traders as quickly as possible. To that end, Vogel enlisted a fellow Lutheran merchant with greater influence named Lambert Van Tweenhuysen. The feud between the competitors soon involved a widening circle of interests in Amsterdam. Even Prince Maurice of Orange who, as *stadholder*, was the leading citizen of the Dutch Republic soon became a party in the dispute.

In 1613 Vogel's group, now headed by Van Tweenhuysen, sent out two ships, the *Fortuyn* and the *Tijger*. Hans Claesz prepared to send one, the *Nachtegael*. Negotiations between the parties failed to resolve the issues.[6] Both groups had armed their ships with additional cannons and entered legal actions against the competition before sailing from the Netherlands. In New Netherland the traders resumed competitive bidding for the Indians' furs. Captain Adraien Block proposed a working solution to share the trading. Then things happened. The agreement broke down. The *Tijger* burned to the water line, a man was shot, the *Nachtegael* was seized by the *Tijger*'s mutinous crew, Block was abandoned ashore, and the crew of the *Tijger* took off on a brief (and probably piratical) voyage to the West Indies in the commandeered *Nachtegael*. A few months later the *Nachtegael* returned to the Hudson Valley, but the mutineers sailed off again, eventually abandoning the vessel in Ireland. The reported details are confusing. At that point, two new ships of competitors arrived in the Hudson River—the *Vos*, out of Amsterdam, and the *Fortuyn*, from Hoorn. Arriving too late in the season to trade, the newcomers demanded an equal share of the furs traded by Block in exchange for a return passage to the Fatherland.[7]

On arrival home in Amsterdam all the parties immediately headed to the courts once more. In the legal turmoil that ensued, the provincial governments became involved. As each province sought advantage for their local merchants, a political wrangle inflamed the issues. The altercations were only resolved in October 1614 when the central governing body, the States General, issued a "Grant of Exclusive Trade" to a chartered monopoly named the New Netherland Company.[8] A new set of players from Amsterdam took control. Foremost among the company's directors were Gerrit Jacobsz Witssen, his brother Jonas Witssen, and their associate, named Simon Morrissen. These new men combined powerful political, mercantile, and insurance interests with extensive finances, ships, and warehouses at their command. Vogel, Van Tweenhuysen, and their partners became relatively minor players. The new company prepared to brush aside all opposition. Then, in what was becoming a standard situation, it was immediately engaged in challenges and litigation. Merchants who had been excluded from the new company protested the monopoly. The managers were obliged to resolve these issues by buying off the plaintiffs.

When the New Netherland Company got down to the business of fur trading, it established a permanent trading post named Fort Nassau. Located within the present Port of Albany, at the head of navigation, the "factory" was well situated for the fur trade on the North (Hudson) River. Standing far upstream, it was a site easily defended from European naval assault, and yet very accessible to the interior sources of the fur trade. It was a tenuous position nevertheless. Overland to the north, the company's claims abutted the French in Canada. Furthermore, in the three years of its life the company undertook exploratory missions to enlarge their territory into the South (Delaware) River, the Jersey shoreline, Long Island, and the Fresh (Connecticut) River. These extended investigations into the unsettled territory were conducted primarily by Cornelius Hendrickson and Cornelius Jacobsen Mey.[9] These Dutch explorations carved a wedge of territory between the lands claimed and chartered by the English.

The New Netherland Company's charter expired in 1618, however, the partners conducted trading operations in the Hudson Valley into the 1620s. They had a workable system. A few outposts at key locations tapped the supply of furs. The charter protected the merchants from outside competition. There were no permanent settlers seeking to obtain Indian land. Situations that could disrupt amiable relations essential to a profitable trading environment were avoided. Nevertheless, the venture was not permitted to continue. Powerful forces in the Netherlands were at work to establish a new company that would supersede all previous chartered operations, put an end to all private trading, and create a western equivalent to the VOC to exploit the Western Hemisphere.

In 1621 the Twelve Year's Truce ran out. The major powers of Europe were already embroiled in the Thirty Years' War. Fighting soon resumed in the Low Countries. The Spanish initiated a series of sieges in an attempt to conquer the Dutch Republic and regain the seven "lost" provinces that comprise the "United Provinces of the

Netherlands." Spain would not formally recognize Dutch independence until after the war ended in 1648. The Dutch were prepared to resist, ever eager to settle old scores. Traditions, dating to the previous century, glorified the exploits of the "Sea Dogs." These Dutch contemporaries of the English sea rovers Sir Francis Drake and Martin Frobisher became legendary by straddling the fine line between piracy and patriotic swashbuckling. They became rich and famous sacking Spanish settlements, capturing Spain's treasure fleets, carrying the war home to the heart of the Spanish Empire in the Western Hemisphere, and boldly taking away the treasures that the Spanish had looted from their American colonies. The idea of getting rich while financing the Dutch war effort with Spanish gold had the aura of Divine justice and Divine retribution. In this heady atmosphere, the founding of the Westindisch Compagnie (Dutch West India Company) was less a commercial venture to develop trade and more a license to go treasure hunting on the "Spanish Main."

From the start the Dutch West India Company focused on the territory frequently referred to as "beyond the line" (of Papal Demarcation) in the American holdings of the then-temporarily united Iberian crowns of Spain and Portugal. The major concern to the directors was a series of get-rich-quick schemes. These began in 1624 with the attempt to conquer the Brazilian stronghold of Soa Salvador de Bahia de Todos os Santos. It was a fiasco. A second invasion fleet was dispatched. In 1626 the Dutch were able to establish a colony in Brazil which they called New Holland. It never worked. The company's one real moment of profit and glory occurred in 1628. That year Admiral Piet Heyn captured the Spanish treasure fleet and brought home loot estimated to be worth 11.5 million florins. The sum was almost equal to the entire original capital subscription that established the company in 1621. Ongoing imperial adventures in Brazil proved to be an unmitigated disaster, a hemorrhaging sore that sapped the company's energy and attention, wasting both the capitalization funds and the treasures captured by Heyn. Privateering raids into the Caribbean, the establishment of a profitable West African slave trade, even the sale of territory on the Delaware River to the City of Amsterdam to create the colony of New Amstel in 1656 for 700,000 guilders could not offset the Brazilian losses.

In 1654 the company finally abandoned the New Holland adventure. The thirty-year struggle had brought the company to the brink of financial collapse. The New Holland losses probably sealed the fate of New Netherland as well. West India stock's prices dropped dramatically. Stock once quoted at 206 percent of the issue price dropped to 28 percent of original value in 1650 and was down to 11 percent by 1661.[10] Commercial activity by the company had almost come to a halt prior to the English takeover of New Netherland in 1664. The experience pointed up a major flaw in the European concept of the chartered trading company monopoly. Whereas a nation state has the obligation to govern territory in the nation's interests at all costs, a trading company's primary obligation is to make a profit for the stockholders at the least expense.

When the States General authorized publication of the charter of the Dutch West India Company on July 7, 1621, New Netherland was not even mentioned by name. From the start the North American territory was a peripheral concern to the directors of the company. Despite an initial capitalization of 7.5 million guilders, virtually nothing was allocated to the trading posts on the North River. As early as 1624 the directors of the Dutch West India Company (called the *Heeren XIX* or the College of the Nineteen and addressed by the somewhat bumptious title of "High Mightinesses") chose to delegate management of the affairs of New Netherland to the company division known as the Amsterdam Chamber. The corporation was divided into five "chambers" with headquarters in the individual provincial capitals.[11] The leading province was Holland and its capital was Amsterdam. The Amsterdam merchants, who had from the start been most active in the affairs of New Netherland, continued to see to the operations of the colony until its eventual loss to the English. The Amsterdam Chamber delegated actual governing of New Netherland to a committee called the New Netherland Commission. The commission was in turn dominated by a small circle of business associates who demonstrated the keenest interest in developments in the Hudson Valley.

The founding of the Dutch West India Company and increased Dutch activity in the Hudson Valley led to rising English concern. In February 1622 the English ambassador to The Hague, Sir Dudley

Carleton, reasserted English rights by prior discovery. Carleton alleged that English settlement at James Town extended north across the virgin wilderness as the "precincts of Virginia" and abutted the territory of the Plymouth Company. The Dutch West India Company re-stated the Dutch position of 1609: Claims based upon first discovery alone were invalid and English explorations in the contested territory had never been followed up by permanent settlement or continuous occupation. Furthermore the Hudson Valley was far from the "precincts" of Virginia. In the years following 1609 the English had not ventured into the Dutch holdings on a consistent basis, nor had they attempted to assert their claim, whereas the Dutch had established "factories" to conduct trade on a regular basis. The company had firmly stated the argument for its continued hold on the Hudson Valley, but had also identified a weakness in its position: There were virtually no colonists in New Netherland. The experience of the New Netherland Company had shown that fur trading and colonization are mutually exclusive activities. Nevertheless, once the Dutch West India Company had staked the legitimacy of its title on the basis of settlement, it needed to introduce permanent settlers to help validate Dutch claims in the entire area from the Delaware River to the Connecticut River valleys.

The company's first voyage to its new holdings on the Hudson had been dispatched in Fall 1623 when they sent the *Mackereel* to trade in North America. The Mackereel was in the East River when the *Unity* and the *Nieu Nederlandt* arrived from Amsterdam with the company's first group of colonists early in 1624.[12] Previous offers by volunteers to settle in the area had been rejected by the directors of the Dutch West India Company. Under pressure, the company selected a group of thirty Walloon families to settle in the colony. These French speaking Calvinist refugees from Spanish aggression in the southern Netherlands were to be landed at strategic sites chosen by the company's home office. Serving at the company's interest, the settlers were sent to points clearly marking claims rather than to areas chosen for easy settlement. One party was deposited on the Delaware River, another on the Connecticut River. Two other groups were planted on the North River—one at Fort Orange; another at the tip of Manhattan Island, where the first European child, Jean Vigne, was born in one of the hastily built huts of the new settlement.[13]

The first Director-General, Wilhelm Verhulst, was replaced by Peter Minuit a Huguenot who was born in the French city of Cleves. Minuit arrived in May 1626 aboard the *Little Sea-Mew (Meewtje)*. That summer Minuit formally legalized the settlement. It was now a cluster of thirty-six dwellings huddled around a small fort with six stone buildings with reed thatched roofs.[14] Apparently to the Indians' complete satisfaction, Minuit purchased unimproved Manhattan Island real estate for the then generous sum of 60 guilders worth of greatly desired European trade goods. By 1628 some 270 colonists lived around Pearl Street, which was then at the tip of Manhattan Island, in a village of some thirty houses and a scattering of huts. Eight families settled up river at Fort Orange. From the beginning, Dutch settlers typically lived in scattered homesteads which proved difficult to defend and fatal when troubles erupted with Native Americans. The Fort Orange settlers were evacuated to Manhattan between 1626 and 1628 when a war broke out between the Algonquian Mohican and the Iroquoian Mohawk Indians. Many of the Walloon families gave up the effort to settle and drifted back to the Netherlands at that time. When the Indian war ended, several families moved back to Fort Orange. A large contingent of settlers, this time Dutch as well as Walloons, arrived the following year when the colony became more secure. However, the colony remained basically two small and widely separated settlements, with a scattering of isolated homesteads, to the end. As late as the 1660s, Director Stuyvesant had to order settlers at Esopus to fortify their settlements.

In 1633 Wouter Van Twiller arrived as Director-General. A nephew of Kiliaen Van Rensselaer, Van Twiller served between 1633 and 1638. He gave evidence of being an alcoholic, but he probably was not as incompetent as the figure ridiculed in Washington Irving's tales of early New York. Van Twiller was smart enough to further his uncle's interests in developing Rensselaerswyck, and clever enough to grant himself extensive tracts of company land. Following his main priorities as director, Van Twiller presided over a fur trade that increased from 6,500 to 7,500 pelts a year shipped from New Netherland. And, he kept the peace and cultivated Indian relations in the colony. In later years, the Indians fondly recalled Van Twiller as a fair and just man. During troubles with Van Twiller's successor Director-General Williem Kieft the Indians were reported to have chanted in a call for justice: "Wouter, Wouter."[15] Early attention to Indian affairs were closely attended to by the secretary of the colony, Cornelius Van Tienhoven, and the influential settlers David De Vries and Adriaen Van der Donck. These men won the respect and trust of most of the Valley inhabitants with their efforts to keep the trade prosperous by maintaining a good neighbor policy.

Early Indian relations involved only the Algonquin tribes of the Hudson Valley. In winter of 1634-1635 additional contact was established with the Iroquois. In that year Harmen Van den Bogart and two other men were sent from Fort Orange to meet with an Iroquois council at one of the Oneida villages a hundred miles up the Mohawk River. The contact reinforced the long-lasting partnership between the Iroquois and the Dutch known as the "chain of friendship." The "chain" outlasted the Dutch era and was maintained by the English Crown through the Revolutionary War.[16] Maintaining the bond of friendship was assisted by the fact that the Iroquois lived at locations remote from the early Dutch settlements. Opportunities for friction were kept to a minimum. The company's officers were prepared to trade guns and ammunition to the Iroquois for furs, whereas they never countenanced the sale of weapons to the Algonquian tribes. Private traders were never legally permitted to sell any guns to the Indians, although enforcement of the laws was intermittent and difficult and many of the Alonquian tribes in the New Amsterdam area had become "dangerously" armed by the 1640s. Empowered with a near monopoly of the latest weaponry, the Iroquois soon became the most feared and respected of all Indians. In later years the Iroquois confederation of tribes known as the Five Nations was essential to the Dutch for access to the fur trade with inland tribes. The Iroquois' strategic location and feared reputation was an effective buffer between the Hudson River settlements and the French and their Indian allies to the north.

In 1638 William Kieft replaced Van Twiller. The new governor avoided conflict with the Iroquois, but Kieft was always ready to clash with the Algonquian tribes as tensions developed with the settlers in the lower Valley. Dutch livestock wandered among the unfenced Indian crops; the Indians slaughtered the "trespassing" cows and hogs for food; and a *kultur kampf* developed where the two peoples came into frequent contact. Insensitivity and heavy-handed methods under Governor Kieft exacerbated the situation. In 1639 he provoked unrest when he attempted to levy taxes on the Indians. In 1641 a Dutch farmer named Claes Swits, called *rademaker* (wheelwright), was murdered without apparent provocation. Kieft's responses were inept. Problems developed. The Governor ordered a raid of reprisal in March 1642. The Dutch managed to get lost in the woods. Nobody was hurt, but two abandoned villages of Wecquaesgeeks and Wappingers were burned and the matter left hard feelings on both sides. The next year the same tribes sought shelter among the Dutch from Iroquois raids. In February 1643 Kieft took the opportunity to slaughter the Indian refugees. The Indians struck back at isolated Dutch farmers in New Jersey, Long Island, and Westchester. Unaware and unwarned, the *boeren* were surprised and massacred. [17] The settlers called for revenge. War erupted in 1643. Two raids by the Dutch in the winter of 1644 broke the Indians resistance. In 1645 peace finally was restored but the colony was in turmoil. The colonists held Kieft responsible. Complaints and pleas for Kieft's recall were sent to the company; two attempts to murder the discredited governor failed. [18] His replacement arrived in 1647.

The new Director-General, Pieter Stuyvesant, was a professional soldier and a strict Reformed Church congregant who had previously served the company as governor of Curacao. He was a mixed blessing who brought both stability and repression to the colony. When he arrived, Stuyvesant was young, arrogant, and tyrannical. With the passage of the years he became older but mellowed little. A moody and argumentative bully, Stuyvesant went out of his way to create problems with the Lutherans, Quakers, and Jews. Each episode resulted in official censure. However, he was an honest, conscientious, and diligent representative of the company, neither a Van Twiller nor a Kieft. Faced with the unceasing expansionism and arrogance of the English—Cromwell, Crown, and colonies—Stuyvesant demonstrated a temperance and restraint that he seldom employed in dealings with his own colonists. In 1650 the Director-

General pragmatically settled border conflicts by abandoning Dutch claims and outposts on the Connecticut River and surrendering the eastern half of Long Island to the English in the Treaty of Hartford. He avoided embroiling the colony in the First Anglo-Dutch War of 1652 to 1654, but in 1656 the Swedes' tiny settlement on the Delaware River, which had grown to three forts and 400 colonists, became more than a minor distraction. The bellicose governor could no longer avoid the temptation to invade and conquer the tiny, irritating, and vulnerable colony of New Sweden. Stuyvesant barely enjoyed his triumph, however, before he was hurriedly recalled from the Delaware by fresh and unanticipated Indian troubles on the Hudson. He returned and firmly put down the tribes in the fighting known as the Peach Tree War. In the 1660s Stuyvesant permitted frictions to get out of hand between settlers and Indians at present-day Kingston, resulting in the bloody Esopus Wars of 1659-1660 and 1663. In the north of his domain Stuyvesant followed his predecessors' wise precedent and avoided conflict with the Iroquois. He kept them loyal and friendly by continuing to supply them with guns and ammunition and presents of trade goods.

Beginning in the 1640s, the English became a growing menace to New Netherland. Heading up a series of confrontations with the Dutch, the small English colony of New Haven joined with its larger English neighbor of Connecticut in an attempt to wrest control of eastern Long Island and the lower Hudson Valley from the company. The goals of New Haven paralleled the objectives of Cromwell and then, following the Restoration in 1688, King Charles II's brother James, Duke of York. Stuyvesant managed to play for time. He diplomatically avoided confrontation in the face of relentless English pressure and overwhelming strength. Then with certain knowledge of failed diplomacy and an impending attack, the Dutch frantically repaired and expanded their defenses as a last desperate measure. It was too late, although as Washington Irving wrote, every man busied himself mightily "putting things in confusion, and assisting the general uproar."[19] On September 1, 1664, the invaders arrived. The English naval force commanded by Richard Nicolls consisted of three men-of-war and a troop transport sailed into the harbor. Demands were made to surrender. Generous terms were offered to the settlers.

The governor reportedly assumed a dramatic pose on the bastion of his decaying fort but it was all over. Stuyvesant could only growl and glare impotently at the English warships until he was led away and escorted home in the hands of solicitous friends.[20] Without firing a shot the Director-General was obliged to surrender the Fort and City of New Amsterdam to the Duke of York's representatives on September 8, 1664. The Duke's actions anticipated the Second Anglo-Dutch War of 1665-1667, a technicality of little importance to James, the Duke of York, or his brother Charles II. Stuyvesant returned briefly to the Netherlands to explain the loss of the colony to the company and to the States General. Defeated and retired, Stuyvesant returned home to his *bouwere* on Manhattan and lived out his life as a private citizen in the English colony of New York.

In the Third Anglo-Dutch War of 1672-1674 the Dutch returned. In 1673 Cornelis Evertsen commanded an invasion that re-took the colony. Evertsen renamed the city New Orange in honor of the principal family of the Netherlands. The Dutch remained for fifteen months but finally were evicted by the terms of the Treaty of Westminster. The Glorious Revolution in 1688 brought the final Dutch reprise. James II's Protestant daughter Mary had married William, Prince of Orange. They ascended to the English throne, and an Anglo-Dutch dual monarchy tenuously renewed a symbolic Dutch tie which lasted until the death of William III in 1702.

Map of Dutch and English Land Grants 1629 - 1708

Legend:

1   Mohawk Patent: 1697
2   Kayaderossa Patent: 1704
3   Saratoga Patent: 1684
4   Hoosic Patent: 1688
5   Schenectady Patent: 1661
6   De Halve Maen: 1664
7   Schaghticoke: 1686
8   Albany: 1686
9   Rensselaerswyck Patroonship: 1629
    Rensselaer Manor: 1685
10 Coeyman's Patent: 1673
11 Debruyn Patent: 1688
12 Nuttenhook: 1667
13 Kinderhook: 1686
14 Bronck's Patent: 1662 (Confirmed 1667; re-patented 1687)
15 Lunenberg: 1667
16 Catskill Patent: 1674 (Purchase from Indians 1684; confirmed 1688)
17 Loveridge Patent: 1667. Originally Thummissen: 1653 (Sold several times and re-patented. Repurchased from Indians 1682; re-patented 1686)
18 Claverack: 1704 (Purchased and originally a part of Rensselaerswyck: 1649-1708)
19 Van Hoesen Patent: 1665 (Purchased from Van Rensselaer's Claverack Tract in 1664)
20 Livingston Manor: 1686
21 Hardenburgh Patent: 1708 (Not purchased from Indians)
22 Esopus: 1653 (Stuyvesant established the independent Village of Wiltwyck: 1662; renamed Kingston: 1669)
23 Fox Hall Manor: 1672 (Added to Kingston in 1787)
24 New Paltz: 1677

25 Schuyler Patent: 1688 (Two sections: 25A at Red Hook and 25B at Poughkeepsie)
26 Little Nine Partners Patent: 1706
27 Great Nine Partners Patent: 1697
28 Rhinebeck Patent: 1697
29 Aertson-Roosa-Elton/Kip Patent: 1688 (Purchased 1686)
30 Fauconnier Patent: 1705
31 Beekman Patent: 1703
32 Poughkeepsie Patent: 1697
33 Rombout Patent: 1685
34 Pawling Patent: 1689 (Confirmed 1696)
35 Philipse's Highland Patent: 1686 (Present-day Putnam County)
36 Van Cortlandt Manor: 1697
37 Philipsburgh Manor: 1693 (Purchased 1672-1692)
38 Colon Donck/Philipsburgh Manor: 1639. (Purchased from Indians in 1639; reconfirmed 1666)
39 Pavonia: 1630
40 Long Island Towns (Five Dutch towns, all in present-day Brooklyn): 39A Brooklyn 1646/1657; 39B Midwout (Flatbush) 1651; 39C New Utrecht 1657; 39D Bushwyck 1661; 39E New Amersfoort (Flatlands) 1667
41 Staten Island: 1630 (Originally a part of Pavonia); Dutch West India Company: 1635; DeVries: 1636, massacred; Melyn: 1642; Bentley Manor (Southern Half): 1687/Castleton Manor (Northern Half): 1687

Courtesy of R. H. Blackburn.

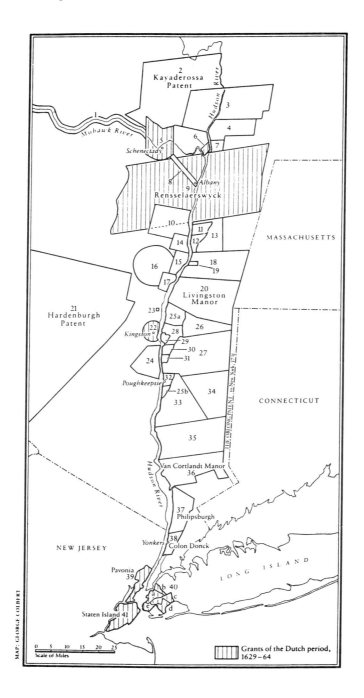

2
Kayaderossa
Patent

3

Hudson River

1

4

Mohawk River

5

6

7

Schenectady

8   9   Albany

Rensselaerswyck

10

11

13   MASSACHUSETTS

14   12

16   15   18
19

17   20
Livingston
Manor

21
Hardenburgh
Patent

23   25a

22   28   26

Kingston   29

30   27
31

24

32

Poughkeepsie   25b   34

33   CONNECTICUT

THE ORIGINAL PATENT OF NEW YORK, 1674

35

Van Cortlandt Manor
36

37
Philipsburgh

NEW JERSEY   38
Yonkers   Colon Donck

Pavonia   b   40
39   a   c

e
Staten Island 41   d

LONG   ISLAND

0   5   10   15   20   25
Scale of Miles

Grants of the Dutch period,
1629–64

MAP: GEORGE COLBERT

Building styles from the Netherlands illustrating the historic and cultural background for Hudson Valley settlers.

Photographs are by the author unless otherwise noted.

Clockwise from facing page top:

Windmills at the Zaanse Schans Museum. Typical scene in early polder lands with windmills pumping water to drain reclaimed lowlands for farming and habitation.

Village at the Zaanse Schans Museum. Museum restoration by Jaap Schipper of seventeenth-century houses in the rural architectural style common to the Zaan region of North Holland. The wooden weatherboarded buildings with steep pitched pantile roofs resemble building types that were common in New Netherland. The bridge over the small drainage canal to farmland in foreground is a typically Dutch setting.

The Nun's House in the Nuns' Court adjacent to the *Spui.* This wood-and-brick building, claimed to be the oldest house in Amsterdam, reflects the typical Dutch urban building gable-front orientation and steeply pitched roof.

Small house in Nuns' Court with curved baroque gable.

Nuns' Court town houses with baroque gables and cranes.

Clockwise from facing page top:

The *Spui,* Amsterdam, just outside the Nun's Court. The small elbow-and-gable brick dwellings with red pantile roofs are typical of seventeenth- century Dutch urban architecture once seen in Hudson Valley houses.

Amsterdam Warehouse showing an early and typical commercial building with gable peak crane to lift goods to upper level doors. This type of building likely would have graced the waterfronts and commercial streets in any Dutch colonial town. Examples survived into the nineteenth century at Brooklyn, Manhattan, and Albany.

Zaanse Schans Museum baroque-gabled wooden house with pantile roof.

Amsterdam stepped-gable building dated 1627.

Amsterdam house dated 1642 with raised baroque gable and crane.

Clockwise from left:

Amsterdam house 'in flight' with façade canted out. The feature is designed to prevent damage when goods are hoisted to upper levels by the crane at the gable peak. Building has step-gable front and spout-gable rear. The anchor irons that join the internal wood frame to the bricks are clearly visible.

A view from the garden of the Bloemracht house —spout gables at the rear on houses fronted with stepped gables.

The Orphanage at Arnhem dated 1617 with steeply pitched pantile roof, spout gables, and cross-framed windows with lower shutters and the anchor irons can be clearly seen at each floor level. A small formal garden occupies the foreground. Except that the building has upper floors, it is typical of the early upper Hudson Valley style.

Right: Amsterdam step gables on Bloemgracht, viewed from front canal. Henk J. Zantkuyl restored these early seventeenth-century buildings for the City of Amsterdam. The brick dwellings have gable-end cranes and warehouse loft doors and originally had shops fronting the canal. The lower section of the ground-floor shutters could be set horizontally and used as display shelves for merchandise. The tall windows illuminate the interior's central-gallery-level rooms.

Below: Close-up view of shutter arrangement of Bloemgracht houses and urban *stoep* with railing.

Left: Netherlands' building showing vertical board siding typical of many early small Dutch dwellings. Courtesy of R. H. Blackburn.

Right: Amsterdam baroque gable with crane and crane housing.

Below right: Early stepped gables built 'in flight' to facade peak with crane, double-height windows at the lower level to illuminate the interior gallery space, and cross-framed leaded windows with shutters only on the lower sections. Originally many of these shuttered openings could be found without glazing.

Below left: An early Amsterdam building with the elbow based spout gables with crane and the pantile roof found on many Albany area rural homes. The orientation of the building is in the urban manner with the entry at the high gabled front but a secondary door is placed similarly to rural houses along the eave side. The building has been blackened by tar to reduce dampness from the adjacent canal penetrating the masonry.

Dutch gristmill at Philipsburg Manor,
North Tarrytown, New York.

CHAPTER II

The Dutch People
in the Hudson Valley

URING ITS HISTORY, the Dutch colony in North America faced several fundamental problems. The most basic weakness was the lack of settlers in sufficient numbers to make the colony credible to its aggressive neighbors. Major difficulties were encountered in any attempt to attract settlers. In the seventeenth century the Netherlands was experiencing a period of economic prosperity. A relatively tolerant enclave in a world of religious fanaticism, it was the refuge of choice for many Europeans escaping persecution and religious intolerance. French, German, and Walloon refugees, as well as English Dissenters (such as the Pilgrims), fled to the Netherlands. Many chose to become permanent residents in the United Provinces. As the Dutch themselves felt little urgency to emigrate, it was difficult to entice colonists to a raw and hostile wilderness. Few among them could be induced to serve as company tenants and live under more repressive laws than those obtained in "Fatherland." Whereas during the 1620s and 1630s England experienced a time of rising religious, political, and economic discontent. The period immediately preceding the English Civil War engendered the mass transatlantic movement known as the Great Migration that attracted thousands of settlers to New England. While many English immigrants sought religious self-expression many more came for economic opportunity. The English did not come to America to be tenants of a company or a landlord; they came for the chance to obtain freehold land to homestead.

The faction within the Amsterdam Chamber of the Dutch West India Company that favored investment and settlement centered in the New Netherland Commission. The member Kiliaen Van Rensselaer who was a wealthy diamond merchant frequently influenced the commission. From the beginning Van Rensselear made the greatest personal financial commitment, and demonstrated the keenest interest, in the colony's long term potential. He realized that a strong agricultural base was essential for the colony's development. Agriculture called for settlement. Commission members finally prevailed upon the company to stimulate privately sponsored colonization because their "Mightinesses" had already learned how quickly expenses could mount. Between 1624 and 1625, colonizing expeditions cost the company an estimated 100,559 florins. In *Holland on the Hudson*, Oliver Rink, provides the following table for the cost of expeditions in the referenced years: [1]

Colonization costs (florins) 1624-1625

Freightage (Chartering fees calculated per ton)	18,620
Insurance premiums (at 5 percent value of vessels)	4,994
Wages (Ship crews: average per ship 15)	19,320
Wages (Dock workers: Amsterdam day laborer rates)	8,000
Passage for colonists (Company rate = 50 fl. one way)	15,000
Livestock (Hoorn wholesale prices = 125 fl. average)	12,625
Trade goods (calculated per ton)	14,000
Total	100,559

The directors were ready to listen when the commissioners advocated the establishment of a system of patrons, or patroons who would recruit colonists and develop private settlements in exchange for large grants of land. In 1639 the patroons gained the additional economic incentive that permitted them to engage in the fur trade in competition with the company. The system created rivalry between the conflicting interests and intermittently resulted in problems.

Commission members Kilian Van Rensselaer, Samuel Godijn, and Samuel Blommaert began making colonization plans early in 1629. Another commission member named Michel Pauw soon joined them as did Albert Burgh, another long-time ally of Van Rensselaer in the Amsterdam Chamber. Most of the schemes ended stillborn. Only three patroonships developed beyond planning stages and were actually established: Swanendael on the Delaware shore; Pavonia at the confluence of the Passaic and Hackensack Rivers by Staten Island; and Rensselaerswyck along both banks of the Hudson River at Fort Orange. The one successful patroon was Kilian Van Rensselaer who devoted unceasing effort and apparently endless finances to secure his investment. But it took a multigenerational commitment for the payback to be achieved in rents, fees, and revenue. Rensselaerswyck was worth the effort—an enormous tract of land that eventually totaled over a million acres surrounding the present state capital at Albany.[2]

Only Rensselearswyck outlasted the Dutch era and achieved any success. Despite the frequent references to patroons in the early history of the Hudson Valley, the other patroonships were failures. Samuel Godijn formed a partnership with Van Rensselaer, Johan de Laet, and Samuel Blommaert to establish Swanendael. Michael Pauw founded Pavonia, but quickly sold it back to the company. Later a well-known ship captain named David Pietersz De Vries became patroon of Pavonia. Swanendael and Pavonia both met tragic and dramatic fates: De Vries records in his book, *Voyages From HOLLAND TO AMERICA, A.D. 1632 to 1644*, "that on account of trifling with the Indians we had lost our colony in the South river at Swanendael, in the Hoere-kil, with thirty-two men, who were murdered in the year 1630."[3] De Vries wrote that the entire Dutch colony was put at risk by ill-conceived and mismanaged Indian policies of Director-General Williem Kieft.[4] De Vries added "that in the year 1640, the cause of my people being murdered on Staten Island was a

difficulty which (Kieft) had with the Raritaense Indians"[5] and Pavonia, too, ended in smoking ruins.

On March 22, 1648 the patroonship of Rensselaerswyck came
under the direction of a troublesome crank named Brandt Aertsz.
van Slechtenhorst; Van Rensselaer's new agent soon attempted to
take control of the company's up-river fur trade based at Fort Orange
on the present-day site of Albany. The fort was located surrounded
by the patroonship of Rensselaerswyck and Slechtenhorst began
encroaching on the fort and the small trading village named Bevers-
fuyck -- locally known as the *fuyck* (trap) -- clustered near the walls.
The agent precipitated a showdown in 1652. When he attempted to
expel the Company's men by force and physically obstruct their
trading operation Director-General Stuyvesant was forced to personally intervene.[6] The matter was settled on April 8, 1652 when
Stuyvesant officially declared the land around Fort Orange separate
from the patroonship of Rensselaerswyck. The governor authorized
the establishment of a court, reaffirmed the company's jurisdiction
over the town, and renamed the village Beverwyck. Freed from the
nettlesome patroonship the town prospered and for many years
served as the cultural center for Dutch in the Hudson Valley. When
the English arrived in 1664 Fort Orange and Beverwyck became the
City of Albany.

Later the English colony of New York came to be dominated by
landlord grandees. In *A History of Agriculture in the State of New York*,
Ulysses Prentiss Hedrick provides a listing entitled "Important Patents in the Eastern Part of New York" that covers the years 1723 to
1775 and specifies the larger grants (11,250 to 100,000 acres) given
away. The listing of the chosen few among the elite of the colony
covers four pages leaving little land for the small-scale settler. The
lone remaining Dutch patroon had by then become a "Lord of the
Manor" and was joined by other English land grant patentees. The
"Lords of the Manor" were never peers or titled aristocracy, because
the "Lords" held their land in freehold, and the tenants' leases were
generally not subject to the "feudal" obligations of a manor. In 1691
the British dual monarchs William and Mary directed a General
Assembly be held in New York. At that time it was declared: "That
all lands within the Province, shall be esteemed and accounted Land

of Freehold and Inheritance, in free and Common Soccage, according to the tenour of East Greenwich in their Majesties' realm of England."[7] In *Historic Houses of the Hudson Valley*, Harold Donaldson Eberlein asserts, "The term 'Lord of the Manor' is a technical one, and means simply the owner—the possessor—of a manor, nothing more."[8]

There were no manorial grants in the section of New Netherland that became New Jersey. The Duke of York created the Province of New Jersey. The Duke then sold it to John, Lord Berkeley and Sir George Carteret on June 24, 1664. [9] New Jersey became a royal province on April 17, 1702, when the proprietors surrendered the power of government to Queen Anne -- but they retained the ownership of the land in freehold.[10] Nine great manors were created under English sovereignty. In Westchester County: Fordham (1671), Pelham (1687), Philipseborough (1693), Morrisania (1697), Cortlandt (1697), and Scarsdale (1701). In Ulster County: Fox Hall (1672). In Albany County: Rensselaer (1685) and Livingston (1686). [11] In addition, there were seven other manors: Gardiner's Island (1639), Plummue Island (1675), Cassiltown on Staten Island (1687), the Manor of Saint George, in Suffolk County (1693), the Manor of Bentley (called Billopp Manor) on Staten Island (1687), Fischer's Manor (circa 1697) north of Newburgh, and Queen's Manor (circa 1697) on Long Island.[12]

Patroonship land grants were specifically for waterfrontage. The tracts ranged up to three leagues along the coast or one side of a river, or half-a-league along both banks of a river. A league is an imprecise measure from 2.4 to 4.6 statute miles. The patroon could keep whatever acreage he was able to claim and hold inland. In addition, he was assured of the necessary right of transferable possession of the title by will to his heirs in perpetuity. Granting large holdings was already a retrogressive move in the seventeenth century. Nevertheless, according to H. R. Eberlein, the patroon system followed manorial land tenure practices current in the Netherlands They did not introduce "feudal" military obligations, which were already obsolete in the Netherlands.[13] In addition to ownership of all minerals, flora, fruits, and water found on the designated territory, the patroon was granted the power to hold civil and criminal court, the right to collect rents up to 10 percent of his tenant's annual income, and the power to require *corvee* labor, mandatory work by the tenants, or to receive paid dispensation. In practice the company and many landlords, were even more demanding. As late as 1640, Alert Teunissen van Putten, a brewer who had leased land at Hoboken, paid rent equal to one-quarter of his wheat harvest. The patroon could conduct direct trade outside the company's control along the Atlantic seaboard with the English and in the Caribbean with the English, French, and Spanish colonies. Direct trade to the Netherlands was permitted with the restriction that all cargo be channeled through the company's offices in Manhattan for audit and fee payment prior to shipment to the homeland. The first patroonship plan offered by the company in 1628 prohibited the patroons from participating in the company's monopoly in the fur trade. It attracted no investors. The second plan, approved in 1629, permitted the patroons to engage in both the fish and the fur trades, the only possible short-term source of profits. In 1639, the company abandoned its fur monopoly completely. The colony prospered, but the company was reduced to relying on the duty charged for pelts and freight.

In exchange for landlord privileges, the would-be patroon made a major investment in the colony: He had to purchase the lands granted by the company from the Indians. He had to recruit and transport at least sixty settlers and establish them on the land. The prospective tenants needed the necessary skills to survive and eventually provide a profit in rents and services to the patroon. Harold Donaldson Eberlein quotes from a letter sent by Kiliaen Van Rensselaer to Dominie Johannes Megapolensis in 1642, outlining the terms for farmers setting out for Rensselaerswyck:

> Each farmer must take with him at least two servants and one boy who understands farming, and himself equip them; the patroon, on his part, provides their board till they arrive in New Netherland at the Island of *manhatans* and once they are in the colony causes them to be provided upon condition of repayment with grain for eating and sowing and with a suitable site on which to establish their farm, where the patroon will once and for all have a good house with (hay) barrack and barn built for them, which according to the custom of that country are usually placed near

the river, the waters of which flow by clear and fresh and full of fish; the patroon causes them also to be provided once with a wagon and plough and what else is needed for farming, the same to be kept in repair and replaced by the farmer; he will further assign them 30 and 40 morgens of land toward the interior, consisting of beautiful woods filled with excellent game, such as deer, turkeys and all sorts of nourishing fowls; he also turns over to them on each farm, from the surplus of animals in the colony, four horses and four cows, of which they are to have half the increase, the other half to be paid to the patroon in money or in kind.[14]

Arnold J. F. van Laer edited the Van Rensselaer-Bowier Manuscripts in 1908 and the work contracts recorded in the archives of the *Gemeentelijke Archief van Amsterdam*. The material, as cited in Oliver A. Rink's *Holland on the Hudson*, included occupational data for 102 immigrants listed as departing for Rensselaerswyck between 1630 and 1644. The material, by revealing the skills needed to make a settlement a success, also notes the class and occupations of people required in the early stages of settlement.[15]

In 1974, the periodical of the Holland Society, *de Halve Maen*, printed a piece on a Rensselaerswyck service contract translated by Dr. W. J. van Hoboken, Director of the Amsterdam City Archives. The Notary Archives include 175 personal service contracts, including twenty-eight agreements for sixty-five individuals destined for Rensselaerswyck, often accompanied by their families. The indenture contract below offers an example.[16]

Rensselaerswyck Service Contract of Jan Theunissen of Leyden,
March 28, 1639

We, the undersigned, acknowledge by these presents and our request, to have agreed with the Seignior Kiliaen van Rensselaer in his quality as Patroon of his colony named Rensselaerswijck, to sail in God's Name with the ship that now lies ready, to the aforesaid colony, to settle there for a term of four years as free colonist and inhabitants of the said colony, without changing our *domicilium* or dwelling place within the same period, unless it were upon the express instruction from our aforementioned Lord and Master; without whose consent also, we shall not be permitted to trade in any manner of pelts of otters, beavers or the like, nor to seek to obtain these either as a gratification or otherwise.

We shall have to provide board, lodging and clothing for ourselves and our families both during our passage and in country and thus are obliged to reimburse the Patroon for all that we require in food and drink on board ship during the voyage, from our readiest means and our first gains, together with such moneys as he moreover might furnish to us in cash coin. It being well understood that we shall make good this ready money with an additional fifty per cent for his risks as interest.

Therefore we shall endeavour to turn our hands to everything, both [on] the land, agriculture, fishery, chase and all other works permitted and conforming to the privileges granted; while holding ourselves bound, should the aforesaid Patroon or his servants require us to work for them and, being paid the proper wage, to use ourselves willingly, loyally and zealously to this end in all things.

We also promise to seek above all other things the advantage of our patroon and safeguard him from loss and to submit ourselves with a will as loyal servants and subjects to all laws and ordinances made or to be made in the aforesaid colony; also to respect its officers and councilors as our lawful superiors; especially acknowledging the detailed Letter Patent of the Chartered West India Company; and in the event that we should find ourselves at variance, either with one another or with someone else, that we shall submit such differences wholly, all in all to neutral "trusty men" or to arbitration by the Court of Law there, without being permitted further litigation or appeal thereafter.

Also that we shall submit a definite statement of everything we have brought with us into that country, so that at the end of the aforementioned four years we can deduct this from the profits and gains that we and our families may have acquired, in order that from the net profit that has been made five-sixth parts will remain for us and for our families and the other sixth part for the benefit of the aforesaid Lord Patroon, in view of the fact that we have made use of his lands and privileges as set out above.

All of which as written above, each and every point thereof, we promise to observe under submission and control of our persons and goods if we should act to the contrary, so that without further legal action we shall be deemed instantly party hereto. All this being accepted by us, the undersigned, this 2nd day of August Anno Domini XVIC six and thirty [1636], in Amsterdam.

Individual Tenant Occupational Distribution

Farmer	(*boern*)	11
Farm servants	(*bouwerijdienaar*)	5
Farmhands	(*bouwerijwerker*)	10
Farm laborers	(*bouwerijarbeiter*)	10
Farmboy	(*bouwereijjongen*)	1
Farmer's apprentice	(*bouwereijleering*)	1
Servant		19
Laborer		7
Magistrate	(*schepen*)	1
Sheriff	(*schout*)	1
Carpenter/mason		1
Wheelwright		2
Journeyman carpenter		1
Carpenter		7
Master carpenter		1
House carpenter		1
Millwright		1
Miller		2
Shoemaker		4
Blacksmith		1
Hog dealer		1
Baker		1
Cooper		1
Clerk		1
Weaver		1
Tailor		4
Wagoner		1
Foreman		1
Brewer		1
Surgeon		1
Minister		1
Skipper		1

All of which abovementioned conditions, points and clauses, having been accepted by the free men preceding us, we, the deponents or undersigned have also at our request and desire accepted the same willingly and will pursue and fulfill them on the pain of the punishments particularized both above and hereafter, besides such others as the Lord Patroon or the Council of the colony might later stipulate to the detriment of contraveners; and to this end and the maintenance of what is written above and follows hereafter with obedience towards all obligatory duties, will affirm the same with solemn oath upon arrival in the colony.

We accept at the same time such points of wider extension, further interpretation, restriction and amplification, as the Lord Patroon has been pleased to include therein provisionally and for his further consideration; we have readily submitted ourselves to revocation and further regulation thereof, on the pain of punishment as above.

The immigration data by occupation for Rensselaerswyck from 1630 to 1644 applies only to men. (Single men would be the most cost-effective workers for the patroon to send over.) However, a permanent settlement would require families, and records representing families and, when known, country of origin (Dutch or foreign born) exist for this period. The family and ethnic data has considerable significance affecting the later character of the settlement in the Hudson Valley.[17]

Recruitment and immigration were only two concerns. The patroon's settlers included both tenants and employees. Tenants paid rent and employees received wages. Wages in America tended to run considerably higher than the rates paid in the Netherlands. A carpenter's boy assistant could earn 25 florins a year in Patria but he could demand as much as 40 florins per annum in Rensselaerswyck. A shoemaker who earned 65 florins in Amsterdam could look for 100 florins in America. A master carpenter was able to demand 550 florins instead of the 410 florins a year received in the Fatherland.[18] The patroon also built defenses, established villages, and constantly was confronted with the problems of overseeing distant activities at a six-month remove. Initially, the tenants had to be supported on the land before they could pay rent to the patroon. At the start, both employees and tenants required victuals, housing, equipment, and protection on the frontier. Everything had to be imported that could not be made in the colony -- food, utensils, clothing, blankets, farm equipment, tools, and livestock. Among the patroon's most recurrent difficulties were poor management on the scene and tenants who tended to leave Rensselaerswyck.[19] Eberlein records the problems concerning the relatively simple matter of shipping eight or ten calves to New Netherland on the *Eendracht* in April of 1631: Among other demands the captain claimed the right, if "inconvenienced," to eat or throw the calves overboard without any obligation to compensate the patroon.[20] Items bought in the colony were marked up at an excessive rate over European costs. As late as 1695, an early settler named, Charles Wooley observed in his book *A Two Years Journal in NEW YORK*, that "goods that are brought over commonly return cent. per cent. i.e. a hundred pounds laid out in London will commonly yield or afford 200 pounds" in New York.[21] The main reason for high prices was the ocean crossing which could take months.

The terrified landlubbers packed aboard saw the frail ships as ever verging on disaster and about to sink. Wooley bemoaned: "Oh the passage, the passage thither, *hic labor, hoc opus est*: there is the timorous objection."[22] Many colonists came over as indentured servants in minimal travel conditions. Even the paying passengers with cabin accommodations often had few creature comforts. While never as terrible as the slave ships on the dreaded "middle passage," any crossing by sail in the early colonial era was a two- or three-month ordeal. Supplies and food rotted, water turned green with algae, and the fetid atmosphere on board the crowded ships encouraged contagious disease. The conditions caused high mortality between decks among the people and the animals, where they shared cramped, cold, and sodden quarters. Even though the company had promised to improve transportation, Van Rensselaer eventually had to invest in his own vessel, the *Rensselaerswyck*, to cover this aspect of his investment.

Not surprisingly, immigration records are incomplete for the entire period of Dutch colonization but it is certain that prior to 1622 the population of the colony was restricted to a few young men who served as agents, or factors, at the company's trading posts. In a report to the Lords Privy Council dated April 5, 1627, Sir Dudley Carlton reported from The Hague that English investigations could produce no evidence of settlement prior to 1622 or 1623. "I cannot learn of any colony either already planted there by these people, or so much as intended." In 1628, the colony probably had no more than 270 men, women, and children, who lived near the fort in New Amsterdam.[23]

New Amsterdam eventually grew in size and amenities and Director Kieft bragged to De Vries in 1642, that the city's new stone tavern met the accommodation needs of New England travelers and

Total Immigration to Rensselaerswyck 1630-1644

Ship	Year	Total	Families	Foreigners	Dutch
Eendracht	1630	15	1	4	5
Eendracht	1631	11	2	2	4
Zoutberg	1633	5			4
Eendracht	1634	12		2	2
Rensselaerwyck	1637	35	1	5	15
Harinck	1638	4	1		2
Chalmer Sletel	1638	6			6
Wapen van Noorwegen	1638	19	2	1	6
Harinck	1639	6	1	1	1
Waterbondt	1640	13			10
Eijkenboom	1641	3			1
Coninck David	1641	7	1	1	2
Houttuijn	1642	22	4	5	7
Wapen van Rensselaerwyck	1644	12	1	1	9

traders. In 1657, there were twenty-one-licensed taprooms and tav-erns. Nicasius de Sille observed in 1653 that everyone drank in New Netherland from the moment they were able to "lick a spoon." The "most famous" hostelry in the city was the Wooden Horse at the corner of Whitehall and Stone Street. The "most popular" was the Blue Dove on Pearl Street.[24] Municipal improvements followed. In the 1650s, the town appointed a measurer of apples, twelve butchers, inspectors of bread, a controller of weights and measures, and a "rattle watch," the town cryers, to check for fires and stray Indians roaming the streets after curfew. In 1653, an area was cleared and a palisade was erected across the island, later known as the "Wall Street," to protect the northern, or landward, side of the city from Indian attack. The village streets were no longer permitted to be lined with privies, nor could the houses be built unaligned. Several streets were paved. A windmill was erected. Then, between 1657 and 1659, that most Dutch amenity appeared. A canal *(gracht* in Dutch) called the *Heer-engracht*, was dug at the site of today's Broad Street. A small hospital was established in 1656. A post office opened in 1660, although residents were still advised to send three copies of any letter to the

Netherlands: via Virginia, Curacao, and England. Docks were finally built along the East River, so workers no longer had to off load all ships with rowboats and canoes. Several streets of Dutch-style houses were built in brick, with pantile roofs, tall stepped gable facades, and stoops with benches, where a citizen could sit in the evening, smoke a pipe, and gossip with passersby. The town began looking less like a frontier settlement and more like a small city in the Fatherland. Eventually, the settlement of New Amsterdam became a city with a charter and an official seal.

In 1652 the City of New Amsterdam numbered 800 inhabitants. Jacob Jansen Huys, master of the *Nieuw Amstel*, wrote his employers on September 30, 1660: "This place, the Manhattans, is quite rich of people, and there are at present, full over 350 houses, so that it begins to be a brave place."[25] An official census that year actually counted 342 houses with 1,500 citizens. Other towns still remained little more than outposts and settlements upriver; even Beverwyck was a mere cluster of houses along the river with a small fort. The colony's Dutch population lived in a few isolated enclaves. They built settlements on the Hudson River; occupied the narrow 140-mile long strip called the "Old Mine Road" -- built in the 1650s through a howling wilderness southwest from Esopus to the Delaware Water Gap; and in a few villages clustered on western Long Island near the East River. [26] The Dutch colony remained small in both total and relative terms compared to the neighboring English settlements. Even after New Netherland experienced a population surge during its final decade, the total number of settlers remained low. When the English took over in 1664, the colony still had no more than 9,000 people. In contrast the United Colonies of New England had more than 25,000 settlers by 1647. In 1664, the City of Boston had a population of 5,000 to 6,000 citizens. According to the Reverend John Miller, who wrote *A Description of The Province and City of New York, in 1695*, the colony of New York still numbered only about 3,000 families whereas Connecticut had a population of 5,000 families.[27]

Nevertheless, the Labadist Fathers, who visited in 1679-1680, affirmed that "As soon as you pass through the *Hoofden* (the Narrows, called after the *Hoofden* [Headlands] in the English Channel between England and France) the city presents a pretty sight."[28] They

Population of New York in 1695

County	Church	Families
New York	Anglican Church at the Fort	90
	Dutch Calvinists	450
	Dutch Lutherans	30
	French	200
	Jews Synagogue	25
	Haarlem Dissenters	40
Richmond	Meeting House	
	English	40
	Dutch	44
	French	36
King's	Chiefly Dutch	
	Flatbush	300–400
	Utrecht	
	Brookland	
Queen's	Mostly English	
	Dissenters	
	Some Dutch	
	Meeting Houses	300–400
	Jamaica	
	Hampstead	
	Newtown	
Suffolk	Meeting Houses	
	Dissenters	500–600
Westchester	Meeting House	
	Mostly English	
	Dissenters	200–300
	Some Dutch	
Orange	English and Dutch	20
Dutchess	English and Dutch	30
Ulster	Calvinist	
	Mostly Dutch some French	300
Albany	Dutch Calvinist	400–500
	Dutch Lutheran	12–14
TOTAL		3017-3519

noted that the fort was situated on a point between two rivers. "When the garrison sees a ship approaching, they raise a flag on the bastion, and people come out from shore each inquiring and searching after his own profit."[29] The City was by now an alert commercial center that continued to grow. Harbor activity mirrored the increasing business. By contrast with the 35 vessels of 1687, 99 cleared the port in 1746, and 726 ships did so in 1772.

The Dutch in New Netherland formed a uniquely cosmopolitan society from the start. It was not always an advantage. By contrast, the English colonies were indeed English and culturally homogenous (entire congregations frequently being transplanted as a unit). The English "Johnnies" or *"Janikens"* (Yankees) formed what would later be termed a "fifth column" who eventually outnumbered the Dutch in large sections of their own colony. The English forced the Dutch from the House of Good Hope trading post on the Connecticut River at Hartford, completely took over the eastern half of Long Island, then absorbed the rest as their settlements rapidly spread west, and finally took control of Westchester between 1658 and 1662.

As reported by the Reverend John Miller who gave a first-hand account, the population remained unevenly distributed, as late as 1695, among ten counties from Albany south to New York and thence east to the end of Long Island (see chart).[30]

Inhabitants in the Several Counties of New-York, 1698

County	Men	Women	Children	Negroes	Total
In ye County and Citty of Albany	380	270	803	23	1476
In ye County of Ulster & Dutchess County	248	111	869	156	1384
In ye County of Orange	29	31	140	19	219
In the City & County of New York	1019	1057	2161	700	4937
In Richmond County also Staten Island	328	208	118	73	727
In ye County of West Chester	316	294	307	146	1063
In Suffolk County within Nassau Island	973	1024	124	558	2679
In King's County within Nassau Island	308	332	1081	296	2017
In Queen's County within Nassau Island	1465	1350	551	199	3565
Totals	5066	4677	6154	2170	18067

In 1698, the Governor of New York, the Earl of Bellomont, ordered each High Sheriff and Justice of the Peace to conduct a survey in their respective county.[31]

The numbers suggest that not all the children were counted in several areas and that some of the black population may have been missed as well in the enumeration of 1698. Some fifty years later another census of the inhabitants of the province of New York was taken on May 10, 1749:[32]

Census of the Province of New-York, 1749

| County | White Population | | | | | |
| | Males | | | Females | | Total |
	Under 16 Yrs	16 yrs to 59yrs	60+	Under 16 yrs	16 yrs upward	
City & Co New York	2346	2765	183	2364	3268	10926
King's	288	437	62	322	391	1500
Albany	2249	2359	322	2137	2087	9154
Queen's	1630	1508	151	1550	1778	6617
Dutchess	1970	1820	160	1790	1751	7451
Suffolk	2058	1863	248	1960	1969	8098
Richmond	431	420	36	424	434	1745
Orange	1062	856	66	992	899	3874
Westchester	2511	2312	228	2263	2233	9547
Ulster	913	992	110	810	979	3804
Total White						62756

| County | Black Population | | | | | |
| | Males | | | Females | | Total |
	Under 16 Yrs	16 yrs to 59yrs	60+	Under 16 yrs	16 yrs upward	
City & Co New York	460	610	41	556	701	2368
King's	232	244	21	137	149	783
Albany	309	424	48	334	365	1480
Queen's	300	386	43	245	349	1423
Dutchess	103	155	21	63	79	421
Suffolk	305	355	41	292	293	1286
Richmond	88	110	20	93	98	409
Orange	62	95	16	84	103	360
Westchester	303	270	66	238	279	1156
Ulster	217	301	50	198	240	1006
Total Black						10692

Total Combined White and Black Population	73448

Even after the Dutch West India Company tried attracting more colonists with the promise of two-hundred acre land grants and right of testament to secure inheritance, native Dutch settlers never numbered more than about fifty percent of the colony's total population.

Even though the Dutch were prodigious breeders who increased in total numbers at a significant rate, after the English took over the colony the percentage of people identifying themselves as Dutch declined sharply.

In *The Dutch-American Farm*, David Steven Cohen reviewed immigration to New Netherland and found, in brief, that among 900 family heads who arrived in New Jersey and New York in the seventeenth century the national origins were as follows: [33]

National Origins of Immigrants to New Netherland

Country of Origin	Total Number	Percent of Total
The Netherlands	459	51.0
North Holland	142	16.0
Gelderland	88	10.0
Utrecht	68	8.0
South Holland	45	5.0
Friesland	25	3.0
Drenthe	22	2.0
North Brabant	16	2.0
Overijssel	21	2.0
Limburg	7	1.0
Zeeland	18	2.0
Groningen	7	1.0
Spanish Netherlands (Belgium)	63	6.0
Walloon Provinces	30	3.0
Flemish Provinces	31	3.0
Brussels	2	0.2
Germany	167	18.0
France	64	7.0
Denmark and Schleswig-Holstein	77	11.0
Sweden	24	3.0
Norway	47	5.0
Poland	3	0.3
Other	6	0.7
Total	1422	100.0

The French Roman Catholic priest Father Jogues reported in 1643 that the Director-General told him that eighteen different languages or dialects were spoken in New Amsterdam. Among the colonists were people from the German states, Norway, Sweden,

Denmark, England, and France. As Helen Wilkinson Reynolds notes in *Dutch Houses In the Hudson Valley Before 1776:*

> Arrivals from the Netherlands rubbed shoulders with Albert Andriesse Bradt from Frederikstadt in Norway, whose son, born on the voyage across the Atlantic, was given the Dutch name of Storm Van der Zee. Bradt was known as de Noorman and the stream in Albany County on which he built a mill was de Noorman's Kil (the Northman's stream). A little south of de Noorman's Kil is Vlauman's Kill, that is: the stream of [Peter Winne] the Fleming. Alexander Lindsay Glen, the Scotchman, was prominent at Schenectady. Thomas Chambers, English-born, was the first purchaser of land at Wiltwyck. Walloons were at New Paltz and Huguenot-French at New Rochelle. Hoffmans from Sweden, Schoonmakers from Hamburg, Ten Broecks from Westphalia, Kiersteds from Prussia all multiplied in Ulster.[34]

D. S. Cohen qualifies the national origins' information. He observes that "only when we look at the cultural boundaries and how they relate to the places of origin of the Dutch settlers can we understand the cultural process that shaped the Dutch cultural area in New York and New Jersey."[35] Several factors modify the apparent diversity. "Germans" came primarily from areas adjacent to the Netherlands and spoke dialects related to the Low German of the Netherlands. The cultural zone from Denmark to Normandy had greater importance than the political boundaries in the seventeenth century. And, the immigrants were primarily Protestants of Calvinist or Lutheran affiliation. There was a broad, but commonly held, heritage of European peoples under Dutch cultural leadership. Assimilation to Dutch culture was a significant unifying factor, and it was easy as most of the settlers basically shared the same cultural roots, while the Dutch tolerated many individual and group idiosyncrasies. One example, noted in *Dutch Architecture Near Albany,* concerns the Moak family. They settled in Feura Bush, New York in 1732, and "provide an example of Palatines (in this case from Switzerland) marrying into local Dutch families," becoming acculturated, and adapting to the prevailing Dutch life style.[36] The colony represented the first American "melting pot" experience. It worked because the common ethnicity and cultural origins of the groups outweighed the differences with others, such as the Native Americans, the English in the Hartford and Connecticut and New England areas, and the French in Canada. In fact, the only assimilation problem came from English settlers in Westchester and on Long Island. When these English grew numerous enough to resist assimilation, their demands to use their own language and maintain a separate cultural identity ultimately contributed to the loss of New Netherland. In the post-conquest period, many of the Dutch turned inward to maintain there own identity and resist absorption by the new masters of the Valley.

From the start, a significant percentage of the population was black. Probably the first known "settler" in the Valley was Juan Rodrigues. A mulatto native of San Domingo, he had jumped ship from the *Jonge Tobias* and lived among the Indians during the winter of 1613.[37] The first blacks to arrive in numbers were a "parcel" of eleven slaves in 1626. Many more blacks came from the West Indies; and after 1655, others landed directly from Africa. With an early start, the colony remained the center for slave holding in the North until after the Revolution. By 1664, there were as many as 700 blacks among the total population of 9,000 persons. In the beginning, after a term of service, a small number of the private and company slaves were manumitted; others were released to a conditional "half free" status; and in time more were free-born. In numbers, if not influence, the black population was significant. Among the members of the free black community were a few early property holders, including Domingo Antony, who received a land patent in 1643 for Bouwery No. 5, and Catelina Antony, who took title to land across the road. In 1679 Jasper Dankers reported in *Journal of a Voyage to New York* that on both sides of Broadway "were many habitations of negroes, mulattoes and whites. These negroes were formerly slaves . . .[but] they have obtained their freedom and settled down where they thought proper, and thus on this road, where they have ground enough to live on with their families."[38] These properties were apparently in a desirable location near the *Bouwerie*, the country home of Peter Stuyvesant, and formed the nucleus of an identifiable black community in Manhattan by the 1640s.

Recent black studies programs have uncovered many previously ignored chapters in our history about free and slave communities in early America. It is worth noting that a free black community existed at the end of the eighteenth century in Rockleigh, New Jersey, developed under the leadership of a man named Jack Earnest and recorded by Reginald McMahon of the Bergen County Historical Society. Upstate New York also had a significant black population, but most blacks lived and were buried at the homes of their masters rather than in separate black communities. Unlike the South, where slave gangs worked large plantations, on Northern farms blacks often were found in small numbers and lived in their master's extended household, participating in many aspects of daily life and, for that matter, afterlife. Dutch family cemeteries typically held all household members, including free blacks and slaves. *Early Architecture in Ulster County,* records that at the Evert Terwilliger House, "Evert Terwilliger was buried, along with 20 slaves on the hill at the rear of the house."[39] In a booklet entitled "History of the Village of Port Chester New York"[40] there is a reference to the Brown family homestead in Port Chester, where a small cemetery has a stone that reads:

> In memory of Cuff Brown
> Born November 1799 Died Mar I, 1822
> A slave (illegible[born?]) in the family of the
> late John Brown

Colonial family histories relate incidents about specific individuals. Eype Schouten, saved her master Garret Storm from hanging by Tories during the Revolution; Dina, the family slave of Matthew Van Keuren, saved their homestead by bribing the English soldiers sent to burn down the homestead with her fresh baked bread. In these special situations the women's contributions were recognized and they were eventually granted freedom.[41] Johannes DeWint's farm was attacked during the Revolutionary War with the loss of a slave boy and a herd of cattle. It was naturally assumed that the raiders were responsible, but "the next day the black boy returned from the woods with the cattle whither he had driven them on the first alarm."[42] If Johannes DeWint had been a harsh master, it is unlikely that the boy would have saved his cattle. In part this loyalty by Dutch slaves grew from their inclusion in the master's household. Jasper Dankers reported an incident where a farm family slave died in a horseback riding accident, the event caused "great sorrow . . .to [the farmer], his wife, and his whole family, as also to all his friends . . . [they] had much love for him." From cradle to grave, the household members shared many of life's more meaningful moments. Washington Irving wrote that around the hearth "the whole family, old and young, master and servant, black and white, nay even the very cat and dog, enjoyed a community of privilege, and had each a prescriptive right to a corner."[43] Under the Dutch, blacks even had the right to their day in court. *The Kingston Papers: 1661-1675* records' cases wherein blacks were given equal access to the law. Mingus Manuel, also known as Mingus the Negro, appeared before the Court of Wildwyck on September 21, 1672, to answer charges of theft of a bag. His testimony satisfied the judges of his innocence and the record shows that, "the hon. court orders that Thomas Harmensen shall pay the costs for Mingus the Negro and also his daily wages, because Mingus the Negro proves that he has not stolen the bag."[44]

However, "black family members" were still chattel, items of property, to be disposed of at the whim of the owner. An advertisement on January 6, 1763, in *The New-York Gazette* and the *Weekly Mercury* by the upholster Richard Wenman advised readers that he "Has to sell, Lines and Tossels, Also a Negro Boy, about 15 or 16 Years old, who has had the small Pox."[45] Wills frequently noted the bequest of people and belongings in casual juxtaposition, as in the 1768 will of Caleb Pell of Pelham Manor, which read: "to my dau. Ann Laurence a negro girl and a Mahogany Chest of Drawers and a dining table and a tea table to be made for her. To my wife Mary a negro boy and a woman & child . . . also my two best beds with furniture and a Mahogany tea table and one dozen of my best chairs . . .my silver plate, Looking glass and China."[46] *Old Ulster: An Historical & Geneological Magazine*, published a section in January 1910, entitled "A Reminder Of Slavery Days In New York," which cited a contract, dated 1782, to lease a slave by Dutch owners in the Hudson Valley. The business-like terms quickly dispel any sentimental notions:[47]

This Indenture Witnesseth

That I, Benjamin Bogardus of Dutches County State of New York have Let Matthew Persen of Kingstone County of Ulster and state afforsaid have a Negro slave Named Robin for the term of Nine years next ensuing, and the said Matthew Persen his heirs or afsigns will procure and provide for him the said Negro sufficient meat drink Wearing apparel Lodging and Washing during the said term of nine years.

And at the expiration of Nine years Next ensuing the date hereof, he the said Matthew Persen his heirs or afsigns shall deliver the said Negro slave if alive unto the said Benjamin Bogardus his heirs or afsigns. And for the true performance of the agreements aforesaid, the said parties bind themselves each unto the other firmly by these presents, in Witness whereof the said parties have hereunto set their hands and seals.

Dated the fifth day of November, One thousand Seven Hundred and eighty-two.

Benjamin Bogardus (S)
Matthew Perfen (S)
Sealed and Delivered
in the presence of us
Frantz J. Roggen
Petrus Roosa

The true situation that underlay even the friendliest, kindest, and most "family like" relationships between master and slave was strictly business.

In 1685 the French king moved to repress religious diversity in his realm; Louis XIV revoked the Edict of Nantes that had provided a measure of religious freedom for Protestants. To his surprise 200,000 Protestants fled from France and his policy of religious persecution.[48] "The Huguenots took refuge from the Dragonnades in England, Holland, and Germany; and those countries benefited by the short-sighted policy of a bigoted king."[49] A significant number came to New York, especially at Manhattan, New Paltz, and New Rochelle. French-speaking Walloons and French Huguenots, fleeing from oppression and civil strife in France, joined the population as well. The Walloons settled primarily in Long Island, New Jersey, and the lower Hudson. Although they spoke French, the Walloons were Calvinists and culturally akin to the Dutch, so they easily became part of the Dutch colonial society. Huguenots arrived in large numbers in the later years of the seventeenth century. An example of Huguenot assimilation would be Catheryna Rombout Brett, who lived from 1687 to 1764. Known in later life as Madam Brett, she was the child of a Walloon father, Francois Rombouts, and a Dutch mother, Helena Teller, and she was the wife of an English husband, Roger Brett. She spoke and wrote in a mixture of English and Dutch. Her son, Francis Rombout Brett, married a Dutch wife, Margaret Van Wyck, and her grand-daughter, Hanna Brett, married a Dutch husband, Henry Schenck. All of these family members lived at various times at the Teller Homestead in Beacon, New York, which was the "old farm" or manor house of the extensive Rombout Patent, some 85,000 acres purchased by Madam Brett's father and Gulian Verplanck in 1683. The patent covered most of southern Dutchess County. When the patent was partitioned among the heirs Madam Brett received a large tract along the Vis Kil (Fish Stream). The inheritance made her one of the principal landlords in the county.[50] From all accounts, Madam Brett emerges as a remarkable woman and a major contributor to the settlement of the Hudson Valley.

Another Walloon family that became leaders in the middle valley was the Delamaters, who established the estate of Troutbeck in Amenia, New York. Claude le Maistre of Richebourg, in Artois, France, took refuge in Amsterdam and then moved to New Netherland, first to Flatbush and later (circa 1666) to Harlem, where he died in 1683. His son Jacobus moved to Ulster. His son Isaac moved to Dutchess County with a Dutch wife, Maria Kip, whom he had married in 1752. He used the new name of John Delamater when they built their house in 1761.[51] The Huguenot colonists who arrived after the English had taken over the colony easily assimilated into Anglo-American society.

The Dutch Reformed Church was the official religion of the Netherlands and the colony. Dutch Calvinist orthodoxy was based upon active conformance to the dogma established at the Synod of Dort, but while many of the Dutch settlers were very devout, they

were seldom fanatical and many viewed the austere behavior of the
Puritans as off-putting and aberrant. From the beginning the colony
of New Netherland reflected tolerant Dutch attitudes. The Dutch
avoided interfering in the souls of their fellow citizens, never com-
prehended the psychic torments that lay behind the witchcraft trial
hysteria, and rarely succumbed to the meddling that provided pruri-
ent relief in the morose lives of their New England neighbors.
Although Stuyvesant's minister, Johannes Megapolensis, wrote la-
mentingly to the company that "We have here Papists, Mennonites
and Lutherans among the Dutch, also many Puritans or Independents
and many atheists and various other servants of Baal."[52] In 1685,
William Byrd of Westover, the Virginian patrician, remarked with
some surprise that in Albany "they have as many Sects of religion as
at Amsterdam, all being tolerated, yet the people seem not concerned
what religion their Neighbor is of, or whether he hath any or
none."[53] Toleration was rare in the seventeenth century. Freedom of
conscience was viewed with alarm in the English colonies, unknown
in the French settlements, and vigorously hunted down and purged
from the holdings of Spain.

In early 1654, four Jews arrived from the Netherlands. Within
the year, a party of twenty-three Portuguese Jews reached the City
of New Amsterdam, after fleeing from the company's failed colony
of New Holland in Brazil. Jews were tolerated in the Netherlands
and permitted to engage openly in business and conduct private
religious services. Even four percent of the company's stockholders
were Jews. However, Stuyvesant balked at letting Jews settle in his
domain and made efforts to evict them. He appealed to the Heeren
XIX, the directors of the Dutch West India Company, to approve
his efforts to expel the Jews but was overruled. The company was
desperate for colonists, so the directors decided that these Jews should
stay, having suffered "considerable loss, with others, in the taking of
Brazil,"[54] and Stuyvesant was ordered to provide them with refuge
in the colony. Over the ensuing years, the Jewish settlers in Manhattan established themselves as a part of the larger community. However, few Jews settled outside the urban centers of Manhattan and
Albany until later in the colonial period. In 1714 a trader called
"Gomez the Jew" (Louis Moses Gomez, ancestor of the poetess

Emma Lazarus and Supreme Court Justice Benjamin Nathan Cardoza) built a house near Newburgh Bay at a place later known as "Jews' Creek." The site of his home is now known as Mill House. A pamphlet from Mill House identifies it as the "earliest extant Jewish residence in North America." It was later owned by Wolfert Acker (grandson of the elder Wolfert Acker immortalized by Washington Irving in *Wolfert's Roost*). Gomez and his sons conducted a thriving fur trade for thirty years and prospered in shipping peltries to Spain and Portugal.When Louis Moses Gomez retired to Manhattan he'd become "one of the wealthiest merchants in New York City and was much respected by his fellow citizens."[55] H. W. Reynolds notes that when Samuel Cohen, Moses B. Franks, and his brother Jacob Franks bought the Low-Van der Burgh-Smith-Myers house in Poughkeepsie at a sheriff's sale in 1742, it was the first recorded evidence of any Jewish connection with Dutchess County in the mid-Hudson Valley.[56]

The influx of religiously diverse settlers vexed and bedeviled Director-General Stuyvesant. New Englanders fleeing a surfeit of Puritanism settled in Manhattan, Westchester, and Long Island. Anabaptists, Quakers, and various Dissenters including Anne Hutchinson, Lady Deborah Moody, John Throckmorton, and Francis Doughty moved kin, kith, and congregations to the company settlement. Stuyvesant fought a running battle with the Quakers that resulted in the Flushing Remonstrance, a milestone in America's struggle for religious toleration. He protested to the directors that the Lutherans objected to a key phrase in the oaths of the Synod of Dort, but the oath was adjusted in the Lutherans' favor by order of the Company. Stuyvesant continued to harass the Jews until he was finally ordered to drop his contentions over religious issues and specifically directed to permit private observance of all religious practices by settlers who conducted themselves in a lawful manner.

The multiplicity of faiths in the colony continued to cause some officials distress under the English. On September 30, 1683 the new governor, Thomas Dongan, wrote in "Governor Dongon's Report on the State of the Province" that: "Here bee not many of the Church of England; few Roman Catholics; abundance of Quakers preachers men and Women especially; Singing Quakers; Ranting Quakers;

Sabbatarians; Antisabbatarians; Some Anabaptists some Independents; some Jews; in short of all sorts of opinions there are some and the most part of none at all."[57] He was not amused.

A topic of complaint among religious Dutch settlers was the frequent shortage or even absence of Dutch Reformed Church clergy to minister to the community. David Pietersz. De Vries recorded a conversation in 1642 with the Director-General William Kieft, who allegedly bragged how the colony's new stone tavern offered comfort for both travelers and residents. De Vries supposedly replied that it was a shame established church members had to meet in a barn while drunkards enjoyed a fine new building.[58] He challenged Kieft on the spot to see that a church was built. Soon thereafter, the stone church of Saint Nicholas was erected within the precincts of the fort. Nevertheless, many Manhattanites remained lax in spiritual matters from the start. In 1697, a Boston physician, Dr. Benjamin Bullivant, observed that "the Dutch seemed not very strict in Keeping the Sabbath, you should see some shelling peas at their doors children playing at their usual games in the streets & ye taverns filled."[59] Upriver the Dutch Reformed Church had much greater impact. The Reformed Church was the foundation of rural Dutch cultural identity, and a mainstay of the *boer* life that was to mark New York between 1664 and 1776.

The colony's total population increased slowly: 10,000 in 1680; 15,000 by 1685. In 1676, New York City had grown to 2,200 persons, but in 1679 Albany still claimed little more than 1,000 occupants. [60] People with initiative would not settle where they could not hope to own land; therefore, New York was losing out to Pennsylvania and the Jerseys. By 1683 Long Island had gown to exceed 5,500 people in five Dutch towns and twelve English villages; though, Governor Dongan reported in 1687 that "for these last 7 years past, there has not come into this province twenty English, Scotch or Irish families."[61] In 1700, the governor, the Earl of Bellomont, complained to the Lords of Trade in London that settlement in the upper Valley was hindered by the lease-hold system. H. W. Reynolds quotes the governor's letter of January 2, 1700-1701. "Mr. Livingston has on his great grant of 16 miles long and 24 broad but 4 or 5 cottagers as I am told, men that live in vassalage under him and work for him and are too poor to be farmers, having not wherewithal to buy Cattle to stock a farm. Colonel Cortland has also on his great grants 4 or 5 of these poor families. Old Frederick Phillips is said to have about 20 families of these poor people that work for him on his grant."[62] The inequities of the lease-hold rental system lasted until the Rent Wars of the early nineteenth century (described by Dixon Ryan Fox in the classic history *The Decline of Aristocracy in the Politics of New York,*), but after 1700 the situation began to improve for the small land owner.

While the Dutch remained the most numerous group in the colony in 1703, the size of their plurality decreased significantly after 1677. The English, and their French Huguenot associates, displaced the Dutch as the politically and socially dominant group. Peter Kalm, the Swedish naturalist, observed in his book, *Travels into North America*, in 1749, that most of the young people in the lower valley spoke English by the 1740s. They also tended to "fall off" to the Anglican church. Services in the Dutch language were reported to have rapidly diminished, although the Dutch continued to maintain a firm hold upriver in the Albany area for some years longer. In 1756, Albany numbered some 3,000 people, most of them identifying themselves as Dutch.[63] In *Colonial New York*, the author Michael Kammen writes that "until mid-century, at least 80 percent of all baptisms, marriages, and burials in the Albany church records bore Dutch surnames."[64] After 1760, that proportion declined rapidly: Whereas Dutch names in Albany County were 82 percent of the total in 1720, they had declined to 57 percent by 1763.[65] Dutch traditions persisted even among the Anglo-Dutch New Yorkers late into the eighteenth century. When Maria Farmer of New York City wrote her will on March 3, 1788, she specified that:

> It is my desire to be buried in Trinity Church as near as possible to my late husband; also my funeral to be conducted by a genuine Dutch Minister; also by all the ministers of the Church of England; also by the Reverand Doctor Rogers, and the assistant Minister of his Church; also by his Excellency the Minister of the United Nether-lands; also by the Governor of this State and the Mayor of this City; also by Doctor Charlton, to all of whom I desire that scarves and gloves be given, as well as to my pall-bearers and in order that the procession may be conducted exactly conformable to the old Dutch custom I desire that the advice of Jeronymous Van Alstine be taken.[66]

The lady was insuring that every eventuality related to the afterlife was covered and that her Dutch roots and origins be addressed in every detail in her last social appearance on earth.

The population of the colony had risen to 175,000 persons on the eve of the American Revolution. New York City and downstate towns had attracted an influx of English settlers. The breakdown by group was about 50 percent English, either from England or New England, Connecticut, and Rhode Island. There were also at least 20,000 blacks, most of whom lived in the lower Valley, including some 5,000 in Manhattan. New Dutch immigration of any significance had come to a halt in 1664; nevertheless, the total population still identifying themselves as "Dutch" numbered at least 20,000 by the middle of the eighteenth century. They increased generation-by-generation solely from the fertile loins of the deceptively placid-appearing valley inhabitants. The balance of the population were French Huguenots, Scots and Scots-Irish, Welsh, Swedes, and Germans.

The Dutch remained clustered along the Hudson River at Kingston and westward along the Old Mine Road, and they continued to dominate the Albany area for generations. In the Hudson Valley, the large land grants, the tenant system, and an antipathy to new immigration slowed change. However, the generous terms granted by the English enabled the Dutch to continue the practice of their distinct culture long after the conquest. Governor Nicolls addressed the specific needs of the three segments of the Dutch colony: New York and Long Island, the Delaware region, and the upper Hudson Valley. Michael Kammen notes that Nicolls permitted the valley communities' considerable continuity with the pre-1664 circumstances. The terms and conditions of surrender, allowed in 1664, were reconfirmed after the reconquest in 1675. The Dutch cultural identity was insured. The business and property rights were unhindered, the patroon system of land tenure was maintained, the Dutch Reformed Church continued to enjoy a privileged position in parishes with a Dutch majority, and the Dutch schools, customs, and language continued much as they had been before the English arrived.[67]

The tenacity of the Dutch culture is partly due to a siege mentality that blossomed after 1664. The strongly held traditions were a product of the isolation in the upper valley and their alienation under the increasing cultural Anglicization.[68] Some Dutch settlers actually relocated from the lower valley to the upper reaches of the River, where they could more easily maintain their traditions.[69] In *Dutch New York*, Esther Singleton states that "in the second quarter of the eighteenth century there was a noticeable migration from Long Island to Dutchess County, when the sons of long established Dutch families bought large acreages in Dutchess under the sound title of the Rombout Patent."[70] An example of the trend was the move by Abraham Schenck to the town of Wappinger in Dutchess County, where a branch of the family resided for some years. The Schencks were long-time residents of Flatlands in Brooklyn. Two of the family homes, restored and reconstructed, are on display at the Brooklyn Museum. Although the Dutch patricians had lost power over the destiny of New York, "ten families in general and five in particular, the Schuylers, Cuylers, ten Broecks, Rosebooms, and Wendels"[71] dominated the Albany Common Council and the Albany hinterland well into the English period. The existence of a Dutch elite helped to sustain the community.

The Valley *boeren* found their real sense of community in the Reformed Church and in the home. The people were not typically grandees and aristocrats; they were merchants and farmers. They lived a hard, but potentially rewarding life along the very fringe of western civilization. They were making a new home thousands of miles from their fondly "remembered," but probably never seen *Patria*. They were not the subjects of painters of royalty and nobility of the Golden Age and did not engage the attention of courtly artists, such as Van Dyke. To see the faces of the Hudson Valley *boeren*' one must look at Jan Vermeer's sturdy and plain *Kitchen Maid,* Michael Sweeters' fresh and innocent *Portrait of a Boy,* and Pieter Codde's young tough in *A Smoker*. One can find the face of a settler matriarch in the ancient and pius *vrouw* depicted in Nichlaes Mae's sympathetic rendering of *An Old Woman Saying Grace*. Frans Hals captures the young and lusty face of the pioneer-type in his *Laughing Fisher-boy,* in his fresh faced *Gipsy Girl*, and in his rendering of the stolid woman in *Nurse and Child*. One would certainly find in a Dutch settlement along the Hudson between 1609 and 1776 one of the "pack of vagabonds" noted by Peter Kalm resident at Albany in the 1740s such as the delightful and riotous lout captured by Adriaen Brouwer in *The Bitter Draught*. These are the faces of New Netherland and the *boers* of the Hudson Valley.

A "remembrance of *patria*" found a deep vein of expression in the home. Today, the small homes of the early settlers stand as the principal memorial to the generations of families who followed the traditions of the Fatherland in the Hudson Valley. The Dutch-style townhouses described by Madam Sarah Kemble Knight in 1704 as "very stately and high. . .the bricks. . .of divers Coullers and laid in Checkers"[72] with the distinguished appearance of the Fatherland have disappeared. New Amsterdam, Esopus, and Beverwyck are gone almost without a trace. Early examples of the rural style houses are rare, a special survivor still stands in Brooklyn. The Pieter Claessen Wyckoff house in East Flatbush, partly built between 1638 and 1640, is the oldest house in New York State, and has been restored by the Preservation Commission. Other contemporary houses in that area, once built as isolated farms, stood on land that has long since been urbanized. The majority of the remaining small Dutch farmhouses in the Hudson Valley were actually built between 1664 and 1776. They reflect the traditions of a flourishing *boer* community that resisted assimilation. A few of the lucky survivors, such as the Luykas Van Alen house, built in 1737, are protected from the onslaughts of "progress." Other houses often stand in relative safety in rural districts of the Hudson Valley, but they are now at risk from the encroachments by developers, and would-be "improvers" of various sorts, who want to erect tract housing and malls everywhere. To lose these homesteads would be a shame and to ignore them a pity. They are practical and functional dwellings with few pretensions and real warmth and charm.

The gradual assimilation of the Valley Dutch into Anglicized British Crown subjects and then into American citizens marked a loss in the region's distinctive character. Washington Irving wrote in "The Author's Apology" to the 1848 revised edition of his *A History of New York* that when he began to write in 1809, he "was surprised to find how few of my fellow-citizens were aware that New York had ever been called New Amsterdam, or had heard of the names of its early Dutch governors, or cared a straw about their ancient Dutch progenitors."[73] As a people we have not changed on this score: Americans are all-too-often ignorant of our past and unaware of our cultural roots. The Dutch era, the early settlers who developed the region, and the homes they built are a part of the Hudson Valley heritage and a distinctive contribution to the American experience.

If only for their down-to-earth humanity, the Dutch settlers deserve remembrance. Whereas, other peoples named every river, rock, and cluster of hovels after saints, monarchs, and bits of promotional puffery, the Dutch knew their ships by the name of *Milkmaid*, *Brindle Cow*, *Horse*, *Sheep*, *Good Beer*, *Cat* and *Parrot*. Their farms and homes were called *Bonte Koe* (Spotted Cow), *Crailo* (Crow's Wood), and *Kost Verloren* (Money Thrown Away). Resisting temptations of grandiosity, they knew the stretches of the Hudson River as Clay Reach, after the clay banks on the east side, the Dance Chamber, for an Indian ceremonial dance ground in the mid-valley, and *Wolven Hoek* (Wolf's Point) opposite Albany. They named the two guardians of the Hudson Highlands for a hay barrack, the *Hoyberg*, and a mound of butter, the *Boterberg*. Later day pretensions led to a loss of much of this original forthrightness: Cow Neck became Manhasset, Long Island; and Saw Pit became Port Chester, New York.

Henry Noble MacCracken wrote, in his history of early Dutchess County, *Old Dutchess Forever!* of the Dutch in America: "Their contribution to American life has been all out of proportion to their numbers in the United States census."[74] The Dutch heritage should be admired and emulated. It is a tradition of moderation and tolerance that has, in many ways, remained central to the widely admired American traditions of a liberality of spirit, an endangered heritage that has been a central part of the American way-of-life and self-image. Their emphasis featured a generosity and openness that stands in marked contrast to the English pretentiousness in the Southern colonies and the mean-spirited attitudes in early New England. Therefore, it is in fond memory of those early Dutch settlers and the delightful homesteads that they built in the Hudson Valley that the following text is addressed.

Building styles that illustrate the cultural
zone of the settlers.

Photographs by the author unless otherwise noted.

Above:

Zuiderzee Museum, Enkhuizen restoration of a pantile-roofed, spout-gable brick, rural-type house with side entry.

Facing page, top left:

Zaanse Schans Museum restoration of seventeenth-century small merchants' cottage with vertical-board siding and a pantile roof. The windows have wooden casements; shutters are like those in the Hudson Valley with 'cigar' bolts and 's'-shaped keepers.

Facing page, top right:

Zuiderzee Museum, Enkhuizen restoration spout-gable brick shop with *stoep.*

Dutch-style eighteenth-century house at Holbeach (Clough), Lincolnshire, England. Pantile roof, braid-edged spout gables, wooden casement windows, and soldier course of horizontal bricks over the doors and windows. Courtesy R. H. Blackburn.

Above:

Dutch-style brick spout-gable house with elbows, braiding, and casement windows in Normandy, France. This style house is seen frequently in the southern parts of the Netherlands and in the culture zone that extended from Normandy to Denmark and across the English Channel into Lincolnshire and Kent. Courtesy of Donald Carpentier.

Facing page, top:

Arnhem Open Air Museum restored farmhouse that combines a brick dwelling with a wooden cow barn. Thatch roof would be typical of many early buildings in New Netherland.

Facing page: bottom:

Arnhem Open Air Museum thatched-roofed half-timbered wattle-and-daub clay farmhouse. The exterior has been coated with blue tinted limewashed.

Clockwise from facing page, top: Hay barrack, *booiberg*, at Arnhem Open Air Museum.

Arnhem Open Air Museum Dutch-style fence materials for making a woven sapling fence.

Colonial-style rail snake fence at Philipsburg Manor, North Tarrytown, New York.

The Dutch barn at Mouny Gulian, Dutchess County, New York. Courtesy of G. Huber.

Dutch barn at Philipsburg Manor.

CHAPTER III

Land Tenure, Title, and Valuation

T HE PATROONS AND PATENTEES who were granted land title by the Dutch West India Company, the English monarchs, or the royal governors still needed to purchase the granted lands from the Native Americans and secure titles from the tribal occupants and owners. The prices may appear absurdly low today but that was market value in the seventeenth and eighteenth centuries for unimproved wilderness. The famous "twenty-four dollar" price that Peter Minuit paid for Manhattan was agreeable to the parties at the time.

Facing page: "Widow" Sturdevant House, Albany, New York. An early eighteenth century dwelling in the traditional Netherlands' urban style with a brick façade and wooden eave walls. The anchor irons can be seen where they hold the frame and brickwork together and the *stoep* design and hand railing follow traditional precedents', as do the simple batten shutters. The upper windows flanking the 'ghost' of an enclosed garret door have the original Dutch frames with later sashes. The main floor windows are later eighteenth-century replacements as is the entry door, but the crane and cock-loft door appear original. Courtesy of R. H. Blackburn.

Even when the Western nations dealt with each other, the prices often appear to be absurdly low in today's terms: The United States bought the vast tract of the Louisiana Purchase from France in 1803 for $3,000,000 dollars, an amount equal to only pennies an acre.

The rich and the well connected purchased most land in blocks and large tracts. Naturally, some imperfect transactions took place, ranging from the erroneous to the scandalous: One example of dubious land dealing occurred when King George I granted 2,000 acres of land in the Mohawk Valley to the Van Slyck family in 1715. The Van Slycks had intermarried for generations with the Mohawk Nation of the Iroquois Confederation and was therefore "family" to the tribe. Through "creative surveying," the tract was enlarged at the Royal Government's expense into 6,000 acres. No one officially complained. The grant was honored at the expanded size. The government in London was not ignorant of the abuses. In 1726 the Board of Trade was advised that encroachment on Royal Land was a common practice and that "many evidences were produced before the Council to prove an encroachment of near Seventy thousand Acres of land" had taken place. [1] Even though the encroachments were illegal, the large tracts were leased, rented, or sold off profitably in small parcels to individual settlers or representatives of congregations and special groups, such as the Palatines, the Quakers, or the Huguenots. The royal government decided against reclaiming the land as "dispossessing so many families would appear so great a hardship that the king would sooner loose his Right than disturb & distress his people."[2]

Therefore the government generally allowed these encroachments and several magnates benefited handsomely from dubious land speculation. Although few settlers ever dealt directly with either the King's governors or the Indians to acquire land a number of small land purchases directly from the Indians did occur. For example in 1662 Pieter Bronck bought 352 acres of land in Coxsackie.[3] Then "on January 13, [1663] negotiations were concluded between Sioketas and Siachemoes, Indian proprietors, and Pieter Bronck for the latters purchase of a large tract of land which the Indians had named Koxhackung."[4]

The Hudson River was the main waterway of New Netherland, passing through the very heart of the colony. The two original boundaries had also been waterways: The Connecticut, or Fresh River, and the Delaware, or South River. The most important land between the head-of-navigation at Fort Orange and the estuary at New Amsterdam lay about mid-way down the river at the junction with a stream known as the Esopus. Long before the arrival of the Dutch, the Indians had settled and farmed the rich, open savannas of the mid-Hudson Valley. Early on, the Dutch had traded among the tribes of the Esopus and observed the hundreds of acres under cultivation. By the 1650s, the Dutch were eager to acquire land in the area for themselves.[5]

The first land patent in the Esopus area was issued by the West India Company to Thomas Chambers on November 8, 1653. The patent comprised thirty-eight morgens of land, or nineteen acres, for which he had obtained the title from the Indians on June 5, 1652. The Dutch "morgan" is an area of land that can be plowed in a morning (about two acres) c. 1674. Over the next few years additional titles were registered: Juriaen Westphael, 38½, August 29, 1654; Cristoffel Davits (Kit Davis), 36 morgens, September 25, 1656; Johannes de Laet, 500 morgens, March 27, 1657; Thomas Chambers, 4½ morgens, March 10, 1662; and Cornelis Barents Slecht, 25 morgens, December 7, 1662.

On June 7, 1663, the Indians burned Wiltwyck (Kingston) and Nieuw Dorp (Hurley). A setback occurred when the First and Second Esopus Wars laid to waste the region and spread terror in the Valley. Many of the inhabitants were massacred. At one time, sixty-six women and children were taken captive among the Indians; it took six months to rescue the last captive. The rescue operation, however, introduced the settlers to new lands, west of the Hudson River in the fertile Shawagunk and the Wallkill river valleys and in the rich lowlands around present-day Rosendale. The Esopus Wars were the only time when the tomahawk, the torch, and the horrors of Indian captivity were experienced in these peaceful infant settlements.[6] Lesser people might have fled; however, within months of the wars, settlement resumed. New patents were granted until on August 19, 1664 when the last patents under the Dutch were issued to Petrus

Bayard, for 260 acres, and Albert Heymans Roose, for "a plantation" at Esopus.[7]

Concerning the New Paltz Patent it was reported that "no land was wrested from the Indians in 'the Esopus.' It was paid for at Wiltwyck, at Hurley, at the home of 'the old sawer' at Saugerties and at New Paltz."[8] Fourteen years passed before the new lands were acquired by the patentees of Hurley. However, settlement of the Esopus area continued apace, even while the Dutch lost the colony to the English, recovered it, and finally ceded it back to the English. On April 28, 1677, a license was obtained from the English Governor, Sir Edmond Andros, to purchase land along the Wallkill from the Indians. The purchase agreement text exists.[9] (see sidebar).

The Indian Deed
(In September 1677, after the Indians received their compensation, this deed was executed.)

We the undersigned former joint-owners of the land sold to Lewis Dubois and his associates acknowledge to have received from them full satisfaction according to the agreement and therefore convey the said land with a free passage to them and their heirs forever, relinquishing our right and title and freeing them from all further claims: in witness whereof we have signed this with the Justice, Sheriff, Magistrates and others present on the 15th day of September 1677 at *Hurley.*

Signed

Esopus Sachems

Sewakanamy	X his mark	Matsayay	X his mark
Pannerewach	X his mark	Asseneraikan	X his mark
Mamaroch	X her mark	Wachtonck	X his mark
Maheny	X his mark	Wawamis	X her mark
Haroman	X his mark	Machkahoos	X his mark
Pagotaramin	X his mark	Wawesaska	X his mark
Wingawis	X his mark	Namas	X his mark
Wessenach	X his mark	Taomchkapay	X his mark
Maccamossingh	X his mark	Saagarowon	X his mark
		Sawonowis	X his mark
		Machkakamoca	X his mark

The Article Of Agreement

To-day, the 26th of May in the year 1677, an agreement was made by the below-named parties, pursuant to a license from the Hon'ble Governor *Edmond Andros*, dated the 28th of April 1677, with the undersigned *Esopus* Indians concerning the purchase of a certain tract of land on the other side of the *Rondout Kil.*

Matsayay, *Nehakaway, Magahahoos, Assmarakan,* and *Wawawanis* acknowledge to have sold to *Lewis Dubois* and his associates the land within the following boundaries: Beginning at the high hill called *Moggoneck*, thence south-east towards the *Great River* to the point called *Juffrouw's Hook* in the *Long Reach*, by the Indians called *Magaat Ramis*, thence North along the river to the island, lying in the *Crum Elbow* at the beginning of the *Long Reach*, by the Indians called *Waracahaes* and *Tawaeretaque*, along the high hill southwest to *Moggoneck*, including between these boundaries all contained therein, hills, valleys, waters, etc. and a free passage to the *Rondout Kil* as convenient, as it may be found. The Indians shall also have as much liberty and license to hunt all kind of wild animal and tom fish, as the Christians. The land the Indians have engaged to sell for the goods specified here below:

40	Kettles, 10 large 30 small	100 knives	
40	axes	4 ancres of wine	
40	addices	40 guns	
40	shirts	60 duffels coats	

100 fathoms of white wampum   60 blankets
300 "black"   100 nails   [?]
60 pair of socks, one half of them small ones   1 schepel of pipes

100   bars of lead   Wine has been given
       for the horses   [?]
1   Keg of powder

The parties of either part herewith acknowledge to have agreed and have signed this with their hands

Signed:

Lowies Du Booys	Matsayay	X his mark
Christian De Yoo X his mark	Wachtonck	X his mark
Abraham Haesbroocq	Senerakan	X his mark
Andries Lefebre	Mayakahoos	X his mark
Jan Brooq	Wawawamis	X her mark
Piere Doyo	Witnesses:	
Lowie Biverie	Jan Elton	
Anthony Crespel		Jacomintje Slecht
Abraham Du Booys	Jan Mattysen	
Hugi Frere		
Isaak Do Booys	Agrees with the original:	
Symeon Lefebre		De La Montagne Sec'y

On September 29, 1677, fourteen days after the deed was executed, Governor Andros issued the patent to Louis DuBois and his
associates, known as the "Duzine," or the "Twelve Patentees" in the
name of the Duke of York.

Similarly, lands on the opposite bank of the Hudson River were
purchased from the Indians. One of the principal land transactions
in Dutchess County was the Rombout Patent. The records -- including a copy of the 1683 bill-of-sale and the deed to tribal lands along
the Hudson River, as well as the text of the Rombout Patent, granted
by Governor Thomas Dungan in 1685 -- are printed in their entirety
in the *Madam Brett Homestead* literature. The material was published
by the Melzingah Chapter of the D. A. R., Beacon, New York, in
1967.[10] The documents show that the Indians were paid for their land,
and that the patent, dated two years after the bill-of-sale, officially
confirmed the private agreement between the concerned parties.

Because these charters and deeds are typical of the fundamental
legal basis for many Dutch settlements on Native American lands in
the Hudson Valley, it is worth quoting one in its entirety. The
Rombout deed of sale reads as follows:

INDIAN DEED OF SALE

The following Indian Deed of Sale, Recorded for
Mr. ffrancis Rumbout and Gulyne Ver Planke,
the 14th day of August, 1683:

To ALL CHRISTIAN PEOPLE To Whom This Writing
Shall Come, Sackoraghkigh for himselfe, and in the name of
Megriesken, sachem of the wappinger Indians, Queghsjehapaein,
Niessjawejahos, Queghout, Asotews, Wappegereck, Nathin-
deaniw, Wappappee, Ketaghkainis, Meakhahoghkan, Mierham,
Peapightapeieuw, Queghitaeuw, Minesawogh, Katariogh, Kight-
apiuhogh, Rearowogh, Meggrek, Sejay, Wienangeck, Maene-
manew, and Ginghstyerem, true and Lawful Owners and Indian
Proprietors of the Land herein Menchoned, send Greeting,
KNOW YEE - that for and in Consideracon of a Certain Sume
or Quantity of Money, Wampum, and diverse other Goods in a
Schedull hereunto Annexed Perticularly Menconed and Ex-
pressed to them the said Indians, in Hand Payed by Mr. ffrancis
Rumbouts and Gulyne Ver Planke, both of the Citty of New
Yorke, Merchants, the Receipt whereof they, the said Indians,

Doe hereby Acknowledge, and therewith ownes themselves to be fully payed, Contented and Sattisfied, and thereof and of every Parte and Parcell Doe hereby Acquitt, Exonerate and Discharge them, the said ffrancis Rumbouts and Gulyne V. Planke, their Heirs and Assignes, have Given, Granted, Bargained, Sold, Aliened, Enfeoffd, and Confirmed, and by these Presents Doe fully Cleerly and Absolutely Give, Grant, Bargaine, Sell, and Alien, Enfeoffe, and Confirme unto the said ffrancis Rumbout and Gulyne Ver Planke, All that Tract or Parcell of Land Scituate, Lyeing and being on the East side of Hudson's River, at the north side of the High Lands, Beginning from the South side of A Creek Called the fresh Kill, and by the Indians Matteawan, and from thence Northward along said Hudson's River five hundd Rodd bejond the Great Wappins Kill, called by the Indians Mawenawasigh, being the Northerly Bounds, and from thence into the Woods fouer Houers goeing, alwayes Keeping five hundd Rodd Distant from the North side of said Wapinges Creeke, however it Runns, as alsoe from the said fresh Kill or Creeke called Matteawan, along the said fresh Creeke into the Woods att the foot of the said High Hills, including all the Reed or Low Lands at the South side of the said Creeke, with an Easterly Line fouer Houers going into the Woods, and from thence Northerly to the end of fouer Houers Goeing or Line Drawne att the North side of the five hundd Rodd Bejoyand the Greate Wappinger Creek or Kill called Mawenawasigh, together with all the Lands, Soyles, Meadows, both fresh and Salt Pastures, Commons, Wood Land, Marshes, Rivers, Rivoletts, Streams, Creekes, Waters, Lakes, and whatsoever else to the said Tract or Parcell of Land within the Bounds and Limitts aforesaid is Belonging, or any wise Appurteining, without any Resevacon of Herbage, Trees, or any other thing Growing or Being thereupon, To have and to hold the said Tract or Parcell of Land, Meadow, Ground, and Primisses, with their and every of their Apputennces, and all the Estate, Right, Title, Interest, Clayme, and Demand of them the said Indian Proprietors, and each and every of them, of, in, and to, the same, and Every Parte thereof, unto them the said ffrancis Rumbout and Gulyne Ver Planke, their Heires and Assignes, to the Sole and only Proper use, Benefitt and Behoofe of them, the said ffrancis Rumbout and Gulyne Ver Planke, *their* Heirs and Assignes for Ever, and they the said Indians Doe for themsilves and their Heires and every of them Covenant, Promise, and Engage that the said ffrancis Rumbout and Gulyne Ver Planke,

their Heirs and Assigns, shall and may from henceforth for ever
Lawfully, Peaceably, and Quietly have, hold, Possesse, and En-
joye the said Tract or Parcell of Land, and all and Singuler other
the Primisses, with their Appertences without any Lett, Hin-
drance, or Interrupcon whatsoever of or by them, the said Indians, Proprieters of their Heires, or of any other Person or Persons,
whatsoever clayming or that hereafter shall or may Clame, by,
from or under them, or Either of them, And that they shall and
will, upon the reasonable Request and Demand made by the said
Francis Rumbouts and Gulyne Ver Planke, Give and Deliver
Peaceably and Quietly Possession of the said Tract or Parcell of
Land and Primisses, or of some Parte thereof, for and in the Name
of the whole, unto such Person or Persons as by the said ffrancis
Rumbout and Gulyne Ver Planke, shall be Appointed to Receive
the same. In *Witness whereof*, the said Sackoraghkigh, for himselfe
and in the Name of Megriskar, Sachem of Wappinger Indians,
Queghsjehapeieuw, Niessjawejhos, Queghout, Asotewas, Wappegereck, Nathindaew, Wappape, Ketaghkanns, Meakag-
hoghkan, Mierham, Peapightapaeuw, Queghhitaeuw,
Memesawogh, Katariogh, Kightapinkog, Rearawogh, Meggiech,
Sejay Wienangeck, Maenemaeuw, Guighstierm, the Indian Owners and Proprietors aforesd, have hereunto sett their Hands on
Seales in N. Yorke, the Eighth day of August, in the 35th Yeare
of his Maties Reigne, Anno Dom, 1683.

The marke of E Sakoraghuck, (L.S.)
The marke of X Queghsjehapaeiw, (L.S.)

Signed Sealed and Delivered in the p'sen of us
Antho: Brockholls,
P. V. Courtlandt,
John West.
The marke of Claes the Indian X Inter. (verite.)
The marke of Merham, (L.S.)
The marke of & Peapightapaew, (L. S.)
The marke of Queghhitaemw, (L. S.)
The marke of 8 Meinesawogh, (L. S.)
The marke of o Kotariogh, (L. S.)
The marke of) Rearowogh, (L. S.)
The marke of u Rearowogh, (L. S.)
The marke of 9 Meggenksejay (L. S.)
The marke of U Wienargeck, (L. S.)
The marke of o Maenemanew, (L. S.)

The marke of 2 Guighstjerem, (L. S.)
The marke of (- Ketaghkannes, (L. S.)
The marke of V Meakhajh, (L. S.)
The marke of O Oghkan, (L. S.)
The marke of X Niessjaweajahos, (L. S.)
The marke of X Qiejhout, (L. S.)
The marke of X Sjotewes, (L. S.)
The marke of X Wappegereck, (L. S.)
The marke of X Nathindaeuw, (L. S.)
The marke of X Wappape, (L. S.)

A schedull or Particuler of Money, Wampum and other goods
Paid by ffrancis Rumbout and Gulyne Ver Planke for the purchase of the Land in the Deed hereunto annexed.

One hundd Royalls,
One hund Pound Powder,
Two hund fathom of White Wampum,
One hund Barrs of Lead,
One hundred fathom of black Wampum,
thirty tobacco boxes,
thirty Gunns, twenty Blankets,
forty fathom of Duffills,
twenty fathom of stroudwater Cloth.
thirty Kittles, forty Hatchets.
forty Hornes, forty Shirts.
forty p stockings, twelve coates of R. B. & b. C.
ten Drawing Knives.
forty earthen Juggs.
forty Bottles.
forty Knives, fouer ankers rum.
ten halfe, fatts Beere.
two hund tobacco Pipes, &c.
Eighty Pound Tobacco.

New York, August the 8th, 1683.

The above Perticulers were Delivered to the Indians in the Bill of
Sale Menconed in the psence of us

(signed) Antho: Brockhalls,
(signed) P. V. Courtlandt,
(signed) John West.

I do hereby certify the aforegoing to be a true copy of the Original Record, compared therewith by me.

(signed) Lewis A. Scott, *Secretary*

The Rombout Patent granted by Governor Thomas Donhan, two years after the sale of the land, reads as follows:

THE RUMBOUT PATENT

EXEMPLIFICATION OF FRANCs RUMBOUTS PATENT

Dated 17TH Oct. 1685

Rumbout Patent

dated February 8, 1682, given to francis Rumbout and Gulyne Verplanke. It was given when Thomas Dongan was Lieut. Governor and Vice-Admiral under his Majesty James II, King of England, Scotland, France and Ireland. *The People of the state of New York,* By the Grace of God *Free and Independent.* To all whom these presents shall come send *Greeting. Know ye* that in our records in our Secretary's Office of our said State we have seen certain Letters Patent In the words following to wit. "*Thomas Dongan,* Lieut. Governor and Vice Admiral under his Majesty James the second the Second By the Grace of God King of England, Scotland, France and Ireland, Defender of the Faith & a Supream Loard and Proprietor of the Colony and Province of New York & its Dependencyes in America, &c. *To all* to whom these presents shall come *Sendeth Greeting. Whereas* Francis Rumbouts and Gulyne Verplanke of the City of New Yorke, Merchants by virtue of and in pursuance of an order and lysence of the Commander in Chiefe and Council of the said Province of New Yorke bearing date the twenty-eight day of February in the yeare of our Lord one thousand six hundred eighty two, Have according to the Law and practice of the said Province for a valuable consideration purchased of the natives and Indian Owners, their right title interest claime and demand of in and to all that certaine Tract or parcell of land herein after mentioned and expressed for their owne proper use as by the Indian Deed of Sale thereof bearing date the eight Day of August in the Yeare of our Lord one thousand six hundred eighty three remaining upon record in the Secretary's Office of the said Province may more fully and att large appeare. And whereas the said Gulyne Verplanke is since deceased butt before his decease mad his last will

and testament in writing and therein and thereby made constituted and appointed Henrita his widdow and relict his whole and
sole Executrix who hath since the decease of the said Gulyne
Verplanke proved the said Will and taken upon her the burthen
of Exectrix and hath since intermaried with Jacobus Kipp of the
City of New Yorke aforesaid Mercht., by virtue of which Will
and the intermariage as aforesaid, hee, the said Jacobus Kipp is
become interested in and Intitled to such share title and interest
as the said Gulyne Verplanke att the time of his decease had in
the said Tract or parcell of land hereafter mentioned by virtue of
the said purchase as aforesaid. *And whereas* in the life time of the
said Gulyne Verplanke it was agreed between the said Francis
Rumbouts and the said Gulyne Verplanke & Stephanus Van
Courtlandt of the City of New Yorke aforesaid Merchants, that
he, the said Stephanus Van Cortlandt paying the full third parte
of the charge of the purchase aforesaid made by them the said
Francis Rumbouts and Gulyne Verplanke as aforesaid should
have conveyed and assuered to him the one full third parte of all
their right title and interest of in and to the said Tract or parcel
of land hereafter mentioned by virtue of and pursuant to which
agreemt. they the said Francis Rumbouts, Jacobus Kipp and the
said Henrita his Wife have since the decease of the said Gulyne
Verplanke conveyed and assured unto the said Stephanus Van
Cortlandt, his Heirs and assighns for ever, one full third parte of
all their right title and Interest of in and to the said Tract or parcell
of land hereafter mentioned as in and by their certaine writeing
or conveyance bearing date the fifth day of September instant may
more fully and att large appeare.

   Now Know Ye That by virtue of the commission and authority unto me given for and in consideration of the yearly rent
herein after mentioned and reserved and for divers other causes
and considerations me thereunto moving I have granted ratified
and confirmed and by these presents Doe grant rattifie and
confirme unto the said Francis Rumbouts, Jacobus Kipp and
Stephanus Van Cortlandt all that Tract or parcell of land situate
lying and being on the east side of Hudsons River att the north
side of the highlands Begining from the south side of a creeke
called the Fishkill and by the Indians Matteawan and from thence
northward along said Hudsons River five hundred rodd beyond
the greate Wappins Kill called by the Indians Mawenawasigh
being the northerly bounds and from thence into the woods foure
houres goeing, that is to say sixteene English miles, always keep-

ing five hundred rodd distant from the north side of said greate Wappingers Creek however it runns as also from the said Fishkill or creeke called Matteawan along the said Fisj Creek into the Woods att the foott of the said high hills including all the read or low lands att the South side of said Creek with an easterly line four howers goeing, that is to say sixteen english miles into the Woods and from thence northerly to the end of the foure howers going towitt sixteen English miles or linedrawne att the north side of the five hundred Rodd beyond the greate Wappingar Creeke or Kill called Mawenawasigh together with all and all manner of Rivers, Rivolets, Runns, Streams and liberty to build erect and make any Mill or Mills thereon feedings pastures woods under-woods Trees waters water courses ponds pooles pitts swamps moores marshes meadows easiements proffitts and commoditys fishing fowling hunting hawking mines mineralls Quarrayes Roy-all Mines excepted Royalties franchises and apurtenances whatso-ever to the said Tract or parcell of land within the Bounds and lymitts aforesaid belonging or in any wise appurtaineing *To have and to hold* the said Tract or parcell of land and and all and singular other the premisses with their and every of their appurtenences unto the said Francis Rumbouts Jacobus Kipp and Stephanus Van Courtland, their Heirs and Assignes forever unto the only proper use and behoofe of them the said Francis Rumbouts, Jacobus Kipp and Stephanus Van Courtland their heirs and assigns forever. *Yielding and paying therefore* Yearly and every Year for the use of our Soverigne *Lord James the second* by the Grace of God of England Scottland France and Ireland King Defender of the faith &c his heires or Successors or such Officers as by him or them shall be from time to time appointed to receive the same six bushells of good merchantable winter Wheate on every twenty-fifth days of March att the City of New Yorke aforesaid

In Witness whereof I have signed these Presents with my hand & caused the publique Seale of the said Province to be hereunto affixed and these presents to be entered upon Record in the Secretary's Office of the said Province this 17th Day of October in the first Year of his said Maties. Reigne and in the yeare of our lord 1685 Thomas Dongan.

After the Revolution the patent was reconfirmed by the State of New York in 1784 and the papers attached verifing the titles were approved and signed by Governor George Clinton.

> *In Testimony whereof* We have caused the said Letters Patent, to be herein and hereby exemplified, and the Great Seal of our said State to be to these presents affixed.
>
> Witness our trusty and well beloved *George Clinton,* Esquire, Governor of our said State General and Commander in Chief of all the Militia and Admiral of the Navy of the same, this twenty fifth day of June in the eight Year of our Independence, and in the year of our Lord one thousand seven hundred and eighty four.
>
> (Signed) George Clinton
>
> Passed the Secretary's office. . .this twenty-fifth day of June one thousand seven hundred and eighty-four.
>
> (signed) Lewis A. Scott D Secry.

The Duke, later King James II, was given a quit rent by the patentee, usually a token payment unrelated to the true value of the land. In the case of the Rombout Patent, granted in 1685, it was "six bushells of good merchantable winter wheat" delivered to New York every March 25. The Board of Trade eventually awoke to this largess at the Crown's expense. In the "Report to the Board of Trade," 1698, it was pointed out that exorbitant grants of land in New York were a problem. The Council of New-York reported that these grants:

> will be very destructive to that province, which. . . is the safeguard and chief fence of all his Majesty's northern plantations; we most humbly offer that all methods whatsoever allowed by law, be put in practice for the breaking and annulling of them, and that for the future no grants of lands be made under a less Quit Rent to his Majesty than 2s 6p pr 100 acres, as was directed by Sr Edmond Andro's forementioned instructions, nor without an obligation upon the grantees to plant and settle the same within the space of three years at furthest, under the penalty of forfeiture.11

The reasonable recommendations concerning the royal interests and development were seldom enforced. Land was given away or sold off at a fraction of its value to the well connected at the king's loss and to the detriment of the colony. New York landlords held tracts of patented land that remained unrented, unsold, and undeveloped for decades, or they sold or subdivided land without regard to their charter or quit rent obligations. George Clark, a member of the colonial council, wrote to the Lords of Trade regarding the unpaid quit rents and the two acts passed to address the problem.

> An Act regulating the payment of his Majesties Quit Rents, and for the partition of Lands in order thereto without the latter, the first would be defective and leave the Recovery and Collection of the Quit Rents in as bad a condition as ever, and in a worse they could not be; but now the long Arrears for Lands granted to several persons in joint tenancy, or in common, and which have by many Sales been subdivided, and for want of a Partition could not be collected, will be paid, and the growing rents regularly collected; It is an Act which the Government has long been labouring to obtain, both for the purposes aforementioned and for quieting the minds of people, who were often threatned (sic) with prosecutions for the whole Quit Rent, amounting to a large sum, when each man's portion was but small; which has been a great discouragement to the peopling of this frontier Province. [12]

The practice of granting large tracts of land discouraged many potential small scale settlers. The more prosperous settlers moved to Pennsylvania and New England where land could be obtained in fee simple more easily. When a New York landlord did attract a settler, he often preferred to lease or rent his holdings and retain title for himself. As is noted in the *Polgreen Photographs*, renting impacted upon many aspects of life, including house size. Early rental contracts specified small houses built by the landlords (the Van Rensselaers, and, for example, speculators such as Gerrit Teunis Van Vechten and Marte Gerritse Van Bergen), but later rentals permitted the tenant to build his own home. Then larger houses were erected "which reflected. . .[the tenant's] own needs and tastes rather than those of a landlord."[13]

The problem of extensive tracts of land held by a few great landlords remained in New York well into the nineteenth century. A sample rental agreement will help to clarify the terms between the landlord and the tenant. At Fox Hall Manor the policy of rental was as follows:[14]

Feudal Service To Fox Hall Manor

Appeared before me, W. Montagne, secretary for the hon. court, the hon. justice of the peace, Jacob Elberts and Johannes Juriaensen, who admits having leased of the before-mentioned Justice Schambers [a parcel of land] named 'the Brabanter's thicket,' for the length of five consecutive years commencing in October, 1675 and terminating 1680. The lessees shall, for one year, be exempt from paying rent, but the next four years shall pay every year 30 sch. of maize. And they shall fence in their land, or in case of neglect shall have no claim against the lessor.

And if need be the lessees shall be obliged, as it is their duty, to assist in defending Foxhall.

Enter into without suspicion or craft, and subscribed to with their own hand in the presence of the below named witnesses at Foxhall this November 23, 1675

Signed   Thomas Chambers
           Jacob Elbertse
           Johannes Juriaensen Westvaellin

Signed   Jacob Jansen
           Ariaen Fransen

To which testifies (signed)
           W. Montagne, Secrectary
           (from court records)

On a continent where land was often available for the taking, small landholders could find better terms than lease or rent. The possibility of freehold ownership in fee simple was the major attraction to settlers able to purchase. Landlords who were prepared to sell could generally find buyers. Buying and selling in good faith implies a secure title to the land; therefore, governments generally act to insure the validity of titles. Even in the earliest days of the colony, problems arose affecting titles, so the government of New Netherland stated in the Ordinances of New Amsterdam:[15]

The Director General and Council have learned, that various clandestine abuses and frauds are practiced in the sale and transfer of real estate, such as houses, yards, lots, and other land, to the prejudice of older creditors. Therefore they herewith charge their Secretary and in his absence his first Clerk, not to pass and sign any conveyance of real estate, unless the same has first been reported to the Director and Council on a regular Court day and been approved by them; declaring herewith all contracts and conveyances of real estate void and of no value, which are passed and signed after this date without their approval and confirmation.

Thus done, etc, February 7, 1650. Signed ut supra.

In the course of time, the Rombout Patent was divided between the heirs of the patentees. One of the more famous and aggressive heirs was Madam Catheryna Rombout Brett. Instead of leasing or renting her lands, she sold title and acreage to settlers in fee simple. Once the individual settler purchased land from the patentee and deed holder, and registered his title with the local authorities, a legal homestead could be established.

The early settlers were often given sound advice. A book written by the Reverend Jonas Michaelius, *Manhattan In 1628*, spelled out many essential guidelines regarding crops, weather, and conditions in the new land. Cornelius Van Tienhoven's 1650 report on colonization, *Information Relative To Taking Up Land In New Netherland*,[16] also gave practical advice to settlers. He advised:

Boors and others who are obliged to work at first in the Colonies ought to sail from this country in the fore or latter part of winter, in order to arrive with God's help in New Netherland early in the Spring, in March, or at the latest in April, so as to be able to plant, during that summer, garden vegetables, maize and beans, and moreover employ the whole summer in clearing land and building cottages.

All then who arrive in New Netherland must immediately set about preparing the soil, so as to be able, if possible to plant some winter grain, and to proceed the next winter to cut and clear the timber. The trees are usually felled from the stump, cut up and burnt in the field, unless such as are suitable for building, for palisades, posts and rails, which must be prepared during the winter, so as to be able to be set up in the spring on the new made land which is intended to be sown, in order that the cattle may not in any wise injure the crops. In most lands is found a certain root called red Wortel, which must before ploughing, be extirpated with a hoe, expressly made for that purpose. This being done in the winter, some plough right around the stumps, should time or circumstances not allow these to be removed; others plant tobacco, maize and beans first. The soil even thus becomes very mellow, and they sow winter grain the next fall. From tobacco, can be realized some of the expenses incurred in clearing the land. The maize and beans help to support both men and cattle. The farmer having thus begun, must endeavor, every year, to clear as much new land as he possibly can, and sow it with such seed as he considers most suitable.[17]

Land travel, difficult at best, was impossible under many circumstances. Early settlement was along the major waterways. Ship, yacht, and dugout canoe were the primary means of travel in a frontier with no roads and few tracks or trails suitable for wagons through the dense forests, tangled underbrush, and wetlands. Water routes were the only way for early settlers to reach many areas and for bulky farm produce to be brought to market. Few early Dutch homes were more than one mile from navigable waters. Only later in the colonial period were roads opened into the interior.

Discussing the Luykas Van Alen house, Walter V. Miller wrote in *de Halve Maen*:

The siting of this house, its length running approximately north-south, admirably utilizes man-made and natural features of the vicinity. Early settlers had been quick to note and make use of a ford in the nearby creek, close to the village, and a bridle path soon paralleled the stream in a northwesterly-southeasterly direction. The house was erected some 300 feet west of this path, and about one mile from the fording place, atop a gentle rise which with a small brook meandering along its base and a never-failing spring close by, offered an excellent location.[18]

The Van Alen's choice of location proved felicitous; the farm and family prospered. Located near, but set well back from, the Post Road [Route 9H] the Van Alen house escaped the pavement that encroached upon many early houses located on major roads. In the twentieth century, road improvements have overrun many houses and the open space in front of buildings. All too often the best early sites have proven to be the undoing of the houses, because they were demolished for right of ways or more profitable use over the passage of three centuries. In fact, the Post Road in front of the Luykas Van Alen house post-dates the building; the original roadway was a path running close to the creek at the rear of the building. The Post Road was typical of other older roads, which were usually laid out to connect existing houses. It might be noted that many an old road seems to make unexpected curves for no obvious reason, and then returns to the direction of the next old house. In many cases the bend "to nowhere" once led to a house and so it may be a clue to a lost building site.[19]

Although uncleared land was not taxed, it was of limited use to a settler. Of course, even small holders cleared land and built on speculation, in hopes of selling and improving their finances, but most small holders were primarily homesteaders. They sought farmland and home sites to occupy on a permanent basis. Some land was left forested as a wood lot, but settlers clear-cut much of the land for farm fields. They used the method called slash-and-burn, the same wasteful technique used to ravish the remaining indigenous forests of the world today. In environmental terms, the activities of the early settlers were rapacious and the primal forest cover was harvested out of existence. The Catskills were originally known as the "Blue Hills" because of the color of the enormous stands of virgin hemlocks. "Within not much more than two generations, the Catskills were a denuded heap of rocks over which lay the rotting carcasses of trees."[20] The virgin hemlocks were clear-cut for their bark alone which was sold to the leather tanning industry, but re-growth has finally begun to restore the Catskills to their eighteenth-century appearance. When a few hundred settlers struggled at the edge of a virgin continent, it seemed inconceivable that their actions could seriously impact on the apparently "endless" bounty of the environment. It did.

The forests were available for the taking and the settlers used wood at the homestead for building and fuel. The trees were also a cash crop sold as whole trunks, split rails, sawn boards, clapboards and weatherboards, split shingles and shakes for building, and firewood in cords (a stack 4 x 4 x 8 feet or 128 cubic feet). The bark stripped from hemlock trees went to the tanning industry; oak trees were felled for ships' hulls; and entire stands of pine were felled for ships' masts, or reduced to tar and pitch as naval stores for the ship building yards. In the nineteenth century, the timber was used as charcoal in the iron industry and later on as ties for the iron rails and firewood on railroads and steamships. The rest was consumed in bonfires to clear the land, turn the ashes into marketable potash, or simply get rid of the wood that was lying waste. Ash is a good garden fertilizer, so some of the value was returned to the land. The settlers then planted a first crop among the stumps and ashes. Remaining trees were "ringed" by cutting a belt of the growth layer around the trunk to kill the trees for removal at a later date. The tree stumps were hauled out by teams of oxen or, in later days, blasted out with black powder. The Dutch farmers chose the rich bottom lands, which were almost free of large stones but often heavily wooded so even they needed to be cleared of trees. The rocky uplands tended to be farmed by transplanted New Englanders. When the hillside lands were plowed, large stones were hauled to the edge of the fields, where they were later erected into walls. The low stone walls were topped with rails to keep out cattle, hogs, and other animals more often than to fence in livestock. The settlers may have been wasteful of nature's bounty, but they certainly were hard workers. However, not every farmer cleared his own land. In many instances people were hired to open the land for farming. Jonas Bronck arrived in America aboard the ship 'Fire of Troy' in 1639 accompanied by two Danes who had contracted to clear and farm land he had not yet aquired.[21]

Problems frequently arose so the Dutch frequently turned to the courts to resolve issues. A case heard at the Kingston court Ordinary Session of March 2, 1668/9 involved Cornelis Wynkoop, plaintiff versus Harmen Hendricks and Jacob Jansen, defendants. Wynkoop claimed to have contracted for his land to be cleared of all the trees, chopped down and taken away, by the defendants. "Defendants admit having taken the contract to chop the trees surrounding his land, but not the 'strievelle,' [a variant form of the word struweel: brush or shrubs] and they agreed about the trees which are thicker than a leg, but not thinner." The court ordered parties to prove their assertions and directed the defendants "to continue with the work contracted."[22]

When discussing homesteads and Dutch houses, it helps to recall the scope and the scale of settlement and not be misled by twentieth-century concepts of wealth. In 1675 the total evaluation for Breukelen was £ 5,204 pounds Sterling. Michel Hainelle, the clerk who reported the Assessment Rolls for King's County, Long Island noted that the total valuation of the five chartered Dutch villages was £ 20,319 pounds Sterling. He wrote, "Reconing the county rates at 1 penny in the pound, they amount to 84 pounds 13 shillings and 2 pence Sterl'g, or in current pay to 1,015 guilders 13 shillings; property being rated as follows:"[23]

Assessment Roll Valuation: 1675

Each man	@	£ 18.00.	Each cow	@	£ 5.00.0
Each horse	@	12.	Each 3 year old	@	4.
Each 3 year old	@	8.	Each 2 year old	@	2.10.0
Each 2 year old	@	5.	Each yearling	@	1.10.0
Each yearling	@	3.	Each hog	@	1.
Each ox	@	6.	Each sheep	@	0.08.6
Each morgen [1/2 acre] of land	@	2.(pounds Sterling)			

Valuation of the Five Dutch Towns, August, 1763[23]

Pounds. sh.	Guild. st.	Pounds. sh
3,174.10.0 valuation of Boswyck (At 1 stiver in the pound)	158.14.8	£ 13.04.6
5,204.00.0 valuation of Breuckelen	260.04.0	£ 21.13.8
5,079.10.0 valuation of Middelwort	253.19.8	£ 21.03.4
4,008.10.0 valuation of Amsfort	200.08.8	£ 16.14.0
2,852.10.0 valuation of New Utrecht	142.12.8	£ 11.17.8

Total
20,319.00.0 valuation of the 5 Towns (At 1 stiv. per pound)

        1015.19.0   £ 84.13.2

The assessment role for the town of New Utrecht in King's County, chartered in 1661, clearly illustrates the size of a community, the individual holdings in livestock and land, and the scale of settlement in late seventeenth- and early eighteenth-century America.[25] New Utrecht was named by Jacques Courtelyou, one of the founding settlers, in honor of his place of origin in the Netherlands.[26] The farms, or *bouweries*, were typically small, some ten to twenty acres for the most part. The livestock was primarily limited to family needs, which usually included a horse (but, no foals are listed) or a team of horses (the Dutch plowed with horses; the New Englanders plowed with oxen) and a few milk cows, with their heifers and yearlings (but, no calves are listed). Surprisingly only a hog or two was listed in the August assessment role before the fall slaughter of excess stock, and few sheep appear (only two farmers in the community kept small flocks of ten or more sheep each). No fowl are listed, but most people probably kept a few chickens, ducks, or geese for eggs and feathers although wild fowl for eating were plentiful at the time. No crops or croplands were specified, but each farm would have grown grain—either wheat or maize or both. The low flatlands and tidal marsh, which the Dutch called *vly*, were mowed "for hay, which cattle would rather eat than fresh hay or grass."[27] (In the assessment rolls, noted below, Jan Hansen is shown to have "valley" or *vly* land. The fodder or hay would be harvested to winter the animals over to the spring.

In the *Dutch-American Farm*, D. S. Cohen notes that the village of Harlem and the Dutch towns on Long Island were laid out in similar fashion; each house was on a lot, or *erven*, and a cross street separated every four lots. Each house lot was assigned one garden plot, called *tuynen*, measuring five-by-twenty Dutch rods. In New Netherland the standard used was the Amsterdam measuring rod of 13 feet, each of 11.143 Dutch inches (*duimen* or thumbs). The Rhinelander measure rod was 12 Dutch *voeten* or feet of 12.36 duimen. The English rod is the same as the American measure of 16.5 English feet of 12 inches each. In addition, each house was assigned four morgen of farmland, or *bouwland*, in strips as well as marsh or meadow land for salt hay for the cattle. (The Dutch "*morgen*," is equal to approximately two English or American acres in area.) Unfortunately, the records do not enumerate houses, barns, or hay barracks, which would have rounded out the picture of a Dutch farm; however, building contracts list tobacco barns as a common feature of many farms. While tobacco would have provided a cash crop for the purchase of a few goods, it is difficult to judge the scale of the tobacco crop. In early villages, the European tradition of common land still existed, so many of the cattle and sheep might have been tended by a single herdboy in land "reserved as a commons," while the hogs typically ran wild in the woods to forage. "The *brinkdorpen*, common on the Drenthe plateau in the eastern Netherlands, were the same kind of towns "as the pattern of settlement seen in the Five Towns of Long Island and in many villages elsewhere in New Netherland.[28]

Assessment Roll of the Real and Personnel Property of the Inhabitants of New Uttrecht, made up 24 th August, 1675[29]

Jan Hansen: I poll [a hornless ox or dehorned cattle] 3 horses, 4 cows,
                         2 ditto of 2 yrs. I ditto of 1 yr   £ 80.10
                         40 morgens of land and valley   80.00
                                                                         160.10

Barent Joosten: 1 poll, 3 horses, 1 ditto of 2 yrs. 7 cows, 4 ditto of 2 yrs.
                         5 ditto of 1 yr. 3 hogs   114.10

Anthony Theunisse: 1 poll, 1 horse   30.00

Theunes Jansen van Peltt: 2 polls, 4 horses, 4 cows   £ 104.00
                         32 morgens of land   64.00
                                                                         168.00

Jacob Bastiaense: 1 poll   18.00

Crein Jansen: 1 poll, 2 horses, 1 ditto of 1 yr   45.00
                         12 morgens of land   24.00
                                                                          69.00

Jan Gisberttse: 1 poll   18.00

Jean Van Cleff: 1 poll, 2 horses, 2 cows, 1 ditto of 1 yr   55.00
                         40 morgens of land   80.00
                                                                         135.00

Jan Jansen Van Dyck: 1 poll, 2 horses, 2 cows, 1 ditto of 1 yr   53.10
                         16 morgens of land   23.00
                                                                          85.10

Gisbert Theyse: 1 poll, 2 horses, 2 cows, 1 ditto of 3 yrs, 2 ditto of 2 yrs 61.00
                         18 morgens of land and valley   36.00
                                                                          97.00

Hendrick Mattheise: 1 poll, 4 horses, 3 cows, 3 ditto of 2 yrs, 3 ditto of 1 yr 93.00
                         20 morgens of land   40.00
                                                                         133.00

Carel Jansen van Dyck: 2 polls, 2 horses, 3 cows, 3 ditto of 2 yrs. 1 ditto of 1 yr 84.00
                         24 morgens of land   48.00
                                                                         132.00

Huibert Jansen Stock: 1 poll   18.00
Jan Jansen van Rheyn: 2 polls, 1 horse of 2 yrs. 5 cows, 2 ditto of 1 year 69.00
                         20 morgens of land   40.00
                                                                         109.00

Pietter Jacobse:	1 poll, 2 cows	28.00
Theys Jansen:	1 poll, 2 oxen, 2 cows, 1 ditto of 3 yrs. 1 ditto of 1 yr. 1 hog	46.10
	12 morgens of land	24.00
		70.10
Jan Clement:	1 horse, 2 cows, 1 ditto of 1 yr	41.10
Jan Musserol:	1 poll, 2 oxen, 2 cows	40.00
	12 morgens of land	24.00
		64.00
Anthony Van der Eycke:	1 poll, 2 horses, 2 cows, 2 ditto of 3 yrs, 1 hog	61.00
	12 morgens of land	24.00
		85.00
Jan van Deuenter:	2 polls, 2 horses, 1 ditto of 3 yrs, 3 cows, 1 ditto of 1 yr,	
	2 hogs	67.00
	20 morgens of land	40.00
		107.00
Jan Verckerck:	3 polls, 5 horses, 2 ditto of 1 yr, 4 cows, 10 sheep	144.00
	72 morgens of land	144.00
		288.00
Rutger Joostten:	1 poll, 5 horses, 4 cows, 8 ditto of 3 yrs., 2 ditto of 2 yrs.,	
	2 ditto of 1 yr. 13 sheep, 1 hog	144.10
	72 morgens of land	144.00
		288.10
Jan Gerrittse:	24 morgens of land	48.00
Jacob Gerrittse:	24 morgens of land	48.00
Ackeys Jansen:	12 morgens of land	24.00
Laurens Jansen:	1 poll, 2 horses, 2 cows	52.00
	24 morgens of land	48.00
		100.00
Hans Harmense:	1 poll, 3 horses, 5 cows, 3 ditto of 2 yrs., 3 ditto of 1 yr.	
	5 sheep, 1 hog	94.00
	24 morgens of land	48.00
		142.00
Arie Willemse:	1 poll, 4 horses, 6 cows	96.00
	24 morgens of land	48.00
		144.00
Total amount of property of New Uytrecht		2,852.10

Valuation and prices are always a problem. Money changes value, even daily. Old estimates are immediately dated. In 1916, for example, John O. Evjen wrote in *Scandinavian Immigrants in New York: 1630 - 1674*, that: "In New Netherland one guilder beaver was worth $0.40. One guilder sewant was worth one-third of a guilder beaver. A good merchantable beaver skin was worth $3.20 to $4.00." His calculations were in current money in 1916. Evjen also provided a listing of the value of Dutch coins 1630-1674:

Coins

stuiver	$0.02
schelling (6 stuivers)	$0.12
gulden/Carolus gulden (20 stuivers)	$0.40
goud gulden (1⅖ guldens)	$0.56
rilksdaelder (2½ guldens)	$1.00
ducaton (3 guldens, 3 stuivers)	$1.26
pond Vallmsch (6 guldens)	$2.40

To arrive at the 1998 value, we need to recalculate the figures listed by John O. Evjen in 1916. (The results would then be immediately dated, and even then the data is often misleading.) Only the ratios between the various coins have real meaning. To have relevance, "value" must be keyed to a contemporary workman's daily wage. In the Rensselaerswyck service contract of 1639, a workman was to receive food and drink plus "the sum of thirty stivers for a full summer's day wage and in winter or otherwise somewhat less in proportion."[30] We can only say, if a day's wage was 30 stivers in cash at Rensselaerswyck, and bricks sold at 4 gilder per thousand in New Netherland, then a thousand bricks were worth 80 gilders, or somewhat over two-and-a-half summer day's wages. In 1997 bricks have sold for 10 cents each, so 1000 bricks cost $100 dollars. The present day-labor minimum wage of approximately $5.00 per hour, or a day's wage of $40.00, equals the two-and-a-half day rate for the same number of bricks.

In 1794, Thomas Cooper visited the new republic and compared various aspects of material culture in America and Great Britain. He computed an exchange table for dollars to pounds Sterling "reckoning the Dollar at 4s. 6d. English Money."[31] The table reads, in part, as follows:

Table of Dollars and Pounds Sterling: 1794

Dol.	£.	s.	Dol.	£.	s.	d.
100,000	22,500	0	200	45	0	0
50,000	11,250	0	100	22	10	0
5,000	4,500	0	30	6	15	0
1,000	225	0	8	1	16	0
500	112	10	3	0	13	6
400	90	0	2	0	9	0
300	67	10	1	0	4	6

Cooper lists the range of prices at Philadelphia in 1794, which need to be compared to 1999 daily average wage. In America, worker's daily pay was approximately three to four shillings, or about a 1794 dollar from the beginning of the Republic well into the first half of the nineteenth century.[32]

Price Current
Per Quantity.—Dollars 100 cents each.
Philadelphia, Jan. 11, 1794

Item		Dlls.	Cts.		Dlls.	Cts.
Bricks, per M.	from	4	0	to	7	0
Bread, fhip, per cwt.		0	0		2	67
Beer, American, in bottles, pr. doz. bot. includ.		0	0		1	74
Boards Cedar, per M feet		0	0		20	0
New England		10	0		14	0
Oak		14	0		10	0
Merchantable pine		20	0		24	0
Sap, do.		0	0		10	67
Mahogony, per foot		0	0		0	10
The above are the fhallop prices add 1 dollar 33 cents per 1000.						
Candles, Sperm. per lb.		0	0		0	48
Wax		0	53		0	56
Myrtle Wax		0	0		0	18
Mould, tallow		0	0		0	16
Dipped		0	0		0	14
Duck, Ruffia, pr. piece of 42 yds.		0	0		14	0
(Duck) Ravens (do.)		0	0		11	0
Dutch fail duck (do.)		18	0		20	0

Discussing a tax rate in New York, Philip Van Wyck writes in
de Halve Maen, March 1988, that in 1664 "the sum of £ 240 (Pounds
Sterling) would be well over $5,000 present value."[33] In 1673 an
evaluation of condemned houses built too close to the fort walls,
quoted values for the lot and for the loss and removal of the house.
The house values ranged from fl. 80 to fl. 3,340 and replacement lots
ranged from fl. 440 to fl. 562 in "wampum value" each.[34]

In 1710, subsistence was figured at six pence a day for an adult
and at four pence a day for a child under ten, in New York. But, what
is the standard for "subsistence" in 1710? Concerning wages for
labor: "Every Man or Woman above 15 years of age may earn two
shillings and three pence New York Money (which is eighteen pence
Sterling) every day in the year except Sundays. Handicrafts men, such
as Smiths, Joyners, Carpenters, Masons & Bricklayers may earn at
least Five Shillings New York Money every day they will work . .
."[35] A day's pay in 1700 was "about 3 s per day" and "soldiers . . .are
required to work for 1 s per day."[36] On May 13, 1701, it was noted
that "Cloathing and drink are double the price of that in England: a
pot of beer costs 4½p . . .A labouring man at New York has 3s a day
and a soldier's week's subsistence is but 3s 6d."[37] A soldier earned
"one third part of the wages which a Negro slave receives every day
in New York for splitting of fire wood and carrying the hodd."[38] In
1712, "dayly labr is never computed at less than half a cron a day"
and "two thirds for children."[39] In 1722, day wages were quoted as
"very dear" at "earning 3 shillings by the day," so that "this charge
. . . overballances all the advantages which the country naturally
affords . . .[because of] the charge of labor."[40] An advertisement in
The New-York Gazette or the Weekly Post Boy, September 18, 1758
noted a range of wages:

> For the Encouragement of Ship-Carpenters, able Seamen, and
> Laborers, in the Country, and the neighboring Provinces, to
> repair to the City of New-York, The Merchants of this City have
> agreed to give to Ships-Carpenters; Eight shillings per Day, able
> Seamen, Five shillings; and Laborers Four shillings; with the usual
> Allowance of Provisions; and other or grater Wages whatsoever.
> And all Persons liking the above Proposals, may be certain of
> constant Employment.[41]

Priorities, era, circumstance, and situation also affect valuation: A sack of wheat or a musket on the frontier was more valuable to a settler than either item may be worth new in the twentieth century. A banister-back New England chair made in 1700 was worth little at the time; today it has great value. Similarly, labor, skills, and knowledge have different values at different times: A dentist might remove two molars in 1998 for $600.00, but what would Louis XIV have paid for that dentist's skills—and painless modern dentistry—or the skills of a modern doctor, in 1700? The last will and testament of two New York Dutch settlers place land, currency, and possessions in context. Excerpts relating to real property are as follows:

On February 14, 1695/6, Wessel ten Broeck prepared his will:

Will of Wessel ten Broeck

I give to my oldest son Wessel ten Broeck or his order of heirs four morgens of land out of my farmland, now belonging to me, for his privilege of first born, without his claiming any more on that account Item, I give to my said son or his order or heirs only just fourth part of my whole farm besides the four morgens above specified, and my farm shall be divided into four shares by number of morgens and my said son or heirs shall have the choice of them in one piece provided that my said son or heirs shall turn over and pay to my other three sons, named below, what said share shall be apraised higher at by impartial parties under oath, when my sons, mentioned below, shall have come of age; I further give to my said son Wessen ten Broeck or heirs the just eighth part my house and ground in Kingston and all the just eighth part of all my personal estate; it is also my will and wish, that he, my said son, shall be allowed to take for his property a negro, selected from my negroes and he shall therefor be allowed in the inheritance of the personal estate the sum of L38 Courant money. Item, I order, that none of my heirs shall be allowed to prevent or cause to be prevented the damming, to preserve the water, and the use of the ground necessary for the damming, and the run of the water for the use of my said son's mill. It is further my wish and will, that my said son or his order of heirs shall be bound to pay the quantity of 1000 schepels of wheat to my four daughters of heirs, named Maria, Elsie, Geertruy and Sara, each one just fourth part of said sum in the time of four years, one just fourth part every year and if said sum is not paid by inability or for other reason at the prescribed time, then he shall be held to give proper interest, until said sum is paid.

I give to my son Coenraat ten Broeck or his heirs, the just fourth part of my whole farm, except what heretofore has been devised to my son Wessel ten Broeck. Item, I give to my said son Coenraat or heirs the eighth part of my house and ground in Kingston and the eighth part of my whole personal estate and he is bound to turn over and pay to my four daughters or heirs, named Maria, Elsie, Geertruy and Sara 1000 schepels of wheat, to each the just fourth part of said sum during the time of four years, after my said son shall have come of age each year one just fourth part of said sum, and if said sum is by inability or for other reasons not paid at the prescribed time, then he is held to give proper interest, until said sum has been paid.

I give to my son Johannis ten Broeck or his heirs the just fourth part of my whole farm, except what has heretofore been devised to my son Wessel ten Broeck. Item, I give to my said son Johannis or his heirs the eighth part of my house and ground in Kingston and the eighth part of all my personal estate and he is held, to turn over and pay the quantity of 1000 schepels of wheat to my four daughters or heirs named Maria, Elsie, Geertruy and Sara, to each the just fourth part of said sum in the time of four years, after my said son shall have come of age, each year one just fourth part of said sum and if by inability or for some other reason said sum is not paid at the prescribed time, then he is bound, to give proper interest, until said sum is paid.

I give to my son Jacob ten Broeck or his heirs the just fourth part of my whole farm, except what heretofore has been devised to my son Wessel ten Broeck. Item, I give to my said son Jacob or heirs the eighth part of my buildings and ground in Kingston and the eighth part of my whole personal estate and he is held to turn over and pay the quantity of 1000 schepels of wheat to my four daughters or heirs called Maria, Elsie, Geertruy and Sara, to each the just fourth part of said sum in the time of four years, after my said son shall have come of age, each year the just fourth part of said sum. And if by inability or for some other reason, said sum is not paid at the prescibed time, then he is bound to give proper interest until said sum is paid.

I give to my four daughters, named Maria, wife of Charles Bradhead, Elsie, wife of Cornelis Decker, Greertruy and Sara ten Broeck or their order or heirs, to be equally divided among them,

102 acres of land, woodland, lying near the land of Gerrit Aartse, conform to patent belonging to me; also the just half of my buildings and ground in the village of Kingston and the just half of my whole personal estate with the quantity of 4000 schepels of wheat, to be received from my sons in such installments as ordered above.

It is my wish and will that none of my said sons shall be allowed, to sell his share of my farm, except that it be bought by his brother or brothers and that my three youngest sons' shares of said farm shall not be divided until the youngest shall have come of age. . . [42]

On November 6, 1707, Antoine Crespel of Kingston wrote a will dividing his property among his children:

Will of Antoine Crespel

And concerning such worldly estate of land, houses, goods, accounts, money, gold, silver, coined or uncoined and what else belongs to my estate (as the Lord has been pleased to grant far above my merits) I order, give and dispose as follows:

I acknowledge, to have conveyed to the children of the late Pieter Crespel, my oldest son, to wit Antoin, Johannis and Aryaentie Crespel, all that certain parcel of land, situate at Hurley, or within the jurisdiction thereof, beginning at a marked tree near the wagon road and stretching to a certain fountain (spring) called the great fountain, which empties into the great kill, also six acres of woodland on the other side of the path and the third part of my land, (according to calculations made by me) with the privileges, lying within the boundaries of the patent for the village of New Paltz; further a lot in the valley of Hurley, lying between the lot of Jan Elting's heirs and the lot of Pieter Pieterse, all according to the conveyance bearing date of the 27th day of December 1705, without that said children of my said son shall or may claim anything further out of my estate, this, in my opinion, being fully their share.

I hereby make known, that my son Jan Crepel has bought from me my land at Hurley (excepting what hereabove has been devised to the children of the late Pieter Crespel) for the sum or quantity of 100 schepels of wheat, which sum has partly been paid, the said Jan Crespel has further directed, that what is due to him from Walrand du Mont on account of his inheritance from

Mattys Blanchan, shall be received by me in part payment; the said Jan Crespel has also had from me a negro, named Frederick and it is my will and wish, that my said son Jan Crespel shall have and enjoy for himself, his order of heirs forever all, which is due to me from the land purchased and the negro, belonging to me, and he shall have nothing more from my estate nor be allowed to claim it.

I acknowledge, that before now I have given to my daughter Maria Magdeleen, wife of Mattys Slegt, her older of heirs, as I hereby do give, a young negro woman, named Margriet, also that I have conveyed to her the third part of my land (according to calculations made by me), lying within the boundaries of the patent for the village of New Paltz; I further give to my said daughter, her order of heirs as reward for boarding me during several years and for the great services done me (as she continues to do daily), all the money, due me by the mortgage of Moyse Le Cont and all the money due me from Stephanus Gascherie according to mortgage and she shall not be allowed to claim anything else from my estate on this account.

I acknowledge, to have conveyed to my daughter Jannetie, wife of Nicolaes Hofman, all the house and lot, bought by me from Jan Gacherie, upon which is a mortgage, of which L 23 Courant money of New York are still due; it is my wish and will, that this sum of L 23 shall be paid out of my estate excepting what has been devised above and I give to my said daughter Jannetie, her order of heirs the third part of my whole estate, excepting what has above been devised and she shall make no further claim upon my estate.

I acknowledge to have been conveyed to my daughter Elizabeth, wife of Elias Uin, the third part of my land (according to calculations made by me) with the privileges, situate within the boundaries of the patent for the village of New Paltz; I further give to my said daughter Elizabeth with my daughter Jannetie the third part of my whole estate, excepting what has been devised above and she shall make no further claim upon my estate. . . 43

As the wills of Antoine Crespel and Wessel ten Broeck indicate, many people had several properties for investment and occupation. "The pattern of owning both town house and rural farm was as common in the 17th century as it is today." [44] In 1653, Pieter Bronck built a brewhouse and tavern on Broadway in Albany and owned property on North Pearl Street. He sold some property to cover debts and continued to keep a house on Broadway where the family "spent a good part of their time" when not at the Coxsackie homestead.[45] Well-known property owners included Pieter Stuyvesant, who owned a house near the Battery and land at the Bowery north of the city wall. The Rensselaers owned several houses in both their upper and lower manors, while other wealthy families had Albany town houses and rural homes. Smaller farmers, who moved from time to time, owned property at different locations. Discussing the first generation of Van Wycks in America, Philip Van Wyck notes that Cornelius Van Wyck, who arrived in 1660, seems to have owned three farms or land holdings at various times.[46] His properties in Midwout (Flatbush) included a home farm and meadows at the Kills and Canarsie, and, later, the Clarkson and Lenox Road Farm north of Midwout.[47]

Dutch colonial houses in the Hudson Valley.

Photographs by the author unless otherwise noted.

Gansevoort House, Albany, New York, eighteenth century. Watercolor by James Eights (1798–1882) shows two Hudson Valley Dutch-style houses. A small early brick-fronted spout-gable building and the later and larger gambrel-roofed Gansevoort house. Courtesy of R. H. Blackburn.

Clockwise from facing page, top: Cornelus Schermerhorn House, Kinderhook, New York, 1713 after. Courtesy of R. H. Blackburn. The brick house with wooden façade has a basement fireplace and still has the original second flue running up the exterior wall that merges with the main flue smoke box at the garret level. Courtesy of R. H. Blackburn.

Luykas Van Alen House, Kinderhook, New York, 1737. Gable view. House has elbows and spout gable, braiding brickwork, and date anchor irons with iron date, and restored *bolkozijn* windows with batten shutters. Courtesy of R. H. Blackburn.

Slingerlands House, Albany County, New York, eighteenth century. Original *bolkozijn* windows with wood muntin casements and anchor irons, later pediment moldings and missing *stoep*. Courtesy of G. Huber.

Facing page, top:

John Pruyn House, Kinderhook, New York, 1766. Brick center hall structure with a high breaking gambrel and shed dormers. Unusual arch of soldier bricks over the doorway and regular soldier bricks over the windows. Anchor irons show on gable wall as does drip course on foundation wall with step back. Courtesy of R. H. Blackburn.

Facing page, bottom:

Hendrick Van Wie House, Albany County, 1732. Fine brick house that offered three living floors and a garret. It displays elbows and spout gables and unique original peaked dormerss with 'chimney' gables and monk's cowl effect of the molding. Courtesy of R. H. Blackburn.

Below:

Leendert Bronk House, West Coxsackie, New York, 1662-1669 & 1738, stone house with later brick addition. The original stone house has a more German medieval character to it, similar in some respects to the later Jean Hasbrouck stone house in New Paltz, than does the later addition. The 1738 building is a typical Albany-area Dutch house with elbows and spout gables with a marked similarity to its near contemporary the Luykas Van Alen House, but the Bronk house has a center chimney rather than gable flues. The addition of the porch changes the entire character of the building. Courtesy of R. H. Blackburn.

Above:

Ariaantje Coeymans' House as it was in 1997 with sash windows and revised entry and gambrel roof. Courtesy of R. H. Blackburn.

Facing page, top:

The old illustration shows the Ariaantje Coeymans' House, Coeymans, New York, as it was in1716. Originally spout gables were built on the stone house, and it had casement windows and a unique center gable over the entry, later the center gable was removed and the roof converted to a high breaking gambrel with brick gables. Courtesy of R. H. Blackburn.

Facing page, bottom:

Broadhead House, Rosendale, New York, 1680. The house has three rooms, two ground-floor entries, a restored jambless fireplace and an enclosed stairway.

Left: Luykas Van Alen House from the rear. Internal arrangement of the three rooms can be deduced from the placement of the gable chimneys with two rooms end to end in the foreground and the third room (plus a hall with open stairs) to the backgound.

Right: Davis Tavern, Stone Ridge, New York, 1680. Two-room dwelling with an exterior doorway to each room and an original enclosed stairway to upper level and two restored jambless fireplaces. Individual exterior entries to each room was possibly an accommodation necessitated by combining a business and dwelling in the same structure.

Below: Leendert Bronk House viewed from the north east showing the gable view of the 1738 building. Courtesy of R. H. Blackburn.

Facing page:

John De Wint House, Tappan, New York, 1700. Built by Daniel de Clark and purchased by John de Wint in 1746, the house is best known as Washington's Headquarters at Tappan. Owned and recently restored to the period of 1780 by the Masons to better reflect the Commander-in-Chief's Masonic ties, the stone-and-brick house is open to the public. The gable end shows the restored spring eaves clearly and two anchor irons above the garret window.

Clockwise from facing page, top: Jean Hasbrouck House, New Paltz, New York, 1712. Germanic medieval gothic-style stone house with wooden gables. The house is of unique architectural and social importance and is open to the public. Courtesy of the Huguenot Historical Society, New Paltz, New York.

Jacobus Demerest House, close view shows New Jersey masonry, twelve-over-eight windows with wide muntins and shutters with "S" keepers.

Shuart Van Orden House, Ulster County, New York, 1773. A "typical New Jersey House" built by a former New Jersey man in Ulster County. Brick façade, stone walls at gables and across rear. Center hall and symmetrical Anglo-Dutch window arrangement featuring brick arches over the windows. The house has a cellar kitchen with massive beamed ceiling and a garret level fireplace, both interesting features and practically unique to this building.

Jean Hasbrouck House gable view shows the square proportions and the great mass and height of the building. Built in the mid-Hudson Valley Dutch cultural zone it has few Dutch-style markers externally, but within it has Dutch jambless fireplaces and framing. Courtesy of R. H. Blackburn.

Above: Bevier-Elting House, New Paltz, New York, early eighteenth century. It is less massive and square than the Jean Hasbrouck house but similar to its other New Paltz neighbors with stone walls and wooden gables. Courtesy of the Huguenot Historical Society, New Paltz, New York.

Below: Jonathan Hasbrouck House, Newburgh, New York, 1750-1770. Washington's Headquarters in Newburgh. Later but similar in massive appearance to the Jean Hasbrock house in New Paltz. Internally the house follows Dutch practice but the exterior is more German in style. Courtesy of New York State Office of Parks, Recreation & Historic Preservation, Palasades Region, Washington's Headquarters State Historic Site.

Above: Jacobus Demerest House, Bergen County, New Jersey, 1763. High breaking bell-curve gambrel with overhang spring eaves. The end view reveals the stone walls and shingled gable.

Below: Myndert Mynderse House, Saugerties, New York, 1743. Rear of the house showing Dutch shed-style dormers; these do not appear to be original to the house.

Facing page, top: Decker House, Ulster County, New York, Mid-eighteenth century and 1776. A small one-room building that grew into a large house with a center hall addition and a rear wing built in several different stages. A subsequent enlargement preserving shingles and lath that would otherwise be lost enclosed an original section of roof. Courtesy of R. H. Blackburn.

Facing page, bottom: Sylvester Salisbury House, Leeds, New York, 1705. An early house that breaks most of the rules concerning Dutch construction being rarely two stories tall and having a gambrel roof at that date. The porches are additions and the windows are Victorian. The house burned down in 1929. Courtesy of R. H. Blackburn.

Above: Ackerman-Zabrinskie-Steuben House, Historic New Bridge Landing, River Edge, New Jersey, 1732-1752, two views. Gable view shows the roof added when the house was enlarged in 1752 from a saddle roof with a Flemish overhang design; high quality New Jersey masonry with squared stones and common-bond brick-work. Courtesy of G. Huber.

Above: Noah Le Fevre House, Ulster County, 1776. Several interesting features are observable: The farthest section of the house front is the original house, and the join in the masonry is visible where the center hall (probably the 1776 date) was built on later. The original roof would have rested on the masonry wall. The roof was raised as evidenced by the makeshift clapboard band with smaller windows to allow for second-floor headroom when the garret was finished. The peaked dormers are a Federal period or later addition.

Below: Persen House, Saugerties, New York, 1770. Stone center-hall house that was originally only the room and hall in the foreground. The house expanded into a center hall with the addition of the second front room, and then became a stone "saltbox" with the addition of three rooms across the rear, the sequence of events revealed by variations in the cellar walls.

Philipsburgh Manor, Tenant House, reconstruction.

Left: This example represents the typical one-room tenant houses on Hudson Valley manors and exhibits many common features: stone walls, wooden gables, wooden shingle roof, Flemish overhang, and shed at rear. *Right:* Gable view. Door indicates small size of the dwelling. In the colonial era a family with several children and at least one grandparent might occupy a one-room building of this size.

Below: Demerest House, relocated and restored at Historic New Bridge Landing, Rivers Edge, New Jersey, mid-eighteenth century. Two-room stone house with shingle gables and spring eaves. Courtesy of G. Huber.

Above:

Nicolas Schenck House, Carnarsie, Brooklyn, circa 1775. Remodeled circa 1830. Gambrel roof and spring eaves on a shingle-sided center-entrance house. This is the "Dutch Colonial" ideal, which is actually the name of a regional York State antebellum Federal-style that remained current through the Civil War. It is Dutch in heritage and particularly American in design. The Dutch Colonial house in fact has been described as one of two uniquely American architectural achievements, the other one is the skyscraper. Courtesy of The Brooklyn Museum, Gift of the Parks Department, City of New York, 29.1283.

Facing page, top:

Minne Schenck House and Dutch Barn, Originally located in Manhasset, Long Island, 1730. Presently at Old Bethpage Village, Nassau County, New York. Restored house shows spring eaves and typical Long Island-shingle siding and roof reflecting Flemish-style influence that was important in the area. Courtesy of R. H. Blackburn.

Facing page, bottom:

Voorlezer House, Historic Richmond Town Restoration, 1696. One of the earliest Dutch colonial houses surviving. The leaded glass, half shutters, and the early rain-gutter design are restored features rarely encountered in this country but typical of Dutch buildings in the seventeenth century. Courtesy of W. McMillen, Historic Richmond Town Restoration.

Above: Guyon-Lake-Tysen, Historic Richmond Town Restoration, Staten Island, New York, 1740-1820. A large bell-curve gambrel-roofed center-hall house with examples of both early spring eaves and the later porch that developed from them.

Left: Bohem House, Historic Richmond Town Restoration, Staten Island, New York, circa 1760-1780. Typically Dutch one-and-a-half story anchor bent framing, but two rooms deep. Gable view shows uneven clapboards and exposed stone back wall to fireplace.

Courtesy of W. McMillen, Historic Richmond Town Restoration.

Basket Maker's House, Historic Richmond Town Restoration, Staten Island, New York, circa 1810. One-and-a-half story H bent of eight bents. The spring eaves have been extended to form a porch. Courtesy of W. McMillen, Historic Richmond Town Restoration.

Cornelius Van Wyck House, Douglaston, Queens County, New York, 1735. Enlarged 1750–1770. Enclosed spring-eave roofline and shingle siding typical of the region. Batten shutters correct but probably not original.

View of beam and post with corbel from the Jan Martense Schenck
house during demolition. In the backgound can be seen the nogging
infill between posts used as insulation in early buildings.

Courtesy of The Brooklyn Museum of Art, Gift of the Atlantic Gulf and Pacific Company, 50.192.

CHAPTER IV

Construction Fundamentals:
From the Ground Up

HAVING LOCATED, chosen and purchased, or been bequeathed, a homestead site, the settler cleared the land and planted a crop. Then, it was necessary to put up a shelter, of some form, quickly. Style and fashion were not of primary concern. The earliest settlers' dwellings were described by the Reverend Jonas Michaelius as little more than a shallow pit with a plank floor and retaining walls "inside all round the wall with timber" and topped "with bark of trees or green sods."[1] This type of structure resembled the wood-walled cellars unearthed in the upper Hudson Valley in the Albany area by Paul R. Huey in 1966.[2] Similarly a cellar hole sheathed with oak slabs is cited, in the text of *The Polgreen Photographs* by Shirley W. Dunn and Allison P. Bennett concerning a house built in 1681 south of the present city of Rensselaer.[3] A small fireplace with a stick and mud chimney that drew away smoke from the hearth provided the most meager of amenities.

Early records indicate that the next level of comfort attained by many early householders took the form of a dwelling of log and board construction. When given the choice, European woodcutters traditionally felled trees "in late autumn and winter on the day after a full moon" (which affected sap levels). Wood was used green or left on the ground to dry.[4] Research at Jamestown, and other early English sites, and modern recreations at Jamestown and Plimouth Plantation[5] are built in *poteaux-en-terre*. In this method a building is constructed of a frame of vertical logs set directly into the earth, without any foundation or frame sill, and an infill between the posts of mixed clay and straw. In Canada, the vertical posts are usually arranged in the form of a closely placed half-timber studding called *colombage,* but among the Dutch the vertical posts were customarily set further apart. *Poteaux-en-terre* buildings can still be seen in Normandy and in rural Quebec. Examples are illustrated in *La Maison Traditionnelle Au Quebec.*[6] In that book, the authors say of *poteaux-en-terre* construction that "ce type de charpenterie fut tres populaire au premier siecle de colonisation francaise" (this type of construction was very popular in the first century of French colonization) in Quebec.[7]

Poteaux-en-terre buildings exist in the European cultural zone (reaching from Normandy to Denmark) that was home to many New Netherland settlers. In *Dutch Houses in the Hudson Valley Before 1776,* H. W. Reynolds referred to the early pioneer cabin of Pieter Viele (construction date unknown, burned down in 1918). Her description of the "cabin" describes a *poteaux-en-terre* structure: "In construction, the house of Pieter Viele was distinctly that of a pioneer's dwelling. The walls were made of a framework of staves, filled with mud, and were two feet thick; they were sided with broad boards . . ."[8] The word "staves" implied that the logs were set vertically as posts rather than laid horizontally, as in a typical "log cabin." She notes that the staves were covered with weatherboards. Early records of Virginia describe the same type houses. A reconstruction is shown in H. C. Forman's book, The *Architecture of the Old South, The Medieval Style: 1585-1850,* of a what he calls a "puncheoned-cottage."[9] Among the English settlers, the method of construction was called "post and pan," wherein upright timber posts, or puncheons, were set into the earth while the "pans," or panels, between them were filled with wattle-and-daub. The wattles of hazel-withes form a basketwork that is then covered with a daubing of clay mixed with chopped straw, as noted above.

Another type of early primitive structure is called a cruck-house. The design employs the natural curve, or "cruck," of a tree's limbs to build an A-frame shaped house. Many cruck-houses later lost their typical tent shape (new corner posts were frequently added to gain interior headroom by squaring-up the building's sides and raising the roof), but often the original framework can still be traced. Curved wooden braces were called swan's necks, *zwaan nek*, by the Dutch and were used until the mid-seventeenth century in the Netherlands. The type is studied at length in S. O. Addy's book, *Evolution of the English House.* He notes the common roots for the technique in the Anglo-Dutch culture area.[10] American climate conditions demanded that all these half-timber and wattling buildings be covered with plank weatherboards in the Hudson Valley and in Quebec to achieve greater protection from the elements. These early dwelling types were more likely to be the so-called "cabins" of the first English and Dutch settlers than the prototypical log cabin of the Kentucky frontier, which were based upon Scandinavian and German models. However, none of the earliest "cabins" have survived in the Hudson Valley to resolve any questions regarding their exact appearance because after the passage of a few years the temporary shelters that had originally housed the settlers were outgrown, inadequate, and gone.

When ready for a permanent building the settler knew the best location for a dwelling site on his land. R. F. Bailey says that the Dutch usually oriented their house facing south "to obtain the maximum sunlight."[11] However, both Roderic Blackburn and Donald Carpentier, leading authorities on Dutch dwellings in New York, have pointed out (in conversations during research for this book) that many extant Dutch houses in fact face east or even north. In a questionable assertion, Bailey says that the orientation of the house was done "regardless of the direction of the road." However one facet of orientation was consistent: Whereas urban dwellings' gables faced the street and were the location of the entry, farmhouses were oriented to an entry along the eave wall.[12]

The early writer Jeptha Simms says, in his *History of Schoharie County*, that "the Germans and Dutch do not generally display much taste in the selection of a site for, and in the erection of, their dwellings, as do the English. Frequently a Dutchman's house fronts its owner's barn, instead of fronting a public highway'.' A study by Greg Huber and Ursula C. Brecknell on farm siting in Somerset County, New Jersey, in the eighteenth and early nineteenth centuries, notes several basically consistent features in Dutch farm arrangements. They report that the barns built in the eighteenth century "as a rule fronted southward" and that Dutch farms they studied had the house's eaves (long-side) entry facing the road with the barn's gable (the long-side on a three-bay barn) entry are similarly sited. Approximately two thirds of all the barns studied face the southeast quadrant. Generally barns were placed to the right (the left side when viewed from the road) of the house (71% of examples). In all but one example the Dutch barns studied were located between 140 feet and 242 feet from the house.[13] Simms does not say if he noted the compass points in relation to the orientation of the houses. He does observe that the Dutch farmer had more taste in locating outbuildings than the Englishman, who often fronted his home with a wagon shed or corncrib that was "literally covered with sheep, raccoon, or skunk-skins."[14]

Apparently, these authors were referring to isolated country homes, because the Dutch were attentive to siting city or town dwellings in accordance with roads and property lines. Early laws in New Amsterdam and other Dutch settlements specified an orderly arrangement of buildings. David Baker, a local historian in Ulster County, emphasized the careful alignment of the early houses in Hurley in relation to road and property lines, when we walked the town in early 1995. Within the confined property lines of towns and villages it was necessary to maximize the efficiency of building arrangements. Especially within a fortified town (common in both the Netherlands and the early Hudson Valley settlements), land was at a premium, and therefore expensive. Building lots were proportionately narrow to the street and deep. Therefore urban houses were oriented with the gable to the street, and of necessity, entry doors of urban houses were located at the gable end of the houses and opened directly onto the street. Rural houses' entries were placed on the eaves walls. In the Netherlands urban houses often had common walls, but in the Hudson Valley each urban house usually had its own separate walls, often with a narrow space between buildings. The narrow proportions of these buildings resulted in dark interiors without direct access to daylight. To solve this problem, houses in the Netherlands had a setback mezzanine floor and a wall of high mezzanine windows. In New York the solution was achieved by using tall windows but there is no record of the use of the mezzanine floor.

In preparation for the new house, the area was cleared and the materials readied: Trees felled for lumber, stones gathered for a foundation, and the clay for both bricks and mortar taken from the excavation were prepared and fired near-at-hand. The settler's objective was to dig a hole deeper than the frost line. Sometimes a full cellar was impractical, as in the case of the Van Cortlandt manor house: "The house is built on a ledge of rock, and part of this rock remains, a ridge beneath the stairs, never having been excavated or leveled completely."[15] A similar outcropping can be seen in the foundation of the north wing of the Van Alen house; however in that house the rock was apparently unanticipated in the original 1737 construction. When it was discovered in the course of building the addition, the north room's floor was raised to avoid the rock shelving. In the cellar of the Gidney house, a stone outcropping too large to remove intrudes into the floor and wall area and is incorporated into the structure.

The next step was erection of a cellar foundation wall. Some early houses have mortared cellar walls. Mortar was always used when the lower level was intended as a kitchen or dwelling area; however, it was also used in many cases where the cellar was never intended for habitation. The early Broadhead house was built with mortared walls, according to Samuel Phelps who did the restoration work on the building, and it has apparently always been a storage cellar. Indeed, Dutch builders in the Netherlands mortared cellars with a waterproof material called *tras*, German for stone, that Jaap Schipper, the Dutch architect-historian, describes as a mixture of one part chalk and four parts sand and "some" water. He noted a "swimming" cellar in Edam that is below the water table, built with *tras,* that has remained waterproof since the sixteenth century. The swimming cellar is called a "floating cellar" in *Building Amsterdam* and described as "a large brick tank within the walls, which more or less floats on the ground water. This kept the water out of the cellar."

America the water table was rarely high enough to be a problem and colonial Dutch cellar walls were usually bonded with clay or mud, even though the mortar may have subsequently washed out. However, in many houses cellar walls were erected of "dry stone," that is, without mortar to ground level. Today many people look upon a dry stone wall with suspicion. William McMillen of Richmond Town Restoration says that if the stones are well set, no mortar is necessary to keep the wall in place.[16] Furthermore, a dry stone wall is based upon a sound concept: Ground water will pass through the wall rather than buckle it with frost heaves. Water that passes through the wall will drain into the dirt floor or between the unmortared flagstones used as a floor in many storage cellars. In many old homes that have been "improved" by cementing the inner surface of a dry stone cellar wall, the wall will often bulge, buckle, and cave inward from frost heaves after standing unsealed, and unharmed, for centuries. Farmers generally knew how to build, or "raise," a good stone wall years ago, though many old walls were little more than casual heaps of stones disposed along a property line. Anyone who walks through a second-growth wood lot in, say, Dutchess County can testify to the durability of these stone fences. The forest-reclaimed fields have miles of fieldstone walls standing forlorn and abandoned amid the trees.

The hole dug and the cellar walls erected, wooden sills of the house frame were laid above the "damp creep," rising ground moisture, on the dry stone or mortared foundation wall. Up to this stage, the early Dutch and English types of construction were similar. The first buildings were of necessity universally primitive and makeshift shelters. Later, the available materials, local conditions, and traditional practices influenced many of the homesteaders' decisions about the dwelling. Finally, to a large extent, national preferences influenced the appearance of the home above the foundation line. Being Dutch by birth or ancestry, or because a Dutch builder was employed, the inclination was to build a house the "right way" by following the traditions and practices of forebears in the Netherlands.

Early scenes of New Amsterdam and the surrounding area depict typically Dutch urban and rural type dwellings replicated in the new land. These early urban houses number few survivors: The Abraham Yates house in Schenectady (c. 1730) is one of the few Dutch-style town houses to survive in an urban context. The best, and least-altered specimen of a town house type is the Teunis Slingerlands house of 1762 which, however, was built in the country, south of Albany.[17] Extant early Dutch farm houses in the valley are more common. With rare exceptions they are medieval-style folk homesteads that are modest in size and unpretentious in design. These homes were not "high style" architectural exercises, rather, they were reflections of the diverse origins of the settlers. Nevertheless, from 1690 to 1740, a recognizable housing style emerged. Steep roofs, jambless fireplaces, casement windows, divided exterior doors, full stone cellars and a wood frame were the norm. The Dutch imprint was strong across New Netherland, even if, "it is disconcerting to find, as one often does, that what seems to be a typical Dutch farmhouse actually was built by a French or a Flemish settler."[18] A typical Bergen County Dutch house with a single pitch roof and spring eaves, what R. F. Bailey and others call a "Flemish" overhang, was built by Hans George Achenbach, by origin "a Saxon shepherd boy."[19] The Jean Hasbrouck House in New Paltz was noted by the *Architectural Record* in March 1926, "as the finest example of medieval Flemish stone architecture in North America"[20] was built in 1712 by a Dutch man for a French Huguenot settler—in a French speaking village in the English colony of New York. The building was once a two room center chimney structure but it presently has a center entrance and hall in the manner of later English houses, although it has retained the broad form and ample proportions similar to houses of the "Lower Saxon Bauernhaus of North Germany."[21]

Similarly international is Pieter Bronck's house in West Coxsackie, New York. The house was originally built in 1663 as a one room structure with a garret topped by a loft. The oldest part of the structure is the east half of the present building. Bronck was not Dutch, he was a member of the Bronck family of Danish immigrants.

It is frequently stated that Pieter was the son of Jonas Bronck; however, Joseph W. Hammond makes a case in the historic periodical of the Holland Society, *De Halve Maen*, that Pieter was the brother of Jonas Bronck.[22] The Bronck family first settled north of Manhattan, an area later known as "The Bronx." Pieter Bronck made his mark in the upper Valley, where he took a Dutch bride, Hillettje Tysink, and reared two children: Jan and Marretje. The couple's house is typically Dutch in design as it developed in the region. In part, this probably stems from the Dutch housewrights' practices as much as the owner's choices. The result seems to uniquely reflect the intermarrying and intermingling of the settlers in the Hudson Valley; but, in fact, it goes much deeper. The confusion "is not totally colonial . . ." but rather, it reflects an overlapping of European traditions wherein "the peasant cottages of France, Germany, Holland, and the Low Countries—despite regional and national accents—often were strikingly similar . . ."[23] The cultural traditions formed a unit that extended from Normandy to Denmark and from Germany to East Anglia in England.

The very lack of stylistic conceits lends the homes an enduring appeal. However, the simplicity and size of the houses can be socially misleading. Frequently, a small and unpretentious building was the home of an influential and wealthy owner. Even the manor homes of the landed magnates, such as the Van Rensselaers and Van Cortlandts, are "homey" rather than "grand." H. W. Reynolds remarks on this phenomenon in reference to the Jean Hasbrouck house in New Paltz. The family was relatively wealthy and politically influential, nevertheless, they continued to live in the homestead of the founder generation after generation.[24]Later in the colonial era some imposing homes were built along the Hudson.

In many Dutch Hudson Valley homesteads built before the middle of the eighteenth century, the core, or basic house, typically has a ground level interior of one room approximately twenty-by-twenty feet. Some early homes began as two rooms, which joined at one gable end, forming a single unit some twenty feet deep-by-forty feet long. Each interior room has one, sometimes two, garret levels above the living floor. Two living stories were common in Albany and Manhattan, or by exception in a few rural areas, as in the

Coeymans house in present day Albany County, but "the general
rule before 1776 was to build a house only a story and a half high."[25]
According to Reynolds, other than the Francis Salisbury house at
Leeds in Greene County, "no house has been learned of in any other
. . . *rural* part of the river valley which was standing in 1705, two full
stories in height."[26] However, the Francis Salisbury house may be
much later than the date attributed by Reynolds. R. F. Bailey notes
that "for an undetermined reason it was only along the Millstone and
Raritan Rivers in central New Jersey that the Dutch built two story
houses in the country."[27]

Other than the 1716 Coeymans house in Coeymans, New York,
there are only two early "Dutch" homes of two full stories outside
Albany and Manhattan: the Van Campen house on the Delaware
River and the Dey house at Preakness, an Anglo-Dutch building in
the Georgian style.[28] The houses, cited as exceptions to Dutch
colonial practice by Bailey, are attributed to English influence and
the exceptional wealth and prominence of the owners. It is possible
to build a Georgian style building following Dutch construction
techniques. Most gambrel houses in the valley are basically Dutch
H-frame structures. However, both Reynolds and Bailey attribute a
"Dutch" designation to houses owned by persons with a Dutch
surname rather than exclusively to buildings with Dutch design
characteristics. Blood, rather than style, was their defining criteria.

In outward appearances Hudson Valley Dutch homes do not
conform to a single ideal. They share basic structural features and
many distinctive details but exhibit a wide range of forms from one
area and era to the next. The "typical" Dutch home varies by date,
location, available building materials, and almost always by its urban
or rural setting. When Pieter Bronck decided to build in 1663, he
"chose to build in stone. . [but]. . .an analysis of surviving building
contracts and other documents suggests that this was highly unusual."
Joseph W. Hammond says that he could not find "any contract
specifying stone construction, but rather wood framing seems to have
been universally used." He says that only after 1710 and the arrival
of German settlers in the upper Hudson Valley were stone buildings
built with any frequency. Later in the eighteenth century, Albany
area homes were built in the limestone common to the western bank

of the Hudson River and in brick where suitable clay was available. Dutch house builders used brick over an underlying structural wood frame identical to their all-wooden buildings, and preferred brick for its finer appearance and fire retardant qualities.[29]

Some early Albany and Rensselaer County buildings also originally had typically Dutch raised-end gables with steep single pitch roofs. Later, as is seen at the Coeymans house, many roofs had the raised gables removed and rebuilt as gambrels without overhangs when that style became fashionable. Ulster County is the regional center for limestone dwellings with steep single-pitch roofs, although the same design can be found in Greene County and rural Albany County. Dutchess County has early stone houses with brick gable ends, whereas later homes were frequently made of wood and with a gentler roof slope line. From the start, Long Island homes were primarily wooden structures due to the lack of suitable stone, and whereas the early homes had single slant roofs, many later buildings had gambrel roofs. The houses of Rockland county were usually of cut sandstone with steeply pitched gables, many with curved overhanging eaves in the front, as seen on the DeWint House. Several other examples are noted by Bailey, whereas, Staten Islanders covered their long narrow homes of small rubble stone with steep, straight gable roofs. In Bergen County the roofs were typically adorned with curved overhanging eaves whether the roof was gambrel or straight gable.

Within the Hudson Valley, therefore, there is a diversity in the outward appearance of the "Dutch" houses influenced by type and period. Furthermore, C. W. Zink writes (in an unpublished masters thesis entitled "Dutch Frame Houses in New York and New Jersey") "the buildings evolved somewhat differently in each region. In the upper Hudson some Dutch-Americans kept building the urban [brick] house type well into the eighteenth century... In the southern New York and northern New Jersey area, Flemish-influenced buildings began to develop the curving roof overhang which [Thomas Jefferson] Wertenbaker called the 'Flemish gutter.' " Variations of the feature are seen in New Jersey and New York.

Certainly by external appearance the most similar to Dutch colonial homes are found in the province of Friesland and occasionally in Zeeland, Zuid-Holland, and Noord-Holland. Farm houses in Friesland often resemble Albany area raised gable-end brick homes. These houses are illustrated in Ellen van Olst's two volume report on the study of Dutch houses done between 1914 and 1934, entitled *Uilkema, een historisch boerderij-onberzoek*. However, few Dutch examples seem to closely approximate the interior floorplans of Dutch colonial homes in the valley, in part because most early Netherlands Dutch farms were typically connected to barns and outer buildings. Nevertheless, all the homes were recognizably Dutch because they share several elements of construction and esthetics. In an article entitled "Traditional Farm Types of the Netherlands." Ellen van Olst, Director of the Open Air Museum at Arnhem, writes: "Variety is beyond doubt one of the most striking features of Dutch vernacular architecture," but despite the wide number of types of buildings "all Dutch farms have a few things in common." Van Olst cites the common features as timber framing to carry the main load-bearing elements, several cross frames separately raised that bear the weight of the roof, and walls that are generally not load-bearing, but serve primarily as dividing elements. She states that, "By paying attention to construction" — the internal arrangement of the build- ings —all Dutch farm buildings could be traced to "a limited number of basic house groups of late-medieval origins." [30]

The identity of a "Dutch" house rests upon the underlying logic that a Dutch builder used when he built. It is a "Dutch" house because the builder thought of the house in a culturally defined way and worked following culturally distinct traditions.[31] The way people think and build in a specific culture is called "conceptualization." It is a culturally-bound logic "that is native to the builder . . .like language . . . thus national characteristics of building form a national building tradition."[32] Zink cites the English architectural writer Richard Harris, author of *Discovering Timber Framed Buildings*, and *Timber Framed Buildings*, for relating building techniques to a cultur- ally based logic.

In *Historische houtconstructies in Nederland*, G. Berends identifies Dutch "transverse frames" consisting of freestanding wooden posts (arcade posts) coupled by tiebeams below the top of the posts as the principal characteristic of traditional Dutch building methods. However, exactly when what is called "anchor-beam construction" was first employed is uncertain. Berends traces the technique to gothic origins. He cites examples ranging from a house in Utrecht with a pre-1340 date, to a church at Deventer from the early fourteenth century, to a Joanniter convent at Burgsteinfurt, across the border in Germany, which dates from 1398. By the seventeenth century Berends says "anchor-beam trusses are common in large parts of the middle, east and south of the country." The same construction methods are found in the Dutch houses in America.[33]

Identifying the problem-solving logic at work in a building is more informative than examining the elements of its style. Houses that appear quite different, such as the regionally distinct Dutch houses of the Hudson Valley, are often fundamentally similar "under the skin." Specifically, the Van Alen raised gable brick house in Kinderhook has the same H-bent frame construction as the Jan Martense Schenck board-sided house in the town of Flatlands, now a part of Brooklyn, New York. In an historic structure report on the Knickerbocker Mansion, in Schaighticoke, New York, Robert Pierpont discussed late eighteenth-century Anglo-Dutch mansions of the Hudson Valley.[34] While the house is English Georgian in style, he writes, the construction fundamentals remain "tempered by traditional Dutch building characteristics."[35] William McMillen, head of restoration at Historic Richmond Town Restoration, Staten Island, similarly notes that houses built in Staten Island and nearby New Jersey were often based upon traditional Dutch H-bent framing into the middle nineteenth century. This practice was followed even when the house was built in the in Federal and early Victorian guise.[36]

Confronted with the same problem, traditional carpenters from England, the Lowlands, and China would go about the job in different ways because culture influences technology. Berends describes in his book, *Historische houtconstructies in Nederland*, 120 different elements typical of Dutch timber-frame construction, and he provides twenty-six cross section drawings of timber framed buildings, as well as illustrating and naming over a hundred securing techniques for wood joins.[37] Like other traditional craftsmen the Dutch house builder worked in a manner that followed a preconceived idea of what constituted the "correct" way to erect a structure.

Despite differences in materials and style, the Dutch colonial house in the Hudson Valley followed certain patterns in construction and emphasis in detail. Adherence to these traditions links a raised gable-ended brick house with no hall passageway and separate exterior entrances to the front rooms in the Albany area built in 1690 to a stone Ulster County single-pitch roofed house with ground level side hall built in 1720 and to a wooden gambrel roofed house with a center entrance and hall in Bergen County built in 1776.

Dutch wooden framed houses were erected with what is called the Continental or "H-bent" method. It was a different problem-solving approach from the typical English or Anglo-American box frame. In effect, the building's frame components are set up individually, can stand alone, and are the main structural components around which a variety of buildings can be erected."[38] The H-bent is composed of a pair of vertical posts joined by a horizontal beam like the crossbar on a letter "H." The crossbar of the anchor beam, *verdiepingh*, (or loft beam in some early seventeenth-century accounts) is set four to five feet below the top of the uprights. The vertical posts are usually a story-and-a-half tall to the wall plates -- horizontal members that run along the post tops at the eave level. The lower ends of the roof rafters are notched. They rest on, and are nailed to, the wall plate. The individual pairs of bents stand on and are joined at the base by a sill beam and at the top by the wall plate (beam). Once in place all the individual H-bent components form a frame. The individual components are usually much sturdier than those used in the English braced frame, but they are mortised and tenoned and joined with wooden dowels or trunnels in a similar manner.

In *Dutch By Design*, the H-bent design is noted to represent the survival of a medieval tradition widespread throughout Northern Europe. The historian David Steven Cohen wrote in the unpublished manuscript entitled "Defining the Dutch-American Farmhouse" that:

> Unlike the English box frame, the continental frame resembles a series of goal posts, known as H-bents, each consisting of two vertical posts connected by a large anchor beam and reinforced by diagonal corner braces. Atop the posts on either side of the H-bents run horizontal plates, which support the widely spaced

rafters of the pitched roof. The paired rafters are reinforced by
collar beams and joined at the peak by mortise and tenon joints.
. . .there is no ridgepole.[39]

In early houses the cross members, or anchor beams, of the
H-bent frequently have extra support from corbels or anchor beam
braces, as may be seen in the Jan Martense Schenck house.[40] Corbels
were not placed in the bay where the original door and fireplace
existed. Aksel Skov includes diagrams, in his book *Gamle huse pa
Romo*, of Danish wood-framed brick buildings. They illustrate Dutch
and Danish construction methods were based on a similar basic
post-beam-post unit with bracing wooden corbels.[41] The technique
is similar to carpentry practices followed in ship building of the
period with the bracing supports, visible within the interior, to
prevent racking by the elements: wind in the case of houses, and wind
and water in the case of ships.

Additional house frame bracing occurred at the chimney H-bent
where a diagonal windbrace tied the end wall to the rafters and wall
plate in many houses. In the Decker house an exceptional pair of
wind braces reach twenty feet between plate and chimney end wall.
Collar ties hold the rafters across the width of the house. The collar
braces are typically about five to seven feet above the garret floor. A
house in Couse Corners, New York, (with double collar braces) has,
according to Donald Carpentier, one brace at seven feet and a second
brace four feet higher. The double bracing forms a "cockloft" or what
is called in *Building Amsterdam* a "roof plate attic" two feet below
the peak.[42] In America the H-bent frame usually limited rural houses
to one-and-a-half stories; however, Roderic Blackburn observes that
urban houses were frequently several stories tall, and warehouses in
the Netherlands typically rose to seven stories in height. In part, the
additional height was possible because the dense grouping of buildings provided, in effect, a collective wind bracing.[43] Henk J. Zantkuyl
provides a clear presentation of Dutch house construction techniques
in wood and several very helpful drawings in *New World Dutch
Studies*.[44]

Dutch framing methods for houses and barns were closely related. *Dutch Barns of New York* by Vincent J. Schaefer has several
illustrations of barn construction, which clearly show similar prac-

tices. It might be noted that Greg Huber, publisher of the *Dutch Barn Research Journal*, suggests that D. S. Cohen is incorrect regarding the total absence of ridgepoles in Dutch construction. Huber says that there are at least three early, pre-Revolutionary, Dutch barns in Ulster County and one in Orange County known to employ ridgepoles. Barns followed the traditional style into the nineteenth century. Houses evolved earlier and more significantly in design under Anglo-American influence and changing living conditions and fashions.

Basic Dutch-American framing is based on four principles, as reviewed by Zink, that include the following: 45

1. The anchorbent, or H-frame, is the primary and most basic unit of construction. It carries the main forces generated by the structure, by the use of the structure, and by external pressure the buildings dead loading, live loading, and wind loading.

2. The close repetition of anchorbents forms the structure's frame, helps organize the space within the building, and determines, in part, the building's form.

3. The anchorbent joint, between the vertical post and the horizontal beam, is the primary connection within the building's frame. It transfers the floor loads to the posts. Corbels stiffen the frame against racking, i.e. going out of plumb.

4. The size of buildings varies as follows: Longitudinal expansion occurs through repeating anchorbents. Greater length may also be achieved by extension of the longitudinal struts, as seen in the Phillipsburg Manor barn, which has only three bays yet, is fifty feet long. Transverse expansion is achieved by adding side aisles (on one side or both) to the nave formed by the anchorbent. Vertical expansion is accomplished by extending the post at the half-story level.

In Dutch construction, the structural elements originally included exposed posts, beams, corbels, and floor/ceiling boards. Because all the components were open to view, the Dutch carpenters treated the visible elements in a decorative manner. With the development of the English taste, wherein structural elements were covered, fewer framing elements were visible. Hiding the entire frame eliminated the aesthetic importance of the size and spacing of framing members.[46] However, whether exposed or enclosed, the methods remained viable, and H-bent framed houses and barns continued to be built into the nineteenth century. Historic Richmond Town has several Federal era buildings with H-bent frames built in the nineteenth century. In time the H-bent frame was adapted and recast in terms of Anglo-Dutch, and then American, aesthetics, and practice moved away from that based purely upon Dutch precedents. New techniques in building and evolving taste, therefore, eventually put an end to the H-bent frame design in America.

A few skilled and strong workers could raise the house's H-bent frame as a series of individual units instead of the massive bay units of the English box frame. Similarly, the roof of the Dutch house could be assembled without the need for a ridgepole. Nevertheless, as Roderic Blackburn explains, the Dutch method of construction requires a pair of large, cumbersome, long wooden plate beams that were placed atop the erected H-bent posts. In addition heavy planks were nailed across the rafters as cross bracing to keep the house rigid so that the bricks in the chimney wouldn't be racked or broken. Diagonal boards connecting the two rafters near the gable chimney and the roof plate provided additional rigidity in the form of wind braces.

New York house restorer Donald Carpentier says that complete planking of house and barn roofs is common in the Albany area where "the weatherboards are an under surface providing extra strength to bear a snow load or the weight of a worker walking on the roof."[47] The under sheathing continued in the northern area into the 1790s, but it was rare elsewhere. An example of a chamfered plank roof may be seen in photographs taken by Waldron Mosher Polgreen, in 1933, of the Gerrit Vandenbergh house. The house was built in the 1750s in the Domine's Hook area, south of the city of Albany, it was razed about 1950 by the Niagara Mohawk Company when a power plant was built on the site.[48] The roof planks typically employed for sheathing were usually about one inch thick by twelve to fourteen inches wide with bevel lap edges. The edges are cut at a slant so that they smoothly overlap where they meet. The Gibney house in the central Hudson area also has heavy roof sheathing planks but they are gapped rather than bevel edged and lapped as would be the case farther north. In the attic of the Decker house, in Ulster County, is an early roof section that had been covered by later construction. The original roof had light four-inch-wide lath (riven with a maul and froe, not sawn) with nine-inch gaps and early thirty-two- to thirty-eight-inch-long pine shingles (with clipped corners) that were nailed to the lath at the lower edges. The original lath was so widely spaced that the roof appeared more suited originally for pantiles or thatch than shingles. Later roof sections in the Decker house had rough, irregular boards rather than closely fitted weatherboards more typically found in the upper Hudson Valley,

In early Dutch buildings the joinery is typically neat and the fit of tenon into mortise is close; yet construction was based upon a few basic carpentry practices that employed a minimum of tools. As William McMillen of Richman Town Restoration explained: In many instances, the carpenter would cut a "story pole," a long stick marked with the standard units of measure he needed for that job. In this way, all measures from one structural member to the next would be standardized for that house. In addition, both McMillen and Zinc note that "the carpenters laid out a full-size template for the anchor-bent and rafter sections, and then proceeded to make as many of these as they needed."[49]

The carpenter relied on the standard Dutch two-foot long measure stick (which, after 1664, was usually in English twelve-inch rather than Dutch eleven-inch feet.) The measure itself would be two inches wide on one side and one-and-a-half inches wide on the other. It can be noted that most measurements in a Dutch house are in these units. Calculating measurements prior to actually building is called "square rule" and is a practice that began in the late eighteenth century primarily among the English. Earlier, both English and Dutch carpenters also used "scribe rule" measures, that is, many parts were measured as the job progressed.[50]

Scribe rule was essential to "draw boring." When structural members were joined with treenails, *toognagel*, an allowance had to be made for shrinkage when houses were built of green wood. Oak was used in the lower valley and pitch pine in the Albany area until the trees were depleted at the end of the nineteenth century. Then, according to Roderic Blackburn and Don Carpentier, white pine was used instead.[51] The green wood shrank about a quarter-inch per foot in volume; however, wood does not shrink in length. Therefore, when a mortise and tenon were measured, cut, and fitted—and a hole was augered through the mortise—the hole was marked on the tenon but not drilled. The tenon was drawn out of the mortise and a hole was augered back at the inner edge of the mark. When the mortise and tenon were reassembled, the treenail was hammered into the slightly off-centered holes. The pointed trunnel snaked through and was held fast. The scribe rule system insured a tighter join with the passage of time and the shrinking of the materials: Shrinkage tightened the join rather than loosened it as the wood dried. To insure vertical alignment, the carpenter used a plumb bob, a board with a weighted string. Set upright, the bob line falls true. A string bob level was also employed: A tee bar was set cross bar down on the beam to be leveled. The upright of the tee bar had a weighted string bob that fell to true level and indicated if the beam was level or not.

Ellen van Olst notes that the "scribe rule" system, with marked elements, was originally developed in the Netherlands and the practice of pre-cutting and marking the timbers continued in America. The reason behind the practice was that the entire building was prepared at the timber framer's yard before being moved and assembled on site. She says that full-size cross-section patterns were made of planks, rather than plans drawn on paper, mainly to help decide which pieces of the [costly and scarce] available timber would best fit the different elements of the frame. Another consideration was that early joiners used cruks or crotched limbs and had to piece what wood was on hand to the job in progress. Each member of the anchor bent system was then identified with a mark. Following traditional Dutch building practice, the carpenter would lay out his posts and beams "with each piece numbered, before construction began on the actual site," according to William McMillen. The following system was generally followed: The mark was usually a Roman numeral cut with a chisel, or occasionally with a timber scribe or race knife. All south end parts, for example, might be marked with a small number, and the north end parts marked with a capital size number. The numbering followed a pattern for the building, for which each builder had his own personal touch: Some used a chisel, while others used a scribe rule or a gouge for rounded marks rather than chisel cuts. Each element was marked with a number where it would join with other members. A sign such as a "V" or Roman numerals could indicate where a specific member, such as a brace, would go during final assembly. The H-bents were identical except for the chimney bent, which usually had a beam three inches greater in depth than the other bents to help carry the weight of the chimney.[52] Measures on posts ran from the base to the top of the H-bent beam. If all measures were taken the same way, the floors would be level. When all of the pieces were ready and had been pre-assembled to insure fit, the building was erected one H-bent at a time.

Basic Elements

The basic elements of Dutch construction and joinery related to the framing of a house, or a barn, which followed similar practice, included the following:[53]

Sill Plates, *stijlvoetplaat*: The sill plates were members of wood, which were set on a foundation wall that raised the wooden members above the damp. The sill plate formed a horizontal frame under the perimeter of the building that supported the base of the anchorbent posts. In English construction the sill plate was a massive beam. According to Donald Carpentier, early Dutch practice used sill plates only two inches thick. Later Dutch buildings had larger sills mortised into the floor beams set on the stone foundation. The H-bent post tenon passed through the sill plate mortise to rest on the floor beam.[53]

Anchorbent Posts, *gebintstijl*: The anchorbent post was the vertical member of the H-bent frame unit. Each anchorbent has two posts, one at either end of the anchor beam, which supported the beam. About three feet below the top of the post was a mortise, or rectangular hole, cut and squared to receive the anchorbent beam's tenon. In a house each of the posts is about seven to nine feet tall to the beam and three feet more to the top, about twelve feet total. The house anchorbent posts' maximum dimensions range from five-by-seven to six-by-eight inches in cross section. In barns the same principles are followed but the posts are more usually seen with a cross section of ten-by-fourteen inches. The posts stand with the wider side parallel with the wall surface and perpendicular to the narrow underside of the beam of the anchorbent.

Anchorbent Beams, *ankerbalk*: The anchorbent beam, was the horizontal member of the H-bent frame unit. The beam was joined to the post about three feet below the top of the post by squared tenons that projected through the post mortise hole and was secured with a trunnel, or wooden dowel, which passed through an augured hole in both the post and the beam. The anchorbent beams in a house usually have a span of eighteen to twenty-two feet in length and measure about six-by-twelve or eight-by-fourteen inches in section with the vertical section deeper than the width. Barn construction was similar, but the beams measured ten-by-fourteen to ten-by-twenty four inches in cross section, with the larger side the vertical measurement because it carries more weight in that position. Dutch practice is to distinguish the type of anchor by the location of the join and whether it is blind or passes through the post. The blind join, common in American Dutch house construction, is usually simply called a "lower tie beam," or *het tussenbalkgebint*. The join where the beam passes through the post, as is typical of American Dutch barn construction, is called an "anchor beam," or *het ankerbalkgebint*, according to both Ellen van Olst and G. Berends. American usage generally identifies both types simply as anchorbent construction.

Anchorbent Tenons, *tussenbalkgebint*: In houses the anchorbent tenons were cut flush with the exterior surface of the supporting anchorbent post. In Berends it is described as the box-frame truss with a lowered tiebeam that is tenoned into the posts and pegged. In Dutch barns "tusk tenons," or tongues, often extend beyond the post, on average perhaps eight to twelve inches but they may measure anywhere from an inch or two to as much as two feet. These are called *ankerbalkgebint*, a tiebeam truss with a wedged through tenon. Side aisles allowed the rafters to pass above the tusk tenons and be supported by the aisle wall post plates. According to Greg Huber, "Dutch Barn Wood Species" in the periodical *Timber Framing*, December 1997, the end corners were rounded in pine beams and squared in oak beams.

Anchorbent Braces, *gebintbalkschoor*: *Gebintbalkschoor* is the brace between a post and a tiebeam. Generally called corbels, or anchorbent braces, they connected the inner surface of the anchorbent post at a forty-five degree angle to the underside of the anchorbent beam. They were joined at the terminal ends to the post and the beam. In northern Hudson Valley practice the brace employed a tendon fitted into a mortise hole in both the post and the beam. In the lower valley, the brace was often merely a scribed dovetail half-lapped into the post and beam and secured with nails, as described by Donald Carpentier.[54] The brace was secured with trunnels through augured holes at each join of the tenon and the mortise. William McMillen notes that "in early Dutch construction a corbel was placed under each anchor beam, at either end, bracing it to the posts. These were mortised in up tight into the lower corner formed by the anchor beam and post. Corbels were placed at each, or at alternate bents, but never at the bent adjacent to the gable wall. In many buildings the bottom edge of this corbel was cut out in an arch. The cut did not reduce the strength of the brace nor did it reduce the space in the room." Several typical Dutch corbels, *korbeel*, are illustrated *in Zaans Bouwkundig Alfabet* by S. De Jong. [55] Corbels were typically used to brace timbers in shipbuilding; an example may be seen on the reconstruction of the VOC ship "Amsterdam" at the Ship Museum, *Scheepvaartmuseum*, in Amsterdam. Corbels disappeared from house construction over the course of the eighteenth century although the straight lower brace corbel continued in use on the partition bents in later practice.

Plate, *gebintplaat*: The arcade plate was a long horizontal timber member, or beam, about six-by-eight inches in cross section that was placed on top of the anchorbent posts. The anchorbent posts terminated in tenons shaped on their tops. The tenons were fitted into a series of mortises cut in the lower side of the plate to secure it and connect the post tops with one continuous plate beam. In early Dutch houses the plate is not pinned to the posts and was held in place by the mortise, tenon, and gravity alone. The use of one inch thick pins to secure the plate only began after the 1750s in houses that have been examined by Donald Carpentier.[56] However, William McMillen

states that pins were used earlier in the lower valley.[57] The plate was
the beam upon which the lower end of the roof rafters rested.

Plate Sway Braces, *gebintplaatschoor* (brace between post and
arcade plate), and Sill Sway Braces, *gebintstijlshoor* (brace between sill
and post): At the gable end corners and other points where needed,
such as the chimney anchorbraces, sway braces were used to secure
the anchorbent beam to the plate or sill. The join is often above the
anchorbent brace joint, but designed in a manner identical to that
used to secure the anchorbent brace joins. The braces were set
between the anchorbent posts and parallel to the sidewalls. Trunnels
or wooden pegs secured the joins.

Roof Rafters, *spoor*: Rafters were the members set at an angle
from peak to plate that support the roof surface. In Dutch construction the rafters do not usually join at a ridge pole or rooftree. (A
rooftree is a horizontal member at the peak of the roof extending
from gable to gable at the top of the rafters. It was used in Anglo-
American buildings but known in only four Dutch barn roofs.)
Instead, the rafters are typically joined in pairs and secured by a
fork-and-tongue, or "bridle joint," or by a half-lap fitting secured with
a wood peg passed through an augured hole in the ends of both rafters.
Each rafter was sometimes notched at the point where it rested on
the purlin or plate, so it would be firmly set, and then secured with
a wooden peg or an iron spike. Rafters were usually set above the
anchorbent posts, so they did not interfere with the mortise and
tenon securing the post to the purlin or plate. In houses and barns
the rafters typically tapered from base to top, following the natural
taper of the tree from which it was cut, and "that allows them to rest
in perfect balance on the purlin."[58] Collar beams, *sporenhout* or
spantbalk, extend across the span of the garret to provide bracing for
the rafters. A *windschoor* or windbrace was a member frequently used
to secure the rafters from lateral stress. In the Albany area and upper
valley, the upper surfaces of the roof rafters were covered with
overlapping planks and shingled, or lathed with split white pine or
oak designed to carry pantiles, thatch, or shingles. The individual
shingles were hand split from a block of wood with an edged cutting
tool called a froe, which was hit with a mallet, and then smoothed
with a draw knife on a shingle horse. Some early shingles were given

clipped corners on the exposed end, as on the Decker house. Only later, in the nineteenth century, were shingles sawn from white pine or cedar.

Nave and Aisle, *naaf en zijbeuk*: The space below the anchorbent beam span, the interior room space, is called the nave or arcade, *naaf* in churches, barns, and ships, but rarely, if ever, in houses. The space under the roof, but outside the anchorbent posts, is called the aisle or *zijbeuk*. No aisled homes survive in America, but there is evidence for aisles on seventeenth century New Netherland houses, and houses with aisles are common in the Netherlands. Some houses had two aisles but most had none. An aisle was called an *uytlaaeten*. At Richmond Town the Treasure House, built about 1700, has an enclosed aisle "to the rear" as the house does not stand gable end to the road. In some instances, the aisle was merely an outside extension of the roof, without posts or a sidewall, used to shelter animals under the eave.

Houses were usually framed with an odd number of bents, commonly five or seven, with the H-bent's average span of twenty feet. The space between bents is called a bay, with an average spacing of three-and-a-half to five-and-a-half feet in a house (a spacing related to the appropriate width of a bedstead, according to Dutch authority Henk Zantkuyl) or a span of ten to fourteen feet in a barn.[59] Based upon a three-and-a-half foot spacing between the bents, a seven-bent house was approximately twenty-two feet long, and with a four-foot spacing average, a seven-bent house would have an overall length of about twenty-four feet. These dimensions are within the range of common length for Dutch houses in the Hudson Valley, although some houses were larger. The Jan Martense Schenck house as shown in isometric projection in *Dutch by Design* is twelve bents or forty-two feet and five inches in length.[60] Normally, there were five bents to a room, three exposed and two built into the end walls, or one might be a common bent with an adjoining room. Thus a two-room house usually had nine bents and center hall houses twelve bents.

Dutch carpentry uses various joins and a detailed description can be found in G. Berends *Historische houtconstructies in Nederland*. A few basic terms include the following: A mortise, *pen*, is a squared opening that is either cut clear through, or part way through a member (and therefore called "blind"). A tenon, *gat*, is a narrowed end member shaped to fit into mortise openings. A dovetail, *zwaluwstaart*, is a lap joint with wedge shapes which are half-lapped together, rather than fitted fully tenon into mortise. Dovetails were used as braces at collarbeam and rafter intersections. The notches on the plates kept the rafters from sliding. In English or Anglo-Dutch practice "gunstock" braces were sometimes used. They are "swellings" that protrude from the side of a post to form a larger shelf, or rest, for a plate, beam, or brace. A wedge shaped cutback on posts was more typical of Dutch practice. To prevent beams and braces from slipping, the Dutch cut a heel or *hiel* or *tand* for members to rest in. Lap joints, *schuine langsoverdekking*, were used for fitting planks or members smoothly together. Early floors had spline joints, or *aansluiting met losse veer*; later, tongue-and-groove joints, *aansuiting met messing en groef*, were used for floors.

General rules seem to apply regarding the positioning and sizing of timbers. The cross section proportions of anchorbents ranged between one-and-a-half to one and two to one. The rectangular shaped beams were always placed vertically in section, a practice that "takes advantage of the timber's weight-to-strength ratio. . .over long spans."[61] The beams, therefore, are more rigid and the floor does not bounce as much. However, cellar beams did not necessarily follow the rule and may vary in dimensions and be placed closer together than anchorbents. Cellar beams were also laid on their side, if headroom was a problem, and may be round or square in section rather than rectangular. Posts within walls frequently are rectangular in section. They were positioned with the wider side parallel to the wall surface to insure enough support around mortise joints.

The ceiling anchor beams of the H-bents were typically exposed in Dutch construction, and therefore all exposed members were customarily planed to a smooth finish, which was a very important part of the aesthetic. The exposed H-bent beams support planks that are both the ceiling for the lower level and the floorboards of the upper level, so the planks were finished to a smooth surface on both sides. In many cases, the underside is the more smoothly finished because the upper floor was a garret storeroom rather than a living area until the latter part of the eighteenth century. In many instances the upper floor surface shows pit saw or sawmill kerf. Only late in the eighteenth century were ceilings in Dutch houses enclosed and plastered over in the English fashion. In later construction, the beams that were never intended to be exposed were left unfinished and rough like the cellar beams, although cellars used as rooms had planed smooth beams as found on the ground level floor. In dwelling rooms unfinished ceiling beams were never left exposed. Even in early Dutch barn construction on rare occasions members were planed. Generally, Vincent J. Schaefer says, the "massive beams were roughed out with a broad axe and often finely finished with a very sharp adze." However, Greg Huber takes exception asserting: It "is a widely held but patently incorrect myth" that the telltale finishing marks were made by an adze." Close examination shows them "to really be only broad axe marks."[62]

Between the vertical posts of the bents, the Dutch frequently placed an insulating infill called nogging which is rough brick masonry used to fill in the open spaces of a wooden frame. The nogging might be of burnt brick, sometimes lightly fired, or a mud-and-straw mixture simply packed in by the handful and smoothed. Sometimes the nogging is of unburnt bricks (adobe or *pise*) as found in the Mabie "slave" house, and the Brewer-Mesier, Southard, and Swartwout houses in Dutchess County. In *Journal of a Voyage to New York: 1679-80*, Jasper Dankers reported seeing the same practice in houses at Boston "made of thin, cedar shingles, nailed against frames, and then filled in with brick and other stuff; and so are their churches." In *Vielles Maisons Normandes*, Lucile Oliver shows houses with "deux types de remplissages: brique et pise," that is, two types of infilling: brick and *pise*.[63] Brick and earth nogging was a universal practice in wooden framed houses with applied siding of shingles or weatherboards. The use of light lath placed horizontally or woven saplings between posts covered on the exterior with mud is called wattle and daub and is distinct from nogging. According to William McMillen, on Staten Island mud or clay-plus-straw infilling was used in the seventeenth and eighteenth century, and only was switched to brick in the early nineteenth century.[64] In the Abraham Ostrander house of Schodack, Rensselaer County, (now gone, the original section was

built in 1765 and later parts added between c. 1800 and 1820)
photographs by Waldron Mosher Polgreen show "nogging (wall
filling) of unmortared bricks, common in the nineteenth century."[65]
Even in an area well-known for stone houses, like Ulster County, the
exceptional frame building used brick or adobe to block wind from
penetrating the walls. In the gambrel roofed Bruyn homestead built
between 1790 and 1810 at Wallkill, "the walls are of frame, brick-
filled and clapboarded."[66] The house called "Old Hundred" in New
Hackensack, New York, is a frame structure with walls "filled in
with a mixture of reddish clay and long hair"[67] and the Zebulon
Southard house has lath "filled with a mixture of clay and straw and
cornstalks"[68] beneath the clapboard. In the Van Slyck house, formerly in Stone Arabia, New York, the beams apparently were left
exposed and painted. The infilling brick and *pise* was plastered and
whitewashed giving the interior a half-timbered effect. A similar
treatment can be seen in the Jan Martense House now installed in the
Brooklyn Museum.[69] The combination of plaster and exposed beams
was an important characteristic of Dutch framed houses' interiors.
    According to Donald Carpentier three different types of lath
supported plaster or clay infilling in frame houses. In the first method
the posts had a wedge shaped cut to hold large laths up to three inches
thick and roughly split, which were dropped in from the garret level.
The second method was similar, except that the posts had guides
nailed-on rather than wedged-out. The lathes were slid in from above
as in the first method. The third method of securing lath between the
H-bent posts was to gouge out a cup-shaped groove and bend the lath
to fit in the space.[70] William McMillen says that, from his observation, "gouging was the oldest technique, wedged grooves next, and
finally strips were the last method adopted."[71]
    In the Netherlands between 1400 and 1650, building methods
developed that relate to practices in the New World. In masonry
houses corbels or indentions in the walls frequently supported beams.
The framework for both wooden and brick houses was constructed
entirely of wood. Examples of the interchangeable H-bent framing
may be seen in comparing the exposed interior framing of the
brick-veneered Luykas Van Alen house in Kinderhook, Columbia
County, New York, with the wood-sided Jan Martense Schenck

house at the Brooklyn Museum. In true Dutch construction, early brick walls were never load bearing. In Netherland experience the ground seldom was able to bear the weight of load-bearing brick, even with pilings under the building. However, load-bearing brick walls are found in Anglo-Dutch gambrel roof houses and in later construction in the Hudson Valley. In the Netherlands and in early American-Dutch practice a wooden H-bent frame carried the load while the bricks are used in two ways: infill and veneer. The infilling bricks as in clapboard houses served as insulation with plaster applied directly to the bricks without a lath base to form the wall surface finish. The posts were left exposed by about one half inch. The wooden frames for urban houses had thin brick veneer outer walls to reduce the risk of fires and protect the frame from the elements. The timber framing determined the scale, spatial arrangement, and form of the house, whether it was built in brick or wood.

Records refer to the conversion of wooden framed houses to brick: A 1661 contract of sale, from the early records of Albany, specified that "the seller to be holden in the months of September and October at his own expense to face the house on all sides with brick."[72]   These practices follow Dutch precedents for covering timber frames with brick.[73] Fireproofing Dutch buildings in this manner is discussed by Ir. R. Meischke in *Het Nederlandse Woonhuis van 1300--1800*. He notes that wooden houses were frequently converted into brick, so the framework for both types became indistinguishable from one another. However, frames for wooden houses with weather-boarding, *weeg*, often called for the frame to have notches, or *kepen*, cut on the exterior surface, called *kepen in de stijlen*, so the weatherboards would lie closely.[74]

Until the end of the eighteenth century, the wooden frame within a brick veneer was employed by the Dutch builders in the Netherlands in preference to brick bearing walls because the wooden frame is very flexible and better suited to the distortions caused by the structure's weight on the soft soil resulting in subsidence. In the Albany area the use of brick bearing walls became the usual practice by the 1760s. In the historic structures report, prepared by the architect Robert Pierpont, on the Johannes Knickerbocker house called "Schaighticoke," built about 1790, the wooden frame for the brick structure is examined at length.

Robert Pierpont says:

> Perhaps it was the additional cost of the English system combined with the traditional building experience of the Dutch workmen which led to the use of an integrated masonry and wood structure. The hybrid system allowed the use of nine inches of brick in exterior walls, and interior bearing walls only a single brick thick. Additionally, since the brick on the interior walls do not carry the load of the building they could be constructed with unfired bricks. This building system does require cutting and fitting the bricks around the wood framing member; however, it does allow the wood frame of the entire house to be erected independently of the masonry and thus more quickly. This traditional Dutch building technique dates back to the earliest Dutch settlers and may simply have been preferred by the builders themselves.[75]

Cost and experience were probably the two main considerations: Either because an English brick bearing wall building used more brick (affecting cost of materials and labor to build), or because of the Dutch traditions of the builders. Roderic Blackburn noted that because the house was built on a wet site (which has caused the house to suffer from settlement, resulting in one wall falling out) both economy and function might well have motivated John Knickerbocker.[76]

In late Anglo-Dutch brick buildings the posts disappeared and the walls became load-bearing as in English brick buildings that typically employed brick bearing walls. In buildings with brick bearing walls without internal wooden frame posts, a shelf or ridge was let into the brick wall or a bracket or corbel was built out to carry the floor beams.[77]

In early New England practice (which we will use as a basis for comparison with the Dutch H-bent design) the basic structure followed English "box-frame" practice. A frame was assembled on the ground. The subassembly was then erected as an entire wall frame unit onto wooden sills set on the foundation walls. This created a box built around and centrally braced by a massive chimney. The English unit of construction was the "bay," a frame section of some fifteen feet between major posts. Dutch practice used the term "bay" only in reference to the space between H-bent posts, not as a measure, so Dutch houses and barns were said to be so many "bays." American practice, outside the Dutch tradition, was generally derived from English roots, so the braced box frame was the common practice until the advent of the "balloon frame" construction in the nineteenth century.

The two side frame units and the end beams (or girts), which would connect the side frames, were raised by a gang of men, a work crew or a gathering of neighbors. The gathering was oxymoronically named a "work party"or sometimes called a "raising" or a "frolic" which in Dutch is a *vrolijk*. The men literally manhandled the components from the ground to shoulder height, then used pikes to raise the walls upright. The pikes were about sixteen feet long with metal tips to hold the frame steady while the two sides were pinned to the end beams with treenails. The two side frames now formed the front and back of the house. The end beams tied the front frame to the back frame and spanned the gable walls at either end of the house. Once the frame was raised and pinned, the main job was done. The roof rafters, the wall studs, and the floor joists were added to the standing box frame. In the earlier English style houses, a middle upper-floor beam called a "summer" beam was set from the central chimney support to the frame end girt. Intermediate floor joists were laid, linking the summer beam to the sides at the front and rear girts. The Dutch used single floor frame construction from about 1625 and completely abandoned the use of floor joists after 1650, according to Herman Janse in *Building Amsterdam*. Early English homes did not have a rooftree, therefore the rafters were supported and braced by planks laid across them as a sub-roof similar to Dutch practice.

In many cases the Dutch employed English carpenters to build Dutch houses. Documentary evidence exists recording Dutch officials' letters deploring the lack of craftsmen skilled in carpentry, brickwork, and other trades. Roderic Blackburn has suggested the labor shortage resulted from the early Dutch colonists' keener interest in trading than in following manual crafts.[78] Several examples are known of craftsmen who went on to pursue greater wealth in trade. The matter deserves additional study, but it would be very difficult to do more than point to vague anecdotal evidence at this late date.

One known example is Cornelius Van Slyke, recorded as a carpenter when he arrived in 1639, but who actively engaged in the fur trade and land speculation in the Mohawk Valley a few years later

Contracts

On July 18, 1641, Isaac de Forest signed a contract with Jan Habbesen and Jan Meris as follows:

> Contract of Jan Habbesen and Jan Meris to build
> a house, and out kitchen for Isaac de Forest

> Before me, Cornelis Van Tienhoven, secretary in New Netherland appointed on behalf of the General Chartered West India Company, appeared Jan Habbesen and Jan Meris, English carpenters, who promise, as they do hereby, to build as soon as possible for Isaac de Forest a dwelling house, 30 feet long and 18 feet wide, with 2 4-light windows and 2 3-light windows, 4 beams with brackets and 2 free beams, one partition and one passage way tight inside and outside and the entire house tight all around, and to make in the said house a pantry and three doors. . .[and] a small kitchen, 20 feet long and 16 feet wide, covered with clapboards; and an English chimney; the dwelling house to be covered in such a manner as to be secure against water and snow.

> All of which we promise to perform and to do, on condition that Isaac de Forest pay us as wages for the aforesaid work the sum of 300 Carolus guilders, to wit, fl. 100 when the house is raised and the remaining fl. 200 when the work shall be finished to the satisfaction of the aforesaid Foreest. Without fraud or deceit, this is signed by the said carpenters and Foreest in the presence of the subscribing witnesses. Done this 18th of July AO. 1641, in Fort Amsterdam.

> > This is the x mark of Jan Habbesen, above named
> > This is the x mark of Jan Meris, above named
> > > Isaack de Forest

> Maurits Janse, witness
> Acknowledged before me, Cornelis van Tienhoven, Secretary[79]

The house was a two-room building "with one partition" dividing the space. The terms called for *kruiskozyn* style windows with two members forming a cross shaped division, allowing four lights, one in each quadrant of the cross. Usually in the seventeenth century the two upper lights would be stationary and fitted with leaded glass, and the lower two lights would be shuttered unglazed casements that could be swung open. The other two windows were *bolkozyn*: rectangular windows of two parts with a single leaded glass mullion on one side and a shuttered casement on the other side that opened.[80] The two "free beams" were the two end H-bents and the four "beams with brackets" were the interior H-bents with corbels supporting the beams, as in the Jan Martense Schenck house. The passage way could have been within the rooms or a gangway along the outer wall on one side. Passages or side aisles in the dwelling section of the early Dutch hall house were used for storage and bedsteads or built-in bed cabinets. These aisle dimensions eventually became closely linked with the size of the bedsteads, a fact that showed up in Albany contracts.[81] The house's three doors were probably the connecting door between the two rooms and two exterior entry doors. No fireplace was mentioned. A separate kitchen with an English style fireplace was part of the homestead. This kitchen arrangement was similar to the Gibney house in New Paltz, where a summer kitchen, with one entire wall as the fireplace, stands a few feet from the main building.

Contract of Jeuriaen Hendricksen and Pieter Wolphertsen
to build a dwelling house for Thomas Hall

This day [August 29, 1639], date underwritten, Jeuriaen from Osenbrugge and Pieter Wolphersen, of the first part, and Thomas Hall, of the second part, personally covenanted and agreed as follows.

Jeuriaen from Ossenbrugge and Pieter Wolphertsen shall construct for said Thomas Hall a dwelling house, 32 feet long, 18 feet wide, 9 feet in height, enclosed all round, one door and windows with a complete frame, three joists with corbels and one mantel piece . . . provided that the aforesaid Thomas Hall shall furnish everything necessary for the construction. For which the said Thomas Hall shall pay the aforesaid persons, all at the same time, the sum of two hundred Carolus guilders, in addition to free board as long as the work of building shall continue, the payment to be made as soon as the work shall be completed.

The aforesaid carpenters hereby promise honestly to execute the work agreed upon as hereinbefore written; on the other hand,

he, Thomas Hall, promise to pay them as soon as the carpentering
shall be done. For all of which the parties bind their persons and
property, movable and immovable, without any exception, according to law. Done the 29th of August 1639, in Fort Amsterdam.

This is the x mark of Jeuriaen from Osenbrugge
This is the x mark of Pieter Wolphertsen
Thomas Hall
Maurits Jansen

Acknowledged before me,
Cornelis van Tienhoven, Secretary[82]

The details were vague in many contracts because the parties
understood that the house would basically be a typical small Dutch
type building. The size and number of H-bents with braces was one
of the few specifics, aside from the overall dimensions. The one
specified door would be the entry. The one mantle indicated a single
heated room that probably served as a general-purpose room for
cooking, living, and sleeping. A room without provision for heating
could possibly have been an entry, a sleeping room, or a storage space.

Contract between Thomas Chamers and Nicolaes to build
a house and divide Boot's plantation, February 17, 1642

Before me, Cornelis [van Tienhoven, secretary] in New Netherland [appointed] by the General [Chartered West India] Company, appeared Nicolaes Willem Boot and Tames Camers, who
in the presence of the undersigned witnesses declared that they
had contracted in manner as follows, to wit: Tames Camers shall
build a house 32 feet long and 18 feet wide, on condition that
Nicolaes Boot shall assist him during the construction. Parties
shall defray each one-half of the expense of all the materials
necessary for the building and the labor of one shall be counted
against that of the other and neither shall demand anything of the
other therefor, provided that the land which the governor of New
Netherland has granted to Nicolaes and on which the aforesaid
house is to be built, as well as the house aforesaid, shall belong to
both parties, each party having a half share in the true and rightful
ownership thereof; which land shall be divided by parties on the
first of October Ao. 1642. If Nicolaes Boot happen to incur any
expense on the tobacco plantation, either in felling trees, splitting
or setting posts, or otherwise, said Tomes Camers must pay him
one half, it being well understood that the crop which Nicolaes

Shall make next summer shall belong exclusively to him. In witness and token of the truth this signed by parties. Done the 17th of February Ao. 1642, in Fort Amsterdam.

Niclaes Willems Boodt

This is the x mark of Tames Camers

Acknowledged before me,

Cornelis van Tienhoven, Secretary[83]

While this contract provided few specifics concerning the house it gave details about the terms of a building agreement that reflect upon conditions in New Netherland in 1642. Another contract from 1642 made it clear that eight weeks was considered ample time to erect a house and noted that the house's 30 x 20 feet dimensions called for five hundred clapboards. In addition, the owner rather than the builder would supply the nails.

The details refer to an existing house identified as "the mason's" which relates to a point made by Zink in reference to "initial dominance," meaning that early buildings established prototypes referred to in subsequent contracts as models for later buildings. This seems to be the case in the following contract: [84]

Contract of Thomas Chambers to build a house for
Jan Jansen Schepmoes

Tomas Cambers, an English carpenter, promises [and agrees if God] grant him health, [to] erect and build a [house], 30 feet long and 20 feet wide, enclosed all around and covered overhead with clapboards, tight against the rain; inside like the mason's house [with] a partition, a bedstead and pantry, two doors and one double and one single casement window. The carpenter shall furnish five hundred clapboards for the house; Schepmoes shall supply the nails, and board for the carpenter during the construction, which commences this day, for eight weeks, when the house, barring accidents, must be ready; and when it shall be entirely and properly finished, Schepmoes shall pay to Tomas Cambers, in addition to his board, the sum of one hundred and sixteen guilders, reckoned at 20 stivers to the guilder. For which the carpenter and Schepmoes bind themselves under submission to all courts, provided that the carpenter shall hew the timber to the best of his ability. Done the 6th of May Ao. 1642, in Fort Amsterdam.

This is the x mark of Tomas Cambers

This is the x mark of Jan Jasen Schepmoes[85]

Contract of Symon Root and Reinier Somensen to build
two houses for Paulus Leendersen van der Grift

Two houses, each 32 feet long, 18 ditto wide, [the H-bent frames
to be] 9 feet high under the beams and 3 feet from the beams to
the wall plate, with header and trimmers for a double chimney
and the shaft
    5 outside and inside doors
    3 Gothic window frames
    1 window frame with transom and mullion
    2 three-light window frames
    Three partitions as happens to be most convenient
    The roof frame covered with boards
    Doors and window sashes as required.
The contractor shall hew and trim the pine timber in the
woods, about 200 feet from the place where the houses are to
stand.
The owner shall deliver the timber at his own expense on the
ground where the houses are to be erected and fell the trees.
    2 closets with shelves inside the square room
    2 bedsteads
The owner shall pay the contractor sixty winter beavers for
the above mentioned work when it is completed. He shall also
convey the contractor and his partner and servant to the place of
building and furnish the contractor and his partner and servant
during the work with food and drink, free of charge. When the
work is finished, the contractor and his partner and servant shall
depart for the Manhatans at their own expense. Being satisfied
herewith the parties have signed this. Manhatans, the 30th of May
1649.

        This is the S R mark of Symen Root
        Rinier Somensen
        Pouwelis Leendersz van die Gri[ft]
In my presence, H. van Dyck[86]

Several interesting points appear in this contract. It was an early
example of multiple unit development. The contractor would cut the
timbers within two hundred feet of the site showing a "frontier"
location, yet the owner agreed to move the cut wood to the building
site, suggesting that the builders had no draft animals. The contract
clearly called for Dutch H-bents frames by noting that the posts
would to extend three feet above the beams to the plate. The contract

was more specific in many details than other agreements. However, it stated that the houses would have three partitions where "convenient" implying that neither building would to be the owner's personal dwelling or more specific instructions would probably have been given regarding the interior space. Each house would have a room eighteen feet square and a smaller room fourteen by eighteen feet. Writing about this house in *Dutch By Design,* Henk J. Zantkuyl says, "the floor plan shows the normal layout of an entrance hall (with door and two *kloosterkozijnen*), the side room (the living room for special occasions, also with a door), and the daily living room (kitchen) with bed boxes and cupboards."[87] In the "square room" are specified built-in beds and closets, which Zantkuyl places together in one partition in his reconstruction. Mention of a closet at all is rare at this date. In plan these houses were very similar to the Jan Martense Schenck house as it was reconstructed at the Brooklyn Museum. The contract clearly called for casement windows, as would be expected at this time, but it didn't specify the number or placement of windows. Assuming that the interior wall between the rooms had the double chimney, then the large room might well have had a door and a gothic window on the front wall and another gothic window in the rear wall. The smaller room may have had one of the gothic windows on the front wall. The other windows would be near the fireplaces and the doors would be placed between the bents in whichever wall they were located. The contract did not specify the arrangement of the five doors.

Farmhouse—Manhattan Reynier Dominious, 1646

House 30x20 [inside measure], having on one side an aisle 8 ft. wide, right through; the story in the forepart of the house to be 9½ feet and in the rear part, 12 feet high, consisting of 5 bents with corbels and one without [such an arrangement would leave room for a post bed]; purlins and posts as required; strong split rafters for entire roof, and the roof frame to be tied by collar beams; the frame work belonging to the chimney; in fore part of house a door casing with two lights; a bedstead in the aisle; beams 10 x 7. Everything well hewed and planed; boards and wainscot for doors and blinds [probably meaning shutters].[88]

In Europe, the term "farmhouse" often implies a shelter shared by a farmer and his crops and livestock. While we know that such buildings were built in New Netherlands, there are no surviving examples in the Hudson Valley. The description of buildings in the Van Rensselaer-Bowier Manuscripts at Rensselaerwyck includes an early house-barn built in 1643, "eighty feet long, the threshing floor twenty-five feet wide and the beams twelve feet high, up to the ceiling."[89] Built too close to the Hudson River, the farmhouse was washed away in a spring freshet in 1667. One possible example existed up until the 1930s, according to Vincent J. Schaefer, it stood "along the Beaverdam Road in the Helderbergs of Albany County" but Greg Huber says that his study of Schaefer's photographs make its identification as a "farmhouse" unconvincing as the proportions do not look correct. It will remain an unresolved issue however as the building has collapsed and is lost forever. R. C. Hekker discusses the origin and types of various Dutch farmhouses in *Historische Boerderijtypen/Historical Types of Farms*. He traces their development from a number of distinct types: The undivided aisled house, *loshoe*; the connected house-aisle, crop barn and byre, *kop-hals-romp* type; the house and free standing byre, *midstrey* barn; and, the compartmented single span building called the *langgeveltype*.[90]

The following contracts were for "farmhouses" which had much larger dimensions than buildings used exclusively as dwelling houses.

Contract of Jeuriaen Hendricksen to build a farmhouse for Jan Damen, October 2, 1648

Jeuriaen Hendr. agrees to build for Jan Damen a House, 60 Feet long and on each side a passageway throughout, the frame twenty-four feet wide; in front 11 feet high and in the rear 12 feet high, the rear part being one foot above the ground and the front part two feet above the ground. The front room 24 feet square, with a cellar under it. To lay and tongue and groove the attic floor and to wainscot the front room all around; two bedsteads, one in the front room and one in the chamber, and a winding stair, so that one can go from the cellar to the attic; the front gable perpendicular and the rear gable truncated. In the front room a window casing with transom and mullion and also a mantelpiece. Jeuriaen

Hendricksz must provide the roof with split rafters and nail on the laths, and on each beam [put] a loft bent [or a cock loft, as per Donald Carpentier].

Jan Damen is bound to furnish Jeuriaen Hendricksz and his men with food and drink until the work is completed. When the work is finished Jan Damen must pay Jeuriaen Hendricksz the sum of four hundred and twenty-five guilders, once. Furthermore, Jeuriaen Hendricksz is bound to construct everything in proper manner and to commence in eight weeks. This day, the 2d of October 1648, in Fort Amsterdam, New Netherland.

This is the x mark of Jeriaen Hendricksz,
made by himself
Jan Jansz Damen
This is the x mark of Dirck Volcksz, made by himself
This is the x mark of Albert Jansz, made by himself91

The farmhouse described below was built at Otterspoor the manor of Director Williem Kieft in 1642 by Jeuriaen Hendriksen:92

A (Farmhouse) 100 feet long; the barn (part) 50 ft. wide, 24 ft. between the posts and two sides aisles (uytlaeten) which run length of barn, one 9 and one 10 feet wide; the forepart of the house fifty feet long and twenty-four feet wide, with one partition and double chimney [Note: The meaning of a double chimney is two fireplaces on either side of a partition. The house, like practically all Netherlands Dutch farmhouses of that period, consisted apparently of a combination of dwelling house and barn, all under the same roof. The front part, or *voorhuys*, of the building being used for dwelling purposes and the rear part as a stable for houses and cattle], all of which shall be of stone. (He) shall make and lay the cellar and garret timbers with the necessary flooring; also window and doorframes, etc. Cost: 600 Carolus guilders and board.

A final example of the farmhouse structure apparently common in the early years of Dutch settlement appears to be clearly based upon a common building type in the Netherlands: 93

Farmhouse 60 feet long and on each side a passageway throughout, the frame 24 feet wide; 11 feet high in front, 12 feet high in rear, rear part 1 foot above the ground, front part front room 24 feet square, with cellar under it. Tongue and groove attic floor (which was also the ceiling for the downstairs area), wainscot front room all around; 2 [built in] bedsteads, one in front room, 1 in chamber; a winding stair, so that one can go from cellar to attic; front gable perpendicular and rear gable truncated [sometimes called a jerkin-head style roof]. Window in front room to have casing with transom and mullion; also a mantel piece. Roof of split rafters and nail-on laths, and on each beam a loft bent. Cost - food and drink and 425 guilders.

Henk J. Zantkuyl described another farmhouse that was built as a house-barn combination in 1648 at Achter Col, near the New Jersey Meadows.[94] In the *Dutch-American Farm*, David S. Cohen discusses the Friesland House Group and Aisled House Group of the Lower Saxon Peasant House. Both were examples of house-barn combination structures within the Dutch heritage cultural zone of many Valley settlers. He cites a similar building in the connected farmhouse and barn in Biezenstraat, Zeeland.[95] The *Frilandsmuseet* (Open Air Museum) in Denmark has several "farmhouse" buildings. The Hans Petersen farmstead dated 1685, from Ostenfeld, South Schleswig, combined cattle and grain sections and a dwelling with alcove beds. It too was from the cultural zone of settlers in New Netherland and resembled the farmhouses once built in early New York.[96]

Other European examples can also to be seen at such open air museums as the Rheinische Freilichtmuseum, Germany and the Nederlands Openluchtmuseum, in Arnhem, Netherlands. Modernized, but recognizable examples of combined house-barns can still be found in current use throughout the coastal region from Normandy to Denmark. In *Uilkema, een historisch boerderij-onderzoek* E. L. van Olst shows many houses that illustrate the various house-barn combinations typical in each of the provinces of the Netherlands.

Framing

In the days following the raising, a small crew of workmen handled detailing. Although the same framing was used in wood and in early brick houses, American Dutch stone houses omitted the posts in the H-bent. The stone walls, which were usually about eighteen inches thick, carried the horizontals without additional framing. The beams were placed on stone shelves or niches similar to those in buildings with brick bearing walls.[97] The practice in Ulster stone houses was typical: Floor beams were laid into a "shelf" above a leveling plate of wood built at the top of cellar walls. Greg Huber suggests a possible secondary function of the leveling plate in regard to "damp creep". He notes that in old English tithe barns "oak templates" were placed on stone plinths at right angles to the base of the frame posts so moisture would not wick up from plinth to post. The four stone building walls were then extended upward for eleven to twelve feet. Timber leveling plates were placed on top of the front and back eave walls for fastening the roof rafters. The first floor ceiling beams were installed about three feet below the top plates lines and were left exposed below and floor planked above as in brick and timber dwellings.[98] The distance from floor to plate varied a great deal (it was usually higher in older houses and lower in later examples) ranging from one-and-a-half feet to four feet. William McMillen states that in some early stone houses each level had a water table setback (a recession of the wall forming a narrow shelf); the walls above that point were centered and made two to four inches narrower than the lower section. The setback can be clearly seen on the outside wall at the first floor level. Later walls omitted the setbacks.[99] It may be noted that when the Dutch in the Netherlands spoke of "steen" or "stone" they almost always meant brick, or more formally "baked stone." Therefore, early references to "steen" outside the limestone belt were as likely to mean brick as they were to mean stone.

The Dutch practice of canting upper stories outward in urban buildings is not known on surviving American examples. Called "in flight" each story of the facade was inclined outward to allow householders easy use of the roof hoist-beams without damaging the lower floors' walls. "In flight" is the opposite of "in line" or plumb-line walls. "In flight" construction had the added advantage of shedding moisture better than a brick wall in plumb-line.[100]

Internal construction posts and beams were often anchored to the stone walls, just as in the brick houses, by an iron rod that pierced the wall and the internal beams. Where the spikes looped end emerged from the wall it was secured by an iron spear on the outside of the wall. The spears terminated in simple points, date numbers, or *fleur-de-lis.* Loop ended rods with spears can be clearly seen on the northern end wall of the Mynderse house in Saugerties. There are disadvantages to piercing thes walls with iron "cramps" or tie rods. Iron can rust, and rust has a volume seven times greater than that of iron itself, therefore a rusting cramp will crack the masonry. "To solve this problem, the hot cramps were oiled or tarred immediately after being beaten. Iron was also wrapped in Hessian cloth, thus creating sufficient space for any subsequent increase in volume."[101]

Facing page:

Top: Basic Dutch H-bent frame for a story-and-a-half house consists of a series of H-bents that resemble goal posts braced where the cross beam joins the posts by corbels. The anchor bents resting on light sills and are raised individually. The bents are laterally joined by a plate that spans the tops of the H-bent posts about three to four feet above the cross beam. Rafters rest on the plate and are supported by a cross brace.

Bottom: Basic English box frame for a two-story house consists of two eave-wall sub-assemblies that are raised complete and attached to each other with tie beams at the gable ends. The frame attaches to a massive central chimney with summer beams, and the rafters rest on the plate and rise to the peak supported by wind braces. Smaller timbers are added between the main posts and joists are placed between the summer beam and the frame to support the floors.

Dutch exterior construction in the Hudson Valley.

Photographs and drawings by the author unless otherwise noted.

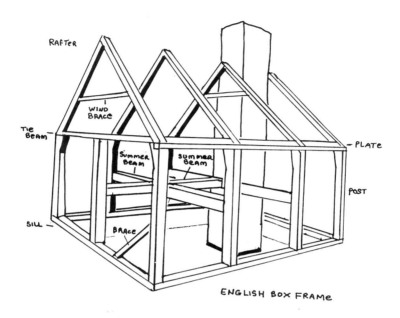

ENGLISH BOX FRAME

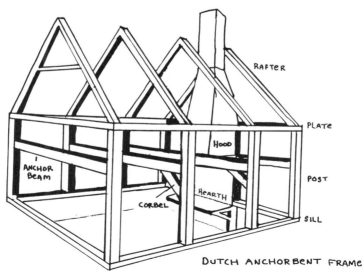

DUTCH ANCHORBENT FRAME

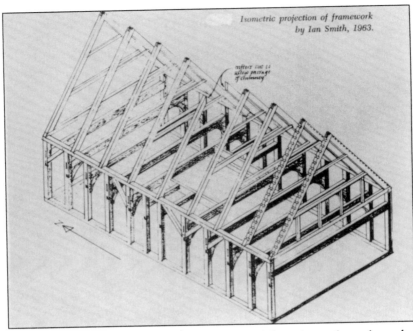

Isometric projection of framework by Ian Smith, 1963.

Above: Isometric projection of framework of a Dutch frame house shows the twelve H-bents braced by corbels. The center bents are closer together and sturdily braced to support the chimney. Joists frame a large open area and mark the location of the chimney rising from the hearth at floor level. The diagram is marked where the chimney passes between the rafters to exit the roof. Courtesy of The Brooklyn Museum: The Department of Decorative Arts.

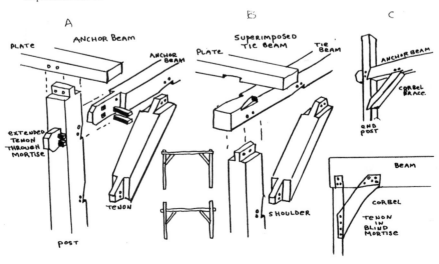

Right: Isometric projection of framework for the Yates House, circa 1730, shows the brick gable wall with elbows and a spout gable and the braiding saw-toothed design of bricks necessary to achieve a weatherproof and finished edge for the raised gable. The little cross-like marks represent anchor irons that joined the H-bent frame to the masonry wall. The arch support for the hearth is just visible and the jambless fireplace can be seen above the hearth. The large central tent-like object is the hood-and-smoke chamber for the back-to-back double fireplaces. As an urban house with a gable wall entry, there

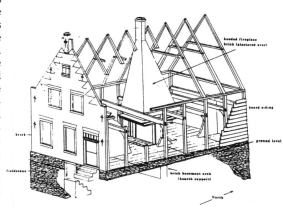

is a side hall with a stairway to a second living level in the garret and a cockloft or upper attic accessed by the small shuttered opening and a crane that would be fitted at the gable peak. A rural house would not have a hall as each room would have its own exterior door. *Below:* Floor plan of the Yates House showing the two rooms and hall with stairway.
Courtesy of R. H. Blackburn

Facing page, bottom: A. Anchor beam assembly shows how the anchor beam is attached to the post and braced by the corbel. The distance between the anchor beam and the plate is generally three to four feet though it appears shorter in the diagram. Barns and some early houses with side galleries used extended tenons and through-mortise joins; generally houses used a blind mortise with the tenon not passing through the post. B. Superimposed tie beams were less common in the Hudson Valley than in the Netherlands. The basic concept is identical, the

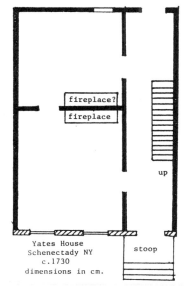

Yates House
Schenectady NY
c.1730
dimensions in cm.

beam joins at the top of the post rather than three or four feet below the top of the post as in the anchor beam design. C. Two methods of seating the corbel in the post and bracing the beam. The first method notches the post to accept the corbel, sometimes the corbel was centered, and other times it was only fitted to half the post. The corbel could also be tenoned into a blind mortise and secured from the side.

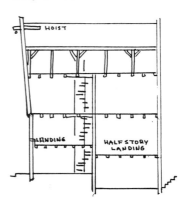

Above: "In Flight" sloping front house frame with circular stair and the half-story interior of urban dwellings. Large ground floor windows would admit light to the half-story room through interior windows.
Left: Corbels as employed in naval practice from the reconstructed East India Company ship *Amsterdam* at the Ship Museum in Amsterdam. The practice was not exclusively nautical and basically reflected period wood joinery techniques.

Above: H-bents and corbels in the reconstruction of the Jan Martense Schenck House, circa 1675. Two corbels are in place, two are not yet installed and the seating cut into the post is visible. Courtesy of The Brooklyn Museum of Art, Gift of the Atlantic Gulf and Pacific Company 50.192.

Below, left to right: Corbel salvaged from early Dutch house by Donald Carpentier and used at his workshops in restoration. Corbel at restored seventeenth-century house at Bloemgracht 91 in Amsterdam. Corbel at the Ariaantje Coeymans' House, Coeymans, New York, 1716. Courtesy of R. H. Blackburn (other photos by the author)

Facing page, bottom: Double anchor beams in a Rensselaer County barn showing extended tenons passing through the post and pegged to secure them in place. Gregory Huber notes the use of double beams is unusual. Courtesy of G. Huber

Above: Jan Martense Schenck house reconstruction view west façade with 1730 door and bay to the south, with supporting cross-beam. Post and brace marked with IIII marks to mate during construction.

Left: Posts taken down from the Jan Martense Schenck house during demolition showing builders markings: VIII and IIIV at tenon end. Note holes bored for tree nails to peg pieces in place.

Facing page, top: View of rafters in kitchen of the Jan Martense Schenck house during dismantling.

Facing page, bottom: Jan Martense Schenck house gable-end detail from collar beam to upper stud with III showing on each piece mated together.

Photos in this spread courtesy of The Brooklyn Museum of Art, Gift of the Atlantic Gulf and Pacific Company 50.192.

Above left: Beam with beading from house in Amsterdam

Above: Beading on edge of deck beam on the ship Amsterdam at the Ship Museum in Amsterdam.

Left. Beam without beaded edge from Broadhead House, Rosendale, New York, 1680.

Reproducing Dutch construction at the John De Wint house in 1997.

Left: Frame raised and roof rafters in place. Fireplace wall with beehive oven shown under scaffolding .

Below: Fireplace wall.

Facing page, top: Frame raised showing plate running across top of H-bent posts and rafters being raised.

Facing page, bottom: Carpenter working on H-bent beam.

Courtesy of the Chairman Paul Dewe-Mathews and Supervisor Harold Jones of the De Wint House, George Washington's Headquarters at Tappan, New York, Property of the Free and Accepted Mason's of the State of New York.

Spring eaves. *Above:* Van Nuyse-Magan House, Brooklyn. Courtesy of G. Huber

Below left: De Wint House. Courtesy of the Director of the De Wint House
George Washington's headquarters at Tappan, New York.

Below right: Kruser-Finnley House, Historic Richmond Town Restoration.

Above left: Join in stone wall where two different periods of construction abut. Unidentified house, Ulster County.

Above right: Join in brick wall where two different periods of construction abut. Luykas Van Alen house, Kinderhook, 1736.

Right: Christopher House, Historic Richmond Town Restoration, Staten Island, circa 1720. Window with soldier bricks and massive early Dutch bearing frame.

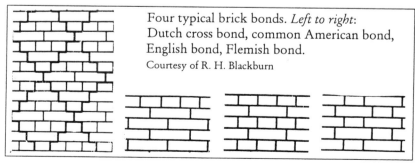

Four typical brick bonds. *Left to right:* Dutch cross bond, common American bond, English bond, Flemish bond.

Courtesy of R. H. Blackburn

Lozenges and date stones. *Top left:* Ackerman-Zabriskie-Steuben House: a wall-mounted lozenge. Courtesy of G. Huber *Top right:* Van Wie House: 1732 date stone. Courtesy of R. H. Blackburn. *Above:* Leendert Bronk House.

Gables. *Left:* Luykas Van Alen House: spout gable, brick braiding. *Below:* Zuiderzee Museum, Enkhuizen: anchor irons, soldier bricks, brick braiding. *Below left:* Arnheim Open Air Museum: *vlechtegen*, anchor iron and thatch roof edge.

Lath used in Dutch houses. *Above:* Bohem House, Historic Richmond Town Restoration, Staten island, circa 1760-1780: riven lath with tapered overlapping ends with one wrought nail. Courtesy of W. McMillen, Historic Richmond Town Restoration. *Right:* Riven lath nailed to post with mud infilling and plaster covering. Courtesy of the Nassau County Museum Collection, Hofstra University Library. Ulster County house with primitive lath used in a frame house made of untrimmed saplings fitted into grooved post channel. Courtesy of G. Huber.

Raamgeheng (similar to ones in Vermeer paintings) from the Cornelus
Schermerhorn House in Kinderhook, New York, circa 1713.
Courtesy of R. H. Blackburn.

CHAPTER V

Exterior Construction Techniques

VIEWED FROM AFAR, the most noticeable feature of many Dutch houses is the roof. Seventeenth- and eighteenth-century Dutch houses often had roofs with high steep-pitched single slants on each side. In *Old Houses of Holland*, Sydney R. Jones noted the "most characteristic essential of domestic architecture in Holland is the steeply-pitched gable." The *Het Houten Huys*, c. 1475, is probably Amsterdam's oldest surviving example of the type; etchings by Frans Hogenberg after Pieter Breughel sixteenth-century paintings show a variety of early high-gabled Dutch houses. The etchings appeared at the Rijksmuseum show titled "Mirror of Everyday Life," February 8 to May 4, 1997, and in the museum publication of the same name. Some excellent American examples of this early gothic style were the houses of Captain Arendt Bradt and Abraham Yates in Schenectady, and the Abraham Glen house in Scotia, New York. The three houses are clearly shown in nineteenth-century photographs reproduced in

Dutch Houses by H. W. Reynolds. Two noteworthy steep-pitched roof houses in Bergen County, New Jersey, are shown in R. W. Bailey's *Pre-Revolutionary Dutch Houses*. They are the Ackerman-Naugle house in Paramus and the Nicholas Varleth house in West-field.[1] The sharp angle of the roof pitch on peaked or what the Dutch call "saddle roofs," *zadeldak*, originally insured the rapid shedding of moisture. In the wet and windy Netherlands the usual pitch for roofs is between 50 and 60 degrees because thatch requires a pitch angle of at least fifty degrees and Dutch pantiles require a pitch of no less than fifty-six degrees.[2]

Thatch is more than just a quaint and picturesque way to cover a roof. It is a practical and a durable organic roofing material. In England, where thatched roofs still are a familiar sight, it is found that reed "if well and closely laid. . .lasts sixty, eighty, and in a few rare cases even as much as a hundred years."[3] Rye straw lasts about thirty years, wheat straw lasts about as long, and what is called "long straw" usually lasts up to twenty years. According to Paul Walshe, "good reed thatch will last for 75–100 years, whereas straw thatch lasts for 25–30 years" and broom or heather "would last a century in any climate."[4] Thatch is also a naturally insulating roof covering: cool in summer, warm in winter.[5] In a traditional society nothing is wasted: Straw used for thatch was readily available, as it is the stalk of a grain crop. Grain was cut at the top of the stalk near the ear of the wheat or rye, the long stalks were left standing as fodder for livestock or, when needed, gathered as thatching material.

Reed grows in marsh and was plentiful. According to Alec Clifton-Taylor, in *The Pattern of English Building*, reed must be cut in mid-winter when all the foliage, or flag, has withered. However, in the *Kingston Papers*, reference is made to cutting reed in Novem-ber.[6] It was a laborious job that often called for wading about in raw weather, cutting the reed, and transporting the bundles through sodden terrain to the building site. It was a task that left the worker exposed and vulnerable as well, David Pietersz. De Vries recorded the fate of a Dutch settler in 1642 who was shot dead while "sitting on a barn thatching it."[7]

Primary documents indicate that thatch, and quite often specifi-cally reed thatch, was used in New York well into the eighteenth century for houses, barns, seasonal buildings, and temporary shelters, and as late as the nineteenth century for hay barracks. A traveling Scot, Dr. Alexander Hamilton, noted that "a great many poor, thatched cottages" were seen on Staten Island in 1744.[8] *Historic Catskill* notes that in 1651 a settler named Van Bronswyck "built a house one story high of timbers, with a huge stone chimney, and thatched with rushes." It was reported that from 1684 Guysbert van den Bogaert "lived for twenty years in a house of logs thatched with reed."[9] Similarly, the first houses in Kingston, then named Wiltwyck, were thatched with reed or straw.[10]

The court records of Kingston refer to thatch. At the November 3, 1665, Ordinary Session of the court, the case of Thomas Chambers, plaintiff, versus Teunis Jacobsen and Andries Pietersen, defendants, was heard. Chambers complained about the "defendants having taken reed off the plaintiff's land." The plaintiff had told the defendants about reed on his property at a place called Pisseman's Corner, and shortly afterward the defendants "mowed the reed for themselves, and had it carted away." At the December 1, 1665, session, the court decreed that the reed be returned to Thomas Chambers and sentenced the defendants to pay the court a fine of twenty-five guilders each.[11] At the March 22, 1670, session, the case of Matthue Blansjan, plaintiff, versus Teunes Jacobs, defendant, concerned 500 sheaves of thatching material that Blansjan "bought of the defendant the roof for a barn for 30 sch. of wheat."[12] (One schepel—"sch."—is equal to 0.764 bushel.) The court ordered Teunis Jacobs, to furnish Blansjan 500 roof-sheaves for the agreed price of 30 schepels of wheat.

Thatch is not just thrown up on a roof. The basics of laying up a reed roof are as follows: Each bundle of reed, which may be as much as seven feet or even eight feet long, curves out from the rafters at the lower end so that the butts form the face of the thatch. The reeds are only cut at the top of the roof; the other reed is tapped into position by hand and then trimmed with a special tool called a leggett. Reed is often laid "to a thickness of 1 m (3 ft 3 in) or more."

"The ridge is a point of weakness for the entry of rainwater, not the least because thatch can slip down the roof over time exposing a gap." Several solutions to this problem traditionally are practiced in the Netherlands: An extra layer of thatch can be laid along the crest,

or the crest is covered with turf, or a capping of lime mortar, clay, is
applied. Picturesquely, in Brittany, Normandy, and into the Lowlands the layer of clay is planted with iris or joubarde. The plants'
roots bind the clay to the roof and a line of flowers' blossom at the
crest in season.

Mr. Jaap Schipper, co-author of *Zaanse houtbouw* and architect
restorer at the De Zaanse Schans museum near Van Zant, Netherlands, noted that Dutch thatch roofs were frequently made of reed.
Because the reed is ridged it will not bend at the crest and therefore
tube-like bales of straw are lain along the crest and covered with *tras*—
waterproof cement—and curved roof-crest tiles are added to create a
weatherproof crest. The practice in New Netherland seems to have
been to use extra thatch or tile with mortar as a crest. Dutch thatched
roofs generally "accomplish their purpose in a straightforward
way."[13]

As the lightest roofing material, thatch was preferred for many
buildings. It only requires "a modest frame work, a foundation of
laths sufficed, or . . . long thin battens of no more than 1¼ in. wide
and ½ in. thick, nailed across rafters at intervals of about . . . 5 in."
In northern France the thatch was supported by a light framework
and held down by braces or spars of wood laid over the under layers
of thatch (and therefore not visible). The spars rest on stepped gables
called *pas d'oiseau* "bird steps" in the Rhone Valley and *pas de moineau*
"sparrow steps" in Cervennes and Pyrennes, while in Britain they're
called "crow steps" and "corbie steps" in Scotland. The raised spout
or stepped gable with parapets often betrays the former use of thatch
as the parapets served to protect the vulnerable edge of a thatch roof
from wind damage. "The stone steps sat on long spars, which held
the thatch-reed, straw, heather or broom in place, and the steps
themselves were designed to give access to the roof for maintenance
work."[14] The steps carried over into later designs from France to
Denmark even when thatch was no longer used, and served a similar
weather edge protective function for brick houses with tile roofs.

Thatch was the original covering for many of the older buildings
in urban and rural colonial America. In crowded urban situations
thatch obviously presented a fire hazard, and early town fire regulations banned thatch. New Amsterdam appointed fire wardens in 1648

because the houses were generally "made of Wood and thatched with Reed," and the chimneys of some houses were made of wood.[15] To limit the fire danger the towns ordered that chimneys be cleaned and thatch banned. A typical ordinance from the magistrates of Albany declared: "In order to prevent accidents (of fire), all inhabitants shall be held to clean their chimneys within the space of eight days, under penalty of fl. 6 [six florins]."[16] Replacing thatch with shingles or pantiles was expensive. Administrative Minutes of New Amsterdam for April 18, 1658, noted numerous petitions requesting postponement for the pulling down the straw roofs, but the Council stood firm. A brief grace period was allowed in which to comply with the new standards. Petitioners were only granted two month's time by the Director General and the Council and ordered to be on their guard against damage in the meanwhile.[17] New Amsterdam thereafter forbid the use of thatch, and after the grace period expired on August 14, 1658, the *schout* was to enforce the regulations and warn everyone, "who has placed thatched roofs on their houses, also who have plaistered chimneys, to remove them."[18] On August 27, the *schout* was back in court declaring, "that pursuant to the orders of the Burgomasters dated 14th August 1658, he was with those, who still have thatched roofs and plaistered chimnies and notified them to remove them, and that they made fun of him." He requested "a penalty be affixed by the Magistrates on those unwilling to obey the order."[19] The Magistrates agreed. The city's roofs were recovered with tiles, planks, or shingles.

Although tile roofs were mandated in Dutch towns for fire prevention, tiles were rarely used in the countryside. The steeply sloped roof design was retained for many years after thatch was replaced by wooden shakes, slate, or tiles, because a steeply pitched roof enabled the tile to shed wind driven rain and snow and helped to preserve wooden shingles from damp and rot.

The most typical tiles were the black or orange "S"-shaped baked ceramic tiles called pantiles. When tiles were used a framework of laths was laid at right angles to the roof rafters. The pantiles were hung on the laths rather than nailed firmly to a solid roof surface.[20] Called single lap tiles, the tiles overlapped only the next course, or row, of tiles below. They also hooked under their neighbor's down

turned bent "S" edge, and, they hooked over the upturned edge of
the tile on their other side. Two types of pantile were common:
Oud-Hollands pan and *gegolfde Friese pan*, Oud-Holland tiles were
single "S" tiles and *Friese* were a triple "S" curved tile. "On most old
Dutch roof tiles the nose fits the next tile to the right. This is known
as covering to the right. In some places, where the southwest wind
can blow rain through the gaps, tiles covering to the left were used.
The top of the roof was closed with special wide curved ridge tiles"
called *vorstpannen*. Spanish tiles with the curved sections lain alternately curved up and down is called *monniken en nonnen*. Dutch
pantiles were usually cemented from the inside, whereas the English
laid them over a sub-roofing base of reeds or hair felt and mortar for
better weather resistance. "Tiles were originally laid without roof
boarding. To keep out snow and rain they were sealed with lime
mortar, sometimes containing cow hair to prevent it from falling out
when it shrank." S. de Jong, in *Zaans Bouwkundig Alfabet*, provides
a clear illustration showing the layering of a top tile, over mortar and
pantile roof surface.[21] After firing, individual pantiles generally measured not less than thirteen-and-a-half inches by nine-and-a-half inches
by one-and-a-half inches. A roof pantile taken from the Abraham
Stats house at the mouth of Stockport Creek in Columbia County
measured fourteen-and-seven-eighths of an inch by nine-and-three-
quarters inches by two inches.[22] The loosely laid pantiles admitted
driven wind, rain, and cold, which was acceptable for a storage garret.
J. Schipper explained that tile eaves were closed from within with
tiles and two boards set at right angles in the gap between eave and
wall: a *wind-veer* and a *waterbord*, and closed the attic from drafts
blown under the eaves. Nevertheless tiles lost favor when New
Yorkers began using their upper floor areas for dwelling space.[23]

Pantiles were imported from Fatherland from the earliest period,
but tiles were soon made at Rensselaerwyck and, as early as 1650, in
Albany. The local clay was not considered entirely satisfactory
compared to the Netherland product, but New Jersey pantiles remained available in the Hudson Valley until the last half of the
eighteenth century. An advertisement in Rivington's *New-York Gazetteer*, on May 19, 1774, announced: "John Campbeel, Potter, At the
upper end of the Broadway, opposite the Negroes Burying-Ground,

Has set up the business of making pantile, and will warrent them to be better than any imported from England or Holland, at 21/10s. per thousand."[24] On July 28, 1774, another advertisement appeared for pantiles, reading: "Weeks and Vallentine, Pan-Tile-Makers, at Middletown; Make and sell pan-tiles of the best quality, at eleven Pounds per thousand for glaz'd and nine Pounds for unglaz'd. Gentlemen may be supplied with any quantity by applying to Mr. John Besnit, Bricklayer, opposite Mr. John Wiley's Distillery, New York. N.B. They will warrent them to stand any weather."[25]

Several factors contributed to the replacement of pantiles as a roofing material in rural New York. Transportating the fragile and heavy pantiles was always a problem. Competition from cheap wooden shingles and shakes, which had been an adequate, if not prestigious, roofing material from the beginning of settlement in the Hudson Valley, finished the tile option by the end of the eighteenth century. The Dutch did not use wooden shingles in the Netherlands, and in America they called them either "wood shingles" in English or *dakspar* or *houtcingel*, according to Charles Gehring of the New Netherland Project. The Decker house in Ulster County has an early section of roof that was covered by an eighteenth-century addition, preserving very early wooden shingles nailed to hand-split widely spaced oak lath. On Staten Island split oak lath ten inches apart was common, but the spacing was as great as fourteen inches between lathes. Many similar examples still exist on Staten Island where split oak lath spaced ten to fourteen inches apart was common, according to William McMillen. The Decker house lath is set at right angles to the rafters and laid at nine-inch intervals. Greg Huber cites a barn from Monmouth County of circa 1780 vintage which originally had cedar shakes (thirty-three inches long by six inches wide and a twenty-three inch overlap) that were nailed to milled oak lath. More frequently, the Dutch used overlapping or feather edge boards laid as full sheathing in the northern end of the Hudson Valley and wide boards closely set but not lapping, farther south in the valley. The wooden shingles used by the Dutch in the lower valley were split from New Jersey cedar or white pine in twenty-four- or thirty-inch lengths laid with a twenty-inch overlap and ten inches exposed. In the upper valley, according to Donald Carpentier, early roofs were made of white pine shingles. William McMillen says that there have been no early white pine shingles found on Staten Island or New Jersey where white cedar shingles of thirty-two to thirty-six inches were the rule.[26] The shingles were riven and then draw-shaved smooth (a draw-shave is a two-handled blade used instead of a plane), with a taper at the end to be overlapped. Wood will last for centuries if split with an axe or adze rather than sawn. This way it splits along the natural cleavage line between soft spring and summer growth and hard autumn and winter growth. Split wood becomes hard and rot resistant and deeply furrowed where the lighter organic material has been dissolved. The northern white pine shingles were typically smooth (unlike today's rough surfaced shingles). Many shingles were "beavertailed" or finished with the corners rounded or taken off at an angle as, for example, on the Madame Brett house in Dutchess County.

Butt nails were common in the early eighteenth century. The nail was driven through the shingle and the lath and left unclenched and exposed to view from within the garret. At the Decker house the nails were driven into the exposed end of the shingle and then through the shingle at two higher points where the upper courses of shingles were laid overlapping.

The Dutch often painted their wooden roofs Venetian red as can be seen in period paintings. Donald Carpentier has red sample shingles he has collected at his restoration center in Rensselaer County.[27] The wooden roof became the American standard on houses built of brick and stone, as well as those of wood, except for town houses and a few large country mansions.

When slate was used in lieu of wood, a heavier frame was needed to carry the additional weight of the stone. Slates had a nail hole punched in them after being freshly removed from the ground, and they were nailed to lath in a manner similar to shingle. Old slates become brittle and fracture under pressure. Roof repairs and expansions are comparable to tile and more difficult and costly than on roofs of wooden shingles or shakes.

Roofing material influenced gable design. The Dutch practice derived from Spanish examples and Mediterranean traditions with Islamic and Roman roots. The parapet gable was a practical solution to the major failing of tiles: Loosely set, the "tiles make poor verges" and therefore are not tight against driven rain and wind. A raised gable provides a better weather seal, and "the tile looks tidier when finished against a parapet instead of as a verge."[28] In addition, the gable solved a significant problem by preventing "thatch or tile being lifted by the wind," which let rain blow in under the roof ends.[29] The Dutch roof with parapet gables, so often seen in house pictures in the Netherlands and early New York, was primarily an urban fashion in America, but tile roofs are still common in rural areas in Europe today.[30]

Town house gables almost always faced the street and were a signature of the Dutch style in the Fatherland. F. R. Yerbury notes, in *Old Domestic Architecture Of Holland,* that the characteristic gable was a natural outgrowth of urban building sites which were often no wider than fifteen feet.[31] The narrow gable front was the only part of the house visible from the street, and therefore, the entry and design focused upon the gable end. Orienting urban houses with an end to the street placed the entry at the gable end, whereas farmhouses had entry doorways along one of the long or eave sides.

The gables assumed various shape and often incorporated the chimney stack in the design as "the chimney was on the inside of the wall" in most Dutch houses.[32] *Tuitgevel* is the Flemish gable, a composition of convex curves, seen in Spanish, Dutch, and Jacobean English designs, as well as in Belgium and Flanders. A *tuitgevel* appeared in the 1721 *Burgis View* illustration of New York and, most famously in America, on Bacon's Castle in Surrey County, Virginia. The *klokgevel* is a concave curve style gable typical of Leiden and was depicted in the 1653 *Dewitt View of New Amsterdam.*[33] The most typical American Dutch gable was the "straight edge with elbows," seen in the Albany area. In the Netherlands today the straight edge gables are still called spout gables. They resemble "the shape of an upside down funnel" with the chimney forming the spout end.[34] As found in the Albany area, the "elbow" is a single "crowstep" at the base of a steeply sloping parapet edge.[35] The style can be seen on the Van Alen House of 1737 in Kinderhook and the Leendert Bronck House of 1738 in Coxsackie.

The straight edge or parapet gable is also typical of Norman French architecture. American examples are found in Quebec where they can be seen on the Maison Marie-Anne Barbel, Maison Milot, and Maison Dumont in La Place Royale, Quebec.[36] Donald Carpentier notes that the typical Albany area Dutch house is very similar to French brick houses found in the area of Calais to Paris; he notes that examples of the gables might even be more frequently found in Normandy than on houses in many areas of the Netherlands.[37] The "step gable requires good maintenance because of the many places where wind and rain can cause damage."[38]

The "crowstep" gable is perhaps the form most Americans associate with Dutch gables. The design was done to excess in Washington Irving's romanticized nineteenth-century modification at his estate named "Sunnyside." In fact, original step gables are unknown on any existing rural house in New York or New Jersey. Frequently quoted as authoritative, H.W. Reynolds erred in claiming that step gables were part of the original design of the 1716 house of Ariaantje Coeymans. Reynolds' statement that the gables were removed when the steep single-pitch roof was modernized to a gambrel in the later eighteenth century is incorrect. Reconstruction drawings of the Coeymans house made by Thomas Nelson in 1986 (shown in *Remembrance of Patria*) are based on a contemporary painting that shows gables "of brick in 'spout' form, the edge laid in a distinctive triangle or braid (*vlechtegen*) pattern."[39]

Outside urban settings and the rural Albany area raised gables rarely appeared in Dutch houses in the Hudson Valley. Instead, the roof ended flush with the wall without an overhang at either gables or eaves. With or without a raised gable, there was a problem to create a smooth edge for an angled brick end wall. A technique was needed to strengthen, weatherproof, and neatly edge straight gables. The problem was resolved by the treatment known to the English as a tumble, or tumbling. The "tumbling" appears as a series of triangles forming a serrated pattern in brick along the gable end. It is incorrectly referred to as mousetoothing or *muizetanden*; the preferred term is "braid" which is called *vlechtegen* in Dutch.[40] Donald Carpentier notes that braid has a long history dating back to the Romans. Angled brickwork "was the best way to give a smooth finish to a straight gable without adding a brick or stone coping so courses of bricks were laid at right angles to the line of the gable, in a series of triangular wedges."[41] An immediately recognizable detail, *vlechtegen* can be seen on the Van Alen House in Kinderhook, New York.[42] Braid brickwork appears in Normandy, in the fens area of Norfolk, and in Jutland.[43]

The origin of the gambrel roof design in America is primarily English. However, gambrel roofs are found in the Netherlands in the eighteenth century and is identified in *Zaans Bouwkundig Alfabet* as "*gebrokendak.*" Gambrel roofs, dated prior to the start of the eighteenth century, are to be seen in Virginia, Maryland, the Carolinas, and especially in New England. Among the earliest Hudson Valley Dutch houses with a gambrel roof was the Rensselaerswyck tenant house known as *Kost Verloren* (Money Thrown Away). Reynolds dates to the house to 1708-1733; however, it could have been built as late as the 1760s as several similar gambrel roofed houses in the area are known to be of that date. The Douw Fonda gambrel roof house Reynolds dates to 1767, and which is possibly a 1730s house, is located near Cohoes. The house is the only Dutch gambrel roofed house with corbels, indicating an early transitional example of the style.

According to D. S. Cohen, there was no precedent for the American use of the gambrel roof in the Netherlands.[44] However, Vincent J. Schaefer wrote, "there is some evidence that earlier barns [in New York] were made with double-slope roofs like those built in the 1600s in the Netherlands."[45] Greg Huber, the editor of the *Dutch Barn Research Journal*, says close examination of the framing indicates early double-pitched barn roofs did not exist. Huber asserts that Schaefer's examples had been modified after the Revolutionary War from steeply pitched roofs.[46]

In domestic architecture the gambrel roof design was popular because it permitted a house to be built two rooms deep and allowed a wider spacing between the anchorbent posts. Although they did not invent the gambrel, the Dutch-American builders enthusiastically adapted the gambrel roof in the eighteenth century to meet their particular requirements. As Dutch-American houses grew in size, Zink says the builders "had to alter their framing to larger loads and longer spans. They retained the one-and-a-half story Dutch form on most of their houses, but the longer span led to the adoption of the gambrel roof. This roof was more efficient than a straight gable, because it did not require exceptionally long rafters, and still provided maximum usable space on the second story."[47]

The gambrel roof house has a strong regional identity with northern New Jersey. In R. F. Bailey's book on Dutch houses in southern New York and northern New Jersey, a significant number of houses have gambrel roofs. Aymar Embury notes that the original models for modern Dutch Colonial Revival houses were frequently found in Passaic, Essex, and Hudson Counties.[48] Furthermore, a third of the houses in Rockland County and most of the large houses in Bergen County had gambrel roofs, which included both the early "high" breaking gambrel and the later low breaking "Dutch Colonial" bell curve gambrels.[49]

The early Anglo-Dutch gambrel roofs had a high break. The roof slope changed angle near the ridgeline in a manner that is virtually indistinguishable from the outside appearance of a contemporary English gambrel roof. Inside, the roofs tend to follow the methods of the builder's cultural roots. D. S. Cohen asserts in *The Dutch-American Farm* that the internal construction of the "two gambrels" was identical.[50] Other authorities disagree: William McMillan at Richmond Town Restoration says that Dutch gambrels follow typical Dutch internal construction practices, and Roderic Blackburn states that "all the [Dutch] gambrel roofs I have seen are based on Dutch, not English, framing."[51]

The low bell-curved gambrel was a later development generally called the "Dutch Colonial" style. However, it was in fact, more typical of the later English colonial period and the Federal era of the new American Republic. The style remained popular in the lower Hudson Valley from the Federal period into the early Victorian era. While this style was most typical of Bergen County, New Jersey, a notable example appears on the Shuart-Van Orden house in Plattekill, Ulster County, New York. An explanation for the apparent anomaly is known: the house was erected by a builder from New Jersey, named John Stevens, in 1773. The low gambrel is the dominant roof design among the 215 extant Dutch houses identified in Bergen County. Timothy D. Adriance, a Bergen County historian, house-restorer, and patentee descendant, notes many fine examples of gambrel roofed houses including the Roelof Westervelt house. He claims that the Westervelt house has "the only original Dutch jambless fireplace remaining in Bergen County," though lacking both hood and cornice.[52] Other examples include the Isaac Naugle house and the Adriance homestead which remain in private ownership. The restorations at Historic New Bridge Landing in River Edge, New Jersey, are located where the tidal Hackensack River meets Coles Brook. The location is the site of a strategic bridge during the Revolutionary War period and it includes three Dutch houses that are open to the public. They are the gambrel-roofed Campbell Christie house of about 1774, the straight roofed Flemish eave Demarest house, and the impressive gambrel roofed Ackerman-Zabriskie-Steuben house, which was built with a single slope roof in 1713 and converted to a gambrel during enlargement in 1752.

Examples of original gambrel roofs on Dutch Hudson Valley buildings were exceptionally rare before the 1720s. Of course stating a general rule invites trouble and calls attention to the exceptions. However the style offered a popular solution for homeowners needing to span a house with deeper rooms. Some true Dutch-style New Jersey houses with steep pitched roofs were converted to gambrels when they were enlarged, according to Timothy Adriance and Kevin Wright, the Curator of the Steuben House. New homes were built in the style between 1725 and 1775 close to New York City. The design spread slowly through the Hudson Valley from about 1700 to approximately 1770. Cherry Hill and the Ludlow house were built even later, in 1786. Gambrel roofs "are noted in Rensselaer County before 1750; north of Albany 1750-1760; in Columbia County in the 1760s in Dutchess in the 1760s and 1770s," but it is unclear if many were built in Westchester before 1776.[53] The gambrel roofed Bethlehem house in Albany County which dates to 1736 originally had a pitched roof; when the house was enlarged in 1795 the roof was converted to a gambrel type.

At the end of the eighteenth century brick gambrel-roofed homes had become popular in Westchester County. In Dutchess County the early practice was to build in stone and complete the gables with brick, as in the Palen-Platt house in Poughkeepsie.[54] The problem with dating roofs is that some homes were revised, enlarged, remodeled, and altered, so a roof is not a true guide to the age of a building. At an unknown date sometime after he had inherited it from his father but before the Revolution, Derick Brinker enlarged the Abraham Brinker house in Dutchess County. "He extended to the east a frame addition, carried up all the walls to two full stories, clapboarded the whole. . .(over stone) and put on a gambrel roof (the latter a clear reflection of the fashion of the day)."[55] Philipse Castle originally had a pitched roof with a single slant to each side, sloping north and south, with the main door in the traditional location on the eave (long) side that faced south. When the house was enlarged, it was also reoriented: The single slant roof was completely replaced with a new gambrel, but the door was now on the gambrel end. Internally the house follows no typical Dutch floor plan and has "an anomalous arrangement throughout."[56]

The straight sloped extended eave roof, without any curve, was often found in the lower Hudson and New Jersey area. The Hendrick Hendrickson house and the Johannes Luyster house in Monmouth County, the Symen Van Wickle house in Somerset County, the Dodd house in Morris County, and the Van Horn house in Bergen County that appear in R. F. Bailey's book most clearly exemplify the extended eave style. One of the finest examples in the Flemish style can be seen in the Gidney house in Newburgh, New York. Dutch house collector Steve Levine described the oldest part of the building as a seventeenth-century one-room homestead, subsequently included within the early eighteenth century building. The deep overhang of the roof, which exceeds three feet, is a functional shelter for the exterior clapboard walls. It also serves to shield the interior from the intense summer sun while admitting lower-angled sunlight to warm the rooms in winter.

Straight slope roofs with eaves that curve at the overhang (which often appears on "Dutch Colonial" houses built in the twentieth century) appears on the authentic colonial Martin Ryerson house in Hunterdon County, New Jersey. The overhanging roof also is seen on the Nicholas Varleth house, the Harmanus Tallman house, the Vreeland house, and the Gerrit Haring house in Bergen County; and on the De Pew house and the Daniel De Clark houses in Rockland

County. The out-curved flaring eave design is frequently called a bell cast or spring eave roof with a "flying gutter" or the rather racy sounding Flemish or Dutch "kick." Originally, the design was used to shed rain from the roof edge, protecting the roof plate (the point where the roof rafters joined to the wall) and the wall surface. The "kick" is a piece of wood curved at the top and notched at the bottom to fit securely against the top plate. Shingled over as an integral extension of the main roof, the kick directs the flow of water outward and away from the structure by creating an overhang at the eave. Either the overhang is short and self-supporting or braced from below by supports from the house wall below the eave line. At its greatest extent of perhaps two to three feet it looks like an embryonic porch roof and undoubtedly suggested that line of development. The design originally appeared in America on the homes associated with settlers of Flemish origin and had a straight-pitch roof with a single slant to each eave. In Normandy the "kick" can still be seen on buildings from cottages to chateaux. Closer to home, the kick can be seen on the Zebulon Southard house at Fishkill, New York. "The Roslyn Landmark Society Annual House Tour Guide, June 1996" included reconstructed elevations of the Van Nostrand-Starkins house (c.1680) -- an English framed Rhode Island 'stone ender' originally occupied by a Dutch family -- that was erected with a straight roofed and about 1730 had a "kick" added to the front eave. In Dutch colonial architecture first impressions are often misleading, the Van Nostrand-Starkins house has a typical Long Island Dutch-Flemish appearance.[57]

In *American Shelter* it is asserted that the flaring eaves design originated in Flanders to protect the plaster on the exterior walls of traditional houses.[58] However the kick was used with gutters and the main purpose of a gutter is to lead water away from cellar walls. The wall material used in Europe was not like typical American exterior hard mortar; rather, it was identical to the perishable interior plaster wall material of houses — a mixture of lime, clay, and straw or animal hair. In American practice mortar was used to bond stones and bricks, and then a layer of whitewash was applied to the outside walls. The extended eave, overhanging a wall sometimes coated with a white-wash of slaked lime and water, perpetuated "a visual resemblance to the Flemish prototype."[59]

The kick on early American Dutch buildings was sometimes a later colonial addition as many early houses built with plain edged roof eaves were modified to Flemish eaves. The Dutch-style Jan Martense Schenck House, built between 1675 and 1677 and modified before 1730, was given a Flemish eave in the early eighteenth century. The Jan Martense Schenck house has been taken apart, moved, reassembled, studied, analyzed, and restored by the Brooklyn Museum since the 1950s. Currently on view at the museum, it is one of the best restorations to date. Similar modifications are seen at the Pieter Wyckoff House in Brooklyn. The Wycoff house is sometimes claimed to have been built between 1639 and 1641 but more probably dates to about 1660. The Wyckoff house's added Flemish eaves date from the late seventeenth century. They are similar to the eaves seen in the Richard Vreeland House built between 1786 and 1818 in Leonia, New Jersey.[60] Identical examples of the style, as original or as later conversions, appeared on Quebecois homes from the middle eighteenth century into the nineteenth century. A construction diagram of the kick appears in *La Maison Traditionnelle Au Quebe.* A caption explains that in Quebecois' practice the curved piece of sawn wood that formed the kick was nailed to the top side of the rafters just above where they rest on the wall plate and the kick extends out beyond the vertical edge of the wall.[61] The design is identical to the eave curve on the Ackerman-Zabriskie-Seuben house cross-section drawings in *The Dutch-American Farm*.[62] A similar curved eave "kick" piece exists on the *Voorleezer*'s house at Richmond Town Restoration. (*Voorleezer* was not an individual's name. It was a Dutch Reformed Church official who served as a reader, church clerk, and *foresinger* who led the congregation in songs, taught school, and was also the catechizer. In the absence of an ordained minister, the *Voorleezer* read the service, but he could not preach nor administer communion.)[63] The spring eves on the restored *Voorleezer*'s house were based upon construction evidence, but according to William McMillen, they were not original and were apprarently added to the house in the eighteenth century.[64]

During the later eighteenth and early nineteenth century, the curved eave was added to the later version of the gambrel roof. The later gambrel had a flattened, longer upper section and a wider lower section than the high gambrel of the 1720s. The combination of a flattened gambrel roof and curved Flemish eaves resembles a bell curve. The Guyon-Lake-Tysen house, of about 1740, at Historic Richmond Town has spring eave ends supported by columns covering the six-foot-wide porch. A good example appears on the Abraham De Peyester House in Beacon.

A French-West Indian style porch and English proportions were then merged with the Flemish eaves and the flattened, bell curved, Dutch gambrel roof to produce the misnamed "Dutch Colonial" design. The "Dutch Colonial" was neither. However, the design was claimed, in fact, to be the first truly original American style.[65] The Nicholas Schenck house restored by the Brooklyn Museum is a good example of the type and is described in detail in *Dutch By Design*. Other examples are the Van Nuyse-Magaw house, and the Lott house, both in Flatlands, Brooklyn. An early example, with a porch and double stairway (added, or restored, in the 1960s), is the Morris Graham house (also called, aptly, the Old Stone House) south of Pine Plains, New York. The most famous example of the French Louisiana or Caribbean style verandah was added in the early nineteenth century to the early Dutch style Van Cortlandt Manor, Croton-on-Hudson. The "Dutch Colonial Style" reached high development in New Jersey, Staten Island, Long Island, and sections of Dutchess County. Noteworthy examples include the Abraham Ackerman house in Hackensack, the Paulus Van Enden house in Bushwick, the Peter De Pew house in Orangeburg, the Jermias Mabie house in Naurashaun, and the William De Clark house in Closter. These later "Dutch Colonials" were built after 1776. The style retained its regional popularity through the mid-nineteenth century.

Gutters, *goot*, were attached below the eave to the H-bent frame members by iron, *goot-ijzer*, or wooden gutter hangers fitted into augered holes. The eave line on an old house will show a series of holes with a drop of about six inches in forty feet of eave line from one end of the house to the other where gutter hangers were hammered into the eave. The gutters were typically hollowed logs about four-by-six inches with a two-inch-deep trough gouged out for rainwater. Gutters were occasionally finished with a decorative bead on the exposed lower edge. In the Netherlands gutters were often supported by corbel shaped brackets. When the eave had no gutter an *ozingplank*, drip plank, often was extended below the roof edge to direct water away from the house siding. In addition, houses built "in flight," or angled outward from the ground up, had drip-stone moldings to shed water from the facade to preserve the brickwork and keep the facade clean.[66]

Early Dutch roofs in America rarely had dormers. If present, early dormers usually were built with a long shed roof placed between the rafters. Early shed dormers appear on the south front of the Mandeville house, Garrison-On-Hudson, on the roof of "Lithgow" near Lithgow Village, and on the Van Loon house, built in 1724, that stands between the Hudson River and the ever-widening road in Athens, New York. Reynolds says: "The longer the slope of the dormer the earlier may be the date ascribed to it, those of the house of Madame Brett (Teller House) illustrating the earliest type."[67] The generalization may be true. The shed dormers on the Mynderse house are "probably original," according to *Early Architecture of Ulster*, although Roderic Blackburn doubts this claim.[68] Donald Carpentier and Roderic Blackburn agree that the shed dormers on the Bronck house are original, and Roderic Blackburn also points to the Van Wie house as another early example of dormers. The dormers of the 1732 Van Wie house were quite unique at that date in America—peaked with a monk's cowl facing and a pseudo-chimney crown.[69] An original pitched or arched dormer on an early Dutch house in the Hudson Valley is extremely rare, but again exceptions are to be found, in this case the roll-gable pediments on the 1729 Marten Van Bergen house. A contemporary illustration can be seen in Pieter De Hooch's painting *A Country Cottage* (c. 1665). This clearly shows a small Netherlands house with both a brick dormer with a pediment roof and classic style pilasters in white along the brick facade facing the garden. Nevertheless, in America a peaked or arched dormer on a Dutch style house tends to suggest an alteration of the roof. Peaked or arched dormers reflect Georgian, Federal, Gothic, or even fantasy Victorian stylistic features rather than typical early Dutch practice.

The small oblong upper windows of story-and-a-half houses just below the eaves known as "eyebrow" or "lie-on-your-stomach" windows were an early nineteenth century alternative to dormers.

They admitted light and air to the upper level between the gable ends on the houses built to a story-and-a-half height. "They came into use in the 1790s . . .and preceded, by a few years only, the introduction of the two-story frame house," according to Helen Wilkinson Reynolds.[70] The windows are most typical of less-costly homes of the 1820s. The narrow oblong windows were very common on houses from the early Greek Revival through the early Victorian period. They are still seen throughout Dutchess and Columbia Counties and other areas developed in the later eighteenth century and early nineteenth century. At times an early Dutch house had its roof raised when the garret was converted to rooms. Small windows were often added to the new upper section. It was a typical renovation on many Ulster County stone homes in the Kingston area, where a wooden strip with windows is clearly identifiable as a later alteration to the house. But it was not an original Dutch design, it was a Federal house detail.

House walls were almost as varied as roofs in design and materials. Most early Dutch houses were built entirely of wood, which was available everywhere in the Hudson Valley. Early contracts, such as the 1649 agreement between Paulus Leendersen and the builders Symon Root and Reinier Somerensen, specified that "the contractor shall hew and trim the pine timber in the woods, about 200 feet from the place where the houses are to stand."[71] Proportionately fewer wooden houses have survived simply because wood is more perishable than brick or stone. Many early wooden homes of the Mohawk Valley disappeared in flames during the several Indian wars when the region was still the frontier.

After the First Esopus War, the Wiltwyck (Kingston) settlers built a cluster of homes within a palisade. Built in haste, these were apparently wood and thatch buildings. In the Second Esopus War, the report of Captain Martin Kreigier noted that on June 7, 1663, the palisade and houses were burnt "and the new village is entirely destroyed except a new uncovered barn, one rick [a hay barrack] and a little stack of reed."[72]

Houses Burnt At Wiltwyck[73]

Of Michiel Ferre	1	Of Hans Carolusen	1
Of Willem Hap	1	Of Pieter van Hael	1
Of Matty Roeloffsen	1	Of Jacob Boerhans	2
Of Albert Gerritse	1	Of Barent Gerretsen	2
Of Lichten Dirrick	1	Of Mattys	1
		Houses	12

These early wooden houses with thatched roofs were quickly reduced to ashes. The same fate awaited houses in the Mohawk Valley during the French and Indian Wars and the Revolution. A rare survivor among the many wooden Dutch houses in the Mohawk Valley was the Van Slyck house of Stone Arabia. It was typical of the early settlers' homes—wood frame, roof, siding, a side entry, two rooms with a garret, and a jambless fireplace. The many small wooden urban houses (similar though usually oriented to the street with a gable end entry and often brick fronted) met more prosaic fate, torn down and built over victims of urban growth.

Externally the frame of Dutch wooden houses was covered with weatherboards called *potdekseling*. Plank siding was used along the Eastern Coast by English, Dutch, and French settlers from an early date. Dutch wooden houses were typical of the southern reaches of the Hudson, Dutchess County, Long Island and Staten Island. Originally, wooden houses were in the majority in Columbia and in Rensselaer County, and they were found through the Mohawk area. Ulster and Greene Counties were the exceptions with a majority of early stone dwellings. In Dutchess County the David Johnson house called "Lithgow" and the Madam Brett house are frame and board buildings. On Long Island the Abraham Wyckoff house at Gravesend, the Minne Schenck house in Nassau County, and the Johannis Schenck house in Brooklyn are also wooden structures.

Mary Mix Foley says: "Characteristically [Netherland] Dutch was the use of vertical or horizontal planking, or clapboards, over a timber frame. In fact, English clapboards—and thus our familiar American clapboard house—probably derive from Holland." The claim of "probably" seems a bit too broad. However, in *The Homes of the Pilgrim Fathers*, Martin S. Briggs shows early board homes in Zaandam (including Czar Peter's Hut) and Broek-in-Waterland, Holland, where imported Baltic timber was commonly used. The museum village at Zaanse Schans features Dutch wooden houses from several locations and periods dating to the seventeenth century. These Dutch houses were usually made of imported wood, floated from Germany or shipped from Scandinavia, according to Jaap Schipper who was the historian architect for the museum. The frame beams in the Netherlands were often notched to lay the weatherboards more closely. This practice— called *potdekseling met/kepen in de stijlen*— was not commonly used in America, probably because it went beyond frontier craftsmanship and priorities. A rare American-Dutch example of notched posts employed to carry weatherboards can be found in the Roslyn Grist Mill, Roslyn, Long Island. It is recorded in an historic structures report prepared for Nassau County in 1994.[74] (The difference between weatherboards and clapboards is that sawn pine clapboards taper toward one edge and riven oak weatherboards are planks of even thickness.) In the same period clapboard houses appeared in Essex, Surrey, and Middlesex counties in England and Briggs also notes that from the start clapboards were exported from Plymouth, Massachusettes, to find a ready market in England. He cites a shipment of lumber for clapboards as cargo in 1621 aboard the *Fortune*, in 1622 aboard the *Little James*, and in 1623 aboard the *Anne*, among others.[75] Early houses with clapboards are still common in England in Kent, Hampstead, Surrey, Essex, and the southeast counties.[76] English examples are virtually indistinguishable from American homes of the same period or later.

Wood was available in American forests everywhere and therefore the typical small American house of Dutch or English origin was likely to be a wooden structure. Weatherboards and clapboards were used in many parts of the country long before 1700, first as riven oak, split like shingles from sections of log five to six feet in length. By 1700 most clapboards were sawn white pine, hard pine, or cedar. New England houses did not normally have siding wider than seven inches according to Donald Carpentier. Dutch buildings, according to William McMillen, were built with siding eight to fourteen inches wide.[77] Like weatherboards, the earliest clapboards were of an even thickness and were not tapered (as later clapboards usually are). Many Dutch weatherboards had a decorative bead line on the exposed edge. An

esthetic detail, the bead line cast extra shadow and gave emphasis to
the edge, dramatizing the visual impact of the boards. Wooden siding
can be applied horizontally as clapboards or weatherboards or vertically, as flat matching boards with butting, rabbeted, or overlapping
edges. According to Henry Lionel Williams, weatherboards came
into use about 1710, but they are commonly found a half-century
later.[78] The Dr. Luke Kiersted house, in the Historic District of
Kingston, New York, has beaded siding laid over brick-lined walls.
A brochure by the "Friends of Historic Kingston" describes it as
"one of the few remaining examples west of Connecticut" with
beaded weatherboards. However, beaded edge boards were the norm
on eighteenth-century houses on Staten Island.[79] At one time, I
owned an early nineteenth-century house with beaded weatherboards in Pine Plains, Dutchess County, New York, and I have seen
many other examples "west of Connecticut."

Wooden siding on the gable was also combined with stone in
many areas and wood sides with brick ends were common in Dutch
urban dwellings. The combined wood and brick houses can still be
found, an example of the type survives in the Cornelus Schermerhorn
house at Kinderhook, Columbia County, New York. Usually the
weatherboard appeared on the upper section of the gable end, which
can still be seen in the Hendrick Kip house at Fishkill. Many Dutch
houses also had siding of both shingles and boards. A handsome
example can be seen in the Symen Van Wickle house, Franklin
Township, Somerset County, New Jersey, which has long rounded-
edge shingles on the front wall.[80]

William McMillen says that the shingle overlap in Staten Island
was typically one third to two thirds on the roof and one half on the
walls. Thirty-inch long roof shingles had nine to ten inches exposed;
side shingles had thirteen to fifteen inches exposed. With twenty four
inch shingles the exposure was seven-and-a-half to eight inches on a
roof and ten to twelve inches exposed on the siding.[81] White pine
roof shingles were observed as typical on Dutch buildings in the
Albany area in 1749 by Peter Kalm, who mentioned them in his book
Travels into North America. According to Bailey, shingle siding made
of cypress was used on the Wyckoff homestead, built in the seventeenth century in Flatlands, Brooklyn, supposedly for Director

Wouter Van Twiller. It was occupied from 1652 to 1694 by Pieter
Claussen Wyckoff.[82] "The shingles were hand hewn from the wood
of the cypress tree; they were 42 inches long and were laid with about
14 inches exposed."[83] The Madam Brett house in Beacon is also "sided
with notable shingles of red cedar" according to Bailey.[84] But, William McMillen says that Bailey is wrong, it was white cedar that came
from the swamps of coast-line southern New Jersey and was a major
item of trade from 1704 through the end of the century.[85] The
shingles were "shipped from ports on the Delaware river and from
Little Egg Harbor on the Atlantic coast and carried by boat to New
York City, whence. . .(they were) re-shipped to the West Indies and
to customers within a radius around New York."[86] Cut with round
edges, the New Jersey cedar shingles were to be seen on the house of
Henry Livingston, torn down in 1910, shown in Reynolds' *Dutch
Houses*.[87] The original white cedar shingles, from 1740, are still on
the Guyon-Lake-Tysen house at Historic Richmond Town. In *Scars-
dale's Heritage Homes*, Mrs. Edwin D. Cox mentions shingle-sided
Wayside Cottage or House, which was the scene of fighting between
the British "cowboys" and the American "skinners" during the
Revolution.

> All the shingles across the front of the house were put on before
> the Revolution and were also severely scarred by raiders, Henry
> N. MacCracken, one-time President of Vassar, who visited the
> house in 1887, recounted that the cottage handyman spent all his
> spare time digging bullets out of the shingles. These shingles are
> unusual in that they are 36 inches long with an 18 inch overlap,
> the edge of which is scalloped..[88]

Shingles were used to cover brick and stone buildings as well.
When the Henry Livingston house in Poughkeepsie was demolished,
the *Poughkeepsie Daily Eagle* editions of May 17 and May 19, 1910,
recorded "that removal of the shingles showed the walls of the house
to be of stone and very thick."[89] A shingle or clapboard covering
was employed to unify a facade built at different times and in various
materials. Among the homes with wood placed over masonry are the
Abraham Lent house, North Beach, Brooklyn, the Simonson-Blake
house in New Springfield, and the Cornelius Van Santvoord-Krusen-
Pelton house in West New Brighton, Staten Island.[90]

Dutch stone houses were an American development. There was little stone for building in the Netherlands. Among the conservative Dutch *boeren* once stone was accepted as a building material availability perpetuated its use. Roderic H. Blackburn writes in *New World Dutch Studies* that: "In effect, what had been the one radical innovation in construction finally came to be the most persistently conservative of Dutch houses."[91] Many stone houses were built of irregular field stone, which the English call rubble stone. When using these stones in a wall, the flattest side must be laid face down and the next flattest side must face out from the wall. The best way to test a stone is to roll it; it will stop on the flattest side. When available, square cut stones were preferred. The quality and quantity of shaped stones employed can help date a building. Squared stones were first used for foundation and corner stones. House fronts frequently were made of square stones, and rubble was used for the rear or sides. Later houses in New Jersey and Ulster County had squared stones all around. In Ulster the stone is often fossil-filled limestone, whereas in New Jersey builders used red sandstone in large and small fragments, chips, and roughly shaped building blocks.

Bailey says, "slight variations in the masonry have become more perceptible in the present day as the use of white lime mortar for repointing has replaced the old . . .binding, which was about the color of the stones."[92] Roderic H. Blackburn describes the mortar as a mixture of buff colored sand and white limestone "often of such a fine grade as to be like mud."[93] William McMillen notes that the color of the pointing depends upon the sand or clay and the amount of added lime.[94] The clay binding was originally pointed over with light mortar, as a weather seal, which would refute Bailey's assertion. Stone construction varied greatly according to the builders' technical skills and the quality of materials used. The De Pew house in New City has rubble stone with carefully dressed corner stones, the Haring house in Tappan has dressed stone on the front and rear walls but rubble stone side walls, and the Tallman house in West Nyack has courses of alternating long and short stones in a pattern common in New Jersey but less often seen in New York.[95] The central area for many Dutch stone homes in the Hudson Valley is in Ulster County along the Old Mine Road west from the Hudson River near Kingston.

Examples range from the fine, large, gambrel roofed Wynkoop-Lounsbery house to the small and charming Davis Tavern in Stone Ridge.

Construction quality varied from the rubble work of an isolated farmer to the contracted work by experienced masons. In Hurley (originally Nieuw Dorp), New York, many of the earliest stone houses show a professional hand with stone courses regularly laid. David Baker, a local authority on Esopus stone houses, says that individual stones were laid in buildings as removed from the ground: The fossil lines and geological evidence are traceable on the individual courses along an entire side, or even completely around the house. The stone was often evenly shaped and squared, especially at the house front. At Richmond Town Restoration, William McMillen explained the details of Dutch stone construction: A foundation wall eighteen inches to two feet thick was built from the cellar footings to the base of the first floor. The top of the foundation wall had a wooden leveling plate set into the top of the masonry. At each floor level of the stone work, another wooden leveling plate was set into the masonry. Usually, there was a leveling plate at the upper course of the cellar wall, so the first floor beams would be level across the building. A second leveling plate was at the ceiling level for the first floor, and a third leveling beam served as a purlin plate where the roof rafters met the top of the wall.

Many of the Dutch were careful masons who paid considerable attention to pointing. A line of mortar often marked the water table line. Each stone had the surrounding mortar pressed in to prevent water from penetrating the joint. Frozen moisture would break down the bond. A raised, inverted "V" shaped ridge will appear where the mortar had been pressed down around two adjacent stones. Then the new masonry was built up to the next level. Frequently, the stone work was indented at each level, leaving space for the beams at floor level. A step-back of several inches on the exterior, called a water table, was created and the next level of wall was centered on that base.

When stone walls were built spaces were left for window and doorframes. The massive pegged together wooden frame members were designed to carry the weight of the masonry above the opening.[96] The early seventeenth-to early eighteenth-century wooden frames had squared, level sills, rather than angled sills that shed water, because the windows normally had shutters for protection from the elements. Stone lintels and sills did not appear until the nineteenth century, when window frames were hollowed for the sash weights and pulleys then coming into fashion.[97]

Helen Wilkinson Reynolds observes: "In building the stone house a custom prevailed of marking one stone of conveniently flat surface with the date of erection or the initials of the owner or builder. The markings are found on lintels, on cornerstones, at the line of the eaves and in the middle of walls and wherever they are placed are almost invariably reliable."[98] This is not necessarily true. Several stones were dated later than the earliest building date and appear on additions to the house. Many Staten Island buildings had dated stones. Five or six are in the collection of the Staten Island Historical Society. Many dates and owner names were also set in iron numbers and letters, like anchor irons, or were incised on bricks, or set in brick patterns in contrasting colors. Date stones can be seen on the Persen house, a stone saltbox-shaped house in Saugerties, New York. The Mynderse house, also in Saugerties, overlooking the Hudson River has a name and date stone. The Daughters of the American Revolution in Poughkeepsie have a 1702 dated-stone from the Van Kleeck house. According to Donald Carpentier, the Slingerland house is dated with a diamond shaped panel in fired clay brick marked "I S 1762."

Stone was chosen in many areas because it provided a defense against Indian attack. Many early homes began as defensive structures on the frontier in The Bronx, Kingston nee Wiltwyck, and the Saugerties-Esopus area. Stone was also a material suitable for the frontier settler because, in addition to its durability and availability, relatively unskilled workers could use it when necessary. A real wooden house, as opposed to a crude cabin, requires a carpenter's skills and tools, and a brick house needs a trained mason. Stone can be gathered and laid up with little training and few special tools, but it requires a very strong back.

Skilled stone masons were available from an early date, and by the middle of the eighteenth century newspapers were filled with advertisements by stone cutters and masons seeking employment.

Men named Lindsey and Sharp, John Norris, and Uzal Ward advertised as masons. Robert Hartley, a stone-cutter from Kingston-upon-Hull, advertised that he executed all stone work in general, and he could cut marble chimney pieces, tombs and head-stones with the greatest dispatch at reasonable terms.[99] In Ulster County the limestone could usually be quarried on site or nearby. Outcroppings could be split with wedges, bars and hammers, or mauls. The rock broke away in long thin slabs and blocks with flat sides, and edges of various shapes. By selecting smoother rocks for the exterior and rubble for the inner mass a builder could quickly raise a sturdy and neat wall.

Early stone houses, such as the DePuy-DeWitt house in Wawarsing, Ulster County, were often crudely built. It has small irregular windows, while the stone walls were bonded with a mixture of mud and straw. "The stones forming the thick walls of the (John) Montross house (ca. 1724) are laid up in clay."[100] Exterior joins were pointed in "fixed limestone mortar. . .designed to prevent moisture from reaching the softer clay bonding."[101] Masonry skills improved with time and peaceful conditions. Later homes often incorporated the older one-roomers and joint lines on a wall surface often are clear indications of additions.

Dutch stone houses usually had chimneys built of burnt brick, which was more heat resistant, lighter in weight, made more even closer fitting joins, and was more weather tight than stone. Brick detailing and front or rear brick walls are common in later stone houses. The Van Cortlandt manor house combines the use of red and yellow brick, fieldstone and red sandstone. "By framing door and window openings with brick in a kind of quoined treatment, these early Hudson Valley builders did away with the laborious task of stone cutting around door and window jambs."[102] Brick gables and end walls are common on early Dutchess County stone houses. The gable end requires a very even fit between the wall and end rafters which was difficult to achieve in stone. The use of brick and stone was also common in New Jersey Dutch houses. "It was a Dutch custom to build the front walls of more carefully finished materials. A logical development was the use of brick for the front walls of the houses" and stone or wood for the back or side walls.[103] The combined materials can be seen, for example, on the Daniel De Clark house in Tappan, built of field stone and brick.

However, the average country mason had much to learn before he could build a brick house. The necessary skills of working in brick are a specialist's craft and beyond the ability of the average farmer or handyman builder.[104] The need for skilled brick workers was a problem in the first years of the colony. The Dutch West India Company's secretary in New Amsterdam, Van Tienhoven, wrote on several occasions in 1658 for "three or four house carpenters who can lay brick." The calls for skilled brick workers continued throughout the Dutch period because brick remained the Dutch material of choice despite the scarcity of trained workers.

To the Dutch bricks were so significant that the early word for brick, *baksteen*, was the same as the word for stone: *steen*. The Dutch always considered lack of bricks as a problem. On August 11, 1628 Jonas Michaelius wrote to Adrian Amoutius about New Amsterdam that "they bake brick here but it is very poor. There is good material for burning lime, namely, oyster shells, in large quantities," but they had problems with several other aspects of production.[105] Vice-Director Alrichs wrote to the Commissioners of the Colony on the Delaware: "I expect that a large quantity of material, such as bricks (steenen), tiles, smith's coals, etc, will be sent out; they are much needed here, as we have not a solitary brick in store to repair an oven which is in ruin."[106]

Ordinances in the colony of New York required brick to control fire hazards in the growing cities. A regulation passed in Albany on July 5, 1676 reads:

> All new buildings fronting on the street shall be substantial dwelling houses, not less than 2 rooms deep (*niet minder als 2 kamers in't vierkant*; literally, not less than 2 rooms square) and not less than 18 feet wide, being built in front on the street of brick or quarry stone and covered with tiles, the commissaries intending and desiring that this provision be strictly observed and ordering the sheriff to keep an eye thereon and to fine those who violate the same according to the exigency of the case.[107]

By 1687 the efforts to secure brick workers and legislate the use of brick in urban settings had yielded results: The governor reported that "the buildings in New-York @ Albany are generally of stone or brick."[108] A sales advertisement for a Manhattan town house in 1767 read:

> Brick and Tile House. ——To be sold, or lett, all that Dwelling-house situated in Stone –Street . . . the dwelling-House is large and commodius, two Stories High, built of Holland Brick, and covered with Tiles, as is also the Kitchen behind said House; there is an excellent Pump and Cistern in the Yard, and a spacious Gang—Way to it, the Lott is 45 Feet in Stone-Street, 75 Feet in Petticoat Lane, and above 200 Feet deep, running from street to street.[109]

In the beginning bricks were imported. An official, called a "Teller of the Bricks and Tiles," recorded the shipments into New Netherland. Baker Cornelis Barensen requested appointment to the post because he was not making enough income as "Measurer of Grain and Lime.". On April 9, 1660, he "was provisionally authorized and qualified as Teller of the Bricks and Tiles which come from *Patria* and other places and for fee. . .(authorized to) draw four stivers per thousand, half of which shall be paid by the purchaser and half by the seller," according to the Administrative Minutes of New Amsterdam.110

Dutch exports of "brick, roof tiles, and paving stones from Rotterdam, Middleburg, or Flushing" arrived regularly as ballast at English ports.111 Brick and tile shipments kept otherwise empty ships from sailing without a cash cargo. The English had been buying imported Low Country bricks at least since purchasing over 200,000 Flemish bricks to repair the Tower of London in 1278.[112] Trade in bricks continued intermittently. In 1628, a single English ship arrived at the English city of Boston with ballast of 3,500 Dutch roofing tiles. At the ports of King's Lynn and Yarmouth, regular shipments of "Flanders brick, pantiles, paving tiles, ridge tiles, millstones, quernstones, dogstones—even gravestones" arrived each year. The demand existed for pantiles and "Dutch clinkers," a hard, yellow, small (six by three by one-and-a-half inch) brick that was often used for paving yards and stables. Called "clinkers" because of "the metallic sound they gave when tapped together" these hard bricks prevent "rising damp" provided they are laid with the waterproof mortar, called *tras*,

and the watertight layer of bricks is still known as a "*tras* course." [113]
"In the Netherlands this yellow brick is called *Gouda steen* and is
made of clay from the old bed of the Rhine near the city of Gouda."[114]
The yellow brick lack iron oxide, which accounts for the pale color,
and it is denser and harder than the red brick, therefore it absorbs less
water and resists wear and freezing damage.[115] In the Netherlands,
and presumably in New York, yellow brick was used on exposed
surfaces as trim and accent, but only rarely for whole walls, therefore,
it was not imported in quantity.[116] William McMillen, of Richmond
Town Restoration, has added the critical detail: The hard yellow
bricks absorbed less water and therefore were practical to use as
ballast. Bilge water in the cargo holds would have doubled the weight
of softer bricks during a long voyage and such a change in lading
would have sunk the carrying vessel.

English trade data confirms an extensive trade in bricks, even
though the recorded quantities were not always great: The trade in
1661-1662 amounted to 57,000 bricks and 57,300 pantiles which is a
quantity sufficient to erect two small houses.[117] Dutch building
materials arrived at the Fens, Dover, Essex, and East Anglia.[118]
Similar cargo arrived as ballast in New Netherland from the colony's
inception. The ship *Fama* arrived at the Dutch settlement in the lower
Delaware Valley with a cargo that included 6,000 bricks, which
would have been enough bricks for an oven and perhaps a few
chimneys.[119] Supply did not keep up with demand. There were not
enough ships to carry the needed bricks.[120] In 1658, for example,
completion of the W. P. De Groot house in Manhattan was delayed
for want of adequate or satisfactory roof pantiles from Holland or
Fort Orange.[121]

In *Dutch New York*, Esther Singleton itemized 1659 building
material prices at New Amsterdam,[122] as follows:

12,000 tiles @ 18 guilder	florins	216.00
100,000 hard brick @ 4 g	fl	400.00
20 hogsheads lime @ 3.5g	fl	65.00
10 chaldron smith's coals	fl	174.00

Brick prices were high compared to Europe, and deliveries were
erratic. H. W. Reynolds, confirms the problems with imported brick

prices, and points out another obvious difficulty: Brick is bulky, heavy, and costly to transport as ballast by sea and prohibitive to cart overland through a trackless wilderness. So what led to claims that so many houses were built of imported brick? To account for the "mystery of the bricks," Reynolds offers the explanation that, because bricks were made to a Dutch or to an English standard, in many cases "if a man built his home of 'Holland brick' his descendants, a few years later, easily inferred that: 'the brick came from Holland'."[123] The Dutch made brick and, less successfully pantiles in Beverwyck and Rensselaerswyck at an early date. Discussing the Van Alen house in Kinderhook, Walter V. Miller, says, "there were, in fact, two kilns operating near Kinderhook when the Van Alen house was built, so that an ample supply of brick and wood seems to have been available locally."[124]

Henk Zantkuyl of the Municipal Office for Preservation and Restoration of Historic Buildings and Sites in Amsterdam, and, Roderic Blackburn, have found, in both the Netherlands and in New Netherland, that "Netherlands bricks of any size were characterized by the same proportions: 6 x 3 x 1 or 6 x 3 x 1.5."[125] The Dutch measures were in "wood measure," in which one foot is equal to eleven inches, but for convenience all measures are given in current units, unless specifically noted. There were three types of Dutch bricks in general use: Large bricks called *moppen,* are nine-and-a-half by four-and-a-half by two-and-a-half inches. Smaller bricks called *drielingen,* were six by three by one inch. And *Utrecht,* or *Vecht*-sized, bricks were eight-and-a-half by four-and-a-half by one-and-three-eighths inches. The *drielingen* bricks were the standard for Amsterdam buildings in the seventeenth century, and they were generally used throughout the Netherlands. The smaller size bricks were particularly suited to Dutch needs, as they "require relatively thin mortar joints that are more watertight because of less shrinkage when curing." In addition, corners "were formed with a quarter brick (a closer) or three-quarter brick (a three-quarter). Corners were made with closers before around 1700 . . . from then on small bricks were considered unwieldy and three-quarters were laid."[126] "In 1683 the General Assembly of New Jersey regulated the size of brick at 9½ inches x 4½ inches x 2¾ inches. This English common brick con-

trasted to the Dutch brick" in both size and color.[127] Similarly, in
1703 the English brick was made the standard in New York. The
New York brick was decreed to be nine by four-and-a-quarter by
two-and-a-half inches; however, brick conforming to Dutch proportions continued in use in rural New York until the 1840s.[128] Dutch
bricks of several sizes, from the small imported yellow "klinkers" to
moppen to eight by eight inch paving bricks are available for inspection at Historic Richmond Town.

An announcement in *The New-York Gazette and Weekly Mercury*
April 6, 1772, published the law for making bricks:

> We are desired to publish the following extract of a law of this
> colony, relative to the making of Bricks, passed the 19th June, in
> the year 1702; the regulation thereby directed, it is said, not being
> duly attended to.
> That no person or persons, shall make or suffer to [be] made,
> in any place or places within this colony, any bricks, or kiln of
> bricks, but such as shall be well and thoroughly burnt, and of the
> size and dimension following. That is to say, every brick to be
> and contain nine inches in length, four inches and one quarter of
> an inch in breadth, and two inches and one half inch in the
> thickness thereof . . .[129]

In some buildings bricks of several sizes and of both English and
Dutch types are found in the same chimney and wall because bricks
were reused by many early builders whenever available. The real
measure of a brick is more basic, as Alec Clifton-Taylor says, "because the determining factor has nearly always been the size of a man's
hand." Brick has always been an important building material because
it is convenient to handle.[130]

Frequently, the clay came directly from the excavated building
site, or nearby. It was used for the mortar and the bricks made on
location. The Rensselaer Nicoll house in Bethlehem, New York is of
locally made brick. H. W. Reynolds says that the yellow brick Van
Schaick house on Van Schaick's Island near Cohoes was made of clay
found "hard by" the site.[131] Roderic Blackburn notes, however, that
he has never encountered any early brick made in the United States
that fires yellow.[132] On-site brick burning took place at the Brick
House Farm (also known as the house of Sarah Tobias Newcomb)

in Pleasant Valley, New York. Today, a duck pond near the house marks the site of the clay pit dug for the bricks made to build the house. H. W. Reynolds comments that: "Sarah Tobias Newcome . . . directed the manufacture of the bricks"[133] which she probably did, but it still took a skilled brick maker to actually do the job.

Some stories claimed that oxen trampled the clay to make it smooth for making bricks. It didn't work quite that way. Trampling oxen could mix sun-dried bricks but baked bricks required expertise and careful handling. Any stones, pebbles, or unmixed clay will cause brick to crack, split, or even explode in the course of firing. Not all clay is suitable for brick making. An experienced person needs to select the clay, because different clay has varying qualities: wet, sticky, "plastic," or over- or under-mineralized. Some clay is more cohesive than others. Frequently, the craftsman mixed clays of different characteristics to produce the correct raw material for bricks. Clay reacts to fire in various ways, and many types of clay will not stand up to the heat in the kiln. The clay may contain to much salt, calcium, or magnesium sulfate. Other clay may just burn to an ugly color unsuitable for domestic use.

Once selected the clay was dug up and thrown into a hole where it was "wetted down" with water poured over it for up to a week. Then the clay or clays were mixed. Under primitive conditions "the treading of the clay, as of the grapes in sunnier climes, was done with bare feet."[135] If oxen were used, they would be yoked to turn a "pug-mill." A pug-mill was a technological advance over stomping the clay. A tube was made, perhaps from a large hollow log. Inside the hollow log a vertical post was mounted, and rods were inserted horizontally to the post in a stepped spiral pattern. Raw clay and sand were dumped in at the top. An ox, donkey, or gang of men then turned the post by pushing or pulling a shaft inserted at right angles to the post in the tube of the pug-mill. As the post turned the rods mixed the clay and sand to a smooth and lump-free batter. The mixed clay was then drawn from the bottom of the pug-mill tube and put into sanded wooden molds. After drying for up to three weeks the clay was removed from the molds as a sun dried adobe. The unbaked adobes were called "green" bricks. They were stacked in a manner that formed long tunnels within a kiln with their headers, or ends, exposed to a central fire. Wood, brush, and branches in the kiln surrounded the green bricks. The wood was then fired and kept burning continuously up to ten days.[135]

Firing affects the bricks in several ways: A chemical change occurs, and the clay is baked into brick. In the process the different clays take on characteristic colors, which vary by region: Albany orange, Schenectady yellow, Maryland and Virginia deep red, and Connecticut River Valley pink. Netherlands brick colors range from a spectrum of yellows and buff through "heavy orange to dark burgundy red." In *Historic Houses of the Hudson Valley* Harold Donaldson Eberlein notes of the Bronck house that "the brickwork of the 'New House' is of beautiful quality, its color a warm orangey pink."[136] The chemical composition of the clay strongly affects color. Because most clay contains iron, bricks commonly have a reddish hue. However, color also varies according to burning. Some bricks may be insufficiently baked, while others were burnt and glazed deep blue, black, or purple. Brick making generated many spoiled bricks that were split, cracked, exploded, and warped but many of the imperfect brick were used anyway. Burnt brick frequently vitrifies and takes on a much-desired sheen for creating patterns in a brick surface. Red bricks were sometimes laid with a row of white or painted stone at regular intervals and this was called "bacon layers" because "the effect is of a rasher of bacon with its strips of red meat and white fat." For visual appeal, skilled workers often varied the brick headers and stretchers into patterns. This patterned work is called "cross-bonding" by the Dutch and "diapering" or "diaper-work" among the English. The patterns included chevrons, zigzags, diamonds, and other designs in colored brick against the plain background of brick bond. "The proportion of length to width was important when laying bricks in Dutch cross-bond pattern. The uniform and subtle decorative diapering pattern of Dutch cross bond required that the length of a brick be exactly twice the width. This proportion is not usually found in English bricks" which are usually narrower and deeper than those used by the Dutch.[138] Patterned brick work may be seen in the gable ends of the Nicholas Vechte-Jacques Cortelyou house in Gowanus, New Jersey, the William and Sarah Hancock house in Salem County, New Jersey, and, as a pattern of graduated diamonds in black headers, on the Ten Broeck *Bouwerij* at Roeliff Jansen's Kill, in Columbia County, New York.

In texture old bricks were rough and irregular, whereas modern bricks are generally smooth and standardized. The visual appeal of old brick comes from the variations in the bricks, as seen in a wall from a distance: New brick appears flat and dead, while old brick has a range of texture and color. Similarly, different batches of bricks varied. Old house walls will show alterations, additions, rebuilding, and repairs with color variation, repair lines, and brick textures. Therefore, brick reveals many more clues about a house's history than does fieldstone or wood, which is usually masked with paint.

Bricks can be laid in several different bonds. The principal bonds were Flemish, English, Dutch cross, and American or common bond. In Flemish bond the bricks are laid in courses with headers (the short ends) alternating with stretchers (the long sides) so each course of bricks would be laid short-long-short. Yerbury states that Flemish bond "is rarely found in Holland" [139] but English bond is seen in several variations in Holland. English bond consists of alternate courses of all stretchers and all headers. Each course of bricks is also vertically bonded by having the joins of one course extend for half-a-length beyond the brick in the course below, called *kruis* or cross-bond. A Dutch style in which the bricks have stretchers immediately below the one above it is called *staad,* or standing. In Holland an example of *staad* can be seen in the town hall of Edam. American bond consists of a course of headers for every fifth or sixth course of stretchers. English Garden bond consists of three courses of stretchers for each course of headers. The use of headers usually indicates a depth of at least two bricks deep.

Similarly, the old brick bonding work tends to be very distinct from current practice. Modern brick is set in thickly laid dark gray cement. Old lime mortar used with old bricks was either white or buff color, having come from the same clay used to make the bricks. The Netherlands' standards in brickwork were very high. Of particular note was seventeenth-century red brickwork that used exceptionally smooth bricks with no visible pointing: "Leiden bricks" were used for this, individually cut and ground and with the backs cut at an angle. "At the front these bricks are laid 'cold' on each other, but a lot of mortar was used between the bricks at the back." Ideally, the mortar in good brickwork was used sparingly, although William McMillen says that many of the early workmen used lots of mortar. They covered the excess mortar by painting the wall with brick-red iron oxide and then applied white paint into a ruled mortise joint, creating the appearance of thin mortar lines. Donald Carpentier similarly notes that a lot of old brick laying was imperfect; it was refinished by overpainting, ruling, and scoring the masonry lines, providing a more unified and smoother appearance than the current practice of leaving old bricks exposed.[140]

In Dutch construction the H-bent frame in early brick buildings was identical to the frame in Dutch wooden buildings, as noted above. Ir. R. Meischke asserts in *Het Nederlandse Woonhuis van 1300-1800* that:

> In masonry houses the beams were sometimes supported by...[frames]...constructed entirely of wood, as was also the case with the houses whose walls were of clay or timber. To reduce the fire risk latter types of houses were provided with thin outer walls of brick. They were in no way supporting walls, their function being solely a protective one, and the interior framework remained unchanged. It was in this period that brick houses with a wooden framework and wooded houses converted into brick became indistinguishable from one another.[141]

In Dutch American practice, such as the Luykas Van Alen house, the timber frame is clearly visible, and the brickwork is a non-supporting wall, just as Meischke describes. Dutch "window frames were almost always put in place first and the brickwork laid around them. In most other countries, a hole was made in the wall into which a thin window frame was set." Then "a stretch or Dutch arch is used as a sort of wide wedge, set fast in the opening to prevent pressure on the underlying woodwork," then a "soldier course"—a row of bricks laid on their ends—was used above small openings. Brick walls were laid three stretcher rows thick with the inner rows bonded to the outer row, which serves as an exterior facing over the bents. Floor and ceiling joists of the Van Alen house in Columbia County, are part of the wooden framework, which was very similar to the Jan

Martense Schenck house on Long Island, even though the two houses were built both miles and decades apart.

In an article entitled "Historical Analysis of the Bronck House, Coxsackie, New York" in *De Halve Maen,* Joseph Hammond writes of the 1738 addition that "in terms of form, construction techniques, and decorative elements, this house represented the continuation of a Lowlands building tradition at least three hundred years old."[142] The design incorporated the characteristic H-frame of heavy posts and beams spanning the building and a brick facing. This system of non-supporting brick facing over a wooden frame created a structure susceptible to movement, water leakage, and collapse. "To help give the frame some strength, the house carpenters frequently used corbels at the junction point between joist and post, a feature often miss-attributed today to ship's carpenters," Hammond writes. He continues, "nonetheless, the frame still lacked lateral stability."[143] The judgment seems unduly harsh. Many small H-bent frame and brick homes have survived both here and in the Netherlands, providing continuous service to families' generation after generation.

In the earliest homes, which were often little more than holes in the ground or huts, the "windows" were true to definition: "The word window means 'wind eye' or 'wind hole', as though its main use was to admit air rather than light."[144] Fiske Kimball writes in *Domestic Architecture* that:

> In the seventeenth century, in the colonies and even in England, glass windows were by no means so universal as may be supposed. The 'current shutting draw windows' of (Samuel) Symond's house (in Ipswich, Massachusetts) in 1638, 'having respect both to present and future use,' were doubtless sliding panels of board, closing windows which were later to be provided with glass.[145]

Occasionally, early settlers made do with simply shuttered apertures. Alternatives included a semi-translucent covering made from "the caul of a new born calf," or framed oil soaked linen called *fenestralls,* or "thin pieces of horn" which could be boiled, scraped thin, and pressed into small panes or lights.[146] In 1621, Edward Winslow, writing from Plymouth, said: "Bring paper and linseed oil for your windows." A little later, in 1629, Francis Higginson advised

Massachusetts Bay settlers to, "be sure to furnish yourselves with. . .
glass for windows."[147]

Being fragile, the glass did not travel well, but small panes were
less likely to break than larger sheets. From the beginning, each
colony tried to make its own glass to meet local needs. The process
was a "mystery," or a craft, which called for special skills and
expertise. To make glass requires sand, soda ash, and lime which were
"cooked" in a beehive shaped clay pot oven with an opening called
a "glory hole" that allowed access to the "metal," as the cooking glass
is called. Window glass was made in two ways: In the first method,
called table glass, a hollow metal tube, called a "blowing rod," was
dipped into the molten metal and withdrawn with a glob of glass on
the tip. The glass worker then blew from the other end of the long
rod to form a bubble of glass. The bubble was transferred to a solid
metal rod called a "punty." The punty was rested on a forked support
before the fiery hot opening of the furnace's glory hole. The bubble
was spun on the end of the rod until it became a large, open-ended
bubble. The opening in the bubble was spun wider and wider until
the sides flew open through centrifugal force and the spinning caused
the sides to form a wide flat disk. This glass pancake was cooled and
snapped from the punty at the central "bull's eye" lump. The disk
was cut into panes, except for the bull's eye, which was occasionally
placed in doors for light and decoration, although it was imperfect
and less desirable, despite the "romance" of bull's eye glass panes
today. The murkier panes nearest the punty sold cheaper, while the
finer quality outer panes went for a dearer price. In the second
method, called cylinder glass, which appeared after 1725, the glass
was blown into cylindrical tubes, cut, and rolled flat. When cool the
sheet was cut into panes.

"Table glass" was the type most frequently used in the colonial
period. With bubbles and imperfections, it was often iridescent with
light green, rosy and bluish colored highlights.[148] Violet colored glass
was usually made in the nineteenth century, green in the seventeenth
century, and blue after about 1700. Several panes of delicately colored
glass appear in the Mynderse house in Saugerties, among other
locations. As late as 1783, an official report stated that the only glass
made in America was for bottles.[149] Reynolds sites advertisements

from 1744 to 1753 for imported English window-glass in all sizes including, "14 per 12; 13 per 11; 4 per 9; 4 per 8. . . and 5 per 7. . . and 8 per 10," (actually seven by nine is most common) and in diamond shapes of various dimensions.[150] An advertisement in *The New-York Weekly Post Boy* on August 18, 1746, announced that Gerardus Duyckinck "sells all sorts of Window-Glasses."[151] On August 7, 1749, John Earl offered to be sold "an assortment of Choice Window-Glass, by the Box, half-Box or single Pane, of all Sizes, at reasonable Rates."[152]

Local works produced glass in America from the settlement of James Town in 1603 throughout the colonial period. During the Revolutionary War, glass was in short supply due at least to difficult circumstances, not just to an exclusive dependence upon imported glass. In the 1780s "glass-factories sprang up in New York, Virginia, Massachusetts and Pennsylvania. . .and thereafter domestic window-glass became more plentiful and Hudson Valley advertisements in the 1790s specifically mention that Albany glass was for sale from 1787 and available in improved quality and in all sizes."[153] Certainly, glass became more available, and the cost dropped dramatically, as seen by the addition of new windows and the enlargement of existing windows in that period. Sheet glass only became popular after 1800 when changes in technology improved the quality.

The oldest part of the Jacobus DePuy house in Rochester, Ulster County, has walls "pierced with windows that are irregular in size, shape and location, —a peculiarity noticeable in structures of an early date."[154] Discussing the Tietsoort house, built about 1710 in Wantage Township, New Jersey, R. F. Bailey observes "the sparsity and small size of the windows" typical in the early homes for defense and economy.[155]

When glass was available in the early years of settlement, it was used in small leaded casements. The Du Bois home in New Paltz still had "a window with leaded panes" of glass when examined by H. W. Reynolds in the 1920s. Very few examples of leaded glass have survived from the earliest times.[156] Paul R. Huey reported on excavations at Schuyler Flatts that unearthed "leaded glass fragments" in an early "wood lined cellar" in conjunction with shutter bolts from the seventeenth century. Early Dutch glass panes were cut in the shape of diamonds and although casements regularly use square or rectangular glass panes "whatever the size or shape, window glass is still known in Dutch as a *'ruit'* which also means diamond."[157] In *Remembrance of Patria*, Roderic Blackburn describes a leaded casement window from the Gerrit Van Bergen house built in Leeds, Albany (now Greene) County, about 1729. The wooden frame still had traces of the original blue-gray paint. Marks of the "double S-shaped hinges" were identical to:

> a casement sash seen in a Pieter De Hooch painting, 'A Dutch Interior.' The construction of the window is evident in the thin glass of varying color and clarity, set in lead cams and then nailed to a frame and secured by iron bars. . .[158]

Existing original S hinges are also to be found on the Schermerhorn house of 1713 in Kinderhook, Columbia County, New York.

Before the middle of the eighteenth century many early casements could not open. Other early windows sometimes had glass lights at the top and shuttered openings without glass at the bottom, which could be opened for air during the day. Night air was suspected of spreading disease, so windows were kept shut after dark. Casement windows with two vertical openings side by side were called *bolkozyn*. The cruciform frames with four window sections—fixed windows above and hinged casements or shutters below—were called *kruiskozym* windows. A third type was the *kloosterkozyn*, which had a fixed leaded-glass window above and a glassless lower section with a hinged shutter. All three types appeared on the Ariaantje Coeymans house in Coeymans, Albany County, New York, built between 1717 and 1720. Gemel-frame windows had a pair of casements next to each other, often with glass on one side and a shuttered glassless section on the other side.159 These windows provided drama to the casements by throwing deep shadows on the lower sections, and F. R. Yerbury asserts, in *Old Domestic Architecture Of Holland*, the Dutch Gothic-style frame is one of the most perfect window designs.[160] The cross-shaped frames were used in the Brooklyn museum restoration of the Jan Martense Schenck house. Early houses without casements almost always have had the windows "modernized," perhaps even more than once. Initial restoration work on the *Voorleezer's* house at Historic Richmond Town on Staten Island resulted in the installation of twelve-over-twelve sash windows. Re-examination of the house in 1981 led to the replacement of the sash windows with the leaded casement windows. The restorer, William McMillen, who has over thirty years experience in the field, says that many restorations were done with double hung windows when the physical evidence suggests that casements were the original window type.

A "sash" is the name for a moveable frame that holds the glass, whether it is in leaded or wooden muntins, or set as double hung or casement. In a casement window the glass was set into small, grooved, lead bars called "cams" or "cames." The leaded glass was then mounted in a square or rectangular iron frame and attached with little lead ribbons twisted around the iron bars of the frame to hold the enclosed panes rigid. Then the frame was fitted into a rabbet, or lipped edge, in a wooden frame called a casement. The glass was held in place by a series of horizontal iron bars across the front of the window nailed to the casement.

In his book on medieval style architecture in Virginia, Henry Forman Chadlee includes several drawings of casements and latches of the seventeenth century. Although his examples were from Virginia and England they are typical of the period.[161] M. S. Briggs, writing about New England, illustrates similar leaded casement windows from Connecticut.[162] If the window opened at all, and many did not, the casements swung inward from hinges on one side. Such casement windows can be seen in Jan Steen's painting *The Merry Family*, of 1668. Jan Vermeer's paintings frequently show interior views of casement windows, opened or closed, as in *The Geographer*, the *Woman With a Water Jug, A Lady and Gentleman at the Virginals, Woman Reading a Letter at an Open Window*, and *Officer and Laughing Girl*.

The glass for casement windows was cut into small panes in diamond, square, or, most commonly among the Dutch, rectangular shape, such as found in the Van Bergen house. According to William McMillen, the most common pane sizes used by the Dutch were four-by-six-inch-long pieces, as opposed to the four-and-five-eighths-by-six inch diamond shaped "square" quarrel used by the English. In

the earliest period most panes were three-by-five-or-four-by-four
inches or less, although some panes were five-by-seven or larger.
There were several reasons for the small size of the panes. First, glass
was expensive; second, most early "table glass" was not more than
two feet wide and could not accommodate a pane larger than eight
inches; and third, the lead cams would not support large pieces
safely.[163] The problem was that the wind or their own weight could
cause the casements to bend, sag, or pull apart because the casement
windows' soft lead cams did not perfectly align and the glass panes
hung at different angles. Early windows could be large, however,
when iron supports were used. The angled panes create complex
patterns of shimmering light reflections (as appear at the Jewish
Museum in Amsterdam) not seen in later window designs.

Yerbury attributes the invention of the sliding sash window to
the Dutch. He says: "The exact date when this invention was brought
into practice has not yet been fixed, and it is probable that it was
found in Holland as early as 1630, although in its most primitive
form, with the upper portion fast, the lower part only being movable."[164] Martin S. Briggs says that "the sash-window . . .(made) its
appearance in Holland. . .about 1630."[165] In *Het Nederlandse Woonhuis Van 1300-1800*, Ir. R. Meischke states that new installations of
"leaded windows disappeared in the second half of the 17th century
to make way for panes in wooden frames, the earliest examples of
which date from 1685." However, "wooden frames" were used for
both casement type windows with larger glass panes and the new
sliding sash windows. Herman Janse, in *Building Amsterdam*, specifically states that wooden "sash" windows appeared around 1685 in
Amsterdam.[166]

Meischke and Janse, however, are writing about urban dwellings
in the Netherlands. Time and culture separated the great merchants,
who were building new townhouses in Amsterdam, from farmers
erecting one-room cottages in the Hudson Valley. Contemporary
paintings almost invariably show leaded glass casement windows
through the seventeenth century. Even a later painter such as Wy-
brand Hendricks (1744-1831) depicts casement windows, rather than
sash windows, in *Interior with a Sleeping Man and a Woman Mending
Stockings,* painted in the mid-eighteenth century.

The restored Jan Martense Schenck house in the Brooklyn Museum shows casement windows with thick wooden muntins. At first these windows might be mistaken for sashes, but they are similar to the early windows in Quebecois homes with thick muntin casements without a center post separating the individual segments.[167] The wooden casements were a late seventeenth- and early eighteenth-century style, but the Slingerland house in Bethlehem, New York, built around 1762, "still has its original wooden casements in great shape" according to Donald Carpentier.[168] The Jan Martense Schenck house, restored to its appearance of the 1730s, uses the wooden muntin casements. A painting entitled *Tea-Party* in the book *Authentic Decor* shows a room "perhaps in Holland" in 1700 with wooden muntin casement windows "in a fashionably furnished middle-class room."[169] The wooden muntins were a transitional design between casement mounting and sash framing.

Bailey mentions the fixed upper sash as typical of New Jersey homes sometime after 1700. But no one has proven whether this useful amenity came from England or the Netherlands. Alec Clifton-Taylor says that this "complicated question" cannot be easily re-solved and probably involves some primal patriotic partisanship. The style appeared in both Holland and Britain and their empires' during the reign of the Anglo-Dutch monarchs William and Mary, but not elsewhere as the sash window found very little general acceptance in other European countries.[170] He says that by 1685

> glass for sash (double hung) windows was already being advertised for sale in the 'London Gazette,' and the next five years were to see the introduction of windows of this kind at Windsor Castle, Kensington Palace and Hampton Court. After royal patronage on such a scale as this, it is not surprising to find that before the death of William III (d. 1702) they had won a sweeping fashion-able success, and in the Home counties were becoming the standard window-type for all new houses. Into other parts of the country they spread more slowly.[171]

Up the Hudson River, double hung windows spread even more slowly. Therefore, the use of double hung windows on the mansion built by Frederick Philipse in 1692, the date when "some writers assert the building's south facade was erected," was "extraordinarily *a la mode*" for the colonies.172 It took much longer for double hung windows to appear on the homes of less grand personages in the Hudson Valley than the Philipse clan. In the then-newly built Coeymans house casement windows were still included thirty years after the Philipse Mansion was erected and it was some time after that before the new-style double-hung windows appeared on the small farmsteads of the valley *boeren*. Houses built before 1725 were not likely to have originally been fitted with the new sash windows. By the later eighteenth century, however, early sash windows were already being updated and "this was especially true after 1770, when panes as large as 8 x 10 inches were becoming generally available."[173] However, all homeowners who modernized, expanded, and remodeled older houses did not necessarily melt down their lead casements to mold patriotic musket balls during the Revolutionary War as some writers have claimed. Many homes were not renovated until after the Revolution. The Coeyman's house waited until the 1790s before being updated.[174]

Use of sash windows became popular in Anglo-Dutch houses of the Hudson Valley in the 1760s, however, Henry Lionel Williams says that the sliding sash window, without counterweights, was introduced in America in 1715. "This sash will have a very light frame with comparatively heavy muntins (the bars that separate the sheets of glass) with the glass set flush, making the tiny panes seem smaller."[175] Early double hung windows were set with panes arranged eight-over-eight or six-over-six. Other configurations are twelve-over-twelve, twelve-over-eight, or nine-over-six. Typically European panes were two inches higher than wide, until panes larger than ten-by-twelve were employed. Seventeenth century panes were often four-by-six inches, but until the end of the eighteenth century common sizes were five-by-seven, eight-by-ten, and ten-by-twelve. At the end of the eighteenth century, panes were available in sizes ranging up to ten-by-fourteen, twelve-by-fourteen, and even twelve-by-sixteen. Frequently, the upper section would not move at all or would travel only a few inches.[176] Unlike the English sash windows, which were often set three panes across, most colonial windows were four panes wide, but these panes were usually smaller and more often square than rectangular.

Alec Clifton-Taylor considers the introduction of the sash window a major advance in style, because every sash window makes a statement clearly visible from a distance with cross bars that are thick and strong, and in no manner either fussy or pretentious.[177] The cross bars were thickest in early Queen Anne windows, gradually becoming narrower in the course of the century. After 1792, six-over-six sashes with seven by nine panes came into favor. They provided more light, but they lacked the strong visual statement of their predecessors. In the nineteenth century the cross bars were made even thinner and reduced to two per sash section leaving windows to appear as empty holes in the walls.

At first shutters were used over openings without any glazing. Sometimes early windows had shutters only in the lower frame sections and glass only in the upper casements. Partially glazed windows of this type can be seen as early as 1504 in the painting *The Seven Acts of Charity* by the Master of Alkmaar. In that painting, both closed and open shutters are shown, and the open shutters reveal casementless "wind holes" rather than glass, which was only used in the upper half of each frame section. Jan Vermeer's *Street in Delft*, painted before 1660, shows upper floor windows with glass paned casements in the top section and wooden shuttered closures below. The master of architectural detail was Pieter Jansz. Saenredam. His painting of *The Old Town Hall of Amsterdam* from 1657 shows casement windows and shutters with both glass upper sections and unglazed lower sections, as well as shutters with fully glazed casements on this important urban building.

The typical early shutter was a heavy batten built unit, but by 1720 the Dutch had already begun to use paneled shutters that "were occasionally large enough to cover the whole window."[178] Shutters served to protect the glass, keep heat in and cold out, and discourage intruders. Shutters were hung and latched with iron hinges and catches. In *Dutchess County Doorways,* H. W. Reynolds includes several good photographs of early solid shutters with the hardware used for mounting them in the eighteenth century and early nineteenth century.[179]

The Dutch eighteenth-century mortised and tenoned panel shutter had a frame with a vertical member called a stile and a horizontal member called a rail that formed the outer edge. It may also have had one or two horizontal cross members dividing the shutter into sections. Often a molding was cut into the solid wood that trimmed the edge of the frame, as separate moldings were not used. One quarter round curved moldings in the rails and stiles were coped to fit at right angles and appear as mitered edges with applied moldings.[180] A paneled shutter had the center framed by the stiles and rails. The early panels had a raised "field," but by the nineteenth century the panels became flat. Batten shutters were made with a flat side of vertical boards seen when the shutters were closed and a supporting side of horizontal rail boards seen when the shutter was opened, as shown in Gabriel Metsu's painting *The Sleeping Sportsman*. Dutch batten-paneled shutters were made with rails and stiles on one side and flat boards on the other; Huguenots also used these in the Hudson Valley, as did the Germans in Pennsylvania.[181]

Early Dutch shutters had vertical boards with horizontal and vertical battens nailed on for a paneled look.[182] A photograph showing a pair of paneled shutters from the 1730s appears in *Remembrance of Patria*, and several earlier but similar Dutch examples appear in *Old Houses in Holland* and *Building Amsterdam*.[183] According to William McMillen, this shutter is actually a battened shutter made to look like it has panels. This type of construction dates from the earliest seventeenth century, whereas eighteenth-century shutters were typically made with fielded panels, i.e. separate panels set in a frame. The shutters were identical to the shutter in Pieter De Hooch's *Courtyard of a House in Delft* painted about 1658. The De Hooch painting also shows hardware like the iron shutter bolt excavated in Schuyler Flatts, in Colonie, Albany County, New York, described by Paul Huey *New World Dutch Studies* [184] The solid style batten panel shutters, and panel shutters, remained popular with many homeowners after louvered blinds came into use after the Revolutionary War and even after 1800 when adjustable louvered blinds came into fashion. When new windows were added and existing windows enlarged on older homes during the later eighteenth century, many homeowners stopped using shutters entirely.

No description of a Dutch house would be complete without mention of the stoop or *stoep*. It was a small raised step or porch that fronted many Dutch homes. The *stoep* appeared on grand dwellings like the Kasteel Middachten, De Steeg, Province of Gelderland, the Netherlands, and in the towns and the rural outlying farms or *bouweries* up and down the Hudson Valley.[185] A "stoop" is still the common name given to a house's front steps in New York City and many rural areas in New York. The stoop was the traditional gathering place for young and old family members who socialized and greeted passersby. Even an early Dutch painting such as *The Seven Acts of Charity*, by the Master of Alkmaar, dated 1504, shows a *stoep* at an entryway. Gabriel Metsu (1629-1667) shows a Dutch doorway with a *stoep* and benches, *perronbank*, forming an "L" in his picture *The Sleeping Sportsman*. Gerrit Berckheyde's *A Street in Haarlem* painted between the 1660s and 1697 shows a street with many houses fronted with *stoeps*, and Jan Vermeer's *Street in Delft* offers another set of *stoeps* that include benches parallel with a house wall and a single side seat and table arrangement. The paintings suggest the universal appeal of the door-side accommodation to Dutch homeowners in the period. Frequently the *stoep* included a roof overhanging the entry step which was flanked by benches and thus a small porch was formed creating a semi-private transition zone at the threshold to the home.[186] None Survive: many early stoops were "improved" into Victorian verandahs during the nineteenth century and the remainder were simply torn off and discarded due to wear, weather, and decay.

The earliest houses' trim, window frames, sashes, doors, and siding were left unpainted. R. F. Bailey remarks that "the seventeenth- and eighteenth-century farmhouses of the Dutch were austere and severely plain."[187] In *Old American Houses and How To Restore Them*, Henry Lionel Williams states that "not much painting of houses was done before 1725, either inside or out."[188] However, gradually increasing security and affluence, as well as a growing interest in the home's appearance, inspired an effort to "dress up" the homestead. Especially among the Dutch, use of paint was manifest early. Pigment was cheap and paint helped preserve the wood.

Generally, before houses were painted they had been whitewashed, a technique that goes back to the Roman *dealbatores* or "dawbers."[189] In any house with clay mortar, the porous whitewash

serves as a weather shield, while permitting the underlying material
to "breath." Whitewash wicks moister out from the walls into the
atmosphere, whereas, the oil and latex paints used today seal in the
moisture, causing problems avoided by limewash.[190] Limewash requires a fresh coat every year or two. Today, the high cost of labor
would discourage frequent coating with limewash, but in early ages
redoing the walls was not considered a major problem. Limewash
was not always pure white. A warmer tone was achieved by adding
an umber tint which prevented the wash from looking gray and cold;
small quantities of carbon black resulted in a pale gray and Venetian
red was used to provide a range of reds from pink to rust.[191] The color
range was limited only by the availability of minerals, earth's, and
plants. In England a popular blue was obtained from the plant
liverwort. The substance known as "archil" or "orchil" is mixed
with limewash to give it a deep blue color[192] Color wash on homes
was common in the homelands of New Netherland settlers. Since
limewash generally lasts only a few seasons, and most early buildings
have been painted over many times, only occasional traces of original
limewash color can be found on the early homes. At the Arnhem
Open Air Museum a particularly striking early house exterior is
limewashed a deep blue and the same wash is used in several other
houses in the restoration, both inside and out.

Henry Lionel Williams writes: "The most popular color of house
paint, for a long time, was Venetian red. This was made by burning
yellow ocher (limonite), then grinding the red clinker into powder."[193] Yellow ocher was used for a similar paint called pumpkin
yellow. The Dutch used linseed oil as the medium to mix their paints.
Williams says that in New England "stone and brick houses sometimes were given a white or yellow wash in the early 1700s."[194] An
examination of the plastered stone walls of the late seventeenth
century Broadhead house in Rosendale, New York, shows traces of
an early yellow ocher pigment in sheltered sections of the exterior
masonry. The original roof shingles on the Van Cortlandt manor
house were painted red.[195] Evidence of paint was found on woodwork on the Van Alen house, in Kinderhook, that closely matched
Venetian red, and similar evidence for use of the pigment exists on
the Van Rensselaer manor house called Crailo. In fact most Dutch

and Georgian brick houses were also stained red with the mortar joints traced in white lines.

In the Netherlands during the seventeenth century "the window-bars were always painted milk white, and frames cream, sometimes both were painted milk white."[196] The white or cream paint made the massive wood frames stand out against the brick work.[197] The white painted wooden glazing bars of a Queen Anne or Georgian window were bold enough to be seen from a distance. They make a positive contribution to any elevation in which they occur.[198] In America, at least, it became fashionable, just before the Revolution, to paint the naturally buff colored putty around window panes in red lead. Later, according to *Old American Houses*, the putty was painted an indigo blue to make the glass pane appear larger.[199]

In the Netherlands shutters, doors and ironwork were mostly painted in a very dark green, and always with the utmost care, so that the flat surfaces shone like mirrors.[200] The special quality of Dutch paint must be seen to be appreciated. Houses at the outdoor museums (the Zuiderzee Museum at Enkhuizen, the Zaanse Schans Museum at Zaandam, and the Open Air Museum at Arnhem) have a rich lustrous glow unduplicated in the United States. The same colors were employed in eighteenth-century England and therefore to an American eye the effect looks very "Georgian" and elegantly formal, especially on a brick house. In addition, in Netherlands Dutch practice, the trim of sandstone lintels and ornamentation was usually painted cream color. The "bricks were treated with oil or tar to prevent moisture from penetrating in the damp Dutch climate, a procedure that darkened the bricks and emphasized the contrast with the light colored trim." [201] Dutch paintings of the seventeenth century confirm that the white and green paint used in conjunction with brick was common practice, softened at times with a blue door or window frames in Venetian red.

Examination of Dutch buildings in America indicates that by the eighteenth century many were far from austere. The Ariaantje Coeymans house in Coeymans, Albany County, New York, was built of stone and brick, but the trim was originally painted and the colors are still visible: "A yellowish white (originally perhaps cream white) on the frame and orange (red lead pigment), yellowish white, and green on the shutters . . . (and) the stoop had a balustrade railing painted cream or white."[202] Shutters on grand Dutch homes in the Netherlands show a variety of painted treatments. White stiles and blue panels are on Kasteel Het Nijenhuis, Wijhe, Province of Overrijssel, the Netherlands; red stiles with the panels painted in saucy red and white chevrons on Kasteel De Haar, Haarzuylens, Province of Utrecht; and black frame and white panels, with a pattern of triangles and squares at Menkemaborg, Uithuizen, Province of Groningen, the Netherlands.[203] The traditions of Fatherland apparently continued in America; but, the *boers* followed the rural traditions of their Dutch antecedents which were occasionally more exuberant than the elegant and conservative taste of the merchants of Amsterdam. In *Remembrance of Patria*, Roderic Blackburn presents a pair of shutters from the Jurriaan Sharp house, Defreestville, Rensselaer County, that were discovered with their original paint: "blue-grey (stile), yellow (molding), and orange (panel)." These colorful shutters were hung on a house "sheathed in red-painted wide clapboards with white casement window frames."[204] In *Historic Houses: Restored and Preserved*, Marian Page, describing the Van Cortlandt manor in the eighteenth century, says that the "porch posts, balustrades, and railings were white. Doorframes were a light gray and the two original shutters were painted gray blue. Handrails, steps, and downstairs doors were chocolate brown with the upper panels picked out in white,"[205] Contemporary illustrations of houses show a similar treatment: Pieter De Hooch's painting *A Country Cottage*, from 1665, depicts a brick building with casement windows. The cottage has red pantiles with white cross-shaped window frames and exposed vermilion-painted opened shutters (inner sides). Jan Vermeer's picture of a *Street in Delft*, done before 1660, shows brick houses whitewashed to door height, red pantile roofs, and green-gray casement window frames. On the ground floor the shutters are red on the inner side and green on the outside surfaces with unpainted wood on the upper floors. A small house to the side has dark blue shutter inner sides and blue and white casement frames. An inner surface of a paneled shutter, painted light red, is prominent in Pieter De Hooch's painting *A Courtyard of a House in Delft*.

An overmantel painting of the Van Bergen farm in Leeds, Albany County, depicts a gray stone house with shutters of red, white, and dark brown, and a roof of bright red tiles or painted shingles. An early painting of an Albany street shows the brick houses fitted with white sashes and frames and blue shutters and doors.[206] When the Jan Martense Schenck was restored, research determined that the house had only been painted once: "The original clapboards had only one coat of paint which proved to have been dark gray. A sand color was used on the window frames, and the shutters were painted green. These colors were used on contemporary structures in the Netherlands."[207] The gray color was revealed "after microscopic analysis" of the clapboards.[208] If the house was painted only once, it probably would have been when the house was modernized in the early eighteenth century.

The Colonial Revival interpretation of early painted houses was more conservative. The typical wood colonial house was assumed to have been white with green doors and shutters. The usual conception of a brick house was even more reserved: Dark green shutters and door with white or buff window frames and sashes is the colonial cliché. However, as Roderic Blackburn remarks: "Variety of color is common in the Netherlands and, apparently, in New York, reflecting Dutch interest in bright multicolored decoration in houses and furnishings." Today, the restored houses at Zaanse Schans, Arnhem, and the Zuiderzee Museum at Enkhuizen are generally painted a deep lustrous green, but as E. van Olst, the Director at Arnhem, and J. Schipper, the restorer of Zaanse Schans, explain: The Dutch policy is usually to restore in a manner that reflects the entire history of a house and rarely to reconstruct a building to its earliest period. Therefore, the green painted dwellings do not reflect the last impressions of home seen by emigrants to the New World in the seventeenth century.[209]

"By 1745 a great many colors were available, such as grays, greens, Spanish brown, and yellow. The greens used for shutters and blinds were made at first from vertigris (copper acetate) and verditer (copper carbonate)."[210] Then, "by 1750, white lead began to be available for making an oil paint," and many houses were thereafter painted white. Always thrifty, American farmers by the mid-eighteenth century began growing flax specifically for the linseed oil.[211] Geradus Duyckinck supplied pigments in the early eighteenth century, as did members of his family before him in the Hudson Valley. In 1799, one of the earliest paint shops opened in the Hudson Valley in Poughkeepsie, New York. Abraham Swartwout advertised in the *Poughkeepsie Journal* of May 21,1799, that he had opened a store for the wholesale and retail sale of paints and oils of the finest quality and could provide "Blue, Green, Yellow, and Black paint or any colour mixed at the shortest notice."[212] By 1800 colors available included: verdigris, yellow ocher, Venetian red, white lead (mostly imported from England), gamboge (bright yellow), verditor, red lead, vermilion, dragon's blood (a dark red tree resin), umber, and Prussian blue."[213]

Dutch exterior construction in the Hudson Valley.

Photographs and drawings by the author unless otherwise noted.

Legends for plans on pages 234-237:

(Pages 234-235: courtesy of E. Van Olst, Director, Stichting Historisch Boerderij-Onderzoek, the Arnhem Open Air Museum; page 236-237: courtesy of W. McMillen, Historic Richmond Town Restoration.)

Page 234

Three combination house and barn "farmhouses" from the Netherlands:

A. Half-timber house and barn combined under a single thatched roof. Plan shows stalls are adjacent to living area with hay above. This is an effective way to maximize utilization of animal-generated body heat and insulate with stored fodder. If the building is kept clean, the predominating scent is of hay.

B. Brick raised-spout gable house with gable-oriented entry and barn under common pantile roof.

C. Brick raised-spout gable house with pantile roof and gable oriented entry attached at gable to a barn with a monk's cowl thatch roof.

D. Brick raised-spout gable house and barn combined under pantile roof.

E. Half-timber house combined with weatherboard-sided barn under common thatch roof.

Page 235

Two combination house and barn "farmhouses" and a house and barn from the Netherlands:

A. Brick spout but not raised gable house with pantile roof and eave-wall-oriented entry abutted to weatherboard sided bar with thatch roof. In this later house the plan shows greater distance between animal and human living areas. The house is typical of the southern Netherlands, Zeeland, and of the Albany area in New York.

B. Brick raised-spout gable house with pantile roof and eave-oriented entry abutted to pantile and thatch-roofed barn. This house is also very similar to Albany-area Dutch houses, however, the gable-wall windows would be rare in early Hudson Valley houses.

C. Brick raised-spout gable house with centered eave-wall-orientated entry and separate weatherboard-sided thatch barn. This format was most typical of Hudson Valley Dutch houses. Most known Hudson Valley Dutch houses are gable-entry with side isles in plan and with a pitch rather than hipped roof design.

Page 236

A. Netherlands Dutch house roof structure in a rare masonry-bearing wall dwelling. Note double stone arch in cellar would be the support for the hearth on the floor above.

B. Netherlands Dutch barn roof structure (dimensions in meters).

Page 237

A. Netherlands Dutch house roof structure in a timber-frame dwelling. Illustration also shows a chimney with bend around gable garret windows. Single arch in cellar would be to support a hearth on the floor above.

B. Treasure House, Historic Richmond Town Restoration, Staten Island, New York, circa 1700. Photo shows a chimney bend. In the house the H-bent posts have been raised at the rear eave wall to allow the roof to be extended over a rear room.

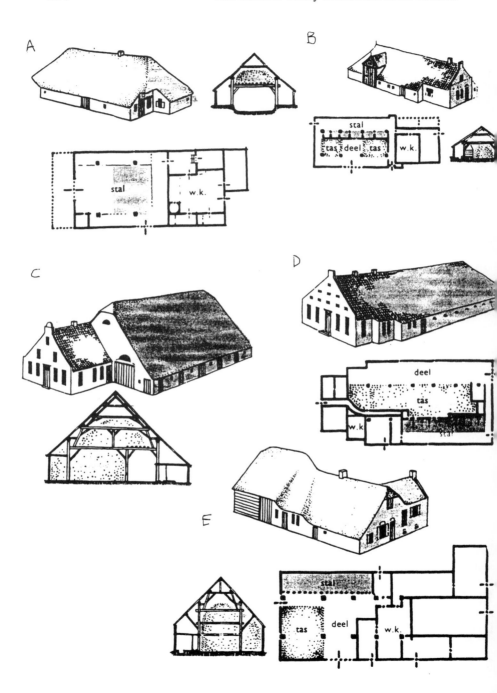

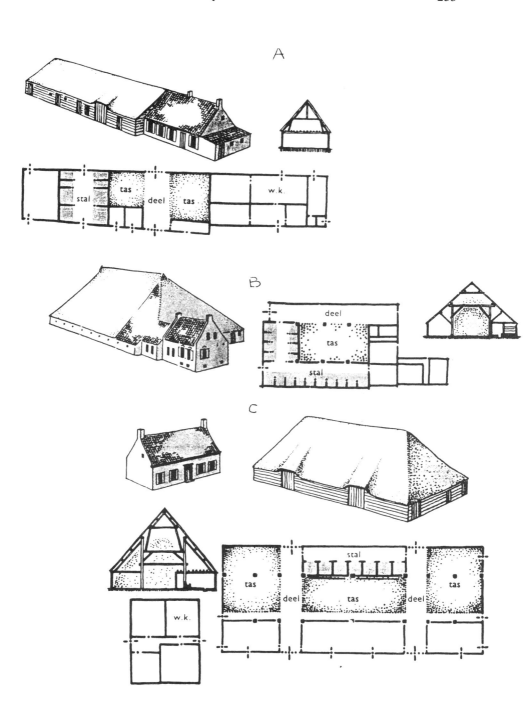

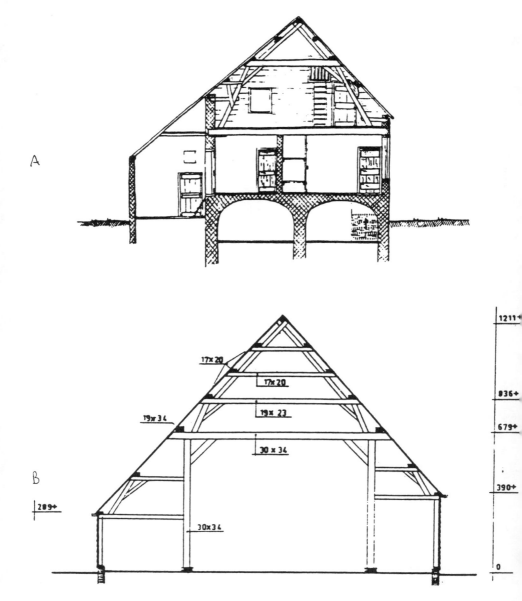

A

B

A

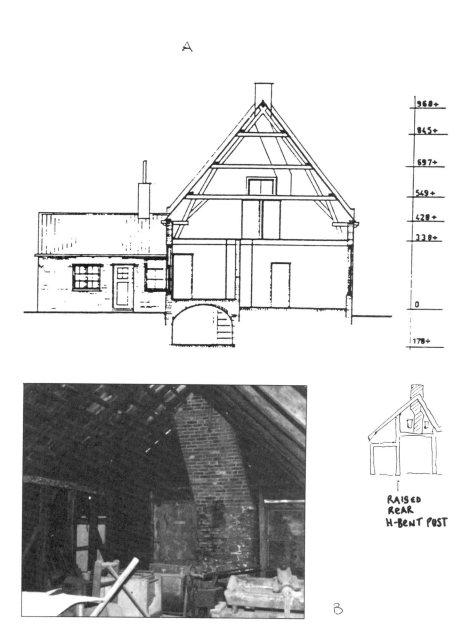

968+

845+

697+

549+

428+

338+

0

178+

RAISED
REAR
H-BENT POST

B

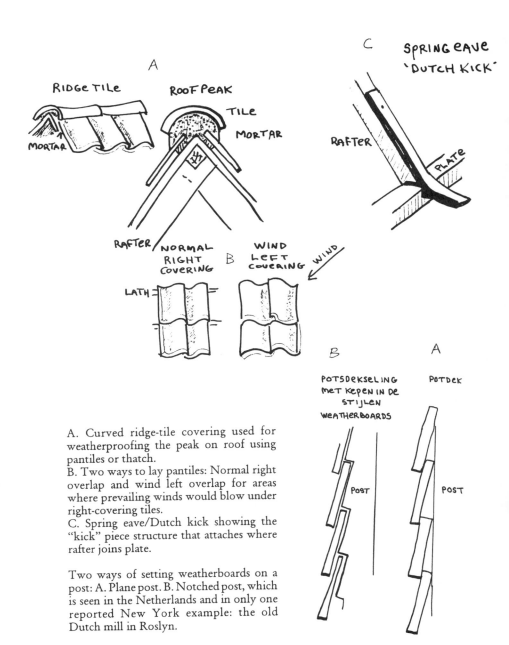

A. Curved ridge-tile covering used for weatherproofing the peak on roof using pantiles or thatch.

B. Two ways to lay pantiles: Normal right overlap and wind left overlap for areas where prevailing winds would blow under right-covering tiles.

C. Spring eave/Dutch kick showing the "kick" piece structure that attaches where rafter joins plate.

Two ways of setting weatherboards on a post: A. Plane post. B. Notched post, which is seen in the Netherlands and in only one reported New York example: the old Dutch mill in Roslyn.

Top left: Dutch colonial-style down spout and hollowed out beam gutter. Voorlezer House, Historic Richmond Town Restoration, Staten Island, New York, 1696.

Top right and above: Two illustrations of thatch roofing: Trimmed edge of thatch on brick and boarded "farmhouse" restoration. Roof crest thatch showing smoke vent and twisted-end bonding on thatch and chimney with anchor iron. Arnhem Open Air Museum.

Left: Close-up view of eighteenth-century wooden shakes with clipped corners and wrought nails showing thirteen inches to the weather (from a private house garret in Hurley, New York). Early shingles were split and planed smooth and laid overlapped two thirds with one third to the weather.

Courtesy of G. Huber.

Below: Exterior view of Nicholas Schenck House, Canarsie, Brooklyn, New York, circa 1775, in 1987 at the Brooklyn Museum. Photograph shows wooden shingles and casement windows as house was remodeled to circa 1830.

Courtesy of Brooklyn Museum of Art, Gift of the Atlantic Gulf and Pacific Company

Exterior view of the Jan Martense Schenck House, Flatlands, Brooklyn, New York, circa 1675, in 1964 at the Brooklyn Museum. Photograph shows weatherboards and reconstructioned wooden casement windows.

Courtesy of Brooklyn Museum of Art, Gift of the Atlantic Gulf and Pacific Company 50.192

A.

B.

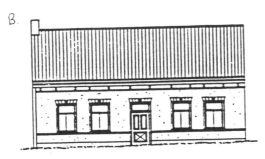

Elevations of houses in the Netherlands from the Arnhem
research project on early Dutch homes.

Above: Cottage with pantile roof showing anchor irons, a "Dutch" door with a
bolkozijn window with shutters, and a door with a leaded light and two simple
three-over-six sash windows. House with eave-oriented center door and four nineteenth-century casement windows. Soldier courses in bricks are shown over the
windows and the doorway. Courtesy of E. Van Olst, Arnhem Open Air Museum.

Facing page: Raised-gable brick house with pantile roof and showing anchor irons
and soldier bricks above and below the windows. Shutters and eight-over-twelve sash
windows. Entry with stovepipe and oriel window not typical of Hudson Valley
houses, although some houses in New York have round gable openings, some of
which are glazed. Raised-gable brick house with pantile roof and showing anchor
irons and soldier bricks above and below the windows. Shutters and eight-over-
twelve sash windows and center entrance with light over door. This style house is a
perfect match to the classic Albany-area Dutch houses. Similar houses can still be
found from Schenectady south along both banks of the Hudson River to Kinderhook and Coxsackie. Courtesy of E. Van Olst, Arnhem Open Air Museum.

A

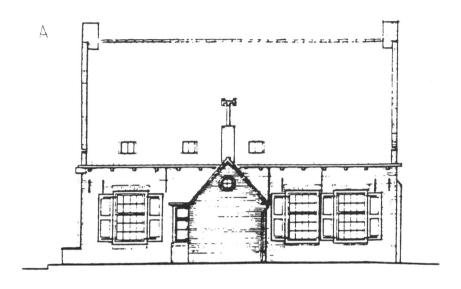

B

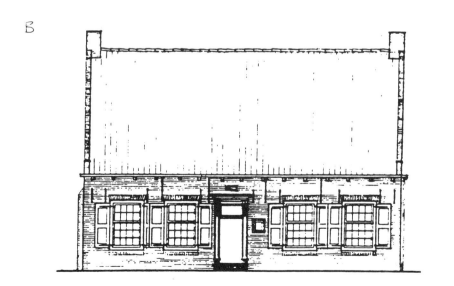

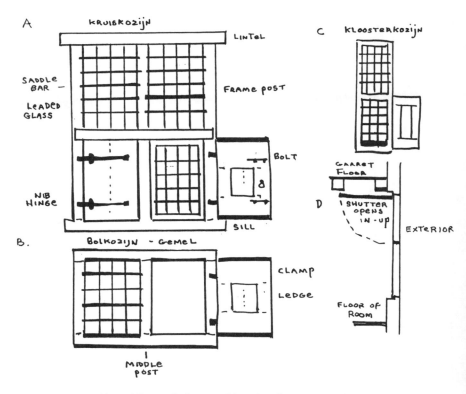

Above: Three windows and interior shutter operation.

A. *Kruiskozijn* window showing the massive weight-bearing outer frame of posts sill and lintel and the "crossed post and beam" that divides the window into four sections. Leaded glass panes are secured with saddle bars of iron to the frame. Exterior shutters below show placement of the hardware in form of nib end strap hinges and bolts.

B. *Bolkozijn Gemel* with middle post and shutter. The shutter has top and bottom clamp and side ledge pieces.

C. *Kloosterkozijn* windows are basically one-half *kruiskozijn* frames.

D. Interior shutters opened inward and up. These are frequently seen in seventeenth- and eighteenth-century pictures.

Facing page: Original Dutch window frames and windows in New York.

Top left: Kruiskozijn window frame with leaded glass and exterior shutters with original red, yellow, and black paint from the Ariaantje Coeymans house. Courtesy of R. H. Blackburn.

Top right: Kloosterkozijn window frame and corbel braced H-bent from the Ariaantje Coeymans house annex. Courtesy of G. Huber.

Below: Casement and frame with shutters from Kingston. Courtesy of R. H. Blackburn.

Above: Leaded windows in the Netherlands:

Interior of upper-floor *kruiskozijn* window in seventeenth-century house in Amsterdam restored by Henk Zantkuyl.

Shutters and fixed leaded glass flush mounted on building dated 1633 in Amsterdam.

Facing page, clockwise from top left:

Massive, original Dutch leaded glass, bearing window frames were built into the framework of the house and supported masonry, unlike later frames that were merely supports for sashes. Note tenon to fit into house beams, pegs, and pintel to hold shutter hinge. Shutter and hardware original and complete, note pivoting peak hole. This complete casement-window assembly is part of the collection salvaged from old houses and used by Donald Carpentier in his restoration workshop seminars.

A reproduction fixed leaded window in the Voorlezer House. William McMillen of Historic Richmond Town Restoration contends that many older restorations have placed sash windows or wooden casements when physical evidence at a site indicates that the original windows were leaded panes. The window is flush on the exterior and does not open. Courtesy of W. McMillen.

Close view of leaded pane as seen on the restored 1696 Voorlezer house at Historic Richmond Town Restoration. The reproduction leaded lights are 4" x 6" and set in lead cams and secured by iron stabilizing bars nailed to the sash frame. Note how the lead ring secures cam to iron bar. Courtesy of W. McMillen.

View of leaded window from Voorlezer house showing entire assembly in place.

Small leaded window from the Jewish Museum in Amsterdam showing leaded cams and iron stabilizing bars, stone sill and soldier brick lintel.

Bolkozijn window at Slingerlands house. Just to the right of the window and below the anchor iron is a date stone marked 1762. The soldier bricks above the window can be clearly seen. Courtesy of G. Huber.

Facing page, top and middle: Sash windows as seen on later Dutch-style houses.

Left: Guyon lake Tyson House, Historic Richmond Town, Staten Island, New York, circa 1740. Original twelve-over-twelve window: frame, sash, and shutters. Courtesy of W. McMillen.

Right: Restored widow in the De Wint House kitchen wing.

Middle: Restored Dutch door and twelve-over-twelve window in the De Wint House, Tappan, New York. Note date: 1700, set into wall with black brick enders and the different types of brick bond seen in the same wall.

Facing page, bottom and below: Shutters were frequently used in the early period.

Left: Reproduction shutter on the 1696 Voorlezer House at Historic Richmond Town restoration. Courtesy of W. McMillen

Right: Reproduction shutter on the 1696 Voorlezer House. Closed.

Below, left to right: Shutter on restored seventeenth-century house at Zaanse Schans, Netherlands. Salvaged shutter from the Hudson Valley. Original shutter on the 1740 Guyon-Lake-Tyson house at Historic Richmond Town.

Bottom: Cellar window guard grill from the Broadhead house showing bars squared and tapered and built into the massive frame that was set in the cellar wall.

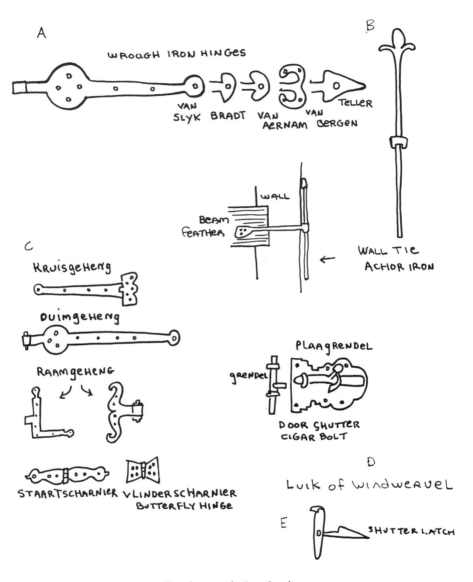

Dutch wrought iron hardware.

A. Frequently seen Dutch strap hinge with pancake nail plate and five representative terminals from the Van Slyk, Brandt, Van Aernam, Van Bergen, and Teller houses. B. Anchor iron attached to wall tie that passed through masonry and was nailed at its flat "beam feather" to a structural beam inside the house. C. Several hinge type with the Dutch names used. D. Door and shutter "cigar bolt." E. Shutter latch.

Top: Dutch iron hardware from the collection of Donald Carpentier: Pancake nail-plate strap hinge shown with open loop end on pintle. The hinge of a shutter pivots on the pintle, which is driven into the window frame; a latch mechanism and its front plate; three typical door pulls and the thumb latch to operate one. Two strap hinges and two bar holders to secure a door.

Right: An original divided Dutch door from the Guyon-Lake-Tyson House, Historic Richmond Town, circa 1740 with all the original hardware: Strap hinges, wood locking bars, iron latch. Note diagonal interior planking, one latch only and placed on the upper half of the door, and all hardware painted in with surrounding surface.

Courtesy of W. McMillen.

Original shutter dog latches: *Right:* Guyon- Lake-Tyson House.

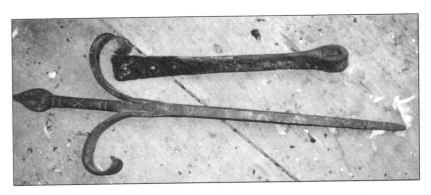

Facing page: Anchor iron and tie bar. Jan Briese House, c. 1720s.

Decorative *Fleur-de-Lis* anchor iron from the collection of Donald Carpentier with tie bar showing beam feather and loop features.

Facing page: Hinges found on Dutch houses.

Duimgeheng from Donald Carpentier collection. The photograph shows the pancake plate for the nails and the unclosed roll of the hinge that drops over the pintel.

Original shutter hinge and pintel circa 1740. Courtesy of W. McMillen.

Basement door hinge with pancake nailing pad circa 1740. Courtesy W. McMillen.

Cellar storeroom door long strap hinge from Donald Carpentier collection.

Dutch exterior door latches combine a knocker with a turning mechanism that is very effective with swollen or stuck doors.

Reproduction knocker latch from the Hasbrouck house in Catskill, early eighteenth century. Courtesy of R. H. Blackburn. *Left:* Reproduction seventeenth-century knocker latch with heart-shaped nail plate from upper half of Voorlezer house door. Note nails clinched over nails from inside. Courtesy of W. McMillen. *Middle:* Reproduction seventeenth-century knocker latch with diamond shaped nail plate from upper half of Voorlezer house door. *Right:* Knocker latch from Broadhead House, Rosendale, 1680.

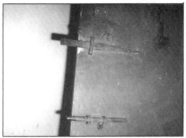

Clockwise from top left: Inside door latch or *klinkstel* from the Guyon-Lake-Tysen House, circa 1740. William McMillen notes this original latch was probably made locally on Staten Island after English patterns. Courtesy of W. McMillen.

A reproduction latch and cigar bolt or *grenolel* from the Luykas Van Alen House, Kinderhook, New York, 1736. The bolt secured the door from the inside. Many doors had several bolts for the door half sections of the exterior doors.

Original cigar bolt from front door of the Guyon-Lake-Tysen House, circa 1740. Courtesy of W. McMillen.

A reproduction door latch bar at Voorlezer House copied from eighteenth-century Austen Cottage, Staten Island, New York. Mechanism is Dutch in origin, simple but sturdy in design. This is the interior mechanism for the knocker latch on the exterior of the door.

Stoeps were a common feature on Dutch houses in both urban and rural settings. A transitional space between the outdoors and the home where people could sit, see, and be seen. Original stoeps exist in the Netherlands but only reproductions are found in America. This is the reproduction *stoeps* at the Luykas Van Alen House, Kinderhook, New York. Based on James Eights' paintings of *stoeps* in the Albany area, c. 1805-1815.

Interiors with fireplaces. *Top left:* Lykas Van Alen House, 1737. *Top right:* Cornelus Shermerhorn House, 1713. *Above:* Broadhead House, c. 1680. Courtesy Geoffrey Gross

CHAPTER VI

Beyond Dutch Thresholds

WEST OF THE HUDSON and along the Mohawk River, Indian raids continued from the earliest period through the end of the Revolution. Difficult as it is to imagine today, in 1663, Kingston, then known as Wiltwyck, was the frontier. Problems between settlers and Indians had begun shortly after the first arrival of settlers, and both sides were probably equally to blame for many disturbances of the peace.[1] On June 7, 1663, Wiltwyck and the surrounding area suffered a surprise attack. The massacre of the *Swannekins*, as the Indians called the settlers, began the Second Esopus War.

The immediate circumstances of the attack, as reported to the Director General Pieter Stuyvesant by the survivors, were as follows: On May 30, 1663, the Director General told the settlers to meet the local Indian chiefs to renew the peace concluded at the end of the First Esopus War. On June 5 the Indians agreed to "sit with them in an open field . . . unarmed."[2] On the morning of June 7 the Indians entered the palisade area professing a desire to trade. Once among the

257

settlers' houses, they launched a surprise attack. The palisaded village of wood and reed thatch houses was burned to the ground within minutes. After the initial fighting was over there followed months of waiting until captives taken by the Indians were rescued. A report by Captain Martin Kregier in his "Journal of the Second Esopus War" provided a firsthand account of the massacre.[3]

In 1970 Ivor Noel Hume excavated the remains of an English settlement called Martin's Hundred. The wood-and-thatch village in Virginia was the scene of burning and massacre in 1622. Circumstances were similar to Wiltwyck. Hume referred to research by Dr. H. A. Bankoff, who found, measured, recorded, and burned a thatched wattle-and-daub cottage in Serbia. The results were used to interpret remains of similar structures in seventeenth-century America. Bankoff reported that

> Within twenty minutes the thatched roof was consumed and the ceiling collapsed, but the fire had died down sufficiently for someone to enter the building and douse whatever flames were still burning. Because heat rises and thatch burns so fast, very little damage had been done to the walls. Clay covering the main posts and wattles had prevented either from catching [fire].[4]

Bankoff let the fires smolder until they consumed the remains of the structure. If the fire had immediately been extinguished, the house could have been rebuilt with little difficulty.

Martin's Hundred was abandoned because so many settlers had lost their lives. In Wiltwyck, however, the buildings were rebuilt and reoccupied shortly after the massacre and many of the survivors went on to settle the inland Esopus region in the following years. After the Esopus Wars, many of the wooden houses of Ulster County were replaced by buildings of stone. The settlers could have viewed stone as a more secure material than wood and thatch for a frontier dwelling.

Entry doors, *deuren buyten*, were usually solid and often double planked. The inner side frequently had boards set diagonally or horizontally to the vertical outer planking with back- boards that overlapped the frame and formed a barrier against the cold. The entry to the Shuart-Van Orden house, built in 1773 in Plattekill, Ulster

County, is an eighteenth-century example with inner boards set at a forty-five degree angle to the exterior boards.

Small farmhouses sometimes had simple latchstrings on exterior doors. This cord passed through a hole in the door attached to a lift bar. In the 1920s, when H. W. Reynolds researched Dutch houses, she found one remaining latch string door on the Madam Brett house and asserted it was "the only latch-string so far observed in a survey of the Hudson Valley."[5] She missed at least one: an interior latch-string remains on a cellar door in the Gidney house, built around 1750 in Newburgh. Doors were secured with large sliding bolts at the top and bottom, and "these are found on houses dating as far back as 1700, but they were far from common then."[6]

The most common Dutch method of securing doors was with iron slide bolts attached to the edge of the upper and lower halves of the Dutch door and the frame. Some early houses had brackets anchored directly into the masonry or wooden or iron sockets firmly secured to the building's wall. More costly than a bolt was a lock, "and rare examples of wood-cased ones have been unearthed in America dating back to the seventeenth century."[7] Locks were common by the eighteenth century even among rural households, and manufactured key locks came into use by the 1820s.

Many Hudson Valley homes had a separate door to the outside from each ground-level room on the front of the house. A New Jersey example is seen at the Henry Doremus house near Towaco, Morris County, where "outside doors open directly into each of the two main rooms."[8] R. F. Bailey has plates showing houses with two outside entries: the Isaac Nagel house in Closter, the Cornelis Lozier house in Midland Park, and the Hendrick Gerritse Blauvelt house in Blauvelt. There are three (not original, according to William McMillen) separate outside entry doors at the Dongan-Christopher house in Willow Brook, Staten Island.[9] Three-door houses include the Broadhead house and the Mynderse house in Ulster County, which have separate entries to the individual rooms from outside; the Van Alen house in Kinderhook, Columbia County; and the Van Wagenen house at Clinton, Dutchess County, shown in an old photo in Reynolds.[10] The broad distribution of this feature indicates that it was a general practice among the Dutch in America, however, it is not a feature seen in homes in the Netherlands. Curiously multiple entry doors are frequently noted in early houses in the French province of Normandy. Lucile Oliver's *Vielles Maisons Normandes* shows one house with Flemish overhang, "spring eave," and three outside doors that apparently open into adjacent rooms. The building, aside from its "traditionnelle a colombage vertical," or vertical post construction, would settle comfortably into the Hudson Valley scene.[11] Many explanations have been offered for these separate entries, but no conclusive data exists to resolve the matter.

The typical "Dutch" entry door was divided like a stable stall door into two halves. The upper can be opened for sunlight and fresh air, while the bottom remains shut to keep small children and a miscellany of farm animals inside or out. The lower half also provided a social barrier for tradesmen and others to talk without having to let them into the house. These doors were commonly mounted into the inner edge of the wall frame, although examples exist mounted at the outer edge of the frame. The top was secured with a *spliegalklamp* and the bottom latched with a *dwars klamp*. A small, plain, and deep-set door without transom windows was used on the small kitchen wing of the Broadhead house. Several Dutch doors appear in H. W. Reynolds' *Dutchess County Doorways*.[12] The doors are shown with interior and exterior mounting placement and often double boarded for weather tight strength. The 1768 Philip Verplanck house entry hung from the frame inner-edge, whereas the Zephaniah Platt house has a door hung from the frame's outer-edge. Sometimes, exterior doors of the second half of the eighteenth century had oval or circular glass lights, as in the Abraham DePyster house, the Philip Verplanck house, and the Doctor Stephen Thorn house. The panes were sometimes thick bull's-eye glass, which can still be seen in a door of the Mynderse house in Saugerties. The thick glass is difficult to see through, but it admits light. Transom windows existed from an early date. The 1737 Luykas Van Alen house has transom windows. By the time of the Revolutionary War more rural homes used over-door lights. The panes were set in a single row of square-shaped glass as can be seen in the Mrs. Zashers Newcomb house, the Obadiah Cooper house, and the house of Richard and Theodorus R. Van Wyck, all in Dutchess County. In some cases, transom lights were added to earlier homes, as probably happened at the 1680 Broadhead house in Rosendale, Ulster County and the Davis Tavern in Stone Ridge, built about 1669. After the Revolutionary War, homes in rural areas began using sidelights and more elaborate over-door lights which had appeared at least a decade earlier on grander homes and town houses. An example can now be seen on the Stinson house, High Falls where Benjamin Hasbrouck added Federal details in 1806 to an early eighteenth-century stone homestead.[13]

Early barns north of the mid-Hudson Valley often had wooden hinges made of oak. About fifteen to twenty barns still have them and they are perfectly functional to their task: The wide and tall doors of the Shuart-Van Orden's Dutch barn retain their original wooden hinges. However, iron hardware was available from the earliest period, hand-wrought by the local blacksmith, who forged all iron products from animal shoes to hinges, tools, cooking utensils, and nails. In addition, Donald Carpentier writes: "a lot of English hardware was brought into the Hudson Valley once the English took over in the late seventeenth century."[14] It should be noted that smith-crafted metal has some irregularities in the placement of nail holes, which were punched rather than drilled, but the surfaces are smooth rather than "rusticated" as is the finish of many reproductions.

Doors were customarily mounted on long iron strap hinges, which could exceed two feet in length. Usually mounted on the inner edge of the entry wall the strap hinges, *duimgeheng*, supported the door. They kept it from sagging by extending across most of the door's width rather than merely attaching along the edge of the stile where it abuts the frame. The "eye" of the hinge that attached to the door was a curved iron loop, but it was not welded, as are reproductions. The hinge dropped over a pivot called a "pintle" set into the doorframe. Forged by the local blacksmith, the hinges frequently were handsomely trimmed with terminals shaped to a spear point, a blunt end, a spade-shaped end, or very rarely, a split end that curved back. Examples appear in H. W. Reynolds *Dutchess County Doorways* from the Van Wyck house, the Obadiah Cooper house, and the Zephaniah Platt house, all in Dutchess County.[15] "An almost universal characteristic of the Dutch [strap hinges] is the large, circular swelling near the inner end called a pancake disk or nail pad. A few

Dutch hinges have German style double disks, one in the normal position and another just before the finial. The pad is usually pierced for four nails, providing extra firm attachment where it is needed most."[16]

Lighter doors were supported by simple H and HL hinges or *raamgeheng;* butterfly hinges, *vlinderscharnier,* were employed for casement windows and furniture. L or T hinges are found before 1750 and thereafter the more familiar H and HL hinges came into general use. These English types of hardware are found in New York and the Netherlands in the eighteenth century.[17] Like other early metalwork, these hinges were handmade, thin and smooth, without the so called "distressing" of modern reproductions. Brass hardware was never used on early small farmhouses.

Hardware to close shutters included iron hinges and latches. Decorative fasteners to hold shutters open came in a variety of shapes, most commonly in S-curved twists of iron pivoting on a pintel set into the wall. Terminals on many of the pieces of hardware were finished with swirls and spirals making them pleasing to the eye. Separate inner latches for each door-half completed the hardware, but the lower half did not have an outside handle. The door was opened first from the top and then from the bottom in two separate actions rather than all at once. When paint became common for household decoration the hardware was always painted to match the surface to which it was attached, it was never picked out in black or left unpainted against a painted surface.

Dutch hardware traditionally included a doorknocker with a drop handle that turned the latch, hence the name "knocker latch" or *klopperklink.* Williams notes that "these latches go back to antiquity and were used all over Europe in the sixteenth century . . . By reason of its construction the Dutch type is much easier to operate and will open weather-stuck doors that . . . [thumb-press latches] will not."[18] The "knocker latch" loop handle had a bar that passed through the door to the mechanism exposed on the inner surface. Lifting and turning the handle moved an inside cam that raised the latch bar.[19] A *deurknop* opened the door, *klinklichters* turned door latches, a *slotploatje* was a key escutcheon over a keyhole, and a *plaatgrendel* was a door bolt.

A number of distinctive internal features identified Dutch houses. The Dutch used an open-hearth fireplace. The hearth had no jambs (sidewalls) and stood with three exposed sides into the room. Only the back wall was masonry. Peter Kalm descibed the jambless hearth as "looking as though they made a fire against the wall itself." Describing the house of Hendrick Gerretse Blauvelt, R. F. Bailey notes: "the foundations of the chimney in the cellar are in the form of a very large arch, giving the impression of a bricked-up fireplace."[20] It's an apt description as examination will usually confirm that the base never had a flue. It is simply a base for the hearth and back wall of the fireplace on the floor above. The foundation did not support jambs or a full chimney stack, the fireplace hearth only required an arch or stone-filled crib and the chimney an H-bent's support to keep it rigid. The Dutch jambless chimneystack was simply seated on an H-bent beam above the fire. A pair of side joists, called trimmers, joined the bent to the fireplace back wall. The more familiar English-type fireplace was often erected on a massive block of masonry that provided the footing for the fireplaces and the chimneystack. In an English braced-frame house, the chimney was built before the house frame was erected because the frame timbers would be fitted around, and often into, this massive stone structure that braced the house frame.

Especially when a house was built into a hillside the lower or cellar-floor level was adapted to the slope and the kitchen was frequently placed in the basement.[21] Examples may be seen at the Van Cortlandt manor house or the Krom house in Accord, New York. Some Dutch houses built on level land, such as the Wynkoop-Lounsbery house in Stone Ridge and the Abraham Hasbrouck house in New Paltz, also had a fireplace and kitchen in the cellar. The north end of the Van Alen house originally had a basement kitchen however the basement chimney was removed in the nineteenth century; exterior brickwork clearly shows where the original flue was removed from the north end wall. A Dutch basement chimney typically had a hearth with a wide but shallow flue that was built stepped out four inches from the exterior of the gable wall behind the first-floor flue. The two flues joined at the garret level and exited as one at the roof level. When a Dutch house did not have a cellar kitchen, the ground-floor fireplace was supported by an arch of masonry extending from the cellar wall or with a manger-shaped crib to hold stones and mortar, serving as a base below the hearth on the first floor.22

A jambless fireplace simply did not provide as much heat as an English fireplace, but even an English fireplace is hard pressed to provide real comfort in a Northeast winter. Wind came down the chimney, and the side of the room opposite the fire was cold. In *Early American Gardens* Ann Leighton cautions about misinterpreting the early fireplaces by size alone. "We do wrong to imagine roaring fires with great logs burning furiously, because the housewife, in order to cook, would have to be able to step or lean into the fireplace herself. And she needed several fires going at the same time, at least three in different degrees of burning: one hotly flaming, one glowing embers, and one of hot ashes with 'coals' on top. With these and hooks on the cranes to hang pots at different heights above the heat . . . she would be able to follow even the most elaborate operations."23

Dutch paintings illustrate the chill of interiors during winter as people commonly appear indoors in heavy clothing, hats, shawls, and even furs. The frequent depiction of Dutch foot warmers (sometimes referred to as a foot stove) also point up poor household heating. The foot warmer was generally called a *stoof*, a wooden framed foot warmer was called a *houten stoof.* Jan Steen's *The Lovesick Maiden, The Sick Lady*, and *The Physician's Visit* all include foot warmers. Peter Kalm records the use of the foot warmers in Dutch households in the Hudson Valley.

Anyone looking up the cavernous interior of a Dutch flue might easily believe the story of Black Peter, the soot-covered chimney sweep boy who was Santa's helper and who brought gifts to children at St. Nicolas' Eve. The wide flue on a Dutch jambless fireplace effectively managed to vent most of the heat and some of the smoke out of the house. Roderic Blackburn states that the large open flue had one unexpected advantage as in the summer it helped to cool the interior of the house by drawing off excessive heat.24 In the warm weather all fires used for cooking were often banished to a separate wing or even to another building used as a summer kitchen. Most hearths were swept clean and many were decorated with a fan, vase, or *objet*. Daniel Marot's drawing of a state bedchamber in Holland, circa 1703 and illustrations in the *Theatrum Europeaun*, from the early eighteenth century, depict ways to garnish a hearth with a display of porcelains. A picture by Gonzales Coques in 1630 shows a burgher's house in Holland with a brass "curfew," or *couvre feu*, for preventing sparks, although in this case the scene must be in warm weather because the brass fire cover is decorated with a lace doily.[25] No example of a brass fire cover remains in America. A simple iron cooking-vessel inverted over the coals would serve the same purpose and go unremarked upon by contemporaries. The decorative embellishment of the hearth also appears in the 1747 English painting *Mr. and Mrs. Richard Bull in their home at Ongar in Essex* by Arthur Devis.[26]

At the Open Air Museum at Armhem there are examples of early hearths laid directly onto the floor without chimneys. The practice continued in fishermen's huts and farmhouses in remote areas of the Netherlands well into the nineteenth century. Fireplaces with chimneys existed from an early date in cities and in larger country dwellings. The Dutch called the urban room with a fireplace a *binnenhaard*, or little room around an inner hearth. Such a room was separated from the entry hall or front room, *het voorhuis* (front of house) and served as a kitchen and living area. A fire on the open hearth was best kept sheltered from outside drafts, for as Peter Kalm observed, "it frequently happened when the door was opened that the smoke was driven into the room" along with soot, ashes, and sparks.[27] An upper room with a fireplace was called a *hangkamer* in the Netherlands, and it accessed the chimney flue rising from a lower floor. These Dutch fireplaces were little more than a fireproofed section of wall and floor with a hood to direct the smoke into a smoke chamber and flue.[28] In *Remembrance of Patria*, a picture of the fireplace in the Van Alen house shows the structure quite clearly. [29] Donald Carpentier cautions that the fireplace is not original: "The original fireplaces in the Luycas Van Alen house were destroyed by Datus Shutaker in 1963 . . . I built those fireplaces in 1973."[30] Photographs in *An Album of New Netherland* show restored hearths in the Billou-Stillwell-Perine house on Staten Island and the Jonathan Hasbrouck house (Washington's Headquarters) in Newburgh. The illustrations of the Jan Martense Schenck house as installed at the Brooklyn Museum also are restored jambless fireplaces. [31]

A jambless fireplace is a sure cultural identifier of a Dutch house. The fireplaces were described by Peter Kalm as being built flush with the wall of the house to a height of about six feet or more from the hearth without side walls or jambs and "it was possible to sit on all three sides of the fire." The chimney began above the anchorbent beam and joists where "the bricks rested upon the . . . on three sides which had been arranged to support them." [32] The Dutch jambless fireplaces continued in use well into the 1760s long after becoming technical anachronisms, thereafter, New York Dutch built hearths in the English manner. Many early Dutch colonial homes have traces of original jambless hearths in their cellars in the form of stone arches or as corbeled half arches springing from a projecting stone in the foundation wall that curves under the hearth and are braced against a first floor joist. At other times, thick planks might be used instead of an arched support might top a pair of vertical stone walls. Sometimes a manger-shaped crib, or cradle, support is found. A ledge in the foundation wall three to five inches deep supports three or four diagonally mounted wood members that project out and up to the first ceiling joist. Planks are laid to form a cradle similar to a hay manger in appearance that was then filled with rock, clay, and earth beneath the hearth.

In addition to the hearth foundation, traces of Dutch jambless fireplaces might be found on the ceiling beams. Sometimes an entire hearth may be discovered within the framework of a later fireplacace as at the De Wint house in Tappan during restoration in 1995. Even after a house has been disassembled, clues remain. Roderic Blackburn describes details of the Van Slyck house built in Stone Arabia. The frame indicates a chimney opening in the roof directly above a large beam in the cellar and suggests that this beam supported a jambless fireplace's weight. The extra sturdy beam avoided the need for a stone support in the cellar.[33] In *Album of New Netherland*, M. E. Dillard notes that the jambless fireplace in the Billou-Stillwell-Perine house on Staten Island, built in the 1660s. It "was later hidden by two fireplaces with jambs and was not discovered until the 1940s, when it was restored to what may have been its original appearance."[34]

English kitchen fireplaces often had a built-in baking oven, whereas jambless Dutch fireplaces rarely had attached ovens. After the mid-1700s; however, Dutch houses with English style jamb-type fireplaces are found with ovens. (It might be noted that a "Dutch oven" is a covered iron cooking-vessel favored by Dutch housewives that was banked with coals on the hearth.) According to Peter Kalm around Albany the Dutch built their ovens for baking separate from the house through the 1740s. English-style fireplace built-in ovens extended outside the walls of the houses. A good illustration of a baking oven in the Berrien(?)-Pumyea house, Plate 129, appears in *Pre-Revolutionary Dutch Houses*.[35] The domed "beehive" oven (a modern term) that extended beyond the exterior wall frequently stands exposed today, but originally ovens were mortared-over to seal the exterior and protected by a roof. According to William McMillen of Richmond Town Restoration, rain and snow could penetrate an unroofed oven's masonry. If the "beehive" absorbed moisture, there was danger the damp walls would crack when heated.[36]

Dutch "beehive" ovens rarely had a separate flue; smoke went up the fireplace chimney. The housewife would build a fire or load the oven chamber with hot coals from the fireplace, and when hot enough for baking, the oven was cleaned of ashes and rested with the door closed for a few minutes to even the heat. The oven was tested with one's arm to feel the heat (generally gauged by experience) or by casting in a few wisps of straw, which would burst into flame if the oven was ready. Then the oven was filled with loaves of bread dough, pie shells filled with fruit or meat, or crocks of beans and bacon and closed with a wooden door, a sheet metal plate, or a flat stone. The bricks held the heat, and the oven baked slowly but consistently timing experience with a particular oven.

Similar to an oven was a room-heating iron box used in some rooms instead of a fireplace. The device was known as a "five-plate stove," front, top, bottom, and two sides, all fitted together. The open rear abutted the masonry wall and as the "stove" had no flue it opened onto a fireplace in the adjoining room. As no weight nor contact with the floor resulted, there was neither a hearth in the room nor necessarily a foundation support under the floor. Fired up like the baking oven, the stove would warm a small room. One of these stoves was probably used in the Van Slyck house, and in the Gemberloing house the east room was likely heated with a five-plate iron stove fueled from the fireplace in the west room. In 1679 Jasper Danckaerts recorded staying in a house with a "warm stove room, which they used to dry their malt in and . . . it was very warm there." Peter Kalm noted that at Albany in the 1740s the people were "unacquainted with stoves," however, he mentions "Newly Invented Pennsylvanian Fire-Places" (Franklin stoves) then becoming available in Pennsylvania.[37] Similar designs were used in the settlers' cultural zone from Scandinavia to France. The early five-plate devices disappeared with the arrival of the improved six-plate stove with its own separate chimney.

The back wall of the fireplace was often fitted with an iron fire-back to protect the masonry from heat damage. A fire-back was a tombstone-shaped cast-iron plate some two-and-a-half feet tall by two feet wide to protect the masonry from the heat. The Livingston firebacks at Ancram in Columbia County have the owners' initials cast into the plate face. The tiles, andirons, and firebacks, as well as many of the chimney cloths used were probably imported from the Netherlands.[38] The Sterling Iron Works in Orange County was one of several American sources for cast firebacks in the Dutch style during the late eighteenth century.[39] The Oxford Furnace in Warren County, New Jersey, was another foundry, operating in the eighteenth century; between 1745 and 1758 it cast the fireback discovered walled into a fireplace in the Nicholas Schenck house.[40]

In the Netherlands the entire wall behind the hearth might be finished with ceramic tiles.[41] F. R. Yerbury's book *Old Domestic Architecture of Holland* shows tiled hearths in Hoorn, Volendam, Edam, Amsterdam, Delft, and Haarlem.[42] Tiles were also used in place of baseboards, as can be seen in seventeenth-century paintings including Vermeer's *The Love Letter, The Geographer*, and *Maidservant Pouring Milk* and Pieter De Hooch's *The Pantry*. Tiles appear as wall facing in De Hooch's painting *Maternal Duty*, where white tile with blue designs covers a wall below an inside window. Yerbury remarks on an interior at Hoorn that had a red-tiled floor and a wall with white-and-blue-patterned wall-tiles. Tiled rooms were unknown in America.[43] The cost of imported tile and the isolation of most

farmsteads precluded extensive use of the traditional material.[44]
Although an important house like Coeymans has tile baseboards as
found in the Netherlands, most Dutch settlers in America "seem to
have limited their use of ornamental tiles to fireplace facings, framed
wall ornaments and hot-plates."[45]

The Netherlands' had a flourishing ceramic industry that served
domestic markets and exported worldwide. They produced red pottery, glazed earthenware and floor tiles known as *plavuizenor* or
estriken. Immigrants from southern Europe introduced the majolica
technique into the Netherlands and by the sixteenth century the
Dutch perfected various techniques to manufacture quality tile on a
quantity scale.

The majolica technique involved a two-step firing process that
Pieter Jan Tichelaar explained in *Tile*. The tile factory, or *gleibakkerij*,
was generally located close to the best source of clay, usually alluvial
sea or river clay. The clay was roughly kneaded for plasticity but not
cleaned of all impurities. A pugmill was used by Frisian brickmakers,
but the clay for tiles was kneaded originally without any mechanical
contrivance. In 1660 an innovation involved the addition of marl to
reduce the danger of tiles cracking, with the result that red tile fired
yellow. About this time the process known as "clay-washing" began,
whereby raw materials were mixed in water to form a "slurry,"
which was sieved, drained, and in later practice it was put into a
pugmill for a final kneading. The kneaded clay was beaten into
oblong slabs and then cut into small squares, which were placed into
a tile-frame to dry thoroughly.

Painting followed the first firing of a piece and then a second
firing softened the sharp line of the brushwork into the characteristic
look of majolica or faience. The tile was usually decorated with
pictures and designs in blue, purple, or polychrome. Traditions
varied by region in the Netherlands. West Friesland tiles were typically white "having animal or floral images. In the Zaan region they
were always . . .decorated with Biblical scenes."[48] The cities of Delft,
Gouda, Haarlem, Makkum, and Maastricht were centers of manufacture.[49] Dutch tiles were exported in quantity, but they were costly
and therefore used sparingly by individuals.

A fragment of an original blue Biblical tile was found below one of the hearths in the Luykas Van Alen house in Kinderhook during a 1970s restoration. The tiles used for the restoration were donated and replicate the original Van Alen designs. The restored single row of tiles trimming the edges of the jambless fireplace back wall were installed by Donald Carpentier in 1973 following typical Hudson Valley practice.

The Wynkoop-Lounsbery house in Stone Ridge has English-style fireplaces with the original tiles of blue, green, or mauve on white. The tiles on each hearth have a unifying theme. "The single scene tiles were made in 'series,' usually 12 to 24 different but related scenes in a set. They can be classified as Biblical, Ships, Cavaliers, Playing-Children, Tradesmen, Seascapes, and Florals and Birds."[50] The Gerret Nieuwkirk house in Hurley has the very popular "blue Biblical tiles" around the fireplace.[51] Dutch tiles "were generally in blue and white, often in Sepia (or plum) and white and sometimes in polychrome."[52] The DeWint house also has Biblical tiles around one of the fireplaces, but in mauve rather than blue. The Mynderse house in Saugerties has seventeenth-century Dutch tiles with polychrome figures of birds and plants on an ivory ground. Tiles were not always elaborately decorated; Van Cortlandt manor has tiles of plain white. That observant traveler Madam Sarah Kemble Knight noted in *The Private Journal Kept by Madame Knight* in 1707 that it was customary in New York that hearths and staircases were laid all with white tile. Even more surprising to Madam Knight: they were always kept clean.[53]

Strange as it seems today, wooden chimneys were common in the early years of settlement and in Europe through the seventeenth century. Vestigial examples remained down to the present century in Britain and probably still remain in areas of Eastern Europe today. Sidney Oldall Addy describes these chimneys as "built of studs and laths, plastered with mud."[54] An illustration of a cottage fireplace at Strata Florida in England clearly shows a jambless fireplace with a "chimney of wickerwork daubed outside with clay."[55] C. R. Morey diagrams examples from England and Virginia of chimneys identical to those described in colonial New Netherland.[56] A similar chimney is shown in *The American Farmhouse* as part of the John Billington house at the Plimouth Plantation restoration. [57] There it is noted as a "Welsh" or wooden country chimney "lathed, filled, daubed and playstered," a type commonly found in early Maryland and Virginia.[58] More substantial chimneys were built of brick as soon as fire regulations in the towns required them and wealth in rural districts allowed them.

The Dutch built their brick chimneys inside the house structure. Chimneys emerged at the roof level rather than appearing externally at gable wall or standing out and away from the house as was the rule in the southern colonies. Sometimes, early fireplaces were centrally located (especially where winters were more extreme). Building back-to-back central fireplaces was more economical and efficient.[59] The central location helped the draft keep the rooms smoke free and the house as warm as possible. As smoke was useful, it was not wasted. Some chimneys had a door accessing the flue at the hood where a smoke chamber could be used to cure meat. No examples of smoke chambers for jambless fireplaces remain in America. However, smoke holes can still be found in Dutch homes with English-type fireplaces at the Crailo, Coeymans, and Bethlehem houses near Albany.[60] Even in fire-conscious towns in the Netherlands "one or two small beams (laths) were allowed in a chimney for hanging meats to smoke," and a diagram in *Zaanse houtbouw* shows an access door to the smoke chamber of a fireplace for smoking meat, when appropriate fuel was available, however, not all smoke is suitable for curing meat: Apple, hickory or oak are good, but the peat or coal fires common in the Netherlands are not. The *Poughkeepsie Journal and Constitutional Republican* reported on February 15, 1815: "Fire—We understand that the house of General Armstrong at Rhinebeck was destroyed by fire on Sunday last . . . The fire is supposed to have originated from a smoke-house in the upper part of the house, connected with the chimney."[61]

With wooden chimneys and thatch roofs in the seventeenth century the danger of fire was always present. Open fires had to be kept up for cooking and heating and then banked down with ashes each night and covered. The fire was "saved" because it was difficult to restart a fire before the friction match was invented in 1833. "Loco

Foco or Lucifer Matches" were first advertised for sale in Poughkeepsie in August 1835.[62]

In Dutch houses the ceiling joists were typically exposed and finished to a smoothly planed surface in rooms used for habitation. Early beams tended to be larger. It was easier to square down a tree trunk than to saw one into several smaller beams. As posts and beams were mortised and tenoned together, the members needed to be large enough for the fitted joints and remain strong enough to do the job. An unusual example for a Dutch American house can still be seen in the cellar of the Shuart-Van Orden house, where the beams form an unusual grid of immense strength, an arrangement more like an English summer beam and joists than the typical Dutch Hudson Valley ceiling. *The Gold Weigher* painted by Cornelis de Man shows a ceiling in a Dutch house with a summer beam as well as exposed joists and planks. Dutch builders had generally abandoned using both cross beams and joists by the mid-seventeenth century. In this instance, the difference probably reflects the availability of large timber in America, while lumber costs in the Netherlands encouraged more economical treatment.

Enclosed stairs appear in most, if not all, of the Dutch houses of the valley. They are usually located in the corners of rooms in the earlier houses. The enclosure saved heat in the winter from escaping the warmer lower living floor to the upper storage garrets and lofts. Donald Carpentier notes the existence of a Dutch stair of circa 1750 "that had two trap doors on the upper section which closed like the hatch on a ship."[63] Enclosed stairs still remain at the Davis Tavern at Stone Ridge; at the Van Antwerp-Mebie house, Rotterdam Junction, in Schenectady County; and, restored, at the Broadhead house in Rosendale.[64] These stairways form a steep flight with a landing and change of direction that takes up very little room. Reynolds, describing the Hoornbeck house, says that the "stairs in the northeast corner of the hall were a crooked, enclosed flight."[65] Three homes with enclosed stairs of different designs are the Broadhead house, which has a restored side entry stairway rising to the second floor. The Gidney house which has an enclosed stair turning at a right angle from a vestibule and backing against a center chimney in New

England fashion. The Shuart-Van Orden house stairway is located at the end of a center hall, with a short exposed handrail that extends beyond a door and a flight of enclosed steps. Primarily designed to conserve heat, the stairways are very inconvenient when moving anything large between floors; Dutch houses occasionally had an exterior garret doorway with a pulley on a crane.

Open stairways were also used in America and in the Netherlands when the upper level was used for living accommodations and heat conservation was of less concern. Several open spiral flights of steps are depicted in *genre* paintings in the sixteenth century. Quirijn van Brekelenkam's *Man Spinning and Woman Scraping Carrots*, c.1653-1654, includes a stair turning on a central post with a wainscoted handrail. Isaack Koedijck depicts a similar two-story spiral stairway, with the upper half fully enclosed, in his painting of *The Foot Operation*, c.1640-1650. Gabriel Metsu's *The Hunter's Gift*, c.1658-1660, shows a spiral flight of steps without any handrail at all. A painting by Cornelis Dusart, entitled *The Pipe Smoker*, 1684, illustrates a makeshift flight of steps in two parts, with half a ladder and half with railed steps, very similar to the cellar steps in the Gidney house in Newburgh. Spiral stairs are found in Dutch houses at all social levels in the Netherlands well into the seventeenth century. A row of small early seventeenth-century houses restored for the City of Amsterdam by Henk Zantkuyl on the Bloemgracht (a canal in Amsterdam) have steep and narrow open flights of spiral stairs between floors. The large home of the hosiery merchant Jan Hartman built between 1661 and 1663, now the Museum Amstel Kring, uses precipitous and narrow stairs for both formal and service flights.

Open stairways in early American houses are usually straight or have one directional change. The baluster members were usually strong and lathe turned. A stairway from the Hendrick Breese house, built in 1726, has been moved and installed at the Luykas Van Alen house in Kinderhook. "In its turnings and moldings it is similar to other surviving stairways in Dutch houses of this period. The balusters are also similar to those on gate-leg tables made in New York in the eighteenth century."[66]

Dutch house walls were usually plastered. In a masonry house, the plaster was often applied directly to the inner wall surface. In

Early Architecture of Ulster County, it is stated that "on the inside of the wall a plumbline was dropped so that it just cleared the point of rock which projected furthest into a room; plaster was then laid directly on the inside rock wall out to the plumbline. Because of the stone irregularities, plaster on any inside wall might range in thickness from just a skim to a respectable number of inches."[67] Brick and nogging was plastered over in the same manner as stone. In wooden houses, according to William McMillen, a lath of large hemlock or oak sticks was slid into place between guide channels nailed to the H-bent post. Sometimes withes, slender flexible branches, were installed, and as the sticks were placed, a filling of clay and straw was put in the wall, then plastered over or white washed.

Early plaster was made from fine sand and lime from seashells. After 1700 fine plaster made with limestone was generally available in America.[68] Lime plaster was made by "cooking" gypsum (hydrous calcium sulfate) with low heat to remove moisture. In the Hudson Valley, the city of Poughkeepsie was a center for both brick and lime production from the early eighteenth century.

The early colonial Dutch practice was to use clay to coat the walls rather than plaster. "The Dutch primarily used one part clay and one part lime" and "applied it directly to the nogging in wooden houses in the Albany area."[69] Anglo-Dutch plaster was applied in three layers: The first coat was a "scratch" coat of lime, fine sand, and a considerable amount of cow hair. The first coat held the plaster to the wall of stone, brick, nogging, or lathe in later Anglo-Dutch houses. A second coat, called the "brown" coat, was then applied. It contained more sand and a considerable amount of cow hair. The finish coat had about the same amount of lime as the brown coat but no cow hair.[70]The hair averaged three bushels to the cubic yard of sand for the "scratch" coat and half as much hair for the "brown" coat. The ratio of lime to sand was one lime to one-and-a-half sand for the first and last coats, and one lime to three measures of sand for the second layer. The finished wall was wavy rather than flat, but the surface was smooth. An adequate plaster could be made with a mixture of three to six times as much sand as lime, according to Alec Clifton-Taylor. Several substances have traditionally been added as binders besides cow hair, including horsehair, chopped hay, straw, and even feathers.[71]

Over the years the plastered wall surface often assumed a scaly look from the repeated coats of whitewash applied to brighten the rooms and cover smoke smutting that could not be washed off the limed surface. Roderic Blackburn notes observing walls with more than twenty coats of wash applied before the middle of the nineteenth century. The walls were never rough as in "quaint olde style" simulations nor were they flat and mechanically smooth as in wallboard. Old walls have a softly undulating surface that can only be duplicated by following the traditional techniques beginning with a base surface that is uneven.

Dutch floorboards were usually held in place with iron spikes or wrought nails called *spijker*. An exception can still be found in the Broadhead house in Rosendale, which has a floor pegged in place and trunnels that show clearly against the lighter color of the floorboards. Floor and wallboards typically in yellow poplar, called "canoewood," or in white pine commonly ranged from 10 to 15 inches in width. Matt Martin of the *Poughkeepsie Journal* noted in a description of the 1750 Neimiah Every house in LaGrange that several floorboards were as wide as 16 to 18 inches. During the passage of years the boards had developed "arches and bows" through the length of the hall.[72] Early floor boards were commonly cut to approximately twelve to sixteen feet in length. William McMillen at Richmond Town Restoration offers two reasons for the sixteen foot length: First, sixteen feet was about the maximum length of a tree trunk that was practical to handle by two men using a frame-saw in a saw-pit. Second, when sawn in a mill, a sixteen-foot-long trunk required a run of about thirty-two to thirty-eight feet for the vertical saw's machinery and these dimensions established a practical limit on small mill size. The boards cut from a single tree vary in width. The widest is the one cut from the center part of the trunk, while each one cut further from the center will be narrower. William McMillen observed that, as tree trunks taper from root end to tip, the boards cut from an unsquared trunk will also taper. When the boards were not rectangular, a builder sometimes laid the taper of each board alternately to achieve a more regular fit and appearance.

Two-man teams using a frame-saw that cut in an up-and-down motion manually sawed wood. The first crankshaft vertical-cut sawmill was erected in Amsterdam around 1600. Powered by wind or water, crankshaft mills converted circular motion into an up-and-down movement like the man-powered saw pit method. These powered sawmills were quickly adopted, and soon timber merchants (*houtkopters*) were establishing timber yards (*houttuinen*) at suitable sites accessible to house and shipbuilders in the Netherlands and then in America at an early date. Colonial sawmills could be relatively large-scale enterprises: In 1662, Jeronimus Bingh, plaintiff, appealed to the Kingston Court and demanded "from Willem Mertense payment of the amount of thirty *schepels* of wheat due in the fall of 1661, on the sale of 150,000 planks." Since the defendant admitted the debt, the court ordered payment by the next fall. Lumber was an important industry, a fact once memorialized in the original name for the town of Port Chester, which was known as Saw Pit until the mid-nineteenth century.[73] Knots in the lumber would make the long vertical saw blade vibrate resulting in visible lines which appear as slightly angled straight-line scorings on the surface of the board. After 1830 power mills used circular saws that cut with a continuous motion and these blades left curved score lines. The distinctive marks are an important dating clue as circular saw cuts would date no earlier than the middle part of the nineteenth century and therefore would not appear on wood originally used in a Dutch house. Early floors were often replaced in the Victorian period with narrow boards, but sometimes a restorer gets lucky: In the Broadhead house, a modernized replacement floor was pulled up and the original wide boards were found to be in good condition.

Different woods were used for various jobs. Pitch pine was used originally for anchor beams, posts, and floors in the Albany area. After about 1760, white pine was used for anchor beams and oak for other purposes into the early nineteenth century.[74] Pine, smooth and free of knots and blemishes, was used for floors and internal paneling; sometimes canoewood (from the tulip poplar tree) was used for the same purpose. Shingles were mostly white pine.

Early Dutch houses rarely had walls with wooden paneling. Paneling only came into fashion later in the Anglo-Dutch period. In the first half of the eighteenth century it was most frequently applied to the walls flanking fireplaces, stairways, and box-beds. Interior doors were made similar to interior paneling. Dutch interior partitions, called *middelschotten*, were dividing walls or enclosing walls. These were often fitted with paneling cut in impressive dimensions. "In one house of the upper Hudson region a beveled panel salvaged from an English style chimney mantle was a single piece of white pine measuring 46 inches by 33 inches, which gives an idea of the material at hand."[75] Boards in panels and English-style chimney breasts were sometimes of prodigious size (one in the Abraham DePyster house measures 48 by 37 inches) and a piece of white pine in the Wynkoop-Lounsbery house measures 33 by 44 inches.[76] Unfortunately, in the nineteenth century many of these wide board chimney breasts were defaced when stove pipe holes were cut through them (as at the Wynkoop-Lounsbery house).

Interior walls occasionally were seasonal. The Wynkoop-Lounsbery house -- which has remained virtually untouched from the eighteenth century to the present day -- had two seasonal wall areas. One wall was on an upstairs landing another in a back kitchen. In the kitchen the "winter wall" boards slid vertically into channels on the ceiling and floor to enclose an entry area against the blasts of cold winter air. In the summer these walls could be removed to improve air circulation. Most of the permanent panels were simple boarding, laid vertically or horizontally or as wainscoting. The *beschieting* was fitted from baseboard to chair-rail height. In the late eighteenth century paneling added at mid-century was frequently removed; so examples are infrequently found although they appear in Dutch paintings. A wall with vertical paneling and a "Dutch shelf" dish rail is shown in Jan Miense Molenaer's 1633 painting entitled *Woman at Her Toilet (Lady World)*, and a chair-rail molding applied without paneling to the plaster wall is illustrated in Nicolaes Maes' *The Account Keeper (The Housekeeper)* of 1656.

The planks used for the *beschieting* could be joined in a number of ways for a smooth mating of two boards or a decorative and patterned meeting. The various board joints, or *aansluiting*, were achieved by changes of angle and plane at the edges. The more common joints were named: Feather edge, *visbek* or *aansluiting met tafel veer*, was an early method of joining when one board had its edges tapered to fit into grooves of the two adjacent boards. Spline, *aansluiting met losse veer*, was produced when two grooved-edge boards were joined by a thin strip of wood that fit into the two abutting grooves. Half-lap, *oplegging*, occurred when two abutting boards were rabbeted, *halfhoutse overdekking*, or *schuine langsoverdekking*, or tapered to one side to overlap an adjacent board's similarly tapered half overlap so the two boards met smoothly. In tongue and groove, *aansluiting met messing en groef* (also *aansluiting met visbek*), one board side was cut in a channel or groove and the other side was cut with two recessed edges and a raised center ridge, or tongue, that fit into the groove of the next board. The edging was firmly fitted but not glued or sealed, a method which lets the boards expand or contract without splitting or buckling. Rough finishing was done with an ax and an adz, a fine finish was achieved with a plane. The surfaces were smoothed leaving only the subtle undulations characteristic of the tools rather than the busy chopped look of "quaint" reproductions.

Because they were open to view, the edges of ceiling beams in the late eighteenth century were occasionally trimmed with a plane into a groove or chamfer, *velling* or *vellingkant*. Some beams had an edge formed with a beading, *kraal*, made with a molding plane, that created a groove near the edge of two adjacent sides. The edge was then rounded resulting in a "reed," or *riet*, as a decorative feature.[77]

In the seventeenth century simple interior doors were often made with two or three vertical boards and three widely spaced horizontal members called battens. In the eighteenth century, interior doors, called *deuren binnen* in Dutch, were of slip panel construction. Flat on one side with raised rails and stiles on the other. These doors were frequently quite thin. The stiles (vertical boards) and rails (horizontal members) of the frame held the inner panels, which were champered to fit into grooves in the frame. The Dutch also used "batten panel" doors, which had flat panels but were constructed like a batten door. Early doors generally were made with the moldings planed from the board in one piece, while nineteenth-century doors were made with applied moldings. Early doors frequently had two or three panels, but later doors may have up to six panels. Both frame- and batten-style doors can be found in the same house: Important rooms had panel type doors, while kitchens and other less formal areas had batten type doors. In all panel doors the frames were held together with small pegs. Batten doors were usually nailed from the batten side, frequently quite crudely, with the nail ends clinched over on the front side. A more substantial door than the batten door was the sheathed door. It was basically a batten door with the battens set at right angles or aslant to the front boards to form a double boarded door.

There was no one basic "Dutch floor plan." It is possible to find a number of alternative room arrangements and floor plans, although rooms with different functions were usually identical in construction. In *The Dutch American Farm*, David Steven Cohen says that he "found four basic floor plans that can be traced to the Netherlands, thus forming the repertory for. . .the Dutch farmhouse."[78] Yet his "Dutch" plans could be English, Danish, or Norman French. Nevertheless, common practice in the Hudson Valley did result in a few predictable room arrangements. Many early Dutch homes only had a single room; others connected additional rooms to the gables of an initial one-room cottage. The dynamics imposed by the H-bent frame determined the configuration of Dutch house floor plans in the seventeenth century, but by the eighteenth century, the growing English influence imposed changes that led eventually to abandonment of the true Dutch house.

Early Hudson Valley Dutch homes were typically a single 18-by18 to 20-by-20 foot room with a floor raised one to three feet above ground level and entered by way of a stoop. Some early homes began as two rooms, which joined at one of the gables, forming a single unit some 20 feet wide by 40 feet long. Each interior room had one, or occasionally two, garret levels above the living floor. The two Schuyler houses built in Albany circa 1670 had two stories with hooded chimneys on the second floor implying that they were planned as living rooms. While two stories were common in urban dwellings at Albany and Manhattan, the general rule before 1776 was to build a house only a story and a half high.[79] According to Reynolds, other than the house of Francis Salisbury at Leeds in Greene County, "no house has been learned of in any other . . . *rural* part of the river valley which was standing in 1705, two full stories in height."[80] However, the Francis Salisbury house appears to be from the 1760s.

The other exceptional two-story country houses were along the Millstone and Raritan Rivers in central New Jersey. [81] The only remaining early "Dutch" homes of two full stories outside the areas mentioned are the Van Campen house on the Delaware River and the Dey house at Preakness.[82] The exceptions are attributed to English influence and the exceptional wealth and prominence of the owners. Both Reynolds and Bailey attribute a "Dutch" designation to houses owned by people with Dutch surnames rather than to buildings with Dutch design characteristics.

From the earliest period Dutch colonial houses assumed several regional forms. The most usual formats found in early houses of Dutch settlers include up to three ground-floor rooms in a row, often with two or more doors opening to the outside, and no internal hallway. In later Anglo-Dutch houses, the plan might include a larger room in the front and smaller room in the rear. Sometimes there was a double set of large and small rooms bisected by a hall. David Baker —a resident of Kingston, New York, and an authority on Dutch houses in Ulster County—identifies one regional type as "Esopus Architecture." The houses consist of a one-room stone homestead with a ground plan of "family room and hall" that sometimes expanded with a second room or parlor into a center hall house. A center hall house typically had only a centered entry door, not separate doors to each room from the outside. Early houses in the Netherlands often had an entry passage along one side of a pair of rooms: Houses with gangs, long shed aisles, remain in the Netherlands but exist only on paper or in restorations in America.

The following examples are Dutch houses that do not conform to stereotypes: The Shuart-Van Orden house, built in 1773, has an Anglo-Dutch floor plan typical of the type of house popularly called "Dutch Colonial" built into the nineteenth century in the Hudson Valley and New Jersey. It has a center hall, two large front rooms, and two smaller rear rooms. However, one rear room has a fireplace, which is less common. The enclosed stairs provide access to a lower half-grade-level kitchen, pantry, and a third room that originally housed five slaves. The cellar has an unusual beam structure with massive interlocking timbers. The second floor level has a large fireplace and originally had three "children's rooms." This is a long list of unusual features for a "typical" Bergen County, New Jersey, gambrel-roofed brick and stone house—that was built in Ulster County, New York.

The wooden-framed and Flemish spring-eave Gidney house in Newburgh, New York, is far more typical of New Jersey, Staten Island, or Long Island than the mid-Hudson Valley. The building seems to contain a seventeenth-century one-room house within its southwest corner that only partially emerges as a wing from the main rear. Internally, it has a center entry and three English fireplaces drawing from one center chimney in typical New England fashion. It probably grew somewhat randomly within a limited number of practical alternatives, following the Dutch principles of construction based upon the H-bent frame core. Discussing the room arrangements at the Jonathan Hasbrouck house in Newburgh, H. W. Reynolds observed that many Dutch houses appear surprising because they were never planned, they were collections of additions to a one- or two-room core. Surprise "arises from an unthinking assumption that the house was built all at one time . . . (whereas) it is an evolution. And as an evolution it is a good example of the way many houses in Ulster grew into their ultimate form."[83]

The Gidney house was originally only a fifteen by twenty feet dwelling. The Van Alstyne house in Chatham Center remains an example of a one-room homestead with an upper half-story attic that never was significantly enlarged. The building is a stone cottage with a tiny shed to one side. Single-room houses served many Dutch colonial families for years, even for generations, such as the original core of the Pieter Cornelise Louw house on Frog Alley Lane in Kingston. H. W. Reynolds specifically cited the Louw house because "the small size of the first unit is significant as an illustration of the living conditions of an early settler."[84]

What we consider a basic two-room arrangement was often called a double house in early New England. Two-room Dutch houses joined at one gable end formed a 20- by 40 foot unit, often having a central chimney with two fireplaces or, in a few cases, a fireplace in one room and a "five-plate stove" in the adjacent chamber. In larger houses there was sometimes a rear room often little larger than a modern walk-in closet with a window. A three-room house might have had two rooms and an "L," or a side passageway, as in the Jan Martense Schenck house built prior to 1730.[85] A four-room house might have duplicated the big front and small rear-room plan either with or without a hall. The Minne Schenck house—originally built in Manhasset, Long Island, and presently located at Old Bethpage Village Restoration—first had a plan found in many Flemish houses in New York—two large front rooms and three smaller rooms across the rear of the house.[86] The smaller rooms were basically storerooms or sleeping chambers, although rooms were not rigidly assigned functions the way they are today. Because the rear chamber rarely had a fireplace, a door would be left open for the warmer air of the front room to circulate. The term "warmer air" is relative. One must suspect that the rear rooms would have been unbearably cold by today's standards and in fact were probably little warmer than the outside temperature.

The typical center-hall Dutch colonial house was a later development, often built or modified in response to English balanced and formal styles that came into fashion during the eighteenth century. Centering the hall resulted in the style generally known as Georgian in America. The Jan Martense Schenck house shows evidence of being revised about 1730 from an original side-aisle design to a center hall. The plan featured two rooms end-to-end and a central chimney with a *gang*, along the west side of the house as an entry passage.[87] Quite a bit of research went into examining the house's changed floor plan for a correct restoration by the Brooklyn Museum of Art. Extensive renovations took place in numerous old homes. Keeping up with the Broncks and the Ten Broeks probably explains many of the additions, rebuilding, and roof raisings done in the eighteenth century. Despite D. S. Cohen's assertion that "it seems highly unlikely that a busy Dutch-American farmer and miller would dismantle a central chimney simply to keep up with the latest style," fashions in home design played a significant role in the evolution of many houses.[88] The editors in *Long Island Architecture* noted that the Roeloff-Minne Schenck house, originally erected in 1730, "was lengthened in the 1760s to provide a center hall," and although a center hall is quite practical, the alteration was clearly a fashion statement without structural necessity.[89]

Originally the word "hall" referred to the main room in a house in medieval times. In later homes the center "hall" was often much more than just a passageway and served to keep interior rooms private and comfortably draft free. In addition the hall frequently served as a summer sitting room, open to the exterior at either end and cooled by the cross ventilation. The hall was also used as an all-purpose room the year round and might be found furnished with a desk, sewing table, or tilt-top dining table. Develpoments reflected both fashion and its modivating functions. The center hall served several functions: It was a passageway, a multipurpose public space, and a way to access special purpose rooms as separate dining rooms, bedrooms, and parlors came into fashion during the course of the eighteenth century.

Between the seventeenth and eighteenth centuries room use changed. Whereas earlier multi-purpose rooms were adequate for even the wealthy, later on even the less well-to-do wanted separate, and specialized, rooms for sleeping, working, and entertaining. In a pair of pictures by Cornelis de Man: *The Gold Weigher*, c.1670-1675, and *The Chess Players*, c.1670, the same room is shown from two different perspectives. A built-in bed occupies a place at right angles to the tiled jambless fireplace, and it is hung with the same fringed green material *en suite* with the cloth hanging on the fireplace. Identical features in the pictures include the draw table with bulbous turned legs, the black-and-white tiled floor, and the details of the paneling. Even the man's hat and the woman's jacket are identical in both pictures. In the first scene a couple plays chess. In the second a man weighs gold, a woman sits by at a domestic chore, and a boy tends to the fire. The importance of the two pictures, in the context of usage, is that it clearly shows de Man was exact in his rendering of the room's details and proportions. We are dealing with a single room that is more than a background prop; it was very likely the artist's home and studio. When de Man shows the room as a setting for different activities, we can be reasonably confident that he took few artistic liberties as the same features reoccur from one painting to the next. To de Man, the room, which we would see as a private bedroom, was a multi-use space in his day. In the seventeenth century, his

viewers found the multi-use situation the norm. In the eighteenth
century or later it was much less likely that a "bedroom" would host
such a wide range of social and business activities. Improved fireplaces
and the new stoves, as well as changing economic and social conditions, created the perceived "necessity" even for "busy farmers" to
remodel their homes to adapt to the new modes of living.

In a report on the Jan Martense Schenck house, several distinct
periods of building and renovation are identified, often dictated more
by fashion than by functional necessity. The trend to specialized
rooms reflected changes in the world far beyond a "busy farmer's"
milieu. Nevertheless, changes in the house indicate a farmer's aware-
ness of the life-style changes. The new "needs" motivated the extensive renovations to the old homestead that were undertaken on
several occasions. Just as de Man's views reflected seventeenth-century practices, the original Schenck house was adequate for seventeenth-century farm life. A century later, the house seemed
out-of-date and "inadequate" and therefore needed to be altered to
meet new eighteenth-century and then nineteenth-century "needs."

From the framework and other elements taken down in 1952, as
well as from the documents. . .we can assume at least five stages
in the construction of the house.

1. About 1675: a 22 by 41 foot story and a half house with central
chimney and symmetrical ends. The west wall was solid, with an
overhang. . .[or possibly an enclosed passageway] The north wall
was probably also without openings. The east side had a door and
window in the north room, a dormer above in the middle and a
window in the south room as well as a door and window on the
south wall. The upstairs area was for storage, with access by an
interior stair.

2. About 1730: the shelter [or passageway] on the west wall was
removed, and windows and a door were put in this side. A door
was installed at the center of the east wall. The large open
fireplaces may have been changed to the more enclosed, safer
English style.

3. About 1800: a three bedroom wing was added and judging from
its early appearance probably soon after the assessment roll of

1796. The chimney was probably removed from the center of the house to create an entrance hall.

4. About 1830-1850: a porch with columns in the Greek Revival style was added to the west side.

5. Late nineteenth century: the attic was divided into bed and storage rooms.90

Our "busy farmer" kept up with all the major developments: center hall, end chimneys, enclosed fireplaces, Greek Revival columns, private bedrooms for family members, and a finished upper level with a bedroom. Few of these changes were "necessities" in the seventeenth century yet the house had apparently adequately served a family's needs from the start. The alterations reflected both changing technology (in heating arrangements) and fashion trends that were seen as important enough to be followed.

In fact, many houses show clear evidence of fashionable renovations. The Minne Schenck house in Nassau County, Long Island, was erected with separate outside entrances to each front room in 1730, but in the 1760s it was converted to a center-hall dwelling.91 Another example of this type of renovation can be seen in the Van Steenburgh house in Kingston. Examination of the facade and interior spatial arrangement reveals that the center door and two of the present front windows (one per front room) were originally doorways. The center hall was also an eighteenth-century modification with space taken from the two adjacent rooms. The house was originally built as two rooms with a separate entry for each room. The facade was further altered by a Victorian gable over the center entrance and, again, extensively remodeled in the 1930s. Nevertheless original Dutch seventeenth- and early eighteenth-century arrangements with the house one room deep and no center hall may still be seen in the Broadhead house, the Mynderse house, and the Luykas Van Alen house. When a center hall appeared, the Dutch preferred to have a door that opened to the outside at either end of the hall, and two large ground floor rooms flanking the hall passage. If additional rooms were part of the basic plan, there was often a pair of smaller rear rooms, as in the Persen house in Saugerties.

Changes were also made in windows unrelated to the centering of front doors. Gothic windows, or *cloosters kusijins*, were converted to sliding sashes. The placement of windows was altered: Windows were frequently added to existing houses during the eighteenth century. In *Dutchess County Doorways,* Reynolds addresses the changes in window placement from 1776 to 1800. In typical pre-Revolutionary center hall houses, the two front rooms usually had only one or two windows facing the front of the house. In the wall opposite the windows, an interior door usually led into a rear room. On the inner side wall a centrally placed door opened into the hall and, opposite, at the gable was a chimney.[92] Early contracts indicate that windows in the gable-end fireplace wall were unusual until after 1800. The single-room-deep Dutch house plan often had a front wall with a door and one window, and a rear wall with a centered window. The jambless fireplace precluded a window opening beside the hearth. When the fireplace was at the gable end of the room there would be no window. If there was no fireplace then there might have been one centered window. In the Broadhead house, for example, the front wall has a window and a door, while the rear wall has a centered window in typical Dutch fashion. However, the gable wall has two later style windows that are different in both dimension and muntin design from the earlier eave-wall windows and are clearly an alteration.

Many houses grew over time. Few old buildings have survived that sprang full-grown from an idealized plan without an alteration or an extension. Additions can be ells attached to an original house or even entirely new, and much larger, structures that dwarf the core building. The contrast can still be seen in two large gambrel-roofed center hall houses built shortly before the Revolutionary War. Both were planned formal main houses but each also exhibits different periods of growth. The Anglo-Dutch Wynkoop-Lounsbery house, a stone building probably built about 1772 in Stone Ridge has a stone "kitchen wing" that was probably the entire original building and appears older than the main structure by a generation or more. The house grew from a modest start to a grand maturity. The Johannis Van Alen house in Stuyvesant is a handsome Albany-area-style Anglo-Dutch brick structure dating from 1765. At the rear of the original Dutch colonial structure is an ell that was a part of the house's growth. Leaving it *in situ* when the house was partially restored by

Roderic Blackburn was a legitimate alternative to replacing it with an imitation in an earlier style. Similarly, recognizing the evolving growth of a structure was a consideration when the Brooklyn Museum restored two of the Schenck family houses, and the circumstances are described at length in *Dutch By Design*. The Jan Martense Schenck house dates from the 1670s, but it was restored to its appearance following alterations dated to 1730. The Nicholas Schenck house restoration traced clues to a building date of about 1771, although the structure may contain elements of another house built by Nicholas' father, Stephen, a generation earlier. The restoration replicated the possible appearance of the building in the 1820s.

Another factor in restoration is when the project was undertaken. Work at Jamestown and Williamsburg is ongoing because early research was either incomplete or conducted prior to later insights and revelations. Similarly, restoration objectives are revised or reconsidered over the course of time. A problem was encountered when researching the origins of Dutch colonial houses in the Netherlands in April 1997. Earlier restorations in the Netherlands, such as Henk Zankuyl's work in the city of Amsterdam, restored buildings to their original appearance. Now, however, while the Arnhem, Zaanse Schans, and Enkhuisen Open Air Museums have examples of various early architectural types, representing many areas within the Netherlands, the original appearance of the buildings is rarely restored. According to Jaap Schipper (who was pivotal in the restoration of Zaanse Schans, where there are several seventeenth-century houses), and Ellen van Olst, Director of Restoration at the Open Air Museum at Arnhem, where many of the houses are also of ancient lineage, the late twentieth-century objective in Dutch restoration is to reflect the entire history of the building. This is a valid sociological goal for the Dutch, but it makes the job of finding examples that clearly illustrate early Fatherland precedents for colonial farm homes much more difficult.

Changing goals in restoration can be seen in America as well. The Grand Lodge of the Masons acquired the De Wint house on November 22, 1931. According to a June 1995 newsletter, "Sixty-Three Years of Restoration/Preservation" by the De Wint curator C. F. William Mauder, a frame addition was taken down in 1932 when the

roof of the main house was replaced with hand-split shingles stained
to look old. The double-hung windows were replaced with casements, and an overhang was created on the east eaves. The building
was painted cream color. Interior tiles that had been removed were
recovered and restored. The building was reinforced and the masonry
and plaster were repaired and painted. Other than routine maintenance, the building endured "benign neglect" by a series of caretakers
and overseers. Then in 1955, "new progress was made on the restoration of the brickwork to its original condition," removing the
cream-colored paint put on in 1932. The roof was reshingled. A series
of "strengthening" and "rehabilitating" measures were undertaken
to the roof and stairway. And the house was repainted and replas-
tered. The 1990s restoration, a more scientifically based project, was
necessary because it was discovered that extensive renovation was
needed to repair termite and rot damage to key structural members.
The work reflected state-of-the-art knowledge, and weighing of alternative priorities, yet the result will undoubtedly be reevaluated by
the next generation of experts in the light of subsequent findings. The
1995 restoration, for example, did not return the house to its earliest
configuration with jambless fireplaces and 1700 woodwork, but to
its appearance in about 1780. The objectives of a restoration affect
the results. The decision was made to de-emphasize the early version
of the house built by Daniel DeClark (de-Klerck), an obscure brewer
who built the brick-and-stone house shortly after the issuance of the
Tappan Patent by Governor Dongan in 1687. Instead, the restoration
recreated the house as occupied by George Washington in 1780 and
stressed Washington's Masonic connections. Supplementing the restoration was a recreation of a kitchen wing, removed in 1932 that was
probably built about 1686. Details about the wing were only discovered in a recent dig.

Quite another story concerns the Glen-Collins house, located on
a small part of a property that once extended to the Mohawk River
known as Claas Graven Hook after the original farmer of the 1600s.
The building now stands on a patch of land divorced from its
agricultural roots. Built as a typical two-room dwelling in about 1730
in the Village of Scotia, the Glen-Collins house is now a branch of
the Schenectady Public Library System. Michelle J. Norris, the Scotia

Village Historian, explains that "this house is loved by just about everyone who has ever lived, worked, or been a part of keeping it going." It has been extensively altered by Victorianisations because historic authenticity was less important than "modern comfort" and "charm" in the Romantic spirit.

Johannes and Maas Van Buren, father and son built the Van Buren farm in Castleton, and the house was inscribed on two red clay tiles:

1763	1763
JVB	MVB
May	May
25	25

Several original Dutch features have survived, including the south gable brick braiding, exposed joists in the north living room, and indications of a jambless fireplace. A historical survey report written by Shirley Dunn, John Mesick, and Paul Huey of the Historical Society of Esquatak after visiting the Van Buren farm on February 8, 1975, notes alterations to the original Dutch house. Changes were made in the Greek Revival style about 1840. Interior detailing dates from the 1860s and the woodwork from the 1870s. Alterations in the 1920s were based upon drawings by Alexander Selkirk dated May 16, 1927. A view of the house in 1876 shows a Romanticized interpretation of the Dutch style after the manner of "Sunnyside," a quaintly picturesque result that evolved from an authentic early Dutch core. Restoring such a house would erase the intervening history, which has a validity all its own. A similar situation prevails at the Vandenburg house, c.1764, in West Coxsackie. Neighboring the Bronck Museum, this privately owned house serves the needs of a contemporary household. The stone exterior and the two principal rooms of the original Dutch homestead were restored, but the kitchen wing was made into a "Shaker-style kitchen," and the upper level was modernized completely. The same approach was used in rehabilitating the Mabie-Holdrum "Old Stone House" in River Vale, Bergen County, New Jersey. This handsome red sandstone Dutch building with a gambrel roof and a kick at the front eave has a recreated *stoep* with benches, twelve-over-twelve windows, and a pair of traditional outside cellar entry doors. It serves as a contemporary dwelling rather than a museum piece. Inside this centerhall house, anything discernibly Dutch is difficult to identify; clearly, the objective was to restore an authentic "Dutch" exterior, while creating a contemporary "country-decorator" interior.

Houses have periods of growth followed by decades of stability. Several reasons motivated alterations. Rising standards of living and expectations, greater security, increased prosperity, and the growth of families, whose members demanded space, contributed to the growth of houses from basic shelters to commodious dwellings. The Noah LeFevre house, originally built in 1776 in Ulster County, typifies this expansion. From the outside, one sees the original small stone house. A larger center entrance was added in the later eighteenth century. Then the current roof over both parts of the house was raised by half a story in clapboard. Low second-floor windows were added between the original stone wall and the new roof eaves, and peaked dormers were later added to the attic in a nineteenth-century style. The Dirck Westbrook house in Accord is a large stone house with Federal details and eyebrow windows, but it is much older with a more complex history than first appearances suggest. "This house has an early rear wing dating back to pre-1700 according to deeds on record. The main stone wing was added at the front in the early 18th century. Finally, in the early 19th century a third addition was made . . . while retaining the earlier twelve light windows," reports *Early Architecture in Ulster County*.[93] The Gidney house in Newburgh was a seventeenth-century one-room homestead that was absorbed into a larger Flemish-eave, center-entry house in the eighteenth century. Even a well-known building like the Van Cortlandt Manor-House is a product of several generations of building activities. The original core was a flat-roofed fort and trading post/hunting lodge built in the seventeenth century. In the eighteenth century, it became the permanent residence of the Van Cortlandts and grew a peaked roof. About 1810 a wing at one corner was added. Then about 1845 the second wing, dormers, and the verandah completed the metamorphosis. The cumulative effect is the result of numerous changes in the appearance of the building we see today.[94] In R. F. Bailey's book, *Pre-Revolutionary Dutch Houses*, one example of growth is the Schuyler-Colfax house in Pompton, New Jersey. Built on a tract of land purchased in

1695 by Arent Schuyler, the original house was erected in 1702 or 1712 by Arent Schuyler or by his son Philip. Several additions from the eighteenth century are attributed to Philip or his son Casparus Schuyler. William Colfax and his wife Hester Schuyler built the present main house in 1783.[95]

One useful approach in unraveling the mysteries of different building dates lies in the phrase "according to deeds on record." Take, for example, the early records of the "*Voorleezer*" house at the Richmond Town Restoration on Staten Island. According to a booklet entitled *The Voorleezer's House: An Illustrated Guide*, published by the Richmond Town Restoration, this house was not considered to be of great historic significance until the mid-1930s. At that time a thorough documentary study and survey undertaken by Raymond L. Saffoed and Rev. Lefferd M. A. Haughwout was combined with the architectural analysis of the Staten Island Historical Society curator Loring McMillen. The researchers established both the great antiquity of the building and its identity as the Voorleezer's House.[96] The records referring to the *Voorleezer*'s house appeared in a deed to adjoining land dated July 17, 1696. Further research confirmed the greater age of a building that had only been known to exist in the family of Rene Rezeau, a French Huguenot, after 1705. It turned out that Hendrick Kroesen occupied the building, when it was a residence and school, during his service as the church lay leader or *Voorleezer* between 1695 and 1718.

Regarding the dating of colonial houses, Donald L. Malcarne of the Essex County Historical Society in Essex, Connecticut, observed: "It is trying to establish an age through land records, probate records, church records, family records, vital statistics, knowledge of architectural styles. And sometimes it comes down to the best guess."[97] Documentation needs to agree with on-the-scene examination. The written record alone may be subject to gaps, omissions, and different interpretations. The dates posted on a house wall may be correct for that aspect of a building but they may only record a rebuilding or renovation. The date may even record a second building on the site or a much later second house on an earlier foundation. Individually, either form of investigation will reveal clues, but dating often requires cross referencing between historians and restoration experts. An opportunity to verify dating occurred when the recent restoration of the De Wint house removed termite-infested cellar beams. Alice Gerard, a local historian, and Gordon Jacoby of the Lamont-Doherty Earth Observatory Tree Ring Laboratory studied the beams. The oak-beam sections were sanded to expose the original tree-growth rings, which were measured and counted on each cross-section of beam. The data was compared to dates for tree-ring sections from the "Big House," a dwelling in Palisades. The two samples cross dated well. They confirmed that the trees used as cellar beams confirmed the date marked by bricks on the house facade when constructed by Mr. De Clark in "1700."

> One section, labeled DEW1, has 142 growth rings. This section is missing the inner most rings but extends out to the bark, The first ring appears to date to the year 1555 and the last measured ring to the year 1697. Beyond this is one ring, possibly only a partial ring, which was not measured. This means that the oak tree from which this beam was cut was probably felled sometime between September 1698 and May 1699. This agrees with the date across the front of the house.
> The second section, labeled DEW3, has 137 rings. It begins at the innermost ring but is missing a number of outer rings, presumably squared off (by Mr. De Clark?). The first ring dates to the year 1535 and the last ring can be assigned to the year 1672.[98]

Whenever possible, both on-site observation and off-site examination of archival data are necessary for specific dating. The improvements in technology and techniques in the past few decades have greatly enhanced our ability to examine and interpret what we find.

Stability is one of the charms of folk custom that stands in sharp contrast to the transitory whims of architectural fancy and stylish chic. The same builder could erect two houses at the beginning and end of his working life that would be practically identical. An even greater span of time could unite two similar homes: The original builder could have had an apprentice or a son building in the same manner for a half-century or more. So similar building techniques and work that appears "from the same hand" could be very misleading for dating. Even a building that initially appears "of a piece" often reveals a number of growth periods on closer inspection. On-site examination will reveal joints in a wall of stone or brick or shingles or weatherboards placed over masonry, different angles to a roofline and variations in window muntin widths, or non-period features that indicate changes.

An article by Harvey Auster in *The Poughkeepsie Journal*, May 28, 1992, describes the 1732 DuBois house in Hurley. He reports that the original house consisted of what today comprises the dining room, lean-to kitchen, and hall. Fifty years later, the house was doubled in size and converted into a center-hall house by the addition of the present living room, and the conversion of the garret, which had been accessed by a ladder, into a true second floor with a flight of stairs. In the nineteenth century, shed dormers were added, giving the house its present appearance.[99]

Similar growth and evolution took place at the Persen house in Saugerties. The following observations apply to the current status of many other early buildings: The house is a single unit without wings, but it has a stone saltbox addition to the rear with a shed roof extending over the rear rooms. A long sloped roof is sometimes called a "cat slide" in New England. There are three distinct foundation areas: A full cellar under one ground-floor front room and the present center hall; a foundation for an English fireplace at the north end wall; and a crawl space under the ground-floor front room on the south side. The mid-eighteenth century date for the house suggests the English chimneys may be original, as jambless fireplaces were going out of style. Where present, they were being converted to English fireplaces when the Persen house was built. Both front foundations still have massive beams, showing rough ax and adz marks, supporting the front floors. Across the rear of the house, facing east, is a third section of cellar. The rear cellar opens on the eastside at a lower ground level making it a partial cellar with full-size windows facing east. The cellar ceiling joists at the rear of the house are smaller than the beams in either front section. In the rear are two large tarred-brick cisterns that once held rainwater channeled from the roof. The cellar floors are dirt with stones laid dry in the rear section.

The first floor front of the Persen house faces west, whereas many Dutch houses faced south. The ground floor front now has two rooms separated by a passage a dozen feet wide. The south room has been divided to create a service section and a bathroom. The massive stone wall of the original house remains between the new end of the south room and a kitchen to the rear of the house. The front part of the house has exposed ceiling beams equal in size to those in the cellar, and very wide original ceiling and floor boards (the floor in the northwest room has been replanked with narrower nineteenth-century boards). In the Dutch manner all ceiling boards are smoothed, and the exposed beams are finished with a bead. The hall that separates the front rooms opens into a rear center room, which has a door that now opens to a porch with steps to the lower ground level. The stairway, mantles, and woodwork all date from the nineteenth century. The upper level has a double-window dormer and a modernized room arrangement. Three very well made, massive Dutch doors with strap hinges remain: one at each end of the centered hall and the third at the side in the present kitchen. Clearly, the house has had three, possibly four, early expansions, and at least two other building periods, one in the nineteenth and another in the middle-twentieth century. What would be the proper period to select if the house were to be restored? The question hinges on the priorities: modern convenience or authenticity? The decision depends upon the objectives of the restorer.

The immediate surroundings of a Dutch house had many distinctive features: The back yard, or *in't state*, was a common feature. Side yards almost never appear in early illustrations of the Netherlands, but some early town houses had about two feet of eavesdrop along the sides. This was "an open space around the house, or *oysendrop*, for the eaves" to shed water.[100] Kitchens for large houses in the Netherlands were often separate buildings called the *achterhuis*, but New World practice limited the idea to separate summer-kitchen houses in rural areas.

Gardens, however, were popular both in the Netherlands and in America. In an article entitled "Dutch Gardens in the Hudson Valley," Ruth Johnson Piwonka writes that in the sixteenth century the Dutch "became Europe's finest horticulturists, and flowers soon came to be known as a characteristic of Dutch gardens." She says that the use of flowers for window gardening and as interior decoration originated in Holland."[101] In *A History of Garden Art*, Marie Luise Gothein states that "there can be no doubt that at the turn of the seventeenth century the standard in Dutch garden art was astonishingly high."[102] Gothein quotes a seventeenth-century traveler's observation that "the love of a garden prevails everywhere, and much money is spent on it. Everybody who can possibly manage it, owns a garden nearer or farther from the town, where he lives with his family from Saturday to Monday."[103] This is in accord with the "Bowery" retreat bought in 1661 for Peter Stuyvesant in the country north of the city of New Amsterdam at present day Third Avenue and Tenth Streets in Manhattan, a short distance from his town house near Pearl Street. An illustration of Stuyvesant's Bowery Mansion in *de Halve Maen* shows a house set in a miniature formal garden in the taste of the late seventeenth century.[104]

There were many books about farming and gardening available to horticulturists, and in 1668 the most important and widely read Dutch works on gardening was published: Van der Groen's *Den nederlandischen Howenier*. It was translated into French and German and widely studied because of its many useful hints to gardeners. "Its two hundred plans of partierres show plainly . . .how very strongly inclined the Dutch taste is towards what is simple and small, even pretty."[105] Space limitations in the Netherlands put an emphasis on compact plantings. Since even the great garden's "merits were more applicable to small scale than large places," Dutch garden methodology was readily applicable to middle class circumstances.[106] "Among the Dutch techniques, one of the best known was trimming and training evergreens, usually box or yew, into fanciful shapes, presuming to create variety of interest on a small area of ground . . .along with proliferation of tulips and the simplifying of ornate French parterre designs into tighter forms." The tulip had been introduced to the Netherlands in the late sixteenth century and was immediately regarded as a desirable object. The bulbs were rare and costly, but they were an investment that could safely be buried in the garden during the troublesome period of the war of independence from Spain. Interest in the tulips fueled speculation in the development of new bulbs, so the price of even a single rare bulb soared. Speculation turned into frenzy as the bulbs rapidly changed hands. In 1637 the saturation point was reached and an economic crash ended "tulipomania" causing a financial shock to those Dutch who had invested heavily in the bulbs. But the flowers remained that still makes the Netherlands the flower capital of the world. [107]

The accession of William and Mary to the English throne made the Dutch style of gardening fashionable in England and *a la mode* in the colonies beyond the Hudson Valley. Queen Mary remodeled Hampton Court Palace and grounds: "The fish-pond and gardens were laid out in the formal Dutch taste, with fountains, clipped trees, hedges, avenues, geometrical beds, an orangery and an aviary of tropical birds."[108] The Dutch garden spread beyond the Dutch settlers' descendants to their Anglo-American neighbors by way of England and an Anglo-Dutch court. Ruth Piwonka observes, "the Hollanders, who loved the out-of-doors, enjoyed vine-covered summerhouses and ate their meals outdoors" in a separate building, called the *tuinhuis* or *speelhuis,* used as a summer dining room. Statuary, of allegorical figures such as "Fame"—an angel with a trumpet—and sundials were favored center pieces. Colored garden globes, shells, stones, and pottery arranged symmetrically were also in demand and soon decorated Dutch gardens on both sides of the Atlantic.[109]

Sharing the garden space, but at a discreet remove, was the toilet or *secreten*. In the show catalog "People at Work: Seventeenth Century Dutch Art" presented by Hofstra University from April 17 to June 15, 1988, it is noted that "the Dutch, almost compulsive about cleanliness, expressed a ribald attitude toward human excrement and urine in some works of art."[110] Close closets, stools, and chamber pots were the amenities for both rich and poor. Jan Both and Hendrick Bary were artists who touched upon the subject. Bary's *Old Woman Emptying a Chamber Pot,* also known as "Sleazy Bessie" (Goore Besje), depicts an everyday activity prior to modern plumbing. Probably few, if any, Dutch outhouses have survived, however, into the 1950s outhouses were still found at many rural homes in the Hudson Valley. Even today many privies remain as "collectibles" or standbys in case of a power or plumbing failure today.

Unfortunately the cultural heritage continues to slip away. In Bergen County, New Jersey, ten Dutch houses have been lost in the last decade. According to Timothy D. Adriance—who records the fate of early buildings in his area—there are only 240 early Dutch stone homes remaining in Bergen County.[111] A similar fate has befallen many of the early homes throughout the Hudson Valley. Kenneth L. Hoadley, Amenia Historical Society Historian, reports on the Hendrick Wenecker, or "Winegar," house in Amenia Union that was built in 1763: "It is now beyond repair, in danger of collapse (back wall gone already, front going) and there seems no way of saving it." The loss was not for want of trying to save the building. In 1972 renovation was begun, but in 1978 "the historical society announced the discontinuation of the project after four years work" for want of sufficient funds to finish the job.

Beyond Dutch Thresholds.

Photographs and drawings by the author unless otherwise noted.

Above: Two sides of a Dutch door from New York State.

Left: Interior of the door showing four strap hinges, two bolts (cigar type on upper and long handled on lower), and two latches (incorrectly the hardware has been painted black).
Right: Exterior of the door showing crude peak hole with bull's eye glass and *peerring* grip (*Peerrings* are pear shaped, and *trekrings* are round) on latch on upper half. Both courtesy of G. Huber.

Facing page: Four variations on a front door theme.

Top left: Dutch front entrance door at the De Wint House, Tappan, New York, 1700. Four-light transom, full complement of hardware: strap hinges, latches and bolts. Note the wear on upper half of the door by knocker latch mechanism. Hardware incorrectly in black.
Top right: Early door from the Donald Carpentier collection that someone saw fit to splice into a one-piece unit.
Bottom left: Entry door with five transom lights from the Broadhead House, Rosendale, New York.
Bottom right: Entry door to the Davis Tavern, Stone Ridge, 1680. Courtesy of R. H. Blackburn.

Three interior doors.
Left: Edge of simple board-and-batten door (the cross brace shown adjacent to the hinge, the hinge set on the pintle). Gidney House, Newburgh, New York, early eighteenth century. *Middle:* Interior door from Gidney house. *Right:* Cellar storeroom door from Donald Carpentier collection complete with frame.

BEPLANKINGEN

A

HALFHOUTSE OVERDEKKING

B

AANSLUITING MET LOSSE VEER

C

AANSLUITING MET MESSING EN GROEF

Three wood joins used in wall panels and floors: A. Rabbet or *halfhoutse overdekking.* B. Spline or *aansluiting met losse vee.r.* C. Tongue in groove or *aansluiting met messing en groef.*

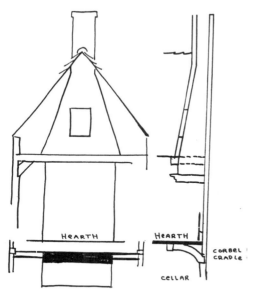

The Dutch jambless fireplace. The fire still stands into the room on a open hearth, unlike an English fireplace with side walls that contained the fire. Most of the heat and smoke managed to exit via the chimney. A small cloth was hung from the fireplace molding to assist in guiding the smoke to the flue, probably a cloth was used because a wooden panel would have been a constant danger to the heads of people working at the hearth. Naturally the cloths smutted quickly, and conscientious housewifes changed the dirty clothes frequently as a matter of pride. The smoke rose to a smoke hood or a smoke chamber at the garret level that was accessible so the smoke could be used to cure meatbefore it exited the chimney. Standing inside a Dutch fireplace and looking up reveals a section of sky, giving credence to the story of Black Peter, the sooty chimney sweep boy who served as the Dutch Santa's helper, coming down the chimney. At the rear of the fire, set before the wall, is a cast iron plate, called a fireback, similar in size and shape to a gravestone. The function of the plate was to deflect heat away from the masonry and protect the wall.

Originally fires were set directly on the earthen floor in the middle of the room like the one in a Dutch farmhouse at the Arnhem Open Air Museum above. Eventually smoke found its way out a draft hole in the roof eventually. The only advantage was unintended as the fumigating smoke discouraged the universally present vermin.

DUTCH CAST IRON FIREBACK

In the cellar the fireplace was supported by arches in masonry (a fireplace-appearing structure) or a cradle for stones and clay. *Facing page, clockwise from upper left:* Jambless hearth support in basement of the Broadhead House in Ulster County, New York (the structure looks somewhat like a hearth, but there is no flue). Jambless hearth support in a home in Rockland County, New York (this arch support is much like the examples in the diagrams of the houses in the Netherlands shown in Chapter Five). Courtesy of G. Huber. Jambless fireplace support in a New Jersey house. The wooden cradle is braced between the basement stone wall and a floor joist and is filled with clay and stones. Courtesy of G. Huber. Jambless fireplace support in a New Jersey house. The wooden cradle is packed with clay. Courtesy of G. Huber. Basement fireplace in the Gidney House, Newburgh, New York, early eighteenth century.

Above the Dutch jambless fireplace was a hood and molding. *Clockwise from upper left:* Jambless fireplace smoke valence attached to hearth at the Jean Hasbrouck House, New Paltz, New York. Courtesy of G. Huber. Fireplace in Amsterdam showing a modern stove placed under the hood as more efficient heating source than open fire (this adaptation leaves the original hearth undisturbed). Small later Dutch jambless fireplace at the Zuiderzee Museum, Enkhuizen, the Nertherlands. The early fireplaces in America would never have been set between windows, note very low mantle hood and smoke chamber. Tiled back is typical of Netherlands, but not of American, hearths; an iron fireback protects the tiles. House at the Zuiderzee Museum, Enkhuizen, Netherlands. Restored fireplace cornice molding at Broadhead House, Rosendale, New York. Jambless fireplace hood with unique cornice adapted for a stovepipe in unidentified house. Courtesy of G. Huber.

Above: Dutch fireplace at the Jean Hasbrouck House, New Paltz, New York, 1712. Fireback and cloth valance in place. A collection of iron pots, Dutch ovens, warming pans, and fire tools stand ready. The mantle provides a place to show china; the molding closely resembled the crown molding on the Dutch linen cabinet called a *Kas.*

Left: Fireplace as shown at the Jan Martense Schenck House as restored in the Brooklyn Museum.
Both courtesy of the Brooklyn Museum.

English-style fireplaces were employed after the middle of the eighteenth century in American Dutch houses, either as original installations or as conversions of earlier jambless hearths. Two English-style units found in Dutch houses. *Top:* Guyon-Lake-Tysen House, Historic Richmond Town Restoration, Staten Island, New York. This kitchen fireplace looks very much like examples of the second half of the eighteenth century in Quebec. Note oven door to side and built-in *pottebank* china shelves. *Above:* Guyon-Lake-Tysen House fireplace showing blue and white replacement tiles. The mantle was built without a shelf as was the rule in the early eighteenth century. Note the 45-degree angle and then the 90-degree angle of the wall within the fireplace—typical of the mid-eighteenth century. Courtesy of W. McMillen.

The exterior walls of fireplaces show as masonry in wooden houses.

Above: Rear wall of hearth at the Britton Cottage, Historic Richmond Town Restoration, Staten Island, New York, circa 1680-1750. Oven emerges from wall, normally roofed over to protect from the elements.

Left: Britton Cottage, section circa 1755, fireplace wall exposed in weatherboard siding. Courtesy of W. McMillen.

Top: Dutch tile depicting a youth fishing. Ideally a fireplace would have all tiles on a single theme, unless constraints limited the availablity to an odd lot. Courtesy of the Nassau County Museum, Long Island Studies Institute, Hofstra University Research Library. Theme tile fireplaces (*clockwise from above*): Mydert Mynderse House (restoration of early English polychrome tiles on theme of birds and flowers. DeWint House, Tappan, New York. Restoration of purple and white Biblical series tiles. Myndert Mynderse House, Saugerties, New York. Restoration of blue and white children's games tiles.

Early Dutch stairways were rarely grand, were usually turned or, in the Netherlands, spiral, and were frequently enclosed in both small and large houses well into the eighteenth century. *Clockwise from top left:* Basic cellar steps from the seventeeth century Broadhead House, Rosendale, New York. Last two turns in cellar steps in Gidney House (these steps are built against an outcrop of rock and the early center-fireplace English-style foundation). Two views of Davis Tavern, Stone Ridge, New York (seventeenth-century enclosed Dutch stairway built into a room corner with a turn over door to cellar steps).

Even the homes of more affluent Netherland merchants used enclosed and spiral stairways in the seventeenth century. *Top and above left:* Three stairways from the Amstel Kring Museum, Amsterdam. *Above right:* Stairway at Bloemgracht 91 in Amsterdam, restoration of mid-seventeenth century flight built in a spiral around a post. Note the rope used as interior banister and rail with wainscot on exterior.

Above left: Open stairway at Ariaantje Coeymans House, Coeymans, New York, 1716. Note massive turnings and members of both balustrades and newel posts. Courtesy of R. H. Blackburn.

Above right: Open stairway in the Luykas Van Alen House, Kinderhook, New York, 1736. Turned balusters and newel post are similar to Coeymans' but less massive. Reconstruction: The stairway is original, but it is from the Van Briese house , not the Van Alen house.

Left: Indoor toilet in white tile, Amstel Kring Museum, Amsterdam, seventeenth century.

Beds were frequently built into the walls in practically any room of Netherland houses.

Above left: Built-in bed in reception room at the Amstel Kring Museum, Amsterdam, seventeenth century. The house has marble floors and walnut woodwork of cabinet quality, yet a bed is built into a quite grand public space.

Top right: Bed at rear in cottage at Arnhem Open Air Museum—a multipurpose use of the space with table and spinning wheel. Similar ladder-back chairs were seen in the Hudson Valley.

Right: Bed at farmhouse at Arnhem Open Air Museum—fire on the floor and cows in the adjacent section of the dwelling. Bedsteads or *niet roken* were short, people slept in a seated position. Similar beds are to be seen in Usant off the coast of Brittany, in Denmark, and in other areas of the English Channel-North Sea culture zone.

South room at the Jan Martense Schenck House, circa 1675, showing the restored stair and ladder-back chair and a table with lathe-turned legs. Note that the floors are smooth but unfinished wood that was scoured and then strewn with sand weekly to maintain its whiteness. Courtesy the Brooklyn Museum Department of Decorative Arts.

CHAPTER VII

Interior Decor

THE DUTCH COLONIAL PERIOD ended in 1664 during the reign of England's Charles II. The colonies of New Jersey and New York were carved out of New Netherland by the new proprietor, the King's brother James, Duke of Albany and of York. New Jersey was sold to two speculators, whereas New York became the personal holding of the Duke and was governed by his appointed representative. However, aside from three brief periods of hostility during Anglo-Dutch wars (1652-1654, 1665-1667, and 1673-1675), the two leading Protestant powers of Europe enjoyed a close material and cultural relationship. Politically, the two countries had cooperated since the reign of England's Elizabeth I, when William the Silent, Prince of Orange, and his son Maurice of Nassau led the Dutch revolt against the Spanish overlords of the Low Countries. The relationship continued, despite trade rivalry, through both the Cromwellian Republic and the Restoration. Following the Glorious Revolution in 1688, and the expulsion of James II (the former Duke of York), the dethroned monarch's daughter, Mary Stuart, and her husband the

Dutch prince, William of Orange, came to the English throne. They reigned in a dual monarchy as England's King William III and Queen Mary II. The two nations were brought closer in cultural harmony though it was not always a happy political union. William outlived his queen, who died in 1694, and he ruled the two counties until his death in 1702. Since William and Mary were childless, her sister, Anne Stuart, became queen and ruled until 1714. But she and her husband, Prince Frederick of Denmark, had no living children, so the English Crown followed the Protestant line of succession to the German Electors and Princes of Hanover, who ascended to the throne of Great Britain. Thereafter German Hanoverians reigned as George I, II, and III through the end of the colonial period.

During the seventeenth and eighteenth century, Hudson Valley homes were furnished in fashions that many Americans in later years would tend to identify by English nomenclature. In twentieth century terms the styles are divided into the categories known as Jacobean, Cromwellian, Restoration, William and Mary ("which in Europe was an international style based on that of Dutch cabinet makers" and known as Dutch Baroque[1]), and Queen Anne. In America the "American Colonial" style that evolved was a provincial interpretation of English fashion derived from Dutch taste through the reign of Queen Anne. Though she only reigned for twelve years, the designs named after her remained current in America until the end of the colonial period. Provincial styles frequently lagged a generation or more behind the *mode* in Europe, but not exclusively because of isolation. Peter Thornton states in *Authentic Decor* that America was a major consumer of the latest in European fashions. He notes that physically moving goods and ideas across the Atlantic from London did not take much longer than moving them to the furthest parts of Britain; therefore, the major port cities of the East Coast were scarcely more provincial than Norwich, Exeter, York, Dublin, or Edinburgh. Thornton quotes Londoner Daniel Neal, who wrote in 1720 in his *History of New England* of the Bostonians that: "Their customs and manners are the same with the English . . . In the concerns of civil life, their dress, (dining) tables, and conversations, they affect to be as English as possible; there is no fashion in London but in three or four months is to be seen in Boston." [2] Thornton observes "much the same could no doubt be said of Philadelphia, Charleston, and Williamsburg."[3] New York had been the most polyglot city of North America from the start, however, up river in Albany most settlers lived in limited economic and social circumstances. Even many New York magnates tended to live more modestly than the social leaders in other colonies. Certainly the average settler was "provincial" and the Dutch *boeren* were even more culturally conservative in lifestyle. This conservatism, more than isolation, explains the persistence beyond the mid-eighteenth century of such distinctive cultural markers as the jambless fireplace, the built-in bedstead, and the medieval linen storage piece called a *kas.*

The interior appearance of settlers' homes evolved from the end of the Dutch administration to the birth of the American Republic. Hudson Valley Dutch material culture in the years before the American Revolution fell into three eras: First came the true Dutch colonial period from 1609 to 1664, beginning with frontier basics and gradually assuming a prosperous provincial replication of the Golden Age of the Dutch Republic. The second was a transitional period from 1664 to 1714, which was difficult politically and economically for many Dutch farmers, fur traders, and merchants, as they adjusted to a second-class role in their co-opted land. The final period from 1714 to 1776 saw Hudson Valley Dutch culture reach its full flowering in the middle years of the century. Material culture in colonial New York paralleled developments in the neighboring colonies and followed the European high-fashion trends, with a strong Dutch influence. [4]

As with house design, the best source of visual material for Dutch rooms in the seventeenth century are the *genre* painters, who recorded scenes of everyday life in the Netherlands. The *genre* pictures present middle-class homes in the Fatherland, not frontier dwellings along the banks of the Hudson. Nevertheless, they represent cultural models for settlers and their descendants, who had ventured from *Patria* to areas as diverse as South Africa, Indonesia, and the Mohawk Valley. The Schenck House brochure, written in the 1960s, notes that "no one knows just how furniture was arranged in a room of the seventeenth century. Even from contemporary Dutch paintings, which are so delightfully precise in every detail, it is impossible to discern the overall plan of an interior, so restorations inevitably have the mark of modern taste in the arrangement of the furniture."[5] However, our knowledge has increased in the past thirty years, so a more reasonably assured reconstruction is possible today. Roderic Blackburn points out that, based on old inventories, it is not only possible to identify items in many individual rooms but "even in some cases the order of their position around the room." While the inventories may not have specified which pieces were placed against the walls and which stood out in the room, we can get good ideas from paintings about room appearances.[6]

As a general rule, in the seventeenth and eighteenth centuries, furniture stood at the walls unless in use. When needed, individual pieces were drawn toward the room's center, then returned to place when no longer in use. Research by Peter Thornton for *Authentic Decor* and *Seventeenth Century Interior Decor* found that candles and candle stands were not generally left out unless in use. Furthermore, they concluded that only one or two candles were the most used at one time unless a special occasion called for an "illumination" and a grand show of light. Probated wills and household inventories identified an owner's house and belongings room-by-room and suggest that Dutch houses were more furnished and decorated than English houses in the eighteenth century. Combining the known contents with illustrations of occupied interiors provides an understanding of how the early settlers lived.

In 1974 Roderic Blackburn undertook the furnishing of the Luykas Van Alen house for the Columbia County Historical Society's Building Committee, a project related to his previous work in creating the Dutch Room display at the Albany Institute. He wrote: "To more accurately furnish the Van Alen house, a composite inventory was created, taken from about 15 inventories of Dutch houses, rural and urban in New York, primarily [from the period] 1700-1730."[7] The composite inventory lists the most frequently mentioned contents of a Dutch house of the period.

Such a project is similar to the Brooklyn Museum's recreation of both Schenck houses. One of the basic resources for this work was wills and inventories of people of Dutch ancestry in the colonial period.

Luykas Van Alen House: A Composite Inventory

Room	Furniture or Item	Quantity
Chamber		
(Fore, Great, or Back)	Bedstead with bedding	1
	Feather Bed	1
	Bolsters	1
	Pillows and Cases	2
	Blankets	4
	Bed Rugg (Cover)	1
	Sheets	4
	Set of Bed Curtains	1
	Valance	1
	Head Cloth	1
	Counterpane	1
	Tester Iron Rods and Bed Rings Set	1
	Small Oval and/or Square Table	
	with Table Carpets	2
	Chairs: Parts of sets in groups of two	
	or three each in leather, cane or matted.	
	Set of Side Chairs	16
	Elbow Chair	1
	Looking Glasses:	
	One Large or One Large and One Small	
	Kas/Cupboard	1
	or Chest of drawers	1
	Trunks or Coffers	1

Small Items: Fireplace equipment in brass or iron trimmed with brass: shovel and tongs and a set of andirons. A warming pan. A set of candlesticks in brass, pewter, or iron. Bible. Psalm books. Other book titles would include religious, history, and song books. Combs with cases. Money scale and weights. Clock. Baskets. Cane. Settle bed. A case and set of glasses. Earthenware, either yellow ware or delft, including cups and (perhaps) saucers. Dishes. Pewter: plates, dishes, tankard. Silver (in a wealthy house): Spoons, tankards, beaker, cup, tumbler, salt, mustard pot, buttons.

Art: Portraits. Scripture paintings. Large and small oil and watercolor paintings, and prints under glass.

Kitchen	(Not enumerated,		
	but essential)	Large Table	1
		small tables	2
		Set of Chairs, Cane or rush ladder back style	16
		(specifically required items)	

Pewter: a dozen plates and dishes, basin, porringers and spoons, quart and pint bottles, tankard. Iron: cooking equipment including hooks and pots, pot chains and trammels, frying pans, drip pan, ladle, smoothing and branding irons. Brass: kettles and pots, sauce pans, pot covers, mortar and pestle, warming pan, ladle, chafing dish. Wood: bowls and platters, (unenumerated: buckets). Glass: Wine glasses and bottles in cases. Tin: pans and pots, funnel. Copper: kettle. Brass, iron, or pewter: pair of candlesticks, brass pail with iron hoops, strainers, knives and forks. Baskets. Lanthorn, milk vessels, butter and soap tubs (wood), flax and wool wheels.

Garret	Bed, casks, trunks, miscellaneous old furniture	
Cellar	Bushels of salt, lumber [8]	

In an article in *de Halve Maen*, Joseph W. Hammond noted the will of Jonas Bronck, whose estate inventory was taken on May 6, 1643. Hammond says that the house contained a wealth of consumer goods that:

> included eleven pictures, a rapier with silver mounting, clothing of satin and damask, alabaster saucers, four tankards with silver chains, silver flat and hollow wares, looking glasses, and other objects not associated with frontier living or subsistence farming. . .[including a]. . .library of some fifty-six titles which included works on Lutheran and Calvinist theology, medicine, law and geography written in Danish, Dutch, Latin and German."[9]

The DeWint House published the inventory of John DeWint "taken and made in the presence of and by direction of Fredericus Blauvelt & John Smith near kinsmen of the said John DeWint deceased" on August 22, 1796, a late but relevant record. The house had a kitchen, two ground-floor rooms, and two upper chambers by the 1790s. The following inventory only partially lists his possessions, and while it did not specify the location of items in the house, it does describe the contents of a small but prosperous household.

Three slaves were listed by name: Jack, Cesar, and Tone. In addition, there was farm equipment, nine head of cattle, four horses, an "old" farm wagon, parts of a small horse drawn carriage known as a *chaise*. Odds and ends of iron and tin in bulk lots were enumerated, also.

The division of public rooms and private bedchambers was a late eighteenth-century development. Instead rooms were identified by their main function or by location, as the "first room," a "room over the parlour," or "north room." In a town house with a shop, the ground-floor front was reserved for business; even grand country houses were known to have used a room for commercial purposes, as at the Wynkoop-Lounsbery house in Marbletown. Designations of "living room" and "dining room" came in the nineteenth century and therefore present-day real estate terminology and preconceptions based upon current practices can be very misleading in terms of original usage. Many early colonial families did all their living in one or two rooms. Frequently only the ground-floor rooms were finished in houses with two floors. Sometimes only a ladder originally ac-

---

Inventory of John DeWint

Furniture or Item: Three mahogany tables, two mahogany chairs and a mahagony desk. Three bedsteads with pillows, bolster, mattress and feather bed, blanket rugs and counterpanes, and a suite of window and bed curtains. A close stool and two looking glasses, two other tables and three more chairs complete the large items enumerated.

Small Items: One pair brass andirons. One pair iron andirons. Three cases with flasks. A lead box & a shaving kit box. A large trunk. Two (fire) screens. One carpet. Two artificial pineapples. One pair brass candle sticks. One pair scales & weights; three weights: 28, 14, 7#; lead weights. One Cruet Stand. Pewter: One basson & one dish, two pewter dishes, 15 pewter plates. Silver: Two silver salt cellars @ 8/6 an ounce, eleven table spoons @ 8/6 an ounce, six tea spoons @ 8/6 an ounce: 2-3/4 ounces, one silver tankard: 44 ounces, one soup ladle: 6 1/2 ounces. China: One decanter; three bowls; five china plates, five china plates, "some china pots" and plates, two china pots. Glass: two lots of glass.

Art: Two pictures, a batch of five pictures, batch of four pictures

Books: Pictet's works in Dutch: Three Volumes (of a possible four religious tract titles in Dutch by this Calvinist author); the balance of the extensive library is listed untitled as two Dutch books; three lots of Dutch books; four lots "old" books; another two books; and two additional lots of books.

Miscellaneous Items: An old wine pipe (a container and unit of measure equal to two hogsheads, one hogshead contains 63 U. S. gallons, or variously measured up to 140 gallons). An old Barrel (31 gallons fermented beverage). One Hogshead. Three old pails. Three iron pots. One frying pan. Two pair waffle irons. One lot of baskets. Decanters. One coffee mill. One skimmer. One iron tea kettle. Three candle molds. Three smoothing irons. One hair sieve. Two apple roasters. Two patty pans. Two augers. One grid iron. One lanthorne. One spit. Three pot hooks or trammels. One candle stick and a block. One fine hatchet. Six pewter plates. Two tongs & shovels. One chisel. One knife case. One watering pot. Three "keelers" (red ocher crayons for marking lines on lumber). The house inventory also mentions a "wind mill" which possibly is a reference to a device that was placed in a chimney and used to circulate air in the warm weather.[10]

---

cessed the upper level. What we might consider a "living room" or a "dining room" was typically a room that combined both functions. Singleton noted that "till comparatively late in the Seventeenth Century, the hall of even wealthy settlers contained a bed as well as dining-room and sitting-room furniture."[11] Warren Johnson said in 1760-61 that "a Dutch Parlor has always a bed in it. & the man & woman of the House Sleep in it. their Beds are good, for they Mind noe other Furniture."[12] Public rooms in Dutch homes contained beds until late in the century. The *groot kamer*, or great room, did not become known as a "parlor" until later. Rural Dutch family members' chambers (the word usually refers to rooms used as bed-sitting rooms) were not commonly placed on the second floor until after the Revolutionary War.

The large homes and town houses of the Dutch had an entry room called the *voorhuis vant grout hus.* The front room was called the *voorhuis,* or fore room, and "the *voorhuis* in New Amsterdam corresponded with the hall in New England and the Southern States."[13] The generic Dutch term for room was *kamer.* Small and early homes seldom dedicated an entire room to the single purpose of a private sleeping area, but many rooms did have special designations. In some houses there was a living room or side room called a *zijkamer.* An example of a *zikamer* was identified in a house built in 1642 for Jan Teunissen. It was described in *New World Dutch Studies* by Henk J. Zantkuyl.[14] The inner room in early Netherlander homes was first called the *binnenhaard* and later the *binnenkamer,* or inner room, which was often a family room and was the location of the fireplace. When this room was also the kitchen, it was called the *keuken.* As in most other early settlers' homes, Roderic Blackburn observes that "kitchens were the most important spaces in Dutch houses. Sometimes this single space was used not only for food preparation, but also as living and working quarters for all other household activities."[15] An *Op solder* was a garret. If it served as a warehouse, it was called a *pakhuis.* An extension to a house might be a side gallery, or a *uytlaet,* as shown on a house built by Juriaen Hendricksen for Adriaen Dircksen Coen in 1649.[16]

The Netherlander practice of using a room exclusively for show and rare occasions was reflected in Dutch-American inventories. If a family were affluent, they might aspire to a *pronkkamer,* or showroom for displaying household wealth, which was a significant aspect of Dutch culture.[17] Most valley Dutch families settled for a *groot kamer,* or great chamber, which did not describe the size so much as the best room in the house, a room intended for hospitality.[18] "Beginning in the third quarter of the eighteenth century the name *groot kamer* was replaced with 'parlour.'. . [But] less pretentious householders—specially in rural areas—retained the custom of the *groot kamer* long past the turn of the nineteenth century."[19] In the restoration of the Jan Martense Schenck house from about 1730 at the Brooklyn Museum, the two rooms are restored as a *keuken* with *bedsteden* and a *groot kamer.*

David Baker, an Ulster County historian, reports that a few years ago an elderly woman at a Hurley Open House Day told him that as a young girl she had lived in the church Parsonage House built in 1790. She remembered that the house only had a ladder from the front hall to the upstairs; the stairs were a twentieth-century addition. Quarters for children were frequently located in the loft level in early houses, as in the Parsonage and the Shuart-Van Orden houses in Ulster County, where the attic floor of the main house was left unfinished and unpartitioned.[20] The garret area often served as the weaving-and-spinning room as well. And under the tall roof of a Dutch house in many instances there was an upper garret (sometimes now referred to by the English name "cockloft") that provided additional storage. The merchant used his garret as a warehouse, while the farmer stored household goods and wheat in the space. Into the early years of the new American Republic a few Dutch houses' upper levels remained storage garrets equipped with a beam and pulley and reached from within by stairway or ladder.[21] With a block and tackle from an exterior beam, heavy burdens could reach the attic more easily than by negotiating steep stairways. The feature can be seen on the Van Schaick house, Cohoes, and the Henrick Van Wie house in Bethlehem. Even on the large and later Wynkoop-Lounsbery house in Stone Ridge the gable end of the house has a now-closed garret door and two recently restored shuttered openings.

Cellars were usually for storing potatoes, beets, apples, and other goods preserved by the cool air although some cellars had kitchens. The Shuart-Van Orden house in Plattekill still has a large cellar kitchen with a massive English-style cooking fireplace and a storage room with the original Dutch hanging racks for provisions. The Wynkoop-Lounsbery house has similar arrangements along with an area with a barrier wall of wooden bars to protect stored goods against theft. An identical cellar with wine casks and stored valuables may be seen in the Margareth de Ruyter's doll house from about 1675 at the Rijks-Museum in Amsterdam.[22] The Shuart-Van Orden and the Wynkoop-Lounsbery houses still have their original cellar stairs as well as exterior doorways to ground level. Many Dutch homes only had outside steps to the cellar.

The most common Dutch interior furnishings in the seventeenth century are best "seen in the innumerable pictures of that day" notes Eshter Singleton.[23] In an article in *de Halve Maen* Lawrence D. Geller states:

> Seventeenth-century Dutch art seems to outstrip most eras in terms of social relevance. As the art historian, Barbara Rose, remarks in her book, *The Golden Age of Dutch Painting* that "in the 17th century there was not art for art's sake as there is today. Art was considered to have specific social, political and economic purposes." Then and now, it should be noted, both the style and subject-matter of the genre painter derive from the realistic re-creation of scenes from everyday life.[24]

Geller traced the origins of a surviving Pilgrim cradle used by Perigrine White (who was born on the *Mayflower* in 1620 at Provincetown Harbor) to cradles in several Dutch *genre* paintings of the seventeenth century. The methodology is sound. The approach is applicable when considering most aspects of Dutch house finish and decor.

Two types of homes commonly appeared in the pictures. One type is of quaint rural peasant houses, which were typically depicted as disorderly shambles, as in Adrien van Ostades *Peasants in an Interior* from 1661. The other types are refined and elegant middle class houses, which were usually clean and serene, as seen in Johannes Vermeer's *Music Lesson* from 1660. Generally, seventeenth-century Netherlands is depicted as an idealized land of middle-class comfort and security. Homes were spacious, but rarely palatial, and even the smaller homes offered both shelter as well as some material comfort. Netherlands' paintings suggest confirmation of New World inventories and wills in regard to interiors and furnishings.

The paintings of the period offer a wealth of detail. Scenes of domestic life show multiple-function rooms. People sew, play music, and entertain in the same room, often with built-in or free standing beds. Gesina Terborch's sketch of her family at home in *A Dutch Bedchamber* shows a room used for sleeping, writing, and childcare. It has a ceiling of unpainted joists and planks, and a bleached bare-wood floor. A map hangs on the rear wall, and a bed with hangings stands in a corner. A table with a red cloth fringed with gold stands in the center of the room, indicating that not all furniture was pushed to the walls, especially not massive draw tables. A row of chairs all covered to match are lined against the rear wall. A child's wicker crib and a chamber pot flank a thin unpainted batten door. A room crowded with activity and people is the setting in Jan Steen's *The Life of Man*: A bed occupies one side of the room next to a hearth, a table across the room has an oriental carpet and a linen cover. The room is filled with musicians, diners, and game players. The tiled floor is littered with food, hats, and flowers. The casement windows are uncurtained, and a shutter is half closed. In Steen's *The Feast of Saint Nicholas,* another room with a bed is filled with activity, ranging from children peering up the jambless chimney flue to the good girl with her doll and the bad boy crying at the sight of a whip. The floor has gray and white tiles and the leaded windows are shuttered at the bottom and unshuttered above. Even in non-*genre* paintings, such as Rembrandt's *The Holy Family with Painted Frame and Curtain*, the rooms have social activity in the foreground and beds in the background.

Jacob Ochtervelt's *A Dutch Lady Dressing* shows a room with a bed curtained in a rich green material, while a matching cover drapes over a large table. The wall has a large map hanging beside a door and an over door framed portrait painting. The floor of scrubbed wooded planks is bare. To the rear, a room appears through the doorway where large windows with leaded casements are hung with simple white curtains. Scattered about the chamber are a silver ewer and tray, books, and writing equipment. In Cornelis de Vos' *Portrait of Antoine Renniers and his Wife* from about 1635, another room is filled with multiple activities. In the painting people dine at an overflowing table covered with a carpet and a linen cloth, a side table is laden with additional viands, at the jambless fireplace a group huddles close to the flames, and nearby a trio plays musical instruments. The room is filled with art: paintings, *objets*, and sculpture. But the floor has bare boards with only a hearth of red and black tiles and the gothic leaded casement windows are shuttered but without hangings.

The seventeenth and eighteenth centuries were different from our own in terms of such basic technologies as artificial light. The

paintings stress the importance of daylight. Women work seated
outside in full daylight in Adriaen van Ostade's 1673 painting *The
Cottage Dooryard and* Isaack van Ostade's 1648 picture *Rest by a
Cottage.* In Gerard Ter Borch's *The Family of the Stone Grinder* a
mother delouses her daughter's hair at the entry to their hovel. Just
within the threshold of an open doorway offered the most direct
sunlight for working indoors as depicted by Cornelis Bisschop in
Woman Peeling Apples. Frequently, people sit elevated at open windows in the direct sunlight on a small wooden platform called a
soldertiev; the *soldertiev* served to stave off the chill damp floor and
offer a better view of the street. In Gabriel Metsu's *Lady Reading a
Letter with her Maidservant,* an unpainted pine, or deal, platform
several inches high and perhaps three by five feet in area sits next to
a leaded casement. Another woman occupies a similar platform in
Dirck Hals' *Seated Woman with a Letter* from 1633. A platform
appears in the background holding a ladder-back chair with a woven
rush seat and pump pillow in Pieter de Hooche's *The Pantry.* In
another example, a chair with a plump pillow, or squab, stands on a
mat (rather than a platform) beside a window and open door in *A
Boy Bringing Pomegranates* by Pieter de Hooch. The platforms appear
in taverns as well; one is depicted where light fills a window over the
shoulder of a peasant in Adriaen Brouwer's *The Smokers* of 1627-1630.

Sometimes the importance of natural daylight is seen in the
simplest actions, as when a woman stands before a pier glass bathed
in light in Vermeer's *Woman with a Pearl Necklace.* In other situations, people use a window to light a table for a meal, as in Adriaen
van Ostade's *Interior of a Peasant's Cottage* from 1668, Jan Steen's
Prayer before the Meal from 1660, and Gerad Dou's *Woman Eating
Porridge.* Pieter de Hooch depicts a *Woman Drinking with Two Men
and a Maidservant* and a *Woman Drinking with Soldiers* at tables set
before large windows. In the paintings *Lady at the Virginals with a
Gentleman* by Johannes Vermeer, *Interior with a Woman at a Clavichord* by Emanuel de Witte, *Elegant Couple in an Interior* by Jan
Verkolje, and *Family Group in an Interior* by Cornelis Troost from
about 1739, all the musical instruments where set so sunlight would
fall upon the keyboards.[25] A *Woman Nursing an Infant, with a Child*

Feeding a Dog by Pieter de Hooch is also set before a window's light. *Interior with a Woman at a Spinning Wheel*, 1661, by Esaias Boursse, *The Account Keeper (The Housekeeper)*, which depicts a woman entering on a ledger, 1656, by Nicholaes Maes, *Man Writing in an Artist's Studio* and a *Girl Chopping Onion by* Gerad Dou all place the action before a window with bright light streaming through the panes. Quirijn van Brekelenkam's *Interior of a Tailor's Shop*, 1665, shows the tailor and two apprentices sitting on a platform. Even a surgeon operates by window light in Isaack Koedijck's *The Foot Operation*, just as a blacksmith labors in a stream of light entering the *Interior of a Smithy* by Gabriel Metsu. In addition, *Authentic Decor,* by Peter Thornton, includes numerous illustrations dating well into the nineteenth century that reveal the importance of daylight for routine activities.[26] We tend to forget the importance of natural light to people in the past, yet many days activities were circumscribed by the available natural light.

When an action takes place at night, the artificial lighting is woefully inadequate by our standards. "It is difficult for us to conceive how little light there normally was in a seventeenth-century house after dark . . . When a large number of candles was lit for some special occasion, it was invariably remarked upon with wonder and delight. For the rest of the time, lights were conserved and life was lived as far as possible in the daylight hours."[27] Outdoors, people used primitive pitch pine torches, which contained a flammable resin, and were known as "candle wood" or "light wood," but a torch was risky indoors. The light of the fire on the hearth was frequently the only night illumination for many households. Willem Duyster illustrates the situation in his painting *Soldiers besides a Fireplace* from 1628-1632, where three men literally sit under the jambless hood in order to see in the darkened room. In Gerard Dou's *Astronomer by Candlelight,* the man holds a candle to read as he refers to his globe in an otherwise pitch dark space. Godfried Schalcken's *Young Girl Eating Oranges by Candlelight* shows a figure sitting at a table with a single candle in a gloom-enshrouded room. In Judith Leyster's painting known as *The Proposition* a woman attempts to concentrate upon her sewing by the light of a single candle while an importuning man, with a handful of coins, is apparently inspired to other activities by the dim light.

The artists show that any nighttime activity occurred within a tiny circle of light from the fewest possible candles. "Candles do not burn steadily either; they moved and pulsed, and what they illuminated seemed to come alive in a manner quite unknown to generations familiar only with the unwinking stare of the electric-light bulb."[28] *In the Cabinet de Brye*, 1665, by Gerad Dou, people in the foreground read and write on a chalk board, while a second group huddles around a dot of light in the background of an otherwise dark interior. In *The Gay Cavaliers* by Judith Leyster, two young men revel by the flicker of the tiniest of candles. In the elegant Parisian society of 1720 the situation was little better. In a painting by Pierre-Louis Dumesnil the Younger, seven candles and a flicking hearth illuminate a spacious *salle*, where an elegant company plays cards in the gloom. Even the goddess *Psyche* is enfolded in the darkness of night in a painting by Simon Voulet, from about 1625; only a flicker of lamp light allows her to engage in a naughty peek at the nude Cupid sleeping on a canopied bed.

The simplest lamps were rushlights with wicks of woven grasses soaked in rendered animal fat from wild deer or bears on the frontier and later from sheep tallow or fish oil. These animal fats smoked and had such a strong odor that even our ancestors' undiscriminating senses were offended by the smell. Occasionally a *blekker*, a typical early lamp resembling oil lamps dating back to the ancient world, or a candlestick hung over the mantel.[29] The early lamps had a small reservoir for oil and a lip for a wick of twisted linen or grasses. The lamp was known among the English as a "betty lamp" (*bettyng* was an Old English word for oil or fat).

There were three principal types of candleholders. Candlesticks were usually placed on a flat surface, sconces were hung on the wall, and chandeliers were suspended from the ceiling. "The Dutch used a number of lighting fixtures: brass and copper chandeliers, silver and brass candlesticks, the *izer knaap*, which was a standing iron receptacle for candles decorated with a brass finial, and wooden stands in which rushes were clipped to their arms."[30] Table candlesticks were heavier in weight than chamber candlesticks, which had a handle and a saucer for wax drippings. In the middle years of the eighteenth century colonial designs "closely followed Queen Anne forms, reflecting the expressed preference of wealthy New Yorkers for silver 'in the latest London fashion' (although, in fact, New Yorkers were often as much as two decades behind trends in the mother country.)"[31] Early candlesticks had a high and wide drip pan, but as the seventeenth century progressed into the eighteenth century, improved candles required smaller and lower drip pans on candlesticks.

Candles made from fat produced a small flickering light and a lot of black smoke. They also dripped a residue of excess fat that pooled in the candlestick's drip pan or a glass *bobeche*. The wick needed constant trimming for maximum illumination. All this effort called for special scissors, wick trimmers, and candle snuffers. Because they needed so much attention, lights were usually set at a convenient height between table top and shoulder level. "Light from such a source was reflected more directly into the eye and thus revealed the fronts of objects (cabinets, vases, tables) rather than their top surfaces."[32] The low position of the light source and the flickering flame were reflected in gilt picture frames, brass andirons and furniture hardware, pier glasses and sconce mirrors in a way that altered the whole appearance of a room and the objects seemed relatively brighter than they would appear in brilliant electric light. [33]

There are two basic ways to make a candle: dipping and molding. In dipping, a linen wick was repeatedly immersed in melted tallow or wax. After each dip, the candle cooled for the new layer of wax to dry before repeating the process. Molded candles were made in pewter or sheet-iron forms shaped like a candle with a wick threaded through the center. Melted tallow was poured into the mold and the candle was removed after it had cooled and shrunk. Because of the cost and labor, candles were used sparingly. Peter Thornton notes that until the end of the eighteenth century neither candlesticks nor candles were left out during the day.[34] Candlesticks were stored, and candles were removed from sticks, sconces, and candelabrum. The candles were often stored in metal boxes, probably to keep them away from mice and rats. The fat used to make tallow candles and soap was identical. The processes were closely related and the same merchant often sold the two products. For example, a frequent advertiser,

Gilbert Ash, offered for sale both "hard Soap and Candles" on April 14, 1763, in *The New-York Gazette or the Weekly Post-Boy*.[35]

In *The Young Mother*, by Gerard Dou, a candelabrum is shown without candles in a sun-lit room. The same situation appears in Gerard Ter Borch's *Curiosity*, even though both pictures show a candle and candlestick. Candles were often placed in wall-mounted sconces and some were provided with mirrored or polished metal backs to magnify the light. When carried, candles were often held in "lanthornes" with thin horn or glass sides to shield the flame from drafts. Other candles stood where needed in candlesticks or suspended over a table in handsome brass chandeliers with arms to hold several candles and a decorative reflecting ball. A chandelier shown in a picture by Emanuel de Witte is suspended by a wire and hung low which "was normal throughout the seventeenth century."[36] Candleholders were very handsome as hardware but provided an inadequate source of night illumination. In the wealthier homes, bee's wax or bayberry candles were employed. An American export the bayberry -- which grows along the East Coast and makes pleasantly scented sage-green candles -- produced superior light with less smoke and mess. The merchant Gilbert Ash advertised on October 22, 1759, in *The New-York Mercury* that he sold hard soap, both brown and white, and had "barbary" (bayberry) wax mold candles.[37]

Several aspects of traditional Dutch colonial homes from the early years of settlement to after the establishment of the new republic are noteworthy: The well-ordered Dutch house was kept spotlessly clean, remarkably so for its time and for ours as well. Books were written about housekeeping, such as *De ervarene en verstandige Hollandsche huyshouldster* (*The Experienced and Knowledgeable Holland's Householder*). Householders were held to a high standard and cleanliness was related to the fundamental values of religion, the state, and an orderly life to such a degree that "travelers to the Netherlands frequently commented on what struck them as an unnatural obsession with cleanliness."[38]

Cleanliness stood for the redemptive ideals of restraint, simplicity, and humility. "The orderly house can thus be seen as a symbolic embodiment of the Dutch people for whom constant vigilance was required against defilement and destruction, whether the source [of danger] was the Spanish, the sea, or the devil."[39] Cleanliness was even a source of inspiration for the painters and many artists made the Dutch interest in household cleanliness a subject of *genre* art. Two examples of the theme from the 1660s can be seen in *Interior with a Woman Playing the Virginals*—where the maid works in the background—by Emanuel de Witte and in *A Dutch Interior*—where another maid labors in the foreground of the picture—by Pieter Janssens. An 1845 book by Jeptha Simms entitled *History of Schoharie County, and Border Wars of New York* makes special note of the cleanliness of the Dutch pioneer settler in the Schoharie valley:

> Twice a year, at least, Dr. Franklin's description of a house cleaning is realized, not only in the primitive Schoharie but also in the Mohawk settlements. Every article of furniture, from the garret to the cellar, is then removed, that the place it occupied may be *scrubbed.* Lime is profusely used on such occasions, especially in the Spring, and it would be difficult to detect the track of a fly on a window, wall, or floor, after the operation. The description given by *Brooks*, in his travels in Europe, of the neatness of the people in some of the Dutch and German countries through which he traveled, is applicable, in many instances, to the people of Schoharie: for as he says—'It is scrub, scrub, scrub from morning till night—where there is dirt, and where there is none.' The Schoharie women usually cleanse their floors daily, sometimes semi-daily, by a process they call *filing*, which is done with a piece of sacking retained in the hands instead of being secured to a mop-stick.[40]

Lorraine Whiting, of Charleston, New York, who is of Dutch descent remembers her "grandmother often talking of 'hand filing' her floors" in the middle twentieth century. In the same theme, Washington Irving's *A History of New York* describes the passion for cleanliness among the Dutch *vrouws*:

> The whole house was constantly in a state of inundation, under the discipline of mops and brooms and scrubbing brushes; and the good housewives of those days were a kind of amphibious animal, delighting exceedingly to be dabbling in water.
> The grand parlor was the sactum sactorum, where the passion for cleaning was indulged without control. In this sacred apart-

ment no one was permitted to enter excepting the mistress and her confidential maid, who visited it once a week for the purpose of giving it a thorough cleaning and putting things to rights—always taking the precaution of leaving their shoes at the door and entering devoutly on their stocking feet. After scrubbing the floor. . . the window shutters were again closed to keep out the flies, and the room carefully locked up until the revolution of time brought round the weekly cleaning day.41

"Some enthusiastic housekeepers—although wealthy—would not allow servants to clean their best rooms, but wielded 'the scrubbing-brush, rubbing towel and floor-cloth.' There are examples of houses where from thirty to forty pails of water a day were used every day, and where the servants did nothing but rub and scrub and scour from morning til night."42 Small wonder exhausted or sleeping maids' were a popular *genre* subject. Paintings such as Nicolaes Maes' *Interior with a Sleeping Maid and Her Mistress* illustrate a worn maid who dozes surrounded by pots and dishes to be cleaned. The mistress seems more bemused than angry, perhaps recognizing that her demands for cleanliness were exhausting. In the Netherlands it was noted that "if the city women keep their houses clean, the farmer's wives are not less particular. They carry this cleanliness even into the stables. They scour everything, even the iron chains and mounts until they shine like silver."43 The *vrouws* of the valley were no less diligent than their sisters in *Patria*. However, in vivid contrast to the well-ordered life were representations of rowdy scenes from the first half of the seventeenth century. These *genre* paintings show a middle-class view of a primal and raucous peasant world, as in Adriaen Brouwer's *Cardplayers Brawling* from about 1625 or Van Ostade's *Carousing Peasants* from 1638.

Observers, however, tended to accentuate the image of brightly-cleaned and polished houses in the Netherlands and the Hudson Valley. As Madam Sarah Kembel Knight observed in 1707 of New York Dutch houses: "the inside of them is neat to admiration; the wooden work. . .[is] planed and kept very white scour'd as so is all the partictions if made of Bords."44 Much of the woodwork was simply scrubbed to the natural pale grain, but furniture was waxed and polished to bring out the deep luster of rare woods. In *Dutch By Design,* the authors quote Adriaen van der Donck, who wrote in his

Description of New Netherland in 1655 that canoewood from the tulip poplar tree was used for the floors "because it is bright and free of knots."[45] Tulip wood was frequently made into spoon racks, painting panels, and other items calling for carved decoration because it is easily worked and does not readily split or splinter. Floors of oak, pine, or tulip poplar were left unfinished, as were beams and panels. After scrubbing, the floorboards were occasionally strewn with sand, which was swept into decorative patterns and swirls.[46]

Walls were whitewashed. Plaster walls were coated with lime-wash from an early date. In some instances, color was added to the whitewash for a blue, gray, ocher, or a pinkish hue. Roderic Blackburn notes that in the Jurriaan Sharp house in Rensselaer County "interior walls were painted a light blue-grey."[47] Henry Lionel Williams in *Old American Houses* remarks that when cleaning old woodwork "if you have the occasion to take down old painted board to the bare wood, you will often find that the first coat is a blue-gray and almost as hard as iron."[48] In his *Old American Houses: 1700-1850*, Williams says that in the colonial period blue-gray paint "appears to have been made of white lead (made by immersing sheet lead in chamber lye) [and] lampblack."[49] However, other recipes using lampblack or charcoal were common, because white lead was not generally available until later in the eighteenth century. At the Broadhead house, which dates from the seventeenth century, an early blue-gray interior paint remains in traces on joists and ceiling-board seams, but the first coat of paint may have been applied years after the house was built. Painted ceiling woodwork was more typical of the late eighteenth century, and blue only became a popular color in the Anglo-Dutch period. Williams says that blue was believed to discourage mosquitoes and flies, an important consideration in an era before screens, when manure was everywhere. However, Roderic Blackburn asserts that black flies are attracted to blue.[50] In addition to blue, the principal colors by the late eighteenth century were blue-gray, yellow ochre, white, and Venetian red, which was the most popular color. After baseboards were introduced in Anglo-Dutch homes in the eighteenth century, they were -- according to Williams in *Old American Houses* -- sometimes painted black or red so the woodwork would not show scuffing and general wear and tear.

Where paneling was installed in Anglo-Dutch homes, it sometimes "became stylish to use two tones in the same room, and often the molding and panels were finished in contrasting colors."[51] A vivid example can be seen in the Brooklyn Museum's yellow and brown paneling in the restoration of the Cupola house stair hall. The contrasting paint was originally used in the Wynkoop-Lounsbery house, where, H. W. Reynolds notes, the central-hall paneling was painted "in pink and blue." It is more likely that she saw woodwork of a faded salmon, which is the color of old oxidized red lead, and a blue-gray.[52]

In line with folk practice in Germany and Scandinavia, a few Dutch houses were dressed with paintings on mantels, doors, and panels. Several examples in *Remembrance of Patria* note this folk-art practice: A woman recalls that in her family's old house in Kinderhook "the door to the parlor had a squirrel painted on it,"[53] and a door at the Wyckoff house in Franklin Park, New Jersey, is painted with a rider and stylized flowers.[54] A door from the Cornelius Cowenhoven house in Pleasant Valley, New Jersey, was painted with doves, flowers, and a view of "a large Netherlands country estate of the late seventeenth century."[55] Overmantles were occasionally painted, even with a picture of the homestead itself, as in the Van Bergen Farm of about 1733 in Leeds, New York, a painting attributed to John Heaten who was active from 1730 to 1745.[56] While painted panels survive in the New World, few examples are found in Dutch paintings of the seventeenth century. The murals that were fashionable in European churches and palaces in the seventeenth century probably inspired the folk painting of walls and panels. A Dutch example remains at the Palace of Het Loo, Apeldorn, Province of Gelderland, which has stairway wall paintings.[57] Reduced to a provincial mantle board or a cottage door, the concept remains a pleasant surprise.

A number of furnishings were consistently found beyond the threshold of a Dutch family's home. Among the traditional items were Delftware ceramics, chimney cloths hung on jambless fireplaces, the storage cabinet called a *kas*, spoon racks, New York and New Jersey chairs, and a distinctive type of religious paintings peculiar to the Dutch among American colonial settlers.

The Dutch used several types of beds. In smaller houses in the Netherlands and in America, they had an enclosed box bed, or *bedsteden*. In *Colonial Days in Old New York*, Alice Morse Earle quotes from the contract for the "Ferry House" -- built in Brooklyn in 1665. The directions order "to wainscot the eastside the whole length of the house, and in the recess two bedsteads (*betste*) one in the front room and one in the inside room, with a pantry at the end of the bedstead."[58] The built-in bed, often considered typically Dutch, was an amenity found in many houses in the Channel Isles, Brittany, Normandy, and Scandinavia. Identical beds appeared in several homes in the Danish *Frilandsmuseet* from Fano, Ostenfeld, Laeso, and Pebringe sections of Denmark. Similarly, in small houses in Normandy and Brittany in France, Paul Walshe notes, "bedrooms were unusual and instead *lits clos*—covered and curtained beds (also found in the Queyras region of Savoy)—were ranged along the wall of the living room."[59] F. R. Yerby notes, in *Old Domestic Architecture of Holland*, that enclosed beds in the Netherlands at Volendam, Edam, and Haarlem.[60] In *Dutch by Design* illustrations show typical examples of early built-in Dutch beds at the Jan Martense Schenck house reconstruction based on Dutch *genre* pictures.[61]

According to Roderic Blackburn the only known original built-in bed to survive in America is at the Mabie house, Rotterdam Junction. The bed was removed from its original location and the wood was reused in the next room at an early date.[62] Built-in beds frequently appear in *genre* paintings, as in Pieter De Hooch's *Mother Delousing Her Child's Hair* and *Mother Lacing Her Bodice beside a Cradle*, c.1661-1663, as well as Esaias Boursse's *The Seamstress at the Fireside*.

Alice Morse Earle notes that "Adam Roelandsen, the first New York schoolmaster, had three *betste* built in his house," and Jan Peech, the founder of Peekskill, had four *betste* in his country home for "a house full of children and more besides."[63] Several house building contracts specified built-in beds.[64] R. F. Bailey claimed, in *Pre-Revolutionary Dutch Houses*, that one of the few extant original box beds still existed in 1936. She'd seen it "in the Westervalt house (Tenafly Road, Tenafly, New Jersey) . . . under the gambrel slope, a small, windowless bed closet which was considered adequate since fresh air was not deemed necessary."[65] *Bedsteden* were sometimes found with a built-in closets and shelves in the Netherlands. These *kasten met plancken* were useful storage places, but they rarely appeared in Anglo-American dwellings. Several basic features of the Dutch boxed bed emerge: The beds were short, because people slept in a semi-seated position. The *betste* could be closed with wooden shutters, or more usually with draw curtains, for warmth and some privacy in the crowded households of the late seventeenth century. The bedsteads were filled with down featherbeds, covers, and pillows that blocked the cold and damp in the marginally heated houses.

The standard freestanding eighteenth-century bed was the tester bed with hanging curtains, known as a canopy bed or a *lit en housse*. It was shaped like a rectangular draped box. In *Masters of Seventeenth Century Dutch Genre Painting*, Cynthia von Bogendorf-Rupprath observes that "before the third quarter of the seventeenth century, Dutch domestic architecture rarely included separate chambers for sleeping, thus beds normally appeared in the public rooms."[66] Similarly, Roderic Blackburn notes that, according to old inventories, beds "were placed in almost any room."[67] Various styles of square canopied beds appear in Jan Steen's *Woman, With a Parrot*; *The Morning Toilet* and *The Sick Lady*; Gerard Ter Borch's *A Company in an Interior*; and Pieter De Hooch's *The Visit*. A four-post bed with a tent-topped canopy can be seen in Gerard Ter Borch's *Officer Writing a Letter, with a Trumpeter (The Dispatch)* from about 1658-1659. A similar bed is depicted in his *Lady at Her Toilet* from 1660, and again in his painting of a *Soldier Offering a Young Woman Coins* from 1662-1663.

Compromise between built-in and freestanding beds was the bed designed to stand in an alcove. Bed alcoves existed in several houses including the Wynkoop-Lounsbery house in Stone Ridge. In *Colonial Furniture In America*, Luke Vincent Lockwood cites Helen Evertson Smith's report of an alcove bed in the Peter G. Stuyvesant house at Eleventh Street and Second Avenue at the turn of the twentieth century. The bedstead was disassembled, but it had been "intended to fit into an alcove, as all the carving was on one side." She observed that "at each corner rose a carved post from six to seven inches in diameter . . . The front posts were square . . .beneath the bed, and round as they rose . . . [and] merged into a carved cornice of over a foot on depth. The two rear posts were halves laid flat against a heavily paneled rear wall." Lockwood states that alcove beds were "frequently mentioned throughout the inventories, which would indicate that they were popular, probably because, being built into an alcove, they took up but little room . . . [but] being built for a particular room, they would have been of little use elsewhere, and when families moved or remodeled their houses these bedsteads would have been destroyed."[68]

Some small homes' inventories included a *sloep-banck*, or *slaw-bunk*, which was a folding bed. It was suspended from the wall at the head and lowered or folded much like the early twentieth-century Murphy bed.[69] Grand or humble, houses had trundle or truckle beds for children. Sometimes called a "rolling coach" this was a low bed stored under a freestanding bed.[70]

Jambless fireplaces in Dutch homes until the second half of the eighteenth century were dressed with a chimney cloth, a short curtain hung by nails or string at the mantle beam. The cloths served a purpose and added a decorative touch. Jambless fireplaces did not draw well, but a cloth hung from the mantle beam helped guide smoke into the open flue. Netherlander housewives used patterned or plain cloths for decoration. Easily smutted by the smoke and soot, the cloths were replaced as necessary. They were called by several specific names referring to their materials, such as *dobbelsteetiens valletje*, "a strong homespun linen checked off with blue or red."[71] In *Dutch By Design* the chimney clothes in the Brooklyn Museum's Schenck house restoration are based upon examples in *genre* paintings and in inventories taken in colonial homes. The 1685 inventory of Jacob de Lange lists a dozen cloths in red, in a coarse blue linen called *ozenbrig*, blue calico, red calico, red pointed lace, red lined fringed blue say cloth, and even carpet work.[72]

The Delft tiles that decorated fireplaces were often complemented by dishes, vases, bowls, and pitchers made of tin glazed Delft earthenware. More affluent homes might have had a rare piece of the oriental porcelain that inspired the Dutch product. In fact, ceramics were widely used in decoration. "In the summer time the pot that was suspended from the crane in the chimney was taken away and replaced by large porcelain vases and beakers" that stood on the swept hearth.[73]

The earliest contacts between Europeans and the orient occurred when the Ming dynasty, founded in 1368, was on the verge of collapse.[74] The ceramic style at that time used an austere blue-on-white palette with dreamy landscapes, solitary figures, and literary scenes. Portuguese and Spanish contacts led the way, but Dutch imports began before the establishment of the Dutch East India Company in 1602. The quality of the pure white hard-paste porcelain, and the appeal of the designs, sparked a terrific trade demand in Europe. "The very substance itself was a delight. Nothing like it had ever been seen in Europe before . . . Naturally the European potters were full of admiration and longed to produce this substance . . . themselves."[75] Immediately, the potters and faience makers of the Netherlands set about attempting to duplicate the fine hard-paste porcelain products of the orient.

True porcelain is made from a type of clay called kaolin. "It is found in China, Japan, Saxony, Cornwall, and Limoges, the clay of China, Japan, and Cornwall being particularly white."[76] European sources of kaolin were not discovered until the early eighteenth century, but the potters of the Netherlands, and especially Delft, developed improved earthenware and soft-paste porcelain, and a glazing method that filled a large measure of the demand for oriental ceramics. In fact, the Dutch product was superior in some ways to the original. W. Pitcairn Knowles observes in *Dutch Pottery and Porcelain* that "no painting on hard-paste china can ever approach the brilliancy of that on Delft earthenware, nor does it equal the effect produced on soft-paste porcelain."[77]

The Dutch product was Delft faience, which was derived from majolica techniques similar to the manufacture of the Delft tiles. Only one early treatise on the manufacture of Delft faience is known: *De Plaateelbakker of Delftsch Aaardewerk Maaker (The Delft Pottery Maker)* by Gerrit Paape, which dates only from 1794.[78] In *Delft Ceramics*, C. H. De Jonge reviews the process which results, as stated by Knowles, in "a high gloss ceramic with a brilliant sheen."[79]

The Delft potters produced imitation oriental themes that were often difficult to distinguish from the originals. They made quaint pseudo-oriental "chinoiseries" and a wealth of decorations based on Dutch painting and graphic arts. Themes included "riverscapes or sea-side landscapes, portraits, interiors, scenes from rural life and other motifs" in blue and white and polychrome.[80] No prosperous Netherlander home was complete without Delftware dishes, serving pieces, or *objets* decorating the top of a *kas* or a mantle shelf. The pieces included ceramic ginger jars; beakers; gourd- or figurine-shaped items; coffee, tea, and chocolate pots; basins; ewers; and many others. Factories in Delft included *De Porceleyne Lampetkan* (The Porcelain Ewer), 1637-1811; *Het Jonge Moriaenshooft* (The Young Moors Head), 1660-1692; *De Grieksche A* (The Greek A), 1674-1722; *De Metalen Pot* (The Metal Pot), 1670-1721; *De Poreceleyn Fles* (The Porcelain Bottle), 1653-1701; *Het Oude Moriaenschooft* (The Old Moors Head), 1761-1793; and *De Roos* (The Rose), 1662-1712 among many others.[81] With the introduction of true European porcelain, the industry died. "The last factory, the celebrated 'Three Bells,' was sold in 1850."[82] At the beginning of the twentieth century a revival of Delftware manufacture took place to meet a reborn demand.

The world was becoming a single trading zone in the seventeenth century. Just as porcelain from the Far East found a ready response, rugs from the Near East were in demand by both Europeans at home and European settlers on the edge of Western settlement. In a small farmhouse an Oriental rug would be a bit presumptuous, but in an urban merchant's house or a manor house of a landed magnate, an Oriental rug would be more appropriate. "Seventeenth-century estate inventories of both New York and New England often list tables together with carpets, indicating that the Turkey carpet was a constant fixture on a properly dressed table."[83] The Dutch traded worldwide, so New Amsterdam was a port of call for vessels heading home via Curacao or outbound for various locations. New York was also a haven for freebooters and pirates in the late seventeenth century, such as the infamous Captain Kidd, and a market for goods from around the world. Godfried Schalcken's *Game of Lady Come into the Garden*, painted in the 1660s, Johannes Vermeer's *Lady at the Virginals with a Gentleman*, and Esais Boursse's *Interior with a Woman at a Spinning Wheel*, all show rugs as table covers. Pieter de Hooch,

Cornelis de Man, Eglon van der Neer, and Michiel van Musscher all included oriental rugs in well-furnished rooms.

Among the oldest oriental rugs imported to Europe, Charles W. Jacobsen writes in *Oriental Rugs: A Complete Guide*, "belong such rugs from Turkey as the Holbein rugs, the so-called Damascus rugs, and the Ushak (Oushak) rugs."[84] Dutch *genre* paintings show oriental rugs in middle class homes as hangings and as table covers, but they were rarely placed on the floor before the mid-eighteenth century. "In rich homes [in Patria] the floor, as a rule, was covered with a fine Spanish matting; and when guests came, a rug or carpet was spread over this, but on their departure it was carefully rolled up and put away."[85] (Emanuel de Witte's *Interior with a Woman at a Clavichord*, c. 1665, comes to mind as a rare seventeenth-century view of a room with a carpet on the floor.) Only in paintings from the mid-eighteenth century did carpets begin appearing on the floor as part of the permanent decoration. In *Authentic Decor* Thornton shows two rooms from the 1740s with oriental rugs on the floor of upper class English homes in William Verelst's *Sir Henry Gough and his family* and in Arthur Devis's *Mr. and Mrs. Richard Bull in their house at Ongar in Essex*, 1747.[86]

By the later colonial period, painted floor cloths, an early predecessor of linoleum, were used in American homes. The Brooklyn Museum shows examples from the mid-eighteenth century, a marbled pattern floor cloth and several patterns designed by the Londoner John Carwitham in 1739. "Although painted floorcloths are almost unknown today, they were common in eighteenth-century decoration in both America and England. Inventories, bills of sale, and household accounts show that they were often used in entries, passages, and halls, and on stairs, indicating that they were thought durable and were considered appropriate for areas of heavy use."[87]

When carpeting came into fashion, women also copied the manufactured items with needlepoint and rag rugs at home. By the start of the nineteenth century, striped woven floor coverings called Venetian carpeting were available. An example appears in the parlor of the Nicholas Schenck house at the Brooklyn Museum. Venetians were relatively inexpensive and were sold by dealers who frequently advertised them along with Brussels, ingrain, and Scotch carpeting.[88]

Advertisements for imported carpeting and rugs appeared in *Rivington's New-York Gazetteer*. Two typical advertisements read:

> May, 19,1774: To be sold at public vendue, on the Coffee House Bridge. . . One very large Persian carpet; six Scotch carpets, of different sizes, and three pieces of Scotch carpeting.

> September 15, 1774: Of the Royal Manufactory at Challiott, which exceed every other kind of carpets for beauty, strength, and duration of colours, Likewise choice of Turky carpets, to be seen at Christopher Miller's [89]

"The Holbein rugs from Turkey. . .got this name when they were shown in paintings by Holbein and other artists of that time. These were purely geometric and the principal designs were squares and stars. Other Flemish painters such as Jan Van Eyck, Memling, Gerard David, and many Italian masters of the same period used Turkish rugs as background for their paintings."[90] The border of the rugs "originally a succession of Kufic characters, is transformed into an elaborate network . . . [and] in the sixteenth century this world of rigid and stylized forms came under the influence of the Persian enthusiasm for plant motifs and related ornaments, such as the arabesque."[91] Another group of popular rugs were the Ushak (Oshak). "These rugs are often depicted in Venetian Paintings of the 16th century and in Flemish and Dutch Paintings of the 17th century. At Williamsburg, Virginia, is displayed an old Ushak in the Governor's Mansion. . . [because] paintings of the day show such rugs."[92]

As seen in the *genre* pictures, the seventeenth-century Dutch were very interested in art. Portraits, landscapes, *genre* themes, religious paintings, and prints were collected and hung in great numbers in Dutch homes. According to Peter C. Sutton, writing in *Masters of Seventeenth Century Dutch Genre Painting*, Dutch art was divided into several categories but *genre* was not a term the Dutch used. The classification of paintings were *portrets* (portraits), *historien* (religious or mythological themes), *landschappen* (landscapes), *stilleven* (still lifes), *geselschap* (merry company), *conversatie* (conversations), *cortegarde* ("*corps de garde*"), *boerenkermis* (peasant kermis), *bambootserytjes* (street or peasant scenes), or *kleyenebeuzelingen* (little trifles).[93] Paintings were filled with allegorical and symbolic meaning, mostly lost to viewers today. Popular Dutch interest in art peaked in the seventeenth century. Even middle and working class homes had paintings or prints displayed on the walls. Roderic Blackburn observes in *Remembrance of Patria* that the cultural identity of the Dutch in New York "suggests that the great New York landowners and the rising middle class would have brought portraits and religious and genre paintings with them, having collected — as Holland burgers did — inexpensive paintings that echoed those of the Golden Age of Rembrant and Vermeer."[94] In addition portraits and religious paintings made in America had begun to appear in wills and inventories of goods.[95] In America the most distinctively Dutch art was the religious theme painting. They reflected Dutch pietism, and they were frequently copied from, or based upon, illustrations in Dutch Bibles. The subjects covered both Old and New Testament stories such as the finding of Moses, Christ on the Road to Emmaus, Philip Baptizing the Ethiopian Eunuch, and Isaac Blessing Jacob.[96]

A number of New York and New Jersey artists are known: Henri Couturier (1592-1672), Gerardus Duyckinck (1695-1746), Pieter Vannderlyn (1687-1778), John Watson, (1685-1768), Nehemiah Partridge (1683-1724), John Heaton (working c. 1730-1740), and many "limners," who are known by name but not by specific paintings. They are discussed at length in a chapter, "Early Colonial Painting of the New York Province" in *Remembrance of Patria* by Mary Black. Artists often sought commissions by the mid-eighteenth century and advertised in *The New-York Mercury*, *The New-York Gazette and the Weekly Mercury*, and *The New-York Gazette and the Weekly Post-Boy* through the 1760s and 1770s.[97]

Portraits, religious paintings, landscapes, still life, and *genre* paintings are mentioned in inventories, but only rare examples survive. They were often based upon prints, etchings, and engravings sold by many merchants in New York and Albany during the eighteenth century. Issues of *The New-York Gazette*, from July 18 to 25, 1736, mention Mr. Waters in Albany and Matthias Creger in New York as seeking subscribers for a view of the City of Albany. *The New-York Gazette Revived in the Post-Boy* on April 24, 1749, advertised prints for sale. Garret Noel and Company advertised in *The New-York Mercury* on March 26, 1759, that they had a wide selection of prints for sale. Noel was still advertising prints in 1773.[98] Gerardus Duyckinck, noted above as a painter, and his son of the same name, offered both paintings and services as japanners, glaziers, and gilders at their house between the Old Slip Market and Coentjes Market in New York in advertisements in the 1740s and 1750s.[99]

The subjects advertised for New York customers included maps of the world, and views of London, New York City, and Albany, as well as views of Niagara, the Battle of Culloden, and Captain Phillip's retaking the *Solebay*. There were also portrait prints of various celebrities and members of the British royal family, horses, the Virgin Mary, Caesar, Apollo, Cleopatra, Cupid, Liberality and Modesty, and the Stuart pretenders.[100] The advertisements are of special interest because the estate inventories enumerate prints and pictures but rarely specify subjects.

As for furniture made in New York, several aspects deserve mention including typical wood stock, individual craftsmen, basic techniques, and the common styles in New York Dutch and Anglo-Dutch homes during the colonial period.

In *Furniture Treasury*, Wallace Nutting says that furniture wood stock was traditionally dried in the open air and then covered without heat because kilns were not used, "thus it required some years to dry thoroughly . . . lumber turned into furniture."[101] Most early American furniture was made with solids rather than veneers. Later veneered pieces used flitches cut with a hand saw (the veneer was thicker modern veneer), and Wallace notes that "it was a tedious, but a satisfactory job."[102] In New York furniture:

> the native woods employed are the usual walnut, maple, and pine, augmented by cherry, beech, red gum, and yellow poplar. The last wood, which came from the tulip tree was called canoewood in New Amsterdam documents; it is found more frequently in draw linings, backs of clock cases, and bracings of tables and chairs than any other one. It is a soft wood, more easily worked than chestnut and ash, which appear in the frames of seating furniture where strength is required. Red gum or sweet gum, known since early times as blisted, was used for wood trim and furniture alike and it is constantly seen in New York work. The inventory of Edward Burling in 1750 mentions a bilsted table and chair. Rosewood and mahogany, brought from the West Indies, were frequently used.[103]

Wallace Nutting says "it should be generally understood that the turned chairs of. . . 1690-1720 are maple. . . Maple was the readily available and excellent wood for this purpose. We get into walnut or fruit wood for fine chairs about 1700. And before 1690 ash persisted to some extent, though maple is usual after 1650."[104] The woods commonly used by cabinetmakers in the eighteenth century were discussed by Joseph Downs in *American Furniture: Queen Anne and Chippendale Periods.* He reported that among the woods chosen for formal furniture and finer cabinet work was black walnut, which was plentiful on the Eastern Seaboard, where trees grew up to eight feet in diameter. European and American furniture was made of solid walnut in the seventeenth century. "The English Age of Walnut was approximately from 1660 to 1730, a span of about seventy years; in the American colonies its equivalent covered the years between 1670 and 1750, with some thirty years more added when characteristically American pieces. . .were made in a design basically Queen Anne."[105] *Colonial Furniture In America* includes a Dutch walnut *kas* long owned by the Beekman family. A massive piece that is richly carved on cornice and case frame, "this kas probably represents the finest of the cupboards in use among the Dutch, and the tradition in the Beekman family is that it came to New York with the first Beekman in Governor Styuvestant's ship in the year 1647."[106] Another great *kas*, owned by the Livingston family, was made about 1670 of walnut solids and veneers with carved festoons and pilasters in a Dutch architectural style. It represented "the highest quality in Dutch kas production."[107]

The extensive use of walnut veneer began with high fashion William and Mary pieces, and it remained popular in New York well into the following century. "The branch figure or swirl crotch of walnut wood enriched plain surfaces, and the root and burl cuts provided an intricate figure for veneering the fronts of desks, chests of drawers, and clock cases frequently seen in northern furniture in the Queen Anne period."[108] Walnut continued to be used south of New York throughout the colonial period in spite of the growing popularity of mahogany.

Santo Domingo mahogany provided timber of unmatched quality. The wood was heavy and solid, and it tuned nearly black with age. Cuban mahogany, imported to England and North America before 1750, was prized for its figure grain, "fiddle back" stripe, and a golden brown color. "Regular shipments of mahogany were made in the early eighteenth century to England and the American colonies."[109] In the will of Thomas Jackson of New York, probated January 19, 1769, there was a bequest of imported wood: "To my dau. Fanny Jackson of Jamaica 50,000 ft. of mahogany, part of 70,000 consigned to me by obligation of Richard Armstrong of Honduras."[111]

Woods for less formal pieces included cherry and maple, which have remained popular in America. Old maple wood takes on a dark honey color that all too often is destroyed by refinishing.[111] In 1990, I examined a tiger maple *kas* at a house in Catskill, New York, which had been found in a Brooklyn cellar, but the only maple *kas* mentioned in *American Kasten* is a painted example from Dutchess County. Dutch chairs from New Jersey and New York were frequently made of maple and often painted. Two are shown in *Remembrance of Patria*: a spindle-back armchair and an armchair with a Queen Anne style back and William and Mary stretcher and details.[112]

The Dutch in the Hudson Valley also favored red or sweet gumwood called bilsted in New York, it is a tall straight tree often five feet in diameter. "The wood was heavy, close grained, and silky; red-brown in color with less grain than cherry."[113] *Remembrance of Patria* shows a number of gumwood pieces, including a candle stand, a Bybellessenaar, or Bible desk, a chest-on-stand, a few tables.[114] In *American Furniture*, a small breakfast table in bilsted of New York origin, between 1725 and 1740 is shown. An inventory of Effingham Townly's possessions taken in Manhattan in October 1730 listed several bilsted pieces:[115]

One round Billstead Table	£ 0.10.0
One Bed stead, Curtains, Iron Rods Calico	6.10.0
One Billstead Cupboard	2.00.0
One large table	0.00.9

"Like tulipwood, [bilsted] was plentifully used for trimming rooms and for furniture in the Hudson Valley. For turnings and moldings it was ideal. Use of gumwood, as much as the style of many

items, would often be a Dutch New York cultural marker in these
pieces. A fine wall of red gum paneling from the Hasbrouck house,
built in 1752 at High Falls, Ulster County, is now in the American
Wing [of the Metropolitan Museum] in New York."116 In America
the Dutch frequently called tulipwood "canoewood because the
Indians made dugout canoes of it."[117] Downs states that "tulip
poplar" in old inventories refered to tulip wood, since poplar was so
inferior that it is now used for packing cases. The Dutch used
tulipwood for floors and panels as well as furniture, many of the
kasten in *American Kasten* are red gumwood.

White, or soft, pine was "common as a secondary wood in
structural members of furniture."[118] Other pine varieties were hard
pine or yellow pitch pine. Loblolly pine or long leaf pine were
southern trees and not important to the New York area. A pine-and-
fir work table, now at the Van Alen house in Kinderhook, displays
a uniquely Dutch style, and "no others with this type of cleat, splay
leg and stretcher arrangement have been seen outside of New York."
The table reflects early Spanish examples that may be the Dutch
tables' design source.[119] "It may represent a Dutch farmer's or even
an unskilled carpenter's attempt at making a proper table."[120] The
pine and fir, as well as the primitive appearance, mark the piece as
provincial but perhaps as recent as nineteenth century in origin.

New York furniture sometimes employed white or red cedar. An
important cedar piece is the fall-front desk at the Museum of the City
of New York, which was originally owned by the Brinkerhoff
family.[121] "Brinkerhoff family tradition claims that this desk was
brought to New Netherland by Joris Dircksen and Susannah
(Dubels) Brinkerhoff, who arrived in New Amsterdam in 1638 . . .
It is made of cedar inlaid with flowers and scrolls of beech and fruit
woods;" but Maus Esther Dillard says that "from all appearances, it
might have been made in New York between 1690 and 1700."[122] A
solid *escritoire* with large ball feet and a fall front covering many small
draws and cubby holes, the desk is a provincial version of the Dutch
inlay style and is a handsome example of a fine and rare cedar
cabinet.[123]

By the late eighteenth century, lumberyards in New York City
advertised domestic and imported lumber for houses and furniture.

Advertisements in New York papers in the 1770s included the following: Abiel Wood of Sheepscut-River offered all kinds of lumber for European, West-Indian, and American markets available in Boston for several cargoes on April 8, 1771. On September 28, 1772, a public vendue was held for a cargo of 60,000 feet of choice "large bay mahogany" that was sold in lots from 5 to 10,000 each. And at George Stanton's Lumber Yard near the North River, "all kinds of Albany board and planck, oak and Jersey pine, timber of all sorts, the best three feet or long shingles" were sold by Philip Hone on July 5, 1773. On March 6, 1775, Hardenbrook and Dominick advertised "red cedar logs, mahogany and Spanish Cedar boards and mahogany and Spanish Cedar for staircases as well as long and short shingles, sawed long oak and pine plank," and a range of lumber for special construction and ship building. Because of problems in the wood trade, legislation to regulate and monitor lumber sales was published on September 13, 1770, in *The New-York Journal or the General Advertiser*.[124]

"By the middle of the seventeenth century the Netherlands had emerged as an important area in terms of the production of furniture . . . [and] veneering and marquetry were used extensively by Netherlandish craftsmen."[125] Both the foreign-trained and domestically-apprenticed woodworkers followed practices from the homeland and as local craftsmen made a wide range of wooden items for the New York market. Unpainted and inexpensive furniture was made by woodworkers called *witwerkers*.[126] Netherlander terminology identifies a skilled craftsman who worked in wood as either a *timmerman* (a carpenter who built buildings and related finishing, such as balusters, paneling, doors, and moldings), a *schrijnwerker* (a joiner who made simple furniture and built various items in wood), or a *meubelmaker* (a cabinetmaker who made fine furniture).

In the late seventeenth century and early eighteenth century, an ever-growing repertoire of techniques evolved that include turning, carving, and veneering. The tools of the trade included a wide range of carving implements, and smoothing and molding planes. Lathes turned by manual, spring-pole, or big-wheel waterpower produced the turned chairs, spindles, and stretchers then in fashion. Mortise and tenon joins were carved, pegged, and glued (good furniture is never nailed together). Veneering covered joins and exposed the highly figured grain of a cabinet wood, while masking the strong, but plain, woods used for framing furniture. In veneering, the Dutch covered the ends of the dovetail on the face of the draw; later under William and Mary, the veneering was put on the board that formed the face while the dovetail was set back "blind" from the face a quarter inch. The early dovetailing had two or three crude tails, but by the end of the seventeenth century it became finer, and the tails increased in number. [127] "This earlier dovetailing will also be found on Dutch pieces, as it was a form of dovetail favored by the Dutch long after it had been discarded by the English."[128] Concerning style, it may be noted that "until the introduction of furniture pattern books about the middle of the eighteenth century the designs of most pieces were based on traditional forms, with such variations as the individual craftsman or his customer may have thought agreeable or necessary."[129]

"The names of some eighteenth-century furniture makers of Dutch descent are known, but most Dutch families probably bought their furniture from British or Yankee craftsmen."[130] Only about a dozen Dutch names were listed among the three hundred woodworking craftsmen on Long Island in the eighteenth century.[131] Ulster county woodworkers included three generations of the Elting family: Jan (1632-1729), William (1685-1744), and Hendricus (bapt. 1722-?). Several other Elting family members, including Hendricus's older brothers, William Jr. (bapt. 1713-after 1770) and Jacob (bapt. 1717-after 1770), were furniture makers and "turners." The Beekman family also included furniture makers among their number: Wilhelmus, who arrived in New Netherland in 1647, his third son Johannes (1656-1751), his son Thomas (1689-1759), Thomas' son Cornelius (1733-1770), and his son Thomas (1761-1814), who was a carpenter and coffin maker by trade. In New Jersey, Matthew Egerton Sr. (1739-1802) and his son Matthew Egerton (1765-1837) were furniture makers who made *kasten*.[132] Among Matthew Sr.'s patrons were "Hardenburgs, Schuremans, Van Artsdalens, Schulers and Frelinghuysens. Kases by Egerton and also his tables, cabinets and other fine pieces went into homes all through New Jersey."[133] However, furniture makers who came to New York, or apprenticed in the Hudson Valley, seldom made elaborate traditional Dutch pieces. Even "after 1664 [the Dutch settlers] continued to import some articles such as clocks, carved cookie molds, ceramics, brass and books in Dutch. Some merchant families had pictures, textiles and elaborate furnishings from the Netherlands."[134] The local demand was for utilitarian pieces until well into the eighteenth century, when the Dutch Baroque style had been superseded by the Anglo-Dutch Queen Anne style. From the high point of the walnut age through the mahogany classics of the middle Georgian period, American colonial style was derived from English rather than Dutch precedents.

Colonial furniture in the Hudson Valley followed the fashions of the neighboring colonies with a few distinguishing characteristics. Many New York pieces were "identifiable by the boldness of the curves and over-all sturdiness of their proportions."[135] In case pieces New York furniture was marked by "straight lines and square shapes."[136] Popular English designs in New York included the spider table, gaming tables, and chairs, but "very few highboys were made in this region; New Yorkers seemed to have preferred the chest-on-chest."[137] "Chippendale is interpreted with great restraint in New York."[138] In eighteenth century examples

many small details have been observed repeatedly until the accumulated evidence determines the characteristics of New York furniture. On the claw and ball foot, the claw grasps the ball firmly, the joints or knuckles standing out with marked prominence, giving in profile almost a right-angle line. The back legs of Queen Anne and Chippendale chairs vary in toe, the square chamfered support appearing as often as the round member, which sometimes tapers to a square or pad foot. Rarely are the side rails of chairs mortised through to the back, as may frequently be seen in Philadelphia seating furniture. A straight cabriole leg having no knee but ending in a claw foot is not infrequently found in tables.

New York furniture is also distinguished by the technique and disposition of its carving. Leaves, shells, and husks are the usual vocabulary of ornament, assisted by gadrooning, Chinese frets, tassels, and scrolls. A peculiar stiffness is evident in the execution of the leaves, and the carved elements are not often accommodated to the structure they adorn. There is none of the airy chinoiserie and the French rocaille spirit of Philadelphia furniture evident, but rather the sobriety of forms evolved by the English school.[139]

Dutch dwellers in the Hudson Valley used traditional Dutch pieces late into the eighteenth century. Rooms furnished by Dutch and Anglo-Dutch New Yorkers often used English and Dutch furniture together in a distinctive New York manner.

The Dutch Period: 1609 to 1664

Few examples of furniture from the Dutch colonial period remain. Designs that originated in *Patria* remained popular among the Dutch in the Hudson Valley region however, and many styles from the colonial scene remained current well into the nineteenth century. In terms of furniture traditionally placed within a typically Dutch room there were a number of pieces seen from the earliest period to the end of the Dutch cultural era. The *kas* was the most prominent furniture in a Dutch house. It was a linen and general storage cabinet. Many homes had more than one. "The 1691/92 estate inventory of Francois Rombouts, a former mayor of New York, lists five cupboards including 'a holland Cubbert furnished with Earton ware and Parsilin' valued at £15."[140] The *kas* was often a dowry, *uitzet* in Dutch, item. It went with a new bride filled with a vast supply of linen, tablecloths, napkins, sheets, and other bedding that was the pride of Dutch housewives at the time. Medieval in origin, but Dutch Baroque in execution, a *kas* was large in size and capacity. Similar to an armoire in dimensions and appearance, and close to the Pennsylvania German *schrank* in most external respects (but with shelves, whereas a *schrank* had both shelves and pegs for hanging clothes), the *kas* was a distinctly Dutch New York, New Jersey, and (occasionally) Connecticut item unlikely to seen in either a New England or a Southern home in the colonial period.

The Metropolitan Museum of Art held a special showing of *kasten* in 1991, and the exhibition catalogue *American Kasten* covers the subject in considerable depth. The ever-practical Dutch design of the *kas* typically, but not invariably, broke the massive piece of furniture down into three or four component parts for easier movement: large cornice, the main carcass, a lower draw section, and large (frequently cannon-ball-shaped) front feet. The Baroque *kas* typically had a massive cornice (frequently similar to a jambless fireplace molding) and a pair of wide doors. Early and rare Holland-made *kasten* were often carved and trimmed elaborately and veneered in rosewood and ebony. American and Dutch provincial *kasten* were more austere, but many were similarly massive. Early American pieces were often oak, but walnut, red gum, or cherry with secondary woods of poplar and pine were typical. A few *kasten* were made in pine and poplar, and painted in *grisaille*, which copied Baroque sculptural and garland forms in gray, black, and white paint. The *genre* painters depicted *kasten* in many scenes of Dutch home life. In Pieter de Hooch's *Woman Drinking With Soldiers of 1658*, a *kas* is viewed through an open doorway. His painting *Interior with Figures* shows a *kas* of ebony and rosewood of *kussenkast*, or "cushion" paneled design, similar to the Brooklyn Museum's example at the Jan Martense Schenck house. Gabriel Metsu's *The Hunter's Gift*, from about 1658 to 1660, depicts a similar rosewood and ebony *kussenkast*. Pieter de Hooch shows a housewife and maid before a *kas* with a stack of clean and pressed linen in his picture *The Linen Closet from 1663*.

   Kasten, or kases, remained a prominent feature in Dutch homes in New York into the present century. When closets replaced free standing cabinets and cupboards, the *kas* lost much of its *raison d'etre*, but it remained valuable as an heirloom. In the course of moving and style changes, however, many *kasten* were left in attics or cellars. Only lately have they emerged as handsome *objets* as well as practical household items.

   Dutch kitchen and *groot kamers* often had a pewter or china cupboard called a *pottebank* (pottery shelf) for open storage and display. Assembled on the scene and "simply nailed together" the cupboard was taller than a doorway. It could be removed only by sawing off the upper section or taking the piece apart. Therefore, many remained *in situ* when a house changed ownership.[141] The base was a cabinet with doors, and the upper part (which has no backboard or cornice molding) was a rack of shelves with scalloped or straight side supports and grooves and crossbars that held platters, dishes, and serving pieces. Usually, the *pottebank* was made of pine. It was frequently painted to match the room in typical Dutch New York colors of red or blue-gray. A blue-gray *pottebank* may be seen in the Philipse Manor house upper kitchen at the Sleepy Hollow Restoration. It displays dishes and other items of household utility. "Curiously, although their name and Hudson Valley ownership have strong Dutch associations, the form is not found in the Netherlands. There, plates were more likely to be displayed on shelves mounted on the wall, or individual plates were hung by ribbons."[142]

Two Dutch Baroque table styles were occasionally seen in Hudson Valley homes. The first was the early massive draw table with expansion leaves built into the top that could be "drawn out" as needed. Massive and set on bulbous legs, with ball-shaped decorative turnings, the draw table is similar to English tables from the Jacobean period. The design appeared in the Flemish furniture design book entitled *Verscheyden Schrynwercknals Portale, Kleerkassen, etc,* written by Paul Vrededeman de Vries and published in Antwerp in 1630.[143] Designed to stand in the middle of a room, draw tables were stationary furniture. Examples appear in the Philipse Manor house, and they frequently turn up in *genre* paintings: Cornelis de Man shows the same uncovered draw table in both *The Chess Players* and *The Gold Weigher*. An uncovered draw table appears in Gerad Ter Borch's picture called *Woman Drinking Wine with a Sleeping Soldier*. Their exposed bulbous legs as seen in Gerard Ter Borch's painting Lady at Her Toilet may identify numerous draw tables covered with oriental carpets. The second table style was the gateleg design with drop leaves. It had six or eight legs, including two hinged sets of legs that swung away from the base frame and supported the raised leaves that were cut squared or oval. Gateleg tables are in rooms at Philipse Manor and at the Brooklyn Museum's Jan Martense Schenck house. Draw tables were usually made in oak, but drop-leaf gate-legged tables can be found in oak, walnut, mahogany, gumwood, and other woods. Other Dutch tables used drawbar leaf supports "which provide greater convenience than, if not as much support as, the common gateleg."[144] Turnings on gateleg and drawbar tables are lighter and more graceful than the bulbous turnings on draw-leaf tables. They commonly used baluster and sometimes spiral turned shapes. "Only in New York was . . . [the] spiral leg attempted, judging from the few surviving examples," but the design was common in England and the Netherlands.[145] Winterthur Museum has a chest-on-stand with spiral twist legs that was found in Dutchess County. It is one of only three known from early New York. Roderic Blackburn reports, in *Remembrance of Patria*, that the chest-on-stand style was typically English and "popular with neither the Netherlands nor the early New York Dutch." [146]

A chair with turned legs, a slat-back (with three to five horizontal back support members), and a rush or reed seat was often found in colonial New York and the Netherlands. It remained current from the seventeenth century well into the nineteenth century. Discussing Bergen County, New Jersey, slat-back chairs, Kevin Wright observed that "generally, eighteenth century models can be loosely distinguished from those of the next century only by their use of bolder turnings and more squat urns with elongated cups. Commercial production in the nineteenth century for a wider market spurred a greater concern for economizing time and materials and hence shallower lathing."[147] These chairs were frequently made of maple and painted black or green and "slat-backs used in combination with turned posts and seats of rush or split were popular . . .until after the Revolution."[148] Both styles may be seen at Philipse Manor in the upper kitchen. The slat-back chair design appears in *genre* paintings from the seventeenth century, such as Esaias Boursse's *Interior with a Woman at a Spinning Wheel*, 1664; Jacobus Vrel's *Woman at a Window*, 1654; Pieter de Hooch's *Mother Lacing Her Bodice beside a Cradle*, 1661-1663; and Abraham Diepraam's *Barroom*, 1665.

At the low end of the social and economic scale, tables with angled or sawbuck braced legs, or medial stretchers were occasionally depicted in Netherlander pictures of taverns and workshops and kitchens. The medial stretcher design was typically Dutch "and reflects a persistent late use of a Dutch medieval style."[149] The one in the Van Alen house resembles the small hexagonal topped table in Adriaen van Ostade's *Interior of a Peasant's Cottage*, 1668. A round topped table appears in two paintings by Abraham Diepraam: *Peasants in the Tavern*, 1663, and *Barroom*, 1665. Both tables have the same angled and braced understructure; possibly they were "the same furnishings."[150] At the bottom of the social structure as depicted by

Diepraam, Ostade, Brouwer, and Cornelis Bega chair seats served as tables, benches were seats or serving counters, and even a board laid across the knees, as in Adrien Brouwer's *The Smokers (The Peasants of Moerdijk)*, c. 1627-1630, was considered "furniture" . . . reminders that our colonial forbears were not all gentile folk.

An early table design, which later gained wide use, was the single-post pedestal. It was used for tables and candle stands and frequently turn up in elegant settings, such as in *Merry Company*, 1620-1622, by Willem Buytewech, which shows a sturdy baluster turned post holding an octagonal table top. Variations appeared as tea tables, English candle and kettle stands, and (by the middle eighteenth century) tilt-top tables and dumb-waiter tables. When the pedestal table with a tilt top was perfected, it was convenient and saved space in the small quarters typical of most colonial homes.

Many small household furniture items are identifiable as Hudson Valley Dutch objects. Low chests stored blankets and other textiles. A blanket chest in red-painted white pine, with black ball turned feet, appears in *Remembrance of Patria*. It has "applied moldings, creating the illusion of slip panels, [which] is a New York Dutch feature found on chests, doors, paneling, and widow shutters. On some other low chests from the Hudson Valley, the illusion of panels on the front and, sometimes, on the top was created by applying moldings or painted *tromp l'oeil* designs."[151] Taller, standing blanket chests with one draw were common in Queens County, New York, with Dutch design influences and "most have ball feet in the same manner as a *kas*, but occasionally they were made with bracket feet and two drawers, especially in the late 18th and early 19th centuries."[152]

The Anglo-Dutch Period: 1664 to 1714

In the earliest period, New World furniture was commonly made in pine, maple, or oak, but by mid-century walnut was used for many better pieces, first in solid wood, and then in veneer and marquetry, but only in the Netherlands. Veneered marquetry was a Dutch craft and, along with oyster-shell parquetry, remained fashionable into the 1690s.[153] English and Dutch pieces look virtually identical.[154] Only a "very few fine pieces from seventeenth-century New York have survived," whether case pieces or chairs. [155] In *Seventeenth Century Interior Decor*, Thornton, shows examples of "the so-called 'fatheringale chair', the commonest form of chair in the seventeenth century, used all over Europe."[156] He shows a typical Dutch example from 1672: a square seat and back on a plain set of legs with minimal turning and plain stretcher. The chairs were called "back stools" in England and sometimes "Cromwell" chairs. "It was the standard chair of its time and was used also for dining—in which case it was covered in leather or turkey work."[157] The chairs appear in *genre* pictures, portraits, and prints through the seventeenth century. A set of the chairs in the north room of the Jan Martense Schenck house at the Brooklyn Museum appear in *Dutch By Design*.[158] Jan Steen's *Easy Come, Easy Go*, c.1660, shows a turkey work chair, Gerard Ter Borch shows a table and set of chairs *en suite* in purple velvet in *Curiosity*, c.1660, and another room *en suite* in red with both a stool and matching back-stool in his painting *Admonition*, c.1654-55.

Later in the century, the Dutch Baroque style, also known (in America) as William and Mary, brought an entirely different design aesthetic to the fore. "The style emphasized the dynamic and dramatic aims common to all aspects of baroque art and these were achieved by a new kind of 'explosive' turning, by large unified shapes, by predominant curves, as well as by vigorous contrasts of color and the 'color' evoked by high relief carving."[159] In chair design, the new fashion called for high backs, rich carving, and frequently oriental cane seats. Laquer, "Japanning,"and Eastern themes became important.[160] These chairs were often referred to as tea chairs. Better chairs were made in walnut, but plain chairs of beechwood were frequently painted black.[161] Chest-on-stand designs with turned legs and stretchers were fahionable case pieces. While more often seen in English homes, they were made through the middle eighteenth century. Luke Vincent Lock cites the first mention of the chest on a table or stand "in the inventory of Dom Nicolas van Rensselaer, January 16, 1678."[162] A walnut and gum wood high chest with turned legs c.1720-1740 (which shows that William and Mary fashions were followed well into the Georgian era), is in the Jan Martense Schenck house at the Brooklyn Museum. In *de Halve Maen*, Roderic Blackburn discussed a chest on frame, c.1700-1740, made of walnut solids and veneers that stood on twist legs and stretcher in the style of the Stuart's.[163]

The Late Colonial Period: 1714 to 1776

The "eighteenth-century farmers and townsmen had New York 'low style' or 'country style' furniture, combining Dutch and English design trends."[164] While traditional designs continued well into the new century, fashion adopted the new *mode* in the Dutch style. "The chief characteristics of the style were the use of the cyma curve in the place of straight lines where possible and the introduction for the first time of the splat, which has become the distinguishing feature of the English and colonial chairs of the Georgian period. The style originated in Holland, but was developed in England and the colonies more than at the place of its birth."[165] Turned legs with Spanish or tassel feet gave way to pad feet and slipper feet (which have pointed terminations to the cabriole leg), or feet with talons grasping orbs. The claw-and-ball foot design was introduced in the early eighteenth century. It reflected Chinese influence as filtered through English and Dutch perceptions and was derived from the Chinese dragon claw grasping a pearl.[166] A range of special tables for tea, dining, and gaming became available and case-piece furniture came in the form of dressers, chests, and bureaus.

A later chair design closely identified with the Dutch was the Hudson Valley Queen Anne chair, a fiddleback or vaseback design that enjoyed a longstanding popularity. The chair was used in New York the way the Windsor chair was used elsewhere for homestead, tavern, and general-purpose seating. It was popular from the mid-eighteenth century until well into the nineteenth century. Although "fiddleback chairs are traditionally associated with the Hudson Valley. . . it seems likely that many fiddlebacks used in the Valley were shipped up-river from New York City."[167] The design is easily identified by a centered, flat vertical back support called a splat and described as "fiddleback" or "urn" shaped. The chair also had a curved crest, turned stiles, stretcher and legs, and feet ending in a pad shape. The seat was typically splint or woven rush. The design had Lowland ball and vase turnings, but it also had English Lancashire and East Anglia leg design dating from 1610 to 1750.[168] "The fiddleback chair is not an expression of naive vision and inferior woodworking skills, as some might think. On the contrary it is an international translation of the elements of the carved mahogany or walnut chair, cabriole legged, Queen Anne-style chair into the vocabulary of the turned chair tradition. The chairmaker who conceived of the fiddleback chair thoroughly understood the aesthetics of the Queen Anne style and adapted them to his craft."[169] The finest fiddleback chairs were made in New York by David Coutant and Jacob and Michael Smith, but the type was made from New Jersey to Rhode Island with varying degrees of success.

A typically Dutch household item was the spoon rack. "These spoon-racks are mentioned in some of the early Dutch records, called by their Dutch name, *lepel-borties*."[170] Small display racks for pewter spoons were made primarily in tulip poplar, easily carved and decorated with chip work, and sometimes painted in various colors including white, green, and red.[171] "It was a folk custom for a man to present a wooden spoon holder to a woman to commemorate betrothal or marriage . . . [and] there is a curious omission of spoon racks in inventories . . . [suggesting that they] may have been considered the wife's personal property and, along with clothing and jewelry, withheld from probate."[172]

The mid-eighteenth century saw the introduction of mahogany and new furniture styles from England. In New York, Queen Anne remained fashionable from about 1740 to 1790 and Chippendale from about 1755 to 1795. "While it has been said that New York furniture is extremely Dutch in feel . . . there are English George II prototypes for most of the developed New York chairs."[173] The fashion moved far from earlier Dutch roots. English taste became the vogue for Dutch New Yorkers as well as their English neighbors. In the late colonial period, a number of rarely, or never before used designs came into fashion among the wealthy. Straight- and camelback sofa designs appeared, as did, dining *suites* and pieces in the French manner. Fashionable homes adapted to the new concept of a room devoted exclusively to dining, with side boards, hunt boards, and console pieces. Aside from several New York features, the general trends in Anglo-American colonial taste applied to the Hudson Valley high-style furniture in the years before the Revolution. Many "typical" New York pieces were actually made and shipped from Boston. Walnut and mahogany remained in demand as primary woods. In New York popular secondary woods included red gum, chestnut, beech, oak, and cherry. Pine and poplar were used throughout the colony as secondary woods.[174]

Furniture was sold newly imported from London, as estate settlements, and as ready-made for those seeking a bargain. An advertisement in *The New-York Gazette* of November 21, 1763, listed a mahogany bookcase, bedstead, mirrors, chairs, tables, and "a curious sett of pictures" that "was the property of the deceased Mr. James Morison (one of the unfortunate Gentlemen, who lately perished in crossing this bay)."[176] Other offerings of ready-made or used furniture in the 1760s and 1770s included "a neat mahogany desk and book case, in the Chinese taste; a Mahogany Clothes Press, a four posted Mahogany Bedstead with fluted pillars, and tea tables, chairs, and desks." Marble slabs for side tables were offered in 1767, "to be sold cheap," and a billiard table, Windsor chairs, and "all the elegant and valuable household furniture of Richard Vassel, Esq."[177]

In *Dutch and Flemish Furniture*, Singleton writes that among the wealthier classes it was a Dutch custom for the bride to go with a few friends and servants to select what was needed for the newlywed's home. "This was called '*ten huisraet vaeren*' (going furnishing), and De Vriij devotes a chapter to this pleasant occupation under the title of '*De vrou vaert ten huysrate*' (the wife goes out to furnish)."[178]

The main distinction between the appearance of seventeenth and eighteenth century rooms and rooms of today is that in the earlier period most furniture, not in use or in unoccupied rooms, was arranged around the walls. Based upon paintings and prints, a Dutch house looked more fully furnished than contemporary English rooms, which seem austere in comparison. Similarly, Dutch houses contained more art and bric-a-brac in the form of plates, prints, pictures on the walls, and ceramics set on furniture tops. *Kasten*, chests on frames, and other casework pieces had garnishes of porcelain or Delft, and on rare occasions a piece of imported oriental ware accented their tops.

Furnishing a Dutch House

Photographs by the author unless otherwise noted.

Top: Placing matting on the floor and oriental carpets on tables were customary practices before the mid-eighteenth century; early pewter candlesticks with low drip pan to catch melting wax (drip pans on candlesticks began in the eighteenth century); Delft and tulip vase on metal foot warmer below the table. Amstel Kring Museum, Amsterdam.

Right: Eighteenth-century French-style mantel, Dutch "Queen Anne"-style chair. In warm weather, when there was no fire, a large Delft vase might decorate the hearth. Amstel Kring Museum, Amsterdam.

Above: Entry hall as viewed in 1971 to the Cornelus Schermerhorn House, Kinderhook, New York, circa 1713. William and Mary-style elbow chair, long case clock and lantern of the period. The house is a private residence and not a museum recreation, a carpet would not have been on the floor in the early eighteenth century.
Courtesy of R. H. Blackburn.

A room in a private residence with Dutch-style period pieces in an authentic manner: Plates and cloth decorate the mantle, fire and iron fireback on the hearth, a pair of Dutch baroque or William and Mary-style elbow chairs, and an early eighteenth-century-style candlestick. A wedding, a funeral, or a visit by the pastor or a suitor might earn entry to such a room, lesser occasions and folk would merit a seat in the kitchen. The single candle (stored away during the day) would be typical of the time. Cornelis Schemerhorn House, Kinderhook, New York.
Courtesy of R. H. Blackburn

Period Dutch linen storage *kas*, gate-leg table typical of the Hudson Valley region, and a chandelier at the John Pruyn House, Kinderhook, New York, 1766. Chairs and tables would be drawn from their usual place along a wall to the center of the room when needed. The chandelier would be hung lower in the eighteenth century. After 1766 it was just possible that the carpet would be laid on the floor when guests were expected, otherwise it would be on the table or rolled and stored safely away from moths. Courtesy of R. H. Blackburn.

Abovve: A *pottebank* with a display of pewter at the Luykas Van Alen House, Kinderhook, New York. *Below, left:* A betty lamp at Historic Richmond Town Restoration. The bowl would be filled with oil or fat and a wick would hang over the pinch lip (no technological advance since the Romans and a smelly, smoky, and inadequate illumination at best). *Right:* Kitchen fireplace and a splat-back chair. Several brushes near at hand would be typical. Broadhead House, Rosendale.

Above: South room showing fireplace with cloth and dishes, massive table that would remain in the center of the room, and a blanket chest with bun feet in the Jan Martense Schenck House. The architectural details relationship to the use of the space are well illustrated with most items set against the walls and a lone candle awaiting sundown. Courtesy of the Brooklyn Museum of Art, Gift of the Atlantic Gulf and Pacific Company 50.192.

Right: Stair hall in the Nicholas Schenck House as remodeled about 1830. The Windsor chair in English style represents an evolution away from Dutch heritage by the later date. Courtesy of the Brooklyn Museum, gift of the Parks Department, City of New York.

Rooms at Philipsburg Manor, North Tarrytown, New York.

Facing page, top: The bed folds up allowing better use of the space during the day; the gate-leg table was another space-saving piece. The *kas* would contain bed linens; many such cabinets were dowery pieces that came filled with sheets, pillowcases, towels, fireplace clothes, napkins and table clothes. Courtesy Philipsburg Manor/Historic Hudson Valley.

Below: Later English-style fireplace. The chair by the window is from New England, the spat-back chairs are Dutch. When not being used, the drop-leaf table would be pushed to the wall. Courtesy Philipsburg Manor/Historic Hudson Valley.

Top: A *pottebank*, sawbuck table, and New York-style splat-back chair. Chimney is of the later English style. Spoon rack on wall next to the casement window was a typical Dutch household item. Courtesy Philipsburg Manor/Historic Hudson Valley.

Above: A table set for us with bowls, clay pipes, and glasses. The items not in use are pushed back, floors are bare as was the practice, but the chandelier is hung too high. Courtesy Philipsburgh Manor/Historic Hudson Valley.

Above: Room at the Minne Schenck House with New York gate-leg table and Long Island yoke-back chairs.

Left: Minne Schenck House, originally in Manhasset, Long Island, presently at Old Bethpage Village Restoration.
Both ccurtesy of Nassau County Museum, Long Island Studies Program, Hofstra University Research Library.

Facing page: The most typical major piece of cabinet work was the *kas*. Three examples of this essentially medieval storage cabinet.

Top left: Dutch *Kas* circa 1650. Courtesy of the Brooklyn Museum, The Department of Fine Atrs.

Top right: New York *Kas* circa 1750. Courtesy of the Brooklyn Museum, The Department of Fine Arts.

Below: Long Island *Kas* circa 1742. Courtesy the Nassau County Museum, Long Island studies Program, Hofstra University Research Library.

Notes

Chapter I
Historic Background

1. Rodman Gilder, *The Battery* (New York: Houghton Mifflin Company, 1936), p. 3. Hereafter cited as *The Battery*.
2. Helen Wilkinson Reynolds, *Dutch Houses: In the Hudson Valley Before 1776* (New York: Payson and Clark, Ltd., 1929. Republished, New York: Dover Publications, 1965), p. 11. Hereafter cited as *Dutch Houses*.
3. *The Battery*, p. 2.
4. Oliver A. Rink, *Holland on the Hudson: An Economic and Social History of Dutch New York* (Ithaca, N. Y.: Cornell University Press, 1986), pp. 30-31. Hereafter cited as *Holland on the Hudson*.
5. Ibid., p. 34.
6. Ibid., pp. 41-42.
7. Ibid., p. 43.
8. Ibid., p. 46.
9. John T. Cunningham, *New Jersey: America's Main Road* (New York: Doubleday & Company, 1966), p. 29. Hereafter cited as *New Jersey*.
10. *Holland on the Hudson*, p. 67.
11. Henri and Barbara Van Der Zee, *A Sweet and Alien Land: The Story of Dutch New York* (New York: Viking Press, 1978), p. 8. Hereafter cited as *A Sweet and Alien Land*.
12. *Holland on the Hudson*, p. 82.
13. *Battery*, p. 5.
14. Ibid., p. 6.
15. *A Sweet and Alien Land*, p. 131.
16. Cadwallader Colden, *The History of the Five Nations* (Originally published Part I [1727] and Part II [1747]). Republished, Ithaca, N. Y.: Cornell University Press, 1964, p. 18. Hereafter cited as *Five Nations*.
17. David Pietersz DeVries, "Voyages from HOLLAND to AMERICA, AD 1632 to 1644," in Cornel Jarey, *Historic Chronicles of New Amsterdam, Colonial New York and Early Long Island* (Two vols: *Empire State Publications Series*, No. 35 and Series No. 36 [Port Washington, New York: Ira J. Friedman, Inc. 1968]), I, p. 103. Hereafter cited as *Voyages/Historic Chronicles*.
18. *A Sweet and Alien Land*, p. 134.
19. Washington Irving, *A History of New York* (Originally published 1809. Republished, New York: Twayne Publishers, 1964), p. 317. Hereafter cited as *A History of New York*.
20. *The Battery*, pp. 16-17.

Chapter II
The Dutch People in the Hudson Valley

1. *Holland on the Hudson*, p. 87.
2. Bruce Bliven, *New York: A History* (New York: W.W. Norton & Company, 1981), p. 23. Hereafter cited as *New York: A History*.
3. *Voyages/Historic Chronicles*, No. 35, I, 103.
4. *Ibid.*, p. 100.
5. *Ibid.*, p. 114.
6. *A Sweet and Alien Land*, p. 206.
7. Ulysses Prentiss Hedrick, *A History of Agriculture in The State of New York* (New York: Hill and Wang, 1933), pp.45-48. Hereafter cited as Hedrick *History of Agriculture*. Harold Donaldson Eberlein, *Historic Houses of the Hudson Valley* (New York: Dover Publications, 1990), p. 28. Hereafter cited as *Historic Houses*.
8. Harold Donaldson Eberlein, *Manor Houses and Historic Homes of Long Island and Staten Island* (Port Washington, New York: Ira J. Friedman, Inc., 1928), pp. 28-29. Hereafter cited as *Manor Houses*.
9. Rosalie Fellows Bailey, *Pre-Revolutionary Dutch Houses* (New York: Dover Publications, 1968). Originally published: William Morrow & Company, Inc., 1936, p. 170. Hereafter cited as *Pre-Revolutionary Houses*.
10. *Ibid.*, p. 18.
11. *Dutch Houses*, p. 16.
12. *Manor Houses*, p. 31.
13. *Ibid.*, p. 26.
14. *Ibid.*, p. 39.
15. *Holland on the Hudson*, p. 151.
16. "Rensselaer Service Contract," *Amsterdam Notarial Archieves*, No. 1054, pp. 60-65, 67-69 as published in *de Halve Maen*, the *Journal of the Holland Society of New York*, XLIX, No. I, April 1974, pp. 11-14 and XLIX, No. 2, July 1974, pp. 15-16. Hereafter cited as *de Halve Maen*.
17. *Holland on the Hudson*, p. 146.
18. *Ibid.*, p. 153.
19. *Voyages/Historic Chronical*, No. 35, note p. 136.
20. *Historic Houses*, p. 37.
21. Charles Wolley, *A Two Years Journal in NEW YORK*, published in Corel Jarey, *Historic Chronicals of New Amsterdam, Colonial New York and Early Long Island*, Two Volumes: Empire State Publications Series No. 35 and Series No. 36 (Port Washington, New York: Ira J. Friedman, Inc., 1968), I, 59. Hereafter cited as *Historic Chronicals* , or as the primary source as Wolley's, *Two Years Journal/Historic Chronicals*.
22. *Ibid.*, p. 60.
23. Bayrd Still, *Mirror for Gotham* (New York: New York University Press, 1956), p. 10. Hereafter cited as *Gotham*.
24. *A Sweet and Alien Land*, p. 354.
25. *Ibid.*, p. 341.
26. *New Jersey*, p. 36.

27. Reverend John Miller, *A Description of the Province and City of New York, in 1695*, published in *Historic Chronicals* , I, 31. Hereafter cited as *Province and City*.

28. Esther Singleton, *Dutch New York* (New York: Dodd, Mead and Company, 1909), p. 325. Hereafter cited as *Dutch New York*. See also, Jasper Dankers, Journal of a Voyage to New York: 1679-80, Henry C. Murphy, ed. (Brooklyn, The Long Island Historical Society, 1867), I. p. 118. Hereafter cited as Journal: 1679-80.

29. *A Sweet and Alien Land*, p. 19.

30. *Province and City*, p. 37.

31. A. J. F. Van Laer, *New York Colonial Manuscript* (Albany: University of the State of New York, 1939-1964), IV, 420. Hereafter cited as *Colonial Manuscripts*.

32. *Ibid*. VI, 550.

33. David Steven Cohen, *The Dutch-American Farm* (New York: New York University Press, 1992), pp. 16-18. Hereafter cited as *Dutch-American Farm*.

34. *Dutch Houses*, p. 13.

35. *Dutch-American Farm*, p. 21.

36. Shirley W. Dunn and Allison P. Bennett, *Dutch Architecture Near Albany: The Polgreen Photographs* (Fleischmanns, New York: Purple Mountain Press, 1996), p115, note #4. Hereafter cited as *Polgreen Photographs*.

37. *Holland on the Hudson*, p. 34.

38. *Dutch New York*, p. 154. *Journal: 1679-80*UI, p. 136.

39. Junior League of Kingston, *Early Architecture in Ulster County* (n.p.: Junior League of Kingston, 1974), p. 106. Hereafter cited as *Early Arch. in Ulster Co.*

40. "History of the Village of Portchester," p. 6.

41. *Dutch Houses*, pp. 377, 395.

42. "De Wint Digest" (Tappan, New York: De Wint House) I, Issue I, November 1994. Hereafter cited as "De Winte Digest."

43. Journal:1679-80, I, p. 290. *A History of New York*, p. 138.

44. Dingman Versteeg, translator, *New York Historical Manuscripts: Dutch: Kingston Papers* (Baltimore: The Holland Society, Genealogical Publishing Company, Inc., 1976), I, 486. Hereafter cited as *Kingston Papers*.

45. Rita S. Gottesman, compiler, *The Arts and Crafts in New York: 1726-1776* (New York: Da Capo Press, 1970), p. 140. Hereafter cited as *Arts and Crafts*.

46. "A Reminder of Slavery Days," *Olde Ulster: An Historic & Genological Magazine*, VI, No. I, January 1910, pp. 41-42. Hereafter cited as *Olde Ulster*.

47. Joseph Downs, *American Furniture* (New York: The Macmillan Company, 1952), plates 305-306. Hereafter cited as *American Furniture*.

48. Thomas J. Archdeacon, *New York City, 1664-1710: Conquest and Change* (Ithaca, New York: Cornell University Press, 1976), p. 42. Hereafter cited as *NYC 1664-1710*.

49. Esther Singelton, *Dutch and Flemish Furniture* (New York: The McLure Company, 1907), p272. Hereafter cited as *Dutch and Flemish Furniture*.

50. *Dutch New York*, pp. 325-330.

51. *Ibid.*, p. 335.

52. *A Sweet and Alien Land*, p. 291.

53. *Dutch New York*, p. 199.

54. *A Sweet and Alien Land*, p. 292.

55. *Manor Houses*, p. 276.
56. *Dutch Houses*, pp. 369-370.
57. *NYC: 1664-1710*, p. 33.
58. *Voyages/Historic Chronicles*, p. 101.
59. *Gotham*, p. 32.
60. Michael Kammen, *Colonial New York: A History* (New York: Charles Scribner's Sons, 1975), p. 91. Hereafter cited as *Colonial New York*.
61. *Ibid.*, p. 41.
62. *Dutch Houses*, p. 15.
63. *Gotham*, p. 22.
64. *Colonial New York*, p. 294.
65. *Ibid.*
66. *American Furniture*, p. 374.
67. *Colonial New York*, pp. 80ff.
68. *Ibid.*, p. 149.
69. *Ibid.*, p. 293.
70. *Dutch New York*, p. 355.
71. *Colonial New York*, p. 293.
72. *Dutch New York*, p. 54.
73. *A History of New York*, p. 350.
74. Henry Noble MacCracken, *Old Dutchess Forever!* (New York: Hastings House, 1956), p. 12. Hereafter cited as *Old Dutchess Forever!*

Chapter III
Land Tenure, Title, and Valuation

1. *Colonial Manuscripts*, V, p. 808.
2. *Ibid.*
3. "Dutch Material Culture: Architecture," Roderic Blackburn, *de Halve Maen*, LVII, No. 1, Spring 1982, p. 1.
4. "An Historical Analysis of the Bronck House, Coxsackie, New York," Joseph W. Hammond, *Ibid.*, LV, No. 2, Summer 1980, p. 6.
5. *Olde Ulster*, I, No. 4, April 1905, pp. 97-99.
6. *Ibid.*, p. 105.
7. *Ibid.*, X, No. 7, July 1914, pp. 204-206.
8. *Ibid.*, I, No. 4, April 1905, p. 98.
9. *Ibid.*, pp. 107-110.
10. "Madam Brett Homestead" (Beacon, New York: Melzngah Chapter, D. A. R., 1957), pp. 18-22. Originally, from the "Rumbout Patent," *Book of Patents* (Albany, New York) V, p. 72. Hereafter cited as "Madam Brett Homestead."
11. "His Majesty's Council of New-York: Report to the Board of Trade, October 19, 1698," *Colonial Manuscripts*, IV, p. 396.
12. "The Lords of Trade," London Documents: XXVI, *Colonial Manuscripts*, VI, p. 215.
13. *Polgreen Photographs*, pp. 10-11, 14.
14. *Olde Ulster*, I, No. 9, September 1910, p. 279.
15. *Ordinances of New Amsterdam*, VI, p. 15.

16. E. B. OCallaghan, *The Documentary History of the State of New York* (Albany: Weed, Parsons & Company, 1850), IV, pp. 22-23. Hereafter cited as Doc Hist of New York.
17. E. B. O'Callaghan, *General Index to the Documents Relevant to the Colonial History of the State of New York* (Albany: Weed, Parsons & Company, 1861), V, p. 367. Hereafter cited as *General Index/Colonial History*.
18. "The Van Alen House of Kinderhook," Walter V. Miller, *de Halve Maen*, XXXVIII, No. 3, Spring 1963, pp. 7-8.
19. Roderic Blackburn conversation, October 17, 1995.
20. *Early Arch. in Ulster County*, p. 21.
21. "Historical Analysis of the Bronck House Coxsackie, New York," Joseph Hammond, *de Halve Maen*, LV, No. 2, Summer 1980, p. 5.
22. *Kingston Papers*, II, p. 425.
23. "Assessment Rolls of the Five Dutch Towns in King's County, L.I. 1675," John Romeyn Brodhead, *Documents Relative to the Colonial History of the State of New York* (Albany: Weed, Parsons & Company, 1853), IV, p. 104. Hereafter cited as *Documents Relative to New York*.
24. *Ibid.*, p. 103.
25. *Dutch-American Farm*, p. 71.
26. *Ibid.*, p. 72.
27. Jasper Danckaerts, *Journal of Jasper Danckaerts: 1679-1680* (New York: Charles Scribner's Sons, 1913), p. 60. Hereafter cited as Danckaerts.
28. *Dutch-American Farm*, pp. 72-73.
29. *Ibid.*, pp. 102-103.
30. "A Rensselaerswyck Service Contract," Contributor, William E. Westbooke, *de Halve Maen*, XLIX, No. I, April 1974, p. 12.
31. Thomas Cooper, *Some Information Respecting America Collected by Thomas Cooper* (Dublin, 1794), p. 149. Hereafter cited as *Cooper*.
32. *Ibid.*, pp. 150ff.
33. "The First Generation of Van Wycks in America," Philip Van Wyck, *de Halve Naen*, LXI, No. 1, March 1988, p. 6.
34. *Colonial Manuscripts*, II, 633-637.
35. *Ibid.*, V, 196.
36. *Ibid.*, II, 707, London Documents: XIII.
37. *Ibid.*, II, 871, London Documents: XIV.
38. *Ibid.*, II, 875, London Documents: XIV.
39. *Ibid.*, V, 343, London Documents: XIX
40. *Ibid.*, V, 688.
41. *Arts and Crafts*, p. 192.
42. *Olde Ulster*, VII, No. 3, March 1911, pp. 86-89, 90-92.
43. *Ibid.*, VII, No. 2, March 1911, pp. 54-57.
44. "An Historical Analysis of the Bronck House," Joseph W. Hammond, *de Halve Maen*, LV, No. 2, Summer 1980, p. 7.
45. *Ibid.* p. 7.
46. "The First Generation of Van Wycks in America," Philip Van Wyck, *Ibid.*, LXI, No. 1, March 1988, p. 7.
47. *Ibid.*, p. 8.

Chapter IV
Construction Fundamentals: From the Ground Up

1. "Manhattan in 1628," Reverend Jonas Michaelius, *General Index/Colonial History*, V, 368.
2. Roderic H. Blackburn, *New World Dutch Studies* (Albany: Albany Institute, 1987), p. 15. Hereafter cited as New World Dutch Studies.
3. *Polgreen Photographs*, p. 13.
4. *Dutch Houses*, p. 16. Paul Walshe and John Miller, *French Farmhouses and Cottages* (London: Weidenfeld & Nicolson, 1992), p. 26. Hereafter cited as *French Farmhouses and Cottages*.
5. Henry J. Kauffman, *The American Farmhouse* (New York: Hawthorne Books, 1975), p. 6. Hereafter cited as *American Farmhouse*.
6. Michel Lessard, *La Maison Traditionnel Au Quebec* (Montreal: Les Editions De L'Homme, 1974), pp. 108-112, 416-417. Hereafter cited as *Masion Traditionnel*.
7. *Ibid.*, pp. 416-417.
8. *Dutch Houses*, p. 402.
9. Chadlee Henry Forman, *The Architecture of the Old South, The Medieval Style: 1585-1850* (Cambridge: Harvard University Press, 1948), pp. 10-11. Hereafter cited as *Medieval Style*.
10. *Ibid.*, p. 9. Herman Janse, *Building Amsterdam* (Amsterdam, De Brink, 1990) p. 48. Hereafter cited as *Building Amsterdam*. William McMillen, conversation August 26, 1995. Sidney Oldall Addy, *Evolution of the English House* (London: George Allen & Unwin, Ltd., 1933. Republished Wakefield, England: EP Publishing, Ltd., 1975), Chapters I, II, and III. Hereafter cited as *English House*.
11. *Pre-Revolutionary Houses*, p. 555.
12. *Ibid.* p. 260. "An Historical Analysis of the Bronck House," Joseph W. Hammon, de Halve Maen, LV, No. 2, Summer 1980, pp. 17-18.
13. Jeptha Simms, *History of Schoharie County* (Albany: Munsell & Tanner, Printers, 1845), p. 604. Hereafter cited as *Schoharie County*.
14. *Ibid.* Brecknell, Ursala C. and Greg Huber, "Farmstead Siting of Dutch Barns: A Study of Somerset County Original Barns" (New Jersey Historical Commission, 1991), pp. 13, 15, 16. Hereafter cited as *Farmstead Siting*.
15. Elise Lathrop, *Historic Houses of Early America* (New York: Tudor Publishing Company, 1927), p. 324. Hereafter cited as *Historic Houses of Early America*.
16. J. Schipper, conversation April 15, 1997. *Building Amsterdam*, p. 78.
17. Joann P. Krieg (ed.), *Long Island Studies: Long Island Architecture* (Interlaken, NY, Heart of the Lakes Publishing, 1991), pp. 69-70. Hereafter cited as *Long Island Studies*. *Polgreen Photographs* p. 14.
18. Mary Mix Foley, *The American House* (New York: Harper & Row, 1980), p. 33. Hereafter cited as *The American House*.
19. *Pre-Revolutionary Houses*, p. 337.
20. William Grimes, *The New York Times* June 30, 1995, "Weekend Section" C p. 1.
21. *The American House*, p. 42.
22. "An Historical Analysis of the Bronck House," Joseph W. Hammond, *de Halve Maen*, LV, No. 2, Summer 1980, p. 5.
23. *The American House*, p. 33.

24. *Dutch Houses*, p. 204.
25. *Ibid.*, pp. 114, 23.
26. *Ibid.*, p. 91.
27. *Pre-Revolutionary Houses*, p. 475.
28. *Ibid*, p. 22.
29. "An Historical Analysis of the Bronck House," Joseph W. Hammond, *de Halve Maen*, LV, No. 2, Summer 1980, p. 8.
30. C. W. Zinc, "Dutch Frame Houses in New York and New Jersey" (Masters thesis Columbia University, School of Architecture, Planning, and Preservation, 1985), pp. 75-76. Hereafter cited as *Dutch Frame Houses*. "Traditional Farm Types of the Netherlands," Ellen van Olst, *Timber Framimg: Journal of the Timber Framers Guild*, Number 27, March 1993. American Guild of Timber Framers. p. 6. Hereafter cited as *Tradional Farm Types*. E. L. van Olst, *Uilkema, een historisch boerderij-onderzoek*, Two volumes (Arnhem, Stichting Historisch Boerderij-Onderzoek, 1991). I, pp. 51, 142-143, 174, 214, 238; II, pp. 31, 75, 223, 255, 329, 336, 375, 459, 481, 609, 631, 641, 719. Hereafter cited as van Olst, *Uilkema*.
31. *Ibid.*, p. 20.
32. *Ibid.*, p. 32.
33. *Ibid.*, pp. 20-21. G. Berends, *Historische houtconstructies in Nederland* (Arnhem, Stichting Historisch Boerderij-Onderzoek, 1996), pp. 132-133. Hereafter cited as *Houtconstructies*.
34. Stana H. Iseman, personal correspondence July 18, 1995; Robert Pierpont "Knickerbocker Mansion Historic Structural Report," 1990. Hereafter cited as *Knickerbocker Report*.
35. *Knickerbocker Report*, p. 42.
36. William McMillen, conversation August 26, 1995.
37. *Dutch Frame Houses*, p. 21. *Houtconstructies*, p. 134.
38. *Ibid.*, p. 29.
39. Kevin l. Stayton, *Dutch By Design* (New York: Brooklyn Museum, 1990), p. 16. Hereafter cited as *Dutch By Design*. Greg Huber, letter of December 6, 1997.
40. *Ibid.*, pp. 16, 17, 25, 26, 45, 49.
41. Aksel Skov, *Gamle huse pa Romo* (Copenhagen: Borgen, 1992), p. 64. Hereafter cited as *Gamle huse*.
42. *Building Amsterdam*, p. 52. Donald Carpentier, conversation September 25, 1995.
43. Roderic H. Blackburn, correspondence July 18, 1995.
44. *New World Dutch Studies*, pp. 143-161.
45. *Dutch Frame Houses*, pp. 58-59.
46. *Ibid.*, p. 59.
47. Donald Carpentier, conversation September 25, 1995.
48. *Polgreen Photographs*, p. 65.
49. *Dutch Frame House*, p. 60; William McMillen, conversation August 26, 1995.
50. William McMillen, *Ibid*.
51. Donald Carpentier, conversation September 25, 1995.
52. *French Farmhouses and Cottages*, p. 62. William McMillan, conversation August 26, 1995. *Traditional Farm Types*, p. 9.
53. William McMillen, *Ibid*. *Houtconstructies*, glossary pp. 135-141.

54. *Houtconstructies*, p. 13. *Traditional Farm Types*, p. 9. William McMillen, conversation August 26, 1995.

55. William McMillen, correspondence April 1, 1996. S. De Jong, *Zaans Bouwkundig Alfabet* (Wormerveer, Stiching Uitgeverij Nord -Holland, 1991), p. 62. Hereafter cited as *Alfabet*.

56. Donald Carpentier, conversation September 25, 1995.

57. William McMillen, correspondence April 1, 1996.

58. Vincent J. Schaefer, *Dutch Barns of New York: An Introduction* (Fleischmanns, NY: Purple Mountain Press, 1994), p. 30. Hereafter cited as *Dutch Barns of New York*.

59. *New World Dutch Studies*, pp. 60-62.

60. *Dutch By Design*, pp. 16, 21.

61. *Dutch Frame Houses*, p. 63.

62. *Dutch Barns of New York*, pp. 23-24. Greg Huber, correspondence December 6, 1997.

63. Journal: 1679-80, I, p. 394. Lucile Oliver, *Vielle Maisons Normandes* (Paris: Editions Ch. Massin, N.D., 1994), p. 17. Hereafter cited as *Maisons Normandes*.

64. William McMillen, correspondence April 1, 1996.

65. *Polgreen Photographs*, p. 124.

66. *Dutch Houses*, pp. 201, 247.

67. *Ibid.*, p. 357.

68. *Ibid.*, p. 365.

69. *Dutch By Design*, p. 49.

70. Donald Carpentier, conversation September 25, 1995.

71. William McMillen, correspondence April 1, 1996.

72. Jonathan Pearson, translator, *Early Records of the City and County of Albany and Colony of Rensselaerswyck* (Albany: 1918), III, 85. Hereafter cited as *Early Records of Albany and Rensselaerswyck*.

73. *Dutch Frame Houses*, p. 48.

74. Ir. R. Meischke and H. J. Zantkuil, *Het Nederlandse Woonhuis Van 1300-1800* (Haarlem: H. D. Tjeenk Willink & Zoon, N. V., 1969), pp. 530-531. Hereafter cited as *Het Nederlandse Woonhuis*. *Houtconstructies*, p. 111.

75. Roderic H. Blackburn, conversation November 22, 1995.

76. *Knickerbocker Report*, pp. 39-40.

77. *Dutch Frame Houses*, p. 75.

78. Roderic H. Blackburn, Research on the Van Slyke family by R. H. Blackburn at The Albany Institute, 1993. Conversations Fall 1993, and November 22, 1995.

79. A. J. F. Van Laer, translator, *New York Historical Manuscripts: Dutch* (Baltimore: Genealogical Publishing Co.,1974) III, 338-339. Hereafter cited as *MMS Dutch*.

80. Roderic H. Blackburn, *Remembrance of Patria* (Albany: Albany Insitute of History and Art, 1987), p. 133. Hereafter cited as *Remembrance of Patria*.

81. *Dutch Frame Houses*, p. 41.

82. *MMS Dutch*, III, 217.

83. *MMS Dutch*, II, 15.

84. *Dutch Frame Houses*, p. 45.

85. *MMS Dutch*, II, 33.

86. *MMS Dutch*, III, 103.

87. *Dutch By Design*, p. 155.
88. *MMS Dutch*, II, 386.
89. *Dutch-American Farm*, p. 42.
90. *Dutch Barns of New York*, p. 69. Greg Huber, correspondence December 6, 1997. R. C. Hekker, Historische Boerderijtypen/Historical Types of Farm, unpaged. Hereafter cited as *Historische Boerderijtypen*.
91. *MMS Dutch*, III, 63-64.
92. *MMS Dutch*, II, 37, 91-92.
93. *MMS Dutch*, III, 63.
94. *New World Dutch Studies*, pp. 158-159.
95. *Dutch-American Farm*, pp. 27-29, illustration and diagrams p. 90 ff.
96. Kai Udall, *Frilandsmuseet: An Illustrated Guide in English* (Lyngby: Denmark, The Open Air Museum, 1966) unpaged. Hereafter cited as *Frilandsmuseet*.
97. Henry Lionel Williams, *Old American Houses: And How to Restore Them* (Garden City, NY: Doubleday & Company, 1946), pp. 78-87. Hereafter cited as *Old American Houses*. Henry Lionel Williams, *Old American Houses: 1700-1850* (New York: Coward-McMann, Inc., 1957), pp. 27-47. Hereafter cited as *Old American Houses: 1700-1850*.
98. *Early Arch. in Ulster County*, p. 25. Greg Huber, correspondence December 6, 1997.
99. William McMillen, conversation August 26, 1995.
100. *Building Amsterdam*, p. 57.
101. *Ibid.* p. 47.

Chapter V
Exterior Construction Techniques

1. Sydney R. Jones, *Old Houses in Holland* (London, Studio Editions, 1986), Originally published: (London, 'The Studio' Ltd., 1912), p. 38. Hereafter cited as *Old Houses in Holland*. The Amsterdam Begijnhof, an anonymously authored pamphlet on "A Women's Island" p.4. Hereafter cited as *Beijnhof*. Eddy de Jongh & Ger Luijten, *Mirror of Everyday Life* (Amsterdam, Rijksmuseum Amsterdam, 1997), pp. 44, 45, 47. Hereafter cited as *Mirror of Everyday Life*. Pre-Revolutionary Houses, plates 73, 107.
2. Alec Clifton-Taylor, *The Pattern of English Building* (London: B. T. Batsford, 1962), p. 284. Hereafter cited as *Pattern of English Building*. Roderic H. Blackburn, conversation September 15, 1995. *Building Amsterdam*, p. 54.
3. *Pattern of English Building*, p. 282.
4. *Ibid. French Farmhouses and Cottages*, pp. 64, 24.
5. *Pattern of English Building*, p. 290.
6. *Kingston Papers*, I, 258.
7. *Voyages/Historic Chronicles*, p. 104.
8. Alexander Hamilton, *Gentleman's Progress: The Itinerarium of Dr. Alexander Hamilton, 1744* (Chapel Hill: University of North Carolina Press, 1948), p. 39. Hereafter cited as *Gentleman's Progress*.
9. J. V. V. Vedder, *Historic Catskill*, pp. 60, 61. N.p., n.d. Hereafter cited as *Historic Catskill*.
10. *Early Arch. in Ulster County*, p. 24.

11. *Kingston Papers*, I, 258, 261.
12. *Ibid.*, II, 440-441.
13. *Pattern of English Building*, p. 288. *French Farmhouses and Cottages*, pp. 99, 104, 138, 150, 152. Jan Schipper, conversation April 15, 1997. *Old Houses in Holland*, p. 32.
14. *Pattern of English Building*, p. 283. *French Farmhouses and Cottages*, pp. 82, 105, 156.
15. *Dutch New York*, p. 50.
16. A. J. F. Van Laer, *New York Colonial Manuscripts: Albany, Rensselaerwyck and Schenectady* (New York: University of the State of New York, 1926-1932), II 281. Hereafter cited as *Colonial Manuscripts*.
17. *Ibid.*, VII, 184.
18. *Ibid.*, II,. 419.
19. *Ibid.*, 424.
20. M. W. Barley, *The English Farmhouse and Cottage* (London: Routledge and Kegan Paul, 1961), p. 200. Hereafter cited as *Farmhouse and Cottage*.
21. *Pattern of English Building*, p. 262. *Alfabet*, pp. 26, 96. *Building Amsterdam*, p. 55
22. *Remembrance of Patria*, p. 126.
23. *Ibid.* J. Schipper, conversation April 15, 1997, also S. de Jong and J. Schipper, *Zaanse houtbouw* (Zaanstad, Stichting De Zaanse Schans, 1976), p. 17. Hereafter cited as *Zaanse houtbouw*.
24. *Arts and Crafts*, p. 84.
25. *Ibid.*, p. 191.
26. Charles Gehring, conversation April 24,1997. William McMillen, correspondence April 1, 1996.
27. *French Farmhouses and Cottages*, p. 69. Donald Carpentier, conversation September 25, 1995.
28. Hugh Braun, *Old English Houses* (London: Faber and Faber, 1962), p. 89. Hereafter cited as *Old English Houses*.
29. *Farmhouse and Cottage*, p. 200.
30. Donald Carpentier, correspondence January 22, 1996.
31. F. R. Yerbury, *Old Domestic Architecture of Holland* (London: The Architectural Press, 1924), p. x. Hereafter cited as *Old Domestic Arch. of Holland*.
32. *Pre-Revolutionary Houses*, p. 418.
33. *The American House*, pp. 34-35.
34. "Colonial Dutch Architecture," Eric Nooter, *de Halve Maen*, LIX, No. 1, July 1985, p. 2.
35. *The American House*, p. 36.
36. *Maison Traditionnelle*, pp. 430-431.
37. Donald Carpentier, conversation September 25, 1995.
38. *Building Amsterdam*, p. 58. *Remembrance of Patria*, p. 135.
39. *Ibid.*, p. 132.
40. *The American Farmhouse*, p. 38.
41. *Farmhouse and Cottage*, p. 200.
42. *Arts and Crafts*, p. 58.
43. *Gamle huse*, pp. 17, 20, 21, 28, 32, 33.
44. Greg Huber correspondence December 6, 1997. *Alfabet*, p.26. *Dutch-American Farm*, p. 34.

45. *Dutch Barns of New York*, p. 30.
46. Greg Huber, correspondence December 6, 1997.
47. *Dutch Frame Houses*, p. 80.
48. Aymar Embury, *The Dutch Colonial House* (New York: McBride, Nast & Company, 1913), p. 111. Hereafter cited as *Dutch Colonial House.*
49. *Pre-Revolutionary Houses*, pp. 34-36.
50. *Dutch-American Farm*, p. 34.
51. William McMillen, conversation August 26, 1995. Roderic H. Blackburn, correspondence July 18, 1995.
52. Timothy D. Adriance, conversation June 26, 1995.
53. *Dutch Houses*, p. 293.
54. *Ibid.*, pp. 323, 425.
55. *Ibid.*, p. 332.
56. *Ibid.*, p. 303.
57. Samuel Chamberlain, *Domestic Architecture in Rural France* (New York: Architectural Book Publishing Company, 1928, 1981), plates ii, vi, xvi, xxvi, xxxi, xxxii. Hereafter cited as *Rural France. Maisons Normandes*, pp. 21-23, 42, 43. *Roslyn Landmark Society Annual Tour Guide: June 1996* (Roslyn, NY, Roslyn Landmark Society, 1996), pp. 16, 32. Hereafter cited as *Roslyn Tour Guide: 1996.*
58. Lester Walker, *American Shelter* (Woodstock, NY: The Overlook Press, 1981), p. 46. Hereafter cited as *American Shelter.*
59. *The American House*, p. 44.
60. *Ibid.*, p. 46.
61. *Maison Traditionnelle*, p. 209.
62. *Dutch-American Farm*, Following p. 90.
63. "The Voorleezer" J. Wilson Poucher, M. D., *de Halve Maen*, XIX, No. 2, April 1944, p. 30.
64. William McMillen, correspondence April 1, 1996.
65. *The American House*, p. 45; *American Shelter*, p. 46.
66. Donald Carpentier, conversation September 25, 1995. *Alfabet*, pp. 36, 38-39. *Building Amsterdam*, pp. 57-58.
67. *Dutch Houses*, p. 322.
68. *Early Arch. in Ulster County*, p. 30.
69. Donald Carpentier, correspondence January 22, 1996. Roderic Blackburn, correspondence October 20, 1997.
70. *Dutch Houses*, p. 322.
71. *New World Dutch Studies*, p. 155.
72. "Journal of the Esopus War: 1663" Capt. Martin Kregier, *Documentary Hist of New York*, p. 32. Hereafter cited as *Esopus War.*
73. *Ibid.*
74. *The American House*, p. 34. J. Schipper, conversation April 15, 1997. *Alfabet*, diagram p. 81. *Zaanse houtbouw*, p. 16. *Houtcostructies*, p. 111. *Roslyn Grist Mill: Historic Structure Report* (Albany Mesick, Cohen, Waite Architects, 1994), Figures 1, 23, 25. Hereafter cited as *Roslyn Grist Mill.*
75. Martin S. Briggs, *The Homes of the Pilgrim Fathers in England and America (1620-1685)* (London: Oxford University Press, 1932), p. 125. Hereafter cited as *Pilgrim Fathers.*
76. *Pattern of English Building*, p. 57.

77. William McMillen, correspondence April 1, 1996.
78. *Old American Houses: 1700-1850*, p. 109.
79. William McMillen, correspondence April 1, 1996.
80. *Pre-Revolutionary Houses*, p. 487.
81. William McMillen, conversation August 26, 1995.
82. *Pre-Revolutionary Houses*, p. 111.
83. *Ibid.*, p. 23.
84. *Dutch Houses*, p. 328.
85. William McMillen, correspondence April 1, 1996.
86. Helen Wilkinson Reynolds, *Dutchess County Doorways: 1730-1830* (New York, William Farquhar Payson, 1931), p. 21. Hereafter cited as *Dutchess County Doorways*.
87. *Dutch Houses*, p. 422.
88. Mrs. Edwin Cox, *Scarsdale's Heritage Homes* (Scarsdale, NY: Scarsdale Board of Education, 1963), unpaged. Hereafter cited as *Scarsdale Homes*.
89. *Dutch Houses*, p. 354.
90. *Pre-Revolutionary Houses*, plates 24, 37, 40.
91. *New World Dutch Studies*, p. 106.
92. *Pre-Revolutionary Houses*, p. 23.
93. Roderic H. Blackburn, conversation January 15, 1996.
94. William McMillen, correspondence April 1, 1996.
95. *Pre-Revolutionary Houses*, plates 49, 52, 65.
96. William McMillen, conversation August 26, 1995.
97. *Ibid.*
98. *Dutch Houses*, p. 20.
99. *Arts and Crafts*, p. 230.
100. *Dutch Houses*, pp. 193, 371.
101. *Early Arch. of Ulster*, p. 25.
102. Marian Page, *Historic Houses: Restored and Preserved* (New York: Watson-Guptill, 1976), p. 53. Hereafter cited as *Historic Houses*.
103. *Pre-Revolutionary Houses*, p. 23.
104. *Farmhouse and Cottage*, p. 189.
105. *Dutch New York*, p. 41.
105. *Colonial Manuscripts*, II, 769.
106. *Ibid.*,II, 18.
107. *Albany MMS*, II, 136.
108. *Documents Relative to New York*, I, 102.
109. *Arts and Crafts*, pp. 176-177.
110. Berthold Fernow, *The Records of New Amsterdam: From 1653-1674 Anno Domini* (Baltimore: Genealogical Publishing Company, Inc. 1976), VII, 250. Hereafter cited as *Records / New Amsterdam*.
111. *Farmhouse and Cottage*, p. 189.
112. *Pattern of English Building*, p. 206.
113. *Ibid.*, p. 231. *Building Amsterdam*, p. 43.
114. *Remembrance of Patria*, p. 127.
115. *Ibid.*
116. Roderic H. Blackburn, correspondence January 29, 1996.
117. *Farmhouse and Cottage*, p. 199.
118. *Ibid.*, pp. 200-201.

119. *Dutch-American Farm*, p. 45.
120. *Pre-Revolutionary Houses*, p. 23.
121. *Dutch New York*, p. 42.
122. *Ibid.*, p. 41.
123. *Dutch Houses*, p. 21.
124. "The Van Alen House of Kinderhook," Walter V. Miller, *de Halve Maen*, XXXVIII, No. 3, October 1963, p. 8.
125. *Remembrance of Patria*, p. 127.
126. *Ibid.*
127. *Dutch-American Farm*, p. 44.
128. *Remembrance of Patria*, p. 127.
129. *Arts and Crafts*, p. 190.
130. *Pattern of English Building*, p. 221.
131. *Remembrance of Patria*, p. 121.
132. Roderic H. Blackburn, correspondence January 29, 1996.
133. *Dutch Houses*, p. 356.
134. *Pattern of English Building*, p. 208.
135. *Ibid.*, pp. 214-231.
136. *Old Domestic Architecture of Holland*, p. xi. *Building Amsterdam*, p. 45.
137. *Historic Houses*, p. 153.
138. *Remembrance of Patria*, p. 127. *Building Amsterdam*, p. 43.
139. *Old Domestic Architecture of Holland*, p. xiv.
140. *Building Amsterdam*, p. 46. William McMillen, conversation August 26, 1995. Donald Carpentier, conversation September 26, 1995.
141. *Het Nederlandse Woonhuis*, pp. 530-531.
142. Building Amsterdam, pp. 64, 46. "An Historical Analysis of the Bronck House, Joseph W. Hammond, *de Halve Maen*, LV, No. 2, Summer 1980, p. 17.
143. *Ibid.*
144. *English House*, p. 131.
145. Fiske Kimball, *Domestic Architecture of the American Colonies* (New York: Charle Scribner's Sons, 1922, reprinted New York, Dover Publications, 1950), p. 27. Hereafter cited as *Domestic Arch. American Colonies.*
146. *English House*, p. 132; *Pattern of English Building*, p. 328.
147. *Domestic Arch. American Colonies*, p. 27.
148. *Historic Houses of Early America*, p. 333.
149. *Dutchess County Doorways*, p. 25.
150. *Ibid.*, p. 26.
151. *Arts and Crafts*, p. 349.
152. *Ibid.*
153. *Ibid.*, p. 27.
154. *Dutch Houses*, p. 191.
155. *Pre-Revolutionary Houses*, p. 578.
156. *Dutch Houses*, p. 199.
157. *New World Dutch Studies*, p. 16. *Building Amsterdam*, p. 67.
158. *Remembrance of Patria*, p. 125.
159. *Remembrance of Patria*, p. 133. *Building Amsterdam*, pp. 64-65.
160. *Old Domestic Architecture of Holland*, p. xi.
161. *Medieval Style*, pp. 32-33.
162. *Pilgrim Fathers*, p. 173.

163. William McMillen, conversation August 26, 1995.
164. *Old Domestic Architecture of Holland*, p. xi.
165. *Pilgrim Fathers*, p. 34.
166. *Het Nederlandse Huis*, p. 531. Building Amsterdam, p. 64.
167. *Maison Traditionnelle*, pp. 131, 180, 188, 339, 430.
168. Donald Carpentier, correspondence January 22, 1996.
169. Peter Thornton, *Authentic Decor: The Domestic Interior 1620-1920* (New York: Crescent Books, 1984), plate 94, p. 78. Hereafter cited as *Authentic Decor*.
170. *Pattern of English Building*, p. 332.
171. *Ibid.*, pp. 131-132.
172. Roger G. Kennedy, *Architecture, Men, Women, and Money in America: 1600-1860* (New York: Random House, 1985), p. 97. Hereafter cited *as Architecture/Money*.
173. *Old American Houses*, p. 89.
174. *Remembrance of Patria*, p. 132.
175. *Old American Houses: 1700-1850*, p. 88.
176. *Pre-Revolutionary Houses*, pp. 28-29.
177. *Pattern of English Building*, p. 332.
178. *Old American Houses: 1700-1850*, p. 92. *Old Houses in Holland*, p. 98.
179. *Dutchess County Doorways*, plates 59-62.
180. Donald Carpentier, conversation September 25, 1995.
181. *Old American Houses: 1700-1850*, p. 92.
182. William McMillen, correspondence April 1, 1996.
183. *Remembrance of Patria*, p. 131. *Old Houses in Holland*, pp. 98, 100. *Building Amsterdam*, p. 65.
184. *New World Dutch Studies*, p. 16.
185. Jorge Guillermo, *Dutch Houses and Castles* (New York: M. T. Train-Scala Books, 1990), pp. 76-77. Hereafter cited as *Dutch Castles*.
186. *Dutchess County Doorways*, p. 137, plate 24, later examples, plates 33, 39, 40,41.
187. *Pre-Revolutionary Houses*, p. 30.
188. *Old American Houses*, p. 203.
189. *English House*, p. 135.
190. *Pattern of English Building*, p. 311.
191. *Ibid.*
192. *English House*, p. 133.
193. *Old American Houses*, p. 203.
194. *Old American Houses: 1700-1850*, p. 115.
195. *Historic Houses*, p. 54.
196. *Old Domestic Architecture of Holland*, p. xii.
197. *Pilgrim Fathers*, p. 34.
198. *Pattern of English Building*, p. 332.
199. *Old American Houses: 1700-1850*, p. 89.
200. *Old Domestic Architecture of Holland*, p. xii.
201. *Ibid.*, pp. xii-xiii.
202. *Remembrance of Patria*, p. 133.
203. *Dutch Castles*, pp. 15, 39, 121.
204. *Remembrance of Patria*, p. 131.
205. *Historic Houses*, p. 55.
206. *Remembrance of Patria*, p. 27.

207. *Dutch-American Farm*, p. 47.
208. *Dutch By Design*, p.18.
209. *Remembrance of Patria*, p. 131. E. van Olst, conversation April 18, 1997. J. Schipper, conversation April 15, 1997.
210. *Old American Houses: 1700-1850*, p. 205.
211. *Ibid.*, 204.
212. *Dutchess County Doorways*, p. 29.
213. *Old American Houses: 1700-1850*, p. 205.

Chapter VI
Beyond Dutch Thresholds

1. *Olde Ulster*, I, No. 4, April 1905, 105-111.
2. "Esopus War," p. 30.
3. *Ibid.*, pp. 31-32.
4. Ivor Noel Hume, *Martin's Hundred* (New York: Alfred A. Knopf, 1995), pp. 249-250. Hereafter cited as *Martin's Hundred*.
5. *Dutchess County Doorways*, plate 3.
6. *Old American Houses: 1700-1850*, p. 109.
7. *Old American Houses*, p. 172.
8. *Pre-Revolutionary Houses*, p. 573.
9. *Ibid.*, plates 30, 42, 96, 98.
10. *Dutch Houses*, p. 439.
11. *Maisons Normandes*, pp. 22-23; *Rural France*, plates xv, xxx, xxxi.
12. *Dutchess County Doorways*, plates 1-32.
13. *Early Arch. in Ulster*, pp. 62-63.
14. Donald Carpentier, correspondence January 22, 1996.
15. *Dutchess County Doorways*, plates 14, 16, 18.
16. *Old American Houses: 1700-1850*, p. 103.
17. Donald Carpentier, correspondence January 22, 1996.
18. *Old American Houses*, pp. 170-171.
19. *Old American Houses: 1700-1850*, p. 105.
20. *Pre-Revolutionary Houses*, p. 234.
21. *Early Arch. in Ulster*, p. 82.
22. Donald Carpentier, conversation September 25, 1995.
23. *Dutchess County Doorways*, p. 34.
24. *Remembrance of Patria*, p. 150.
25. *Authentic Decor*, plate 16. p27.
26. *Ibid.*, plate 146, p. 120.
27. *New World Dutch Studies*, pp. 144-145.
28. *Ibid.*, p145.
29. *Remembrance of Patria*, p. 147.
30. Donald Carpentier, correspondence January 22, 1996.
31. Esther Maud Dillard, *An Album of New Netherland* (New York: Twayne Publishers, 1963), p. 89. Hereafter cited as *Album of New Netherland*.
32. *Dutch By Design*, pp. 30, 31, 46, 48.
33. *Remembrance of Patria*, p. 150. *De Wint Digest*, II 2, No. 5, May 1995. Roderic H. Blackburn, correspondence May 7, 1991

34. *Album of New Netherland*, plate 86.
35. *Pre-Revolutionary Houses*, p. 476.
36. William McMillen, conversation August 26, 1995.
37. Roderic H. Blackburn correspondence May 7, 1991. *Journal: 1679-80*, I, p. 235.
38. *Dutch By Design*, p. 33.
39. *Remembrance of Patria*, p. 165.
40. *Dutch By Design*, p. 77.
41. *New World Dutch Studies*, p. 176.
42. *Old Domestic Architecture of Holland*, plates 71, 75, 76, 77.
43. *Ibid.*, p. xiv.
44. *Remembrance of Patria*, p. 150.
45. *de Halve Maen*, XXVIII, No. 3. October 1953, p. 4.
46. C. H. de Jonge, *Dutch Tiles* (New York: Praeger, 1971), p. 9. Hereafter cited as *Dutch Tiles*.
47. Pieter Jan Tichelaar, *Dutch Tiles* (Philadelphia , Philadelphia Museum of Art, 1984), pp. 9-13. Hereafter cited as Tichelaar, *Dutch Tiles*.
48. *New World Dutch Studies*, p. 180.
49. "Antique Dutch Tiles Are Links to the Past" Charles H. Vanderlaan, *de Halve Maen*, XXVIII, No. 3, October 1953, p. 4.
50. *Ibid.*
51. *Dutch Houses*, p. 213.
52. *de Halve Maen*, October 1953, p. 4.
53. *Dutch New York*, pp. 54-55.
54. *English House*, p. 62.
55. *Ibid.*, p. 129.
56. *Medieval Style*, pp. 18-19.
57. *American Farmhouse*, p. 6.
58. *Medieval Style*, p. 114; *American Shelter*, p. 47.
59. *Remembrance of Patria*, p. 150.
60. *Building Amsterdam*, pp. 84, 85. *Houtbouw*, p. 22. J. Schipper, conversation April 15, 1997. *Remembrance of Patria*, p. 150.
61. *Dutchess County Doorways*, p. 46.
62. *Ibid.*, p. 36.
63. Donald Carpentier, correspondence January 22, 1996.
64. *Dutch Houses*, p. 106.
65. *Ibid.*, p. 208.
66. *Remembrance of Patria*, p. 141.
67. *Early Arch. in Ulster*, p. 25.
68. *Old American Houses*, p. 208.
69. Donald Carpentier, correspondence January 22, 1996.
70. *Old American Houses: 1700-1850*, pp. 120-121.
71. *Pattern of English Building*, pp. 292-294.
72. *The Poughkeepsie Journal*, August 7, 1994, Section C, p. 1.
73. William McMillen, conversation August 26, 1996. *Building Amsterdam*, pp. 40, 41. *Kingston Papers*, I, 26.
74. Donald Carpentier, correspondence January 22, 1996.
75. "Dutch Architecture Over Wide Area," Walter H. Van Hoesen, *de Halve Maen*, XXX, No. 1, April 1955, p. 5.

76. *Dutch Houses*, pp. 237, 338.
77. *Alfabet*, p. 64. *Houtconstructies*, p. 110.
78. *Dutch-American Farm*, p. 38.
79. *Dutch Houses*, pp. 23, 114.
80. *Ibid.*, p. 91.
81. *Pre-Revolutionary Houses*, p. 475.
82. *Ibid.*, p. 22.
83. *Dutch Houses*, p. 206.
84. *Ibid.*, p. 211.
85. *Dutch By Design*, pp. 18-19.
86. "The Minne Schenck House in Nassau County, L.I.," Martha Ashton Vander Veer, *de Halve Maen*, LC, No. 1, April 1975, p. 11.
87. *Dutch By Design*, p. 19.
88. *Dutch-American Farm*, p. 52.
89. Joann P. Krieg, *Long Island Architecture* (Hempstead, NY: Hofstra University Press, 1991), p. 72. Hereafter cited as *L. I. Architecture*.
90. Marvin B. Schwartz, *The Jan Martense Schenck House* (Brooklyn: The Brooklyn Museum, 1964), pp. 14, 15-16. Hereafter cited as *Jan Martense Schenck House*.
91. *de Halve Maen*, LC, No. 1, April 1975, p. 11.
92. *Dutchess County Doorways*, p. 28.
93. *Early Arch. in Ulster*, pp. 86-87.
94. *Dutch Houses*, p. 305.
95. *Pre-Revolutionary Houses*, p. 558.
96. "The Voorleezer's House," (Staten Island, Richmond Town Restoration, 1985), p. 4. Hereafter cited as "Voorleezer's House."
97. *The New York Times*, July 2, 1995, Connecticut Weekly, pp. 1, 8.
98. *De Wint Digest*, June 1995, II, No. 6, p. 4.
99. *The Poughkeepsie Journal*, May 28, 1992, p. 4.
100. *New World Dutch Studies*, p. 144. J. Schipper, conversation April 15, 1997. Building Amsterdam, pp. 78, 79.
101. "Dutch Gardens in the Hudson Valley," Ruth Johnson Piwonka, *de Halve Maen*, XLIX, No. 2, July 1974, , p. 11.
102. Marie Luise Gothein, *A History of Garden Art* (New York: E. P. Dutton & Co, Ltd. undated c. 1900), p. 230. Hereafter cited as *Garden Art*.
103. *Ibid.*, . 221.
104. *de Halve Maen*, XLIX, No. 2, July 1974, p. 11.
105. *Garden Art*, p. 223.
106. Norman T. Newton, *Design on the Land* (Cambridge, MA: Harvard University Press, 1971), p. 198. Hereafter cited as *Design on the Land*.
107. *Ibid.*, p. 197. *Amsterdam Times* (Tourist Pamphlet: April 1997), p. 12.
108. Esther Singleton, *Dutch and Flemish Furniture* (New York:The McClure Company, 1907), p. 282. Hereafter cited as *Dutch and Flemish Furniture*.
109. *de Halve Maen*, XLIX, No. 2, July 1974, p. 12. Zaanse Schans, p. 21.
110. Donna R. Barns, *People at Work: Seventeenth Century Dutch Art* (Hempstead, NY: Hofstra University Press, 1988), p. 37. Hereafter cited as *People at Work*.
111. Timothy D. Adrience, conversation June 26, 1995.

Chapter VII
Interior Decor

1. "Silence is Golden: A Survey of Hudson Valley Dutch Material Culture," Alice P. Kenney, *de Halve Maen*, LVII, No. 1, December 1983, p. 3

2. *Authentic Decor*, p. 87.

3. *Ibid.*, p. 392

4. *de Halve Maen*, LVII, No. 1, p. 1.

5. *Jan Martense Schenck House*, p. 26.

6. Roderic H. Blackburn, correspondence November 15, 1995.

7. *Ibid.*

8. *Ibid.* "Luykas Van Alen House Inventory," Roderic H. Blackburn (Unpublished) Columbia County Historical Society's Building Committee, 1994.

9. "An Historical Analysis of the Bronck House, Coxsackie, New York," Joseph W. Hammond, *de Halve Maen*, LV, No. 2, Summer 1980, p. 5.

10. "Inventory of the goods of the late John De Wint, August 22, 1796," *De Wint Digest*, II, No. 7, p. 3.

11. *Dutch New York*, p. 89.

12. *Remembrance of Patria*, p. 176.

13. *Dutch New York*, p. 89.

14. *New World Dutch Studies*, p. 151.

15. *Remembrance of Patria*, p. 147.

16. *New World Dutch Studies*, p. 156.

17. *Ibid.*, p. 67.

18. *Ibid.*

19. *Remembrance of Patria*, p. 170.

20. *Pre-Revolutionary Houses*, p. 26.

21. *The American House*, p. 35.

22. A. F. E. Van Schendel, *Art Treasures of the Rijksmuseum, Amsterdam* (New York: Harry N. Abrams, Inc. 1966), plates 148-148a. Hereafter cited as *Rijksmuseum*.

23. *Dutch New York*, p. 89.

24. "Pilgrim Artifacts and Dutch Genre Painting," Lawrence D. Geller, *de Halve Maen*, XLV, No. 3, October 1970, p. 11.

25. *Rijksmuseum*, plate 86.

26. *Authentic Decor*, plates 239, 253, 254, 255, 259, 260, 276, 298, 304, 330.

27. Peter Thornton, *Seventeenth Century Interior Decor of England, France and Holland* (New Haven: Yale University Press, 1978), p. 268. Hereafter cited as *17th C. Decor*.

28. *Ibid.*

29. Alice Morse Earle, *Colonial Days in Old New York* (New York: Empire State Book Company, 1938), p. 126. Hereafter cited as *Colonial Days*.

30. *Album of New Netherland*, p. 86.

31. *Remembrance of Patria*, p. 183.

32. *17th C. Decor*, p. 268.

33. *Ibid.*

34. *Ibid.*

35. *Arts and Crafts*, p. 109.

36. *Authentic Decor*, plate 45, p. 42.
37. *Arts and Crafts*, p. 109.
38. Peter M. Kenny, *American Kasten* (New York: The Metropolitan Museum, 1991), p. 6. Hereafter cited as *Kasten*.
39. *Ibid.*, p. 7.
40. *Schoharie County*, pp. 603-604.
41. *A History of New York*, pp. 137-138.
42. *Dutch and Flemish Furniture*, pp. 194-195.
43. *Ibid.*, p 185.
44. *Colonial Days*, p. 98.
45. *Dutch By Design*, p. 33.
46. *A History of New York*, p. 138.
47. *Remembrance of Patria*, p. 131.
48. *Old American Houses*, p. 206.
49. *Old American Houses: 1700-1850*, p. 115.
50. Roderic H. Blackburn, conversation November 17, 1995.
51. *Old American Houses: 1700-1850*, p. 115.
52. *Dutch Houses*, p. 236.
53. *Remembrance of Patria*, p. 170
54. *Ibid.*, p. 28.
55. *Ibid.*, p. 273.
56. *Ibid.*, p. 119.
57. *Dutch Castles*, p. 90.
58. *Colonial Days*, pp. 105-106.
59. *Frislandsmuseet*, plates 2, 4. 63. *French Farmhouses and Cottages*, p. 148.
60. *Old Domestic Architecture of Holland*, plates 72, 75, 76.
61. *Dutch By Design*, pp. 29, 36.
62. Roderic H. Blackburn, conversation March 15, 1996.
63. *Colonial Days*, p. 106.
64. *New World Dutch Studies*, pp. 150-158.
65. *Pre-Revolutionary Houses*, p. 31.
66. Peter C. Sutton, *Masters of Seventeenth-Century Dutch Genre Painting* (Philadelphia: Philadelphia Museum of Art, 1984), p. 177. Hereafter cited as *Dutch Genre Painting*.
67. *Remembrance of Patria*, p. 169.
68. Luke Vincent Lockwood, *Colonial Furniture in America* (New York: Castle Books, 1957), p. 248. Hereafter cited as *Colonial Furniture*.
69. *Colonial Days*, p. 106.
70. *Dutch and Flemish Furniture*, p. 266.
71. *Colonial Days*, p. 125.
72. *Dutch By Design*, p. 33.
73. *Dutch and Flemish Furniture*, p. 182.
74. "Chinese Porcelain of the Seventeenth Century: Landsacpes, Scholars' Motifs, and Narratives," Holland Cotter (A review of a show at the China Institute). *The New York Times*, July 28, 1995, Section C, p. 25.
75. Felicia Schuster and Cecilia Wolseley, *Vases of the Sea* (London: Angus & Robertson, 1974), p. 17. Hereafter cited as *Vases of the Sea*.
76. Pitcairn W. Knowles, *Dutch Pottery and Porcelain* (London: George News Limited, undated), p. 3. Hereafter cited as *Dutch Pottery*.

77. *Ibid.*, p. 5.
78. C. H. De Jonge, *Delft Ceramics* (New York: Praeger, 1970). p. 11. Hereafter cited as *Delft Ceramics.*
79. *Ibid.*, pp. 11-13.
80. *Ibid.*, p. 3.
81. *Ibid.*, pp. 41, 43, 50, 53, 61. 140. 141.
82. *Dutch Pottery*, p. 63.
83. *Dutch By Design*, p. 37.
84. Charles W. Jacobsen, *Oriental Rugs: A Complete Guide* (Rutland, VT: Charles E. Tuttle Company, Inc., 1962), p. 93. Hereafter cited as *Oriental Rugs.*
85. *Dutch and Flemish Furniture*, p. 180.
86. *Authentic Decor*, pp. 121, 120.
87. Donald C. Pierce and Hope Alswang, *American Interiors* (New York: Universal Books, 1983), pp. 47-48. Hereafter cited as *American Interiors.*
88. *Dutch By Design*, pp. 92-95.
89. *Arts and Crafts*, p. 126.
90. *Oriental Rugs*, p. 93.
91. Ignace Schlosser, *The Book of Rugs: Oriental and European* (New York: Bonanza Books, 1962), p. 22. Hereafter cited as *Book of Rugs.*
92. *Oriental Rugs*, p. 93.
93. *Dutch Genre Painting*, pp. xiv-xv.
94. *Remembrance of Patria*, p. 213.
95. *Ibid.*, p. 214.
96. *Ibid.*, pp 253-255.
97. *Arts and Crafts*, pp. 1-5.
98. *Ibid.*, pp. 14-15.
99. *Ibid.*, p. 130.
100. *Ibid.*, pp. 14-15.
101. Wallace Nutting, *Furniture Treasury* (New York: The Macmillan Company, 1949), p 425. Hereafter Cited as *Furniture Treasury.*
102. *Ibid.*, p. 386.
103. W. Valentiner, *Hudson Fulton Celebration: Metroplitan Museum of Art* (New York: Metroplitan Museum of Art Press, 1909), p. xv. Hereafter cited as *Hudson Fulton.*
104. *Furniture Treasury*, II, note plate 1963.
105. R. W. Symonds and T. H. Ormsbee, *Antique Furniture in the Walnut Period* (New York: Robert M. McBride & Company, 1947), p. 118. Hereafter cited as *Walnut Period.*
106. *Colonial Furniture*, pp. 170-171.
107. *Remembrance of Patria*, p. 176.
108. *Hudson Fulton*, p. xxxi.
109. *Ibid.*, p. xxx.
110. Joseph Downs and Ruth Ralston, *A Loan Exhibition of New York Furniture with Contemporary Accessories* (New York: Metropolitan Museum of Art, 1934), unpaged, item #s 340-341. Hereafter cited as *Loan Exhibition.*
111. *Hudson Fulton*, p. xxxii.
112. *Remembrance of Patria*, p. 175.
113. *Hudson Fulton*, p. xxxiii.
114. *Remembrance of Patria*, pp. 173, 174, 178, 180.

115. *American Furniture*, plate 299.
116. *Hudson Fulton*, p. xxxiii.
117. *Ibid.*
118. *Ibid.*, p. xxxiv.
119. "Dutch Material Culture," Roderic H. Blackburn, *de Halve Maen*, LIV, No. 1, Spring 1976, p. 4.
120. *Remembrance of Patria*, p. 164.
121. Louis B. Wright, *The Arts in America; The Colonial Period* (New York: Charles Scribner's Sons, 1966), p. 272. Hereafter cited as *Arts In America*.
122. *Album of New Netherland*, plate 101.
123. *Loan Exhibition*, p. xxxvi.
124. *Arts and Crafts*, pp. 184-185.
125. Christopher Payne, *Sotheby's Concise Encyclopedia of Furniture* (New York: Harper & Row, 1989), p. 38. Hereafter cited as *Sotheby's*.
126. *Kasten*, p. 31.
127. *Walnut Period*, p. 13.
128. *Ibid.*, p. 13.
129. Marshall B. Davidson, editor, *The American Heritage History of Colonial Antiques* (New York: American Heritage Publishing Company, 19967), p. 109. Hereafter cited as *Colonial Antiques*.
130. " Silence is Golden: A Survey of Hudson Valley Dutch Material Culture," Alce P. Kenney, *de Halve Maen*, LVIII, No. 1, December 1983, p. 3.
131. *Kasten,* p. 33.
132. *Ibid.*, pp. 21, 25.
133. *de Halve Maen*, XXVIII, No. 1, April 1953, p. 9.
134. *Ibid.*, LVIII, No. 1, December 1983, p. 1.
135. *Colonial Antiques*, p. 21.
136. *Ibid.*, p. 218.
137. *Ibid.*
138. Mary Jean Madigan and Susan Colgan, editors, *Early American Furniture: From Settlement to City* (New York: Art and Antiques Magazine, Publisher1983), p. 40. Hereafter cited as *Early American Furniture*.
139. *Hudson Fulton*, p. xiv.
140. *Kasten* , p. 16.
141. *Remembrance of Patria*, p. 166.
142. *Ibid.*, pp. 166-167.
143. *Arts in America*, p. 254.
144. *Remembrance of Patria*, p. 174.
145. *Ibid.*
146. *Ibid.*, p. 173.
147. *Antique Furniture Made In Bergen County New Jersey*, A show booklet (New Jersey: Old Stone Church Antiques Show, 1984), p. 12. Hereafter cited as *Bergen County*.
148. *Jan Martense Schenck House*, p. 28.
149. *Remembrance of Patria*, p. 164.
150. *Dutch Genre Painting*, p. 180.
151. *Remembrance of Patria*, p. 178.
152. *de Halve Maen*, LIV, No. 1, Spring 1976, p. 5.
153. *Walnut Period*, p. 58.

154. *Ibid.*, p 17.
155. *de Halve Maen*, LVIII, No. 1, December 1983, p. 3.
156. *17th Cent. Decor*, p. 187.
157. *Ibid.*
158. *Dutch By Design*, pp. 29, 30, 31.
159. *Arts in America*, p. 265.
160. *Ibid.*, pp. 265-269.
161. *Ibid.*, pp. 32-54.
162. *Colonial Furniture*, p. 61.
163. *de Halve Maen*, LIV, No. 1, Spring 1976, p. 3.
164. *de Halve Maen*, LVIII, No. 1, December 1983, p. 3.
165. *Colonial Furniture*, p. 56.
166. *Ibid.*, p. 60.
167. *Early American Furniture*, p. 94.
168. *Ibid.*, pp. 93-97.
169. *Ibid.*, p. 93.
170. *Colonial Furniture*, p. 171.
171. *Remembrance of Patria*, pp. 160-161.
172. *Ibid.*, p. 159.
173. John T. Kirk, *American Chairs: Queen Anne and Chippendale* (New York: Alfred A. Knopf, 1972), p. 42. Hereafter cited as *American Chairs*.
174. *Ibid.*, pp. 43-48.
175. *Arts and Crafts*, pp. 124-125.
176. *Ibid.*, p. 125.
177. *Ibid.*
178. *Dutch and Flemish Furniture*, p. 255.

Glossary

Adobe Sun dried bricks.

Anchor-Iron An iron pin or spike that passes throuh an exterior masonry wall and holds interior framing beams and walls together.

Achterhuis A separate kitchen.

Baluster An upright, handrail support.

Balustrade A row of balusters supporting a rail. "Banister" is a colloquial form of the word.

Batten The strip of board fastening across the join of two boards (as in board-and-batten siding) to hold them together. Also used to hold pantiles or slates to a roof.

Bead A convex molding along the edge of a board or beam.

Bedsteden Also a *betse*, a built-in box bed.

Bent A Dutch or Continental method of building using a series of H-framed units with two vertical posts and a horizontal connector beam.

Beshieting Wainscotting, interior paneling to the window sill height.

Binnenhaard Also a *binnenkamer*, an inner room or family room with a fireplace.

Bonding Mortared, overlapping in brick or stone work in order to hold the individual pieces together. American Bond: Four to five courses of stretchers to one course of headers. English Bond: Alternate courses of stretchers and headers. Flemish Bond: Bricks laid in a course of alternating headers and stretchers.

Bolkozyn **Windows** Two casement windows side by side with a wooden divider.

Brace Frame An English-American style of house box frame building.

Briquete-en-poteaux Vertical framing with brick infilling.

Buttery A pantry used to store kegs and casks. A pantry or larder for "butts" or barrels.

Cames Also cams, groved lead strips that hold glass panes in a casement window.

Camfer A beveled edge cut diagonally from a corner.

Casten Met Plancken Closet with shelves.

Casements Windows hinged to open in or out rather than up and down.

Catslide A lean-to roof , usually a long sloping roof as on a salt-box-style house, a New England term.

Chamber A bedroom.

Clapboard A wedge-shaped siding board that is laid overlapping and horizontal.

Clinch Bending and hammering the protruding ends of nails over to secure the nail to a surface.

Clincher A bent headed nail clinched to a surface.

Cloosters Kusijins Gothic windows placed vertically above another.

Cob English name for an infilling for timber-framed walls of clay with straw for binding, gravel to stabilize the mixture, and cow dung for adhesion. See *torchis*.

Cockloft An upper attic.

Coping A topping or finishing layer for a wall or gable.

Corbel A supporting member diagonally bracing a horizontal H-bent beam to a vertical post.

Crow-Steps A type of gable that appears to be a flight of steps from the side walls to the gable peak. Also called *pas d'oiseau*, 'bird steps,' *pas de moineau*, 'sparrow steps,' and in Scotland 'corbie steps.' Used in brick buildings with tile roofs or with thatch roofs to hold spars to anchor the thatch.

Course A row of bricks horizontally laid.

Cradle/Crib A wooden structure that holds stones or brick. A below-floor support for a hearth stone.

Cruck An "A" framing of curved members. A naturally forked or bent limb used in the frame of a house.

Cylinder Glass Glass window panes cut from a tube and openned flat.

Deuren Binnen Inside doors.

Deuren Buyten Exterior doors.

Diapering Setting bricks in decorative patterns by exposing the burnt ends.

Dormer A vertical window projecting from a roof slope.

Dry Stone A stone wall constructed without mortar.

Duimen Literally "thumb." The Dutch inch.

Dutch Door Door built in two parts, with a top that may be opened separately.

Dutch Kick A curve to the eaves in Flemish or "Dutch Colonial" roofs, also called spring eaves.

Eave A roof edge.

Eyebrow Windows Upper floor quarter-sized windows at the eave level.

Farmhouse A building that is a house barn combination.

Fireback An iron plate used to protect a firplace backwall from heat.

Feather Edge A taper to a board so it fits into a grove in an adjacent board.

Fenestrall An oil-soaked sheet of linen used instead of a glass window pane

Flying Gutter A Dutch kick. Spring eave.

Gable End wall at the roof level.

Gable Elbow A single step at the base of a straight-end gable, one crow-step.

Gambrel Roof A roof with a double angle to each sloping side. Usually a short shallow slope, then a change in angle to a steep or curved slope.

Gang Passageway.

Georgian Styles from the reigns of Kings George I, II, and III.

Glory Hole Opening in a glassmakers' oven.

Gothic Windows Also *cloosters kusijins* and *kruiskuzym*, framed casements .

Green Bricks Dry raw clay bricks ready for the kiln.

Groot kammer Great chamber, main room.

Hangkamer An upper room with a fireplace.

Half-Lap A rabbeting of two boards to fit together by overlapping smoothly.

Half Timber A method of building using exposed frames and in-filling.

Header A brick laid to show the short end in a course of bricks.

Het Voorhuis An entry hall.

Hogshead A U.S. unit of measure equal to a barrel or 63 gallons, a variable measure up to 140 gallons.

Horse Feathers Very large shingles.

In-filling Clay and a binder of lime (see **Cob** and *Torchis)* as daub pressed into a lath base of wattle in a timber-framed building. Known as wattle and daub, also called *hourdis.*

In't State A back yard.

Jambs Sidewalls to an English-style fireplace.

Jambless A Dutch-style open hearth fireplace without enclosed sidewalls.

Joist A small timber used to support a floor or ceiling.

Kamer A room.

Keuken A kitchen.

Klokgevel A concave gable style typical of Leyden.

Kruiskuzym **Windows** Cross-shaped window frames with four casements. A Gothic window.

Lambs Tongue A type of carved teminal trim on a camfered beam with a curve alledgedly shaped like a small tongue.

Lean-to A roof with a single slope, its upper edge abuting a wall or an extension of one side of a pitch roof, as in a New England-style "saltbox" house.

Lath Thin strips of wood attached to a frame to support plaster.

Leggett Also legget or leggatt, a thatchers' tool to tap reed into place on a roof.

Limewash Whitewash, a slaked-lime coating.

Lintel A loadbearing member over a door or fireplace hearth.

Metal A term for molten glass.

Middelschotten Interior walls or partitions.

Mortise A square hold cut to receive a square ended tenon.

Mousetoothing See *Vlechtegen.*

Muizetanden See *Vlechtegen.*

Mullion A vertical bar or a pier between windows.

Muntin A wooden mullion used to hold panes of glass in a sash or casement window.

Ogee An "S" profile curve used on frames and mantles.

Oysendrop An open space between buildings for eaves to shed water, where an "eavesdropper" would listen.

Pakhuis A warehouse.

Pantiles Roof tiles with an S-shaped flange overlapped and hung on battens.

Pise Clay mixed with water used as an infilling in timber-framed houses. See *Torchis* and **Cob,** another form of infilling.

Post A vertical framing member.

Post-and-Pan Upright timber framing with wattle-and-daub in-filling

Poteau-en-terre A half-timber wall of vertical posts set in the ground.

Pronkkamer A showroom for display and ceremonial uses.

Punty A glassmaker's iron rod.

Purlin A horizontal roof member.

Rabbet A right angled groove, like a step, used to join two pieces of wood together.

Rod The English rod is 16.5 feet in length. Two Dutch rod measurements were used: the Rhinelander rod of 12 Dutch *voeten* (feet) of 12.36 *duimen* (thumbs) or 3.7674 meters; and the Amsterdam measure of of 13 *voeten* of 11.143 *duimen,* or 3.6807 meters. Typically, New Netherland measurements are in the Amsterdam standard unless specified as being in Rhinelander or English units.

Rise The vertical section between two step treads.

Rubble Stone Rough stones used in fieldstone walls or as fill for a cut stone wall.

Schouwe-Kleedt Also called a *Schoorsteen Valletje*, a cloth suspended from a mantle to dress a jammless hearth and direct smoke up into the chimney flue. A mantel cloth.

Secretin A toilet.

Shakes Large shingles.

Shingles Thin wedges of wood attached to a building as roofing or siding and laid overlapping.

Sill A horizontal beam at the base of a wall.

Spline A narrow strip of wood used to fit into the groved sides of two adjoining boards as a method of holding them together.

Stile The verticle board in a frame or panel.

Stoep, **Stoop** A small entry step, a small porch often with a bench.

Strap Hinge A long iron hinge used to support and turn a door.

Stretcher A brick laid long side exposed on a horizontal row.

Studs Vertical framing members between posts.

Turn your paid Kykuit admission into FREE admission at other National Trust Historic Sites!

Credit $9 of today's admission* toward a membership in the National Trust for Historic Preservation.

Receive a $20 individual National Trust membership for just $11, or a $24 family National Trust membership for just $15.

National Trust Membership Benefits:

* **Free** or discounted admission to all National Trust Historic Sites

* 10% discount at all National Trust Historic Site shops. *Please note: Philipsburg is not a National Trust site*

* Subscription to the award-winning magazine *Preservation*

* Invitations to participate in Trust study tours

* Discounts on Trust publications

Your membership keeps historic sites open by supporting the National Trust, the only national, private organization chartered by Congress to encourage public participation in preservation.

Sign up today and receive a **Free Tote Bag.** See the Trust membership consultant in the automobile area of the Kykuit Coach Barn.

*One credit allowed per Membership

Speelhuis Also a *Tuinhuis*, a summer house or garden dining room.

Summer The pricipal beam in an English frame house supporting a ceiling or floor.

Tenon The square projection cut to fit into a mortise.

Thatch A roofing material of reeds or straw.

Tie-Beam A beam that holds a pair of roof rafters together.

Top Plate A horizontal member framing the top of a wall.

Torchis A binding of clay, straw, gravel, and cow dung used as in-filling with timber-framed walls. See cob.

Tread The horizontal "step" of a stair.

Trunnels Tree nails, wooden dowels used instead of nails.

Tuinhuis Also *speelhuis*, a garden house or summer dining room.

Tuitgevel A Flemish gable of convex curves.

Uytlaet A side gallery.

Vlechtegen Edge-laid bricks in a distinctive triangular or braid zig-zag pattern on gables to make them watertight and smooth edged. Often miscalled "mousetoothing" or *Muizentanden*, which refers to raised-edge brick work.

Voorhuis Fore room; *Voorhuis vant grout huis*, an entry.

Wainscot Also *beshieting*, interior panelling to window sill height.

Wattle and Daub A filling between posts in a frame made of wicker and clay.

Weatherboard A wide clapboard without a tapper, often with a beaded edge.

Windbeam A brace for rafters.

Voeten The Dutch foot. The standard, Amsterdam, measure of 11.143 inches.

Vrolijk A work party or "frolic."

Zijkamer A side room.

Appendix

Dutch Colonial Museums and Restorations to Visit

THE HUDSON VALLEY and the greater New York metropolitan area have a number of Dutch historic sites. Recent room restorations are worth visiting *in situ* or as recreated in museums. In addition older museum restorations and historic community open house days enable the public to visit genuine colonial structures; however, the interiors are not likely to resemble an authentically decorated Dutch colonial home. Several locations offer individual rooms or entire houses restored to state-of-the-art period appearance. The following are a few site locations:

NEW JERSEY

Historic New Bridge Landing: 1209 Main Street, River Edge. The museum contains The Ackerman-Zabiskie-Steuben House (1713 & 1752), The Demarest House (eighteenth century), the Campbell-Christie House (1774), and a reconstruction of a Dutch out-kitchen with oven and smoke room.

NEW YORK

Nassau County

Old Bethpage Village Restoration: Round Swamp Road, Old Bethpage. Old Long Island buildings. Mostly nineteenth century, but including the Minne Schenck house, probably the oldest Dutch farmhouse in Nassau County, built c. 1740. Moved from Manhasset to Bethpage in 1967.

Bronx County

Frederick Van Cortlandt House: Van Cortlandt Park at 242nd Street. A Georgian-style mansion built in 1748-1749 for an influential family of Dutch ancestry.

Kings County/Brooklyn

Brooklyn Museum: Eastern Parkway and Washington Avenue. Restored rooms and houses. The Jan Martense Schenck House, c. 1675, restored to 1730, and the Nicholas Schenck House, c. 1775, restored to early nineteenth-century fashion, the best and most to be seen in a museum.

Pieter Claesen Wyckoff House: 5902 Canarsie Lane. Museum. A seventeenth-century Dutch colonial frame residence with later additions, the oldest house remaining in New York City.

Wyckoff-Bennett Homestead: 1669 East 22nd Street. A one-and-a-half story Dutch colonial frame residence built c. 1766.

Queens County

Cornell (Creedmore) Farmhouse: 73-50 Little Neck Parkway, Bellrose. Museum and farm. A 1772 Dutch colonial frame residence with later enlargements and alterations.

John Bowne House: 37-01 Bowne Street Flushing. Museum. An English-style house built in New Netherland in 1661 with the main section added 1680-1690. The home was the setting for events related to the Flushing Remonstrance and the history of relgious freedom in America.

Richmond County/Staten Island

Billlou-Stillwell-Perine House: 1476 Richmond Road. House dated to 1680 with several additions from c. 1700 to c. 1830.

Kreuzer-Pelton House: 1262 Richmond Terrace. One-room Dutch colonial c. 1722 and additions of 1770. American Loyalist Headquarters under General Cortladt Skinner.

Poillon-Seguine-Britton House: 360 Great Kills Road. French Huguenot Jaques Poillon frame house built c. 1695. Enlargements in 1730 and 1845.

Historic Richmond Town: 441 Clarke Ave, Staten Island. Arthur Kill Road opposite Center Street. Staten Island Historical Society Museum. Numerous Dutch buildings, including the Voorlezer's House, built c. 1695, a rare two-and-a-half story meeting house and school. Other buildings with early Dutch associations. A wide range of special programs, guided and individual tours, and workshops are offered.

New York County/Manhattan

William Dyckman House: 4881 Broadway. Museum. Dutch colonial stone-and-brick gambrel-roofed house. The only remaining eighteenth-century farmhouse in Manhattan.

Metropolitan Museum of Art: Fifth Aveune at 82nd Street. One of the world's most presitigious museums. Period rooms and colonial arts and crafts. A research library.

Westchester County

Van Cortlandt Upper Manor House: Oregon Road, Cortlandt. The country home of the prominent Van Cortlandt family, 1770s. Much remodeled.

Van Cortlandt Manor: US 9, north of junction with US 9A. Croton-on-Hudson. Museum. Incorporating an earlier building, the Dutch colonial/Georgian stone residence was built in 1748-1749.

Odell House: 425 Ridge Road, Greenburgh. Museum. Built in 1732 by John Tompkins on the Philipsburg Manor. In 1781, it served as the French headquarters during the last phase of the American Revolution.

Miller House: Virginia Road, North White Plains, North Castle. Museum. One-and-a-half story dwelling built in 1732 and used by Washington as his headquarters in 1776 at the time of the Battle of White Plains.

Philipsburg Manor: 381 Bellwood Avenue, North Tarrytown. Museum. The manor house was built of stone c. 1690, enlarged 1749, and after the Revolution, enlarged again by the Beekman family. Historic house with several period rooms. Dutch barn, grainery, dam, and 20-acre site.

Philipse Manor House: Warburton Avenue and Dock Street, Yonkers. A mostly Georgian residence built 1682-1758. Center for Philipburg Manor.

Rockland County

Terneur-Hutton House: 160 Sickelton Road, West Nyack, Clarkstown. Dutch colonial home built in 1731 and added to in 1753.

DeWint House: Livingston Avenue and Oak Tree Road, Tappan. Built c. 1699 with later eigtheenth-century alterations. Recently restored to what is believed to be its 1780s Revolutionary-era look to focus on the period when it was occupied by George Washington. A reconstructed early Dutch-style kitchen was recently added to the house.

Putnam County

Mandeville House: Lower Station Hill Road, Philipstown. Frame residence built c. 1735 by Jacob Mandeville and headquarters of General Isreal Putnam during the Revolutionary War.

Orange County

New Windsor Cantonment: Temple Hill Road, New Windsor.

Hasbrouck House/Washington's Headquarters: Liberty and Washington Avenues, Newburgh. Museum. The 1750-1770 Jonathan Hasbrouck house has several rooms finished in the Dutch colonial manner.

Dutchess County

Teller or Madam Catharyna Brett Homestead: 50 Van Nydeck Avenue, Beacon. Built c. 1715 but extensively remodeled into the Federal period style.

Mount Gulian: 145 Sterling Street, Beacon: Gulian Verplanck House, c. 1730-1740. Extensively rebuilt restoration of important house destroyed by fire in 1931. Garden and Dutch barn on property.

Van Wyck-Wharton House: US9, south of Fishkill. Built by Cornelius Van Wyck c. 1733, modified 1756. Museum.

Ulster County

Locust Lawn Estate: NY 32, southeast of Gardiner Township. Museum. A 1738-colonial stone house operated by the Huguenot Historical Society.

Hurley Historical District: Main Street Hurley. Ten Dutch colonial houses, most built in the early eighteenth century. Yearly open house day to view interiors (private homes not restorations.)

Kingston Historic Stockade District: Downtown Kingston between Clinton Avenue and Main, Green, and Front Streets. Twenty seventeenth-through nineteenth-century buildings. The Senate House on Clinton Avenue dates to the seventeenth century and is a museum.

New Paltz Huguenot Street Historic District: Three-block residentail area of seventeenth- and eighteenth-century private homes and the Jean Hasbrouck House (Huguenot and Front Streets), New Paltz. Museum. Featured is a jambless fireplace in a 1712 residence.

Columbia County

Luycas Van Alen House: NY 9H east of Kinderhook. Museum. A 1737 residence of three ground-level rooms furnished in an authentic Dutch colonial manner. An important raised gable-style building. Said to be the inspiration for the setting of Washington Irving's *Legend of Sleepy Hollow*.

Greene County

Pieter Leendert Bronk House: US 9W, two miles west of Coxsackie. Museum. Built 1663, 1685, and 1738. Important early Dutch colonial house with an interesting history. Combines both early stone and later brick raised-gable wings.

Albany County

Albany Institute: 135 Washington Avenue, Albany. Dutch room, museum, and a major historic resource center for matters relevant to the Dutch and Anglo-Dutch periods.

Quackenbush House: 683 Broadway, Albany. Dutch colonial urban residence built c. 1736 and now a restaurant.

Philip Schuyler Mansion: Clinton and Schuyler Streets, Albany. Georgian residence of a prominent early New York family of Dutch origin, built 1761-1762. Museum.

Rensselaer County

Fort Crailo: 9-1/2 Riverside Avenue, Rensselaer. Museum. A seventeenth- and early eighteenth-century residence of the Van Rensselaer family, an early restoration of an historic structure, claimed to be the location where the song "Yankee Doodle" was written.

Schenectady County

Mabee House: NYbv5S south of Rotterdam Junction. A ten-acre property on the Mohawk River with a c. 1700 house with additions. It is a fine example of a modest Dutch colonial house in the upper valley.

Stockade District: Schenectady along the Mohawk River. Scene of the 1690 French and Indian attack and massacre. Includes several eighteenth-century Dutch houses and numerous other early domestic and commercial structures.

Bibliography

Addy, Sidney Oldall. *Evolution of the English House*, George Allen & Unwin Limited, 1933, London, republished: E P Publishing Ltd., 1975, East Ardsley , Wakefield, England .

Anonymous. *Zaanse Schans, Woudt-Van Staalen*, 1989, Zaandijk, Netherlands.

Archdeacon, Thomas J. *New York City, 1664-1710: Conquest and Change*, Cornell University Press, 1976, Ithaca, N.Y.

Bailey, Rosalie Fellows. *Pre-Revolutionary Dutch Houses*, William Morrow & Company, Inc., 1936, New York, republished: Dover Publications, Inc. 1968, New York.

Barley, M. W. *The English Farmhouse and Cottage*, Routledge and Kegan Paul, 1961, London.

Barnes, Donna R. *People At Work: Seventeenth Century Dutch Art*, Hoftra Museum, 1988, Hempstead, N.Y.

_____. *Street Scenes: Leonard Bramer's Drawings of 17th Century Dutch Daily Life*, Hofstra Museum, 1991, Hempstead, N.Y.

Berends, S. *Historische houtconstructies in Nederland*, Stichting Historisch Boerderij-Onderzoek, 1996, Arnhem.

Blackburn, Roderic H. *New World Dutch Studies*, Albany Institute, 1987, Albany.

_____. *Remembrance of Patria*, Albany Institute of History and Art, 1988, Albany.

Bliven, Bruce. *New York A History*, W.W. Norton & Company, 1981, New York.

Braun, Hugh. *Old English Houses*, Faber and Faber, 1962, London.

Briggs, Martin S. *The Homes of the Pilgrim Fathers in England and America (1620-1685)*, Oxford University Press, 1932, London.

Brodhead, John Romeyn. *Documents Relative to the Colonial History of the State of New York* (14 vols.), Weed, Parsons and Company, Printer, 1853, New York.

Butler, Joseph T. *Sleepy Hollow Restoration*, Sleepy Hollow Press, 1983, Tarrytown, N.Y.

Chamberlain, Samuel. *Domestic Architecture in Rural France*, Architectual Book Publishing Company, Inc., 1928, 1981, New York.

Clifton-Taylor, Alec. *The Pattern of English Building*, B. T. Batsford, Ltd., 1962, London.

Cohen, David Steven. *The Dutch-American Farm*, New York University Press, 1992, New York.

Colden, Cadwallader. *The History of the Five Nations*, Part I (1727) Part II (1747), Cornell University Press, 1964, Ithaca, N.Y.

Cooper, Thomas. *Some Information Respecting America Collected by Thomas Cooper*, 1794, Dublin.

Cummings, A. L. *Framed Houses of Massachussetts Bay*, Harvard University Press, 1980, Boston.

Cunningham, John T. *New Jersey: America's Main Road*, Doubleday & Company, 1966, New York.

Danckaerts, Jasper. *Journal of Jasper Danckaerts: 1679-1680*, edited by Bartlett Burliegh James and J. Franklin Jameson, Charles Scibner's Sons, 1913, New York. See also, edition edited by Henry C. Mirphy, The Long Island Historical Society, 1867, Brooklyn.

Davidson, Marshall B., ed. *The American Heritage History of Colonial Antiques*, American Heritage Publishing Company, 1967, New York.

De Jong, S., and J. Schipper. *Zaanse houtbouw*, Houtvoorlichtinginstituut, 1976, Amsterdam.

De Jong, S. *Zaans Bouwkundig Alfabet. Stichting uitgeverij Noord-Holland*, 1991, Wormerveer, Netherlands.

De Jonge, C. H. *Delft Ceramics*, Praeger, 1970, New York.

_____. *Dutch Tiles*, Praeger, 1971, New York.

De Jongh, Eddy, and Ger Luijten. *Mirror of Everyday Life*, Rijksmuseum/Snoeck-Ducaju & Zoon, 1997, Ghent.

Dillard, Maud Esther. *An Album of New Netherland*, Twayne Publishers, Inc., 1963, New York.

Downs, Joseph, and Ruth Ralston. *A Loan Exhibition of New York Furniture with Contemporary Accessories*, Metropolitan Museum of Art, 1934, New York.

Downs, Joseph. *American Furniture*, The Macmillan Company, 1952, New York.

Dunlap, William. *History of the New Netherlands, PROVINCE OF NEW YORK and STATE OF NEW YORK To The Adoption Of The Federal Constitution: In Two Volumes*, originally published 1839, republished: Burt Franklin, 1970, New York.

Dunn, Shirley W., and Allison P. Bennett. *Dutch Architecture Near Albany: The Polgreen Photographs*, Purple Mountain Press, 1996, Fleischmanns, N.Y.

Earle, Alice Morse. *Colonial Days in Old New York*, Empire State Book Company, 1938, New York.

Eberlein, Harold Donaldson. *Historic Houses of the Hudson Valley*, Dover Publications, 1990, New York.

_____. *Manor Houses and Historic Homes of Long Island and Staten Island*, Ira J. Friedman, Inc., 1928, New York.

_____. *The Manors and Historic Homes of the Hudson Valley*, J. B. Lippincott Company, 1924, Philadelphia.

Ellis, David M. *A Short History of New York State*, New York State Historical Association/Cornell University Press, 1957, Ithaca, N.Y.

Embury, Aymar. *The Dutch Colonial House*, McBride, Nast & Company, 1913, New York.

Evjen, John O. *Scandinavian Immigrants in New York: 1630-1674*, K. C. Holter Publishing Company, 1916, New York.

Fernow, Berthold, ed. *The Records of New Amsterdam: From 1653 to 1674 Anno Domini*, 7 vols., Genealogical Publishing Company, Inc. 1976, Baltimore.

Fried, Marc B. *The Early History of Kingston & Ulster County N. Y.*, Ulster County Historical Society , 1975, n.p.

Foley, Mary Mix. *The American House*, Harper & Row, 1980, New York.

Forman, Henry Chadlee. *The Architecture of the Old South, The Medieval Style: 1585-1850*, Harvard University Press, 1948, Cambridge, Mass.

Forster, Peter, trans. *Travels into North America by Peter Kahm*, The Imprint Society, 1972, Barre, Mass.

Fuchs, R. H. *Dutch Painting*, Oxford University Press, 1978, London.

Furman, Gabriel. *A Brief Description of New York, Formerly Called New Netherlands*, William Gowans (Printer), 1845, New York.

Gerson, H. *Art and Architecture in Belgium: 1600-1800*, Penguin Books, 1960, New York.

Gilder, Rodman. *The Battery: etc*, Houghton Mifflin Company, 1936, New York.

Gothein, Marie Luise. *A History of Garden Art*, Translated from the German by Mrs. Archer-Hind, J. M. Dent & Sons Limited, London/E. P. Dutton & Co., Ltd., New York, 2 vols., undated (c. 1900).

Gottesman, Rita S., compiler. *The Arts and Crafts in New York: 1726-1776*, Da Capo Press, 1970, New York.

Guillermo, Jorge. *Dutch Houses and Castles*, Rizzoli, M. T. Train-Scala Books, 1990, New York.

Guiness, Desmond. *Newport Preserved: Architecture of the 18th Century*, A Studio Book: The Viking Press, 1982, New York.

Halsey, R. T. H., and Elizabeth Tower. *The Homes of Our Ancestors*, Doubleday, Doran and Company, 1935, New York.

Hamilton, Alexander. *Gentleman's Progress: The Itinerarium of Dr. Alexander Hamilton, 1744*, Carl Bridenbaugh, ed. University of North Carolina Press, 1948, Chapel Hill, N.C.

Hekker, R. C. *Historische Boerderijtypen/Historical Types of Farms*, Stichting Historisch Boerderij-onderzoek, 1991, Arnhem.

Hedrick, Ulysses Prentiss. *A History of Agriculture in the State of New York*, Hill and Wang, 1933, New York.

Hume, Ivor Noel. *Martin's Hundred*, Alfred A. Knopf, 1982, New York.

Huber, Gregory. *Dutch Barn Research Journal*, Greg Huber, 1995, Ramsey, N.J.

Irving, Washington. *A History of New York*, originally published 1809, republished: Twayne Publishers, 1964, New York.

Jacobsen, Charles W. *Oriental Rugs: A Complete Guide*, Charles E. Tuttle Company, Inc., 1962, Rutland, Ver.

Janse, Herman. *Building Amsterdam*, De Brink, 1994, Amsterdam.

Jaray, Cornell. *Historic Chronicles of New Amsterdam , Colonial New York and Early Long Island*, 2 vols., Empire State Publications Series No. 35 and Series No. 36, Ira J. Friedman, Inc., 1968, Port Washington, New York.

Jones, Sydney R. *Old Houses in Holland*, Studio Editions, 1986, London. Originally published 'The Studio' Ltd., 1912, London.

Junior League of Kingston. *Early Architecture in Ulster County*, Junior League of Kingston, 1974, n.p.

Kahr, Madlyn Milllner. *Dutch Painting: in the 17th Century*, Harper & Row, 1978, New York.

Kammen, Michael. *Colonial New York: A History*, Charles Scribner's Sons, 1975, New York.

Kauffman, Henry J. *The American Farmhouse*, Hawthorne Books, Inc., 1975, New York.

Kennedy, Roger G. *Architecture, Men, Women and Money in America: 1600-1860*, Random House, 1985, New York.

Kenny, Alice P. *Stubborn For Liberty: The Dutch in New York*, Syracuse University Press, 1975, Syracuse, N.Y.

Kenny, Peter M. *American Kasten,* The Metropolitan Museum of Art, 1991, New York.

Kimball, Fiske. *Domestic Architecture of the American Colonies*, Charles Scribner's Sons, 1922, New York, reprinted: Dover Publications, 1950, New York.

Kirk, John T. *American Chairs: Queen Anne and Chippendale,* Alfred A Knopf, 1972, New York.

Knowles, W. Pitcairn. *Dutch Pottery and Porcelain*, George Newes Limited, London, undated.

Krieg, Joann P. *Long Island Architecture*, Long Island Studies Institute/Hofstra University Press, 1991, Hempstead.

Lathrop, Elise. *Historic Houses of Early America*, Tudor Publishing Company, 1927, New York.

Lessard, Michel. *La Maison Traditionnel Au Quebec*, Les Editions De L'Homme, 1974, Montreal.

Lockwood, Luke Vincent. *Colonial Furniture in America*, Castle Books, 1957, New York.

MacCracken, Henry Noble. *Old Dutchess Forever!,* Hastings House, 1956, New York.

Madigan, Mary Jean, and Susan Colgan, eds. *Early American Furniture: From Settlement to City*, Art & Antiques Magazine, Publisher, 1983.

Meischke, Ir. R. and H. J. Zantkuil. *Het Nederlandse Woonhuis Van 1300-1800*, H. D. Tjeenk Willink & Zoon, N.V. , 1969, Haalem.

Moss, Roger W., ed. *Paint In America*, Natuional Trust for Historic Preservation, 1994, Washington, D. C.

Newton, Norman T. *Design on the Land: The Development of Landscape Architecture*, The Belknap Press of Harvard University Press, 1971, Cambridge, Mass.

Nutting, Wallace. *Furniture Treasury*, 3 vols., The Macmillan Company, 1949, New York.

O'Callaghan, E. B. *General Index to the Documents Relevant to the Colonial History of the State of New York*, Weed, Parsons & Company, 1861, Albany.

_____. *The Documentary History of the State of New York* (4 vols.), Weed, Parsons & Company, 1850, Albany.

Oliver, Lucile. *Vieilles Maisons Normandes*, Editions Ch. Massin, n.d., Paris

Ottenheym, Koen. *Philips Vingboons: Architect 1607-1678*, De Walburg Press, 1989, Amsterdam.

Page, Marian. *Historic Houses: Restored and Preserved*, Watson-Guptill, 1976, New York.

Payne, Christopher. *Sotheby's Concise Encyclopedia of Furniture*, Harper & Row, Publisher, 1989, New York.

Pearson, Jonathan, trans. *Early Records of the City and County of Albany and Colony of Rensselaerswyck*, (7 vols.) 1918, Albany.

Pierce, Donald C., and Hope Alswang. *American Interiors*, Universe Books, Brooklyn Museum, 1983, New York.

Reynolds, Helen Wilkinson. *Dutch Houses: In the Hudson Valley Before 1776*, Payson and Clark, Ltd. 1929, New York, republished: Dover Publications, 1965, New York.

_____. *Dutchess County Doorways: 1730-1830*, William Farquhar Payson, 1931, New York.

Rink, Oliver A. *Holland on the Hudson: An Economic and Social History of Dutch New York*, Cornell University Press, 1986, Ithaca, N.Y.

Rosenberg, Jakob. *Dutch Art and Architecture: 1600-1800*, Penguin Books, 1966, New York.

Schaefer, Vincent J. *Dutch Barns of New York: An Introduction*, Purple Mountain Press, 1994, Fleischmanns, New York.

Schoonmaker, Marius. *The History of Kingston*, Burr Printing House, 1888, New York.

Schlosser, Ignace. *The Book of Rugs: Oriental and European*, Bonanza Books, 1962, New York.

Schwartz, Marvin B. *The Jan Martense Schenck House*, The Brooklyn Museum, 1964, Brooklyn.

Schuster, Felicia, and Cecilia Wolseley. *Vases of the Sea*, Angus & Robertson, 1974, London.

Shaver, Peter D. *The National Register of Historic Places in New York State*, Rizzoli, 1993, New York.

Simms, Jeptha R. *History of Schoharie County and Border Wars of New York State*, Munsell & Tanner, Printers, 1845, Albany.

Singleton, Esther. *Dutch and Flemish Furniture*, The McClure Company, 1907, New York.

_____. *Dutch New York*, Dodd, Mead and Company, 1909, New York.

_____. *Social Life Under the Georges: 1714-1776*, D. Appleton and Co, 1902, New York.

Skov, Aksel. *Gamle huse pa Romo*, Borgen, Copenhagen, 1992.

Slive, Seymour. *Jacob van Ruisdael*, Abbeville Press, 1981, New York.

Small, A. P. *Historic Buildings in Holland*, Rijksdienst voor Monumentenzorg, 1982, Zeist.

Speltz, Alexander. *Styles of Ornament*, Gramercy Books/Random House, 1994, New York.

Stayton, Kevin L. *Dutch By Design*, Brooklyn Museum, 1990, New York.

Still, Bayrd. *Mirror for Gotham*, New York University Press, 1956, New York.

Strictland, J. E., rev. ed. *William Strictland, Journal of a Tour in the United States of America 1794--1975*, New York Historical Society, 1971, New York.

Sutton, Peter C. *Masters of Seventeenth-Century Dutch Genre Painting*, Philadelphia Museum of Art, 1984, Folio Typographers Inc, Pennsauken, N.J.

Symonds, R. W., and T. H. Ormsbee. *Antique Furniture of the Walnut Period*, Robert M. McBride & Company, 1947, New York.

Thornton, Peter. *Authentic Decor: The Domestic Interior 1620-1920*, Cresent Books, 1984, New York.

_____. *Seventeenth Century Interior Decor of England, France and Holland*, Yale University Press, 1978, New Haven.

Tichelaar, Pieter Jan. *Dutch Tiles in the Philadelphia Museum*, Philadelphia Museum Press, 1984, Philadelphia.

Trefois, Clemens. *Ontwikkeling Gescheidenis Van Onze Landelijke Archetecturen*, De Sikkel, 1950, Antwerpen.

Trotter, Alys Fane. *Old Colonial Houses of the Cape of Good Hope*, Bradbury Agnew & Co. Ltd., Printers , 1899, London.

Udall, Kai. *Frilandsmuseet: An Illustrated Guide in English* , the Open-Air Museum, 1966, Lyngby, Denmark.

Valentiner, W. R. *Hudson-Fulton Celebration: Metropolitan Museum of Art*, Metropolitan Museum of Art Press, 1909, New York.

Van Der Zee, Henri and Babara. *A Sweet and Alien Land: The Story of Dutch New York*, Viking Press, 1978, New York.

Van Laer, A. J. F. *New-York Colonial Manuscripts: Albany Rensselaerwyck and Schenectady*, Vol. I, 1926, Vol. II, 1928, Vol. III, 1932, University of the State of New York, Albany.

Van Olst, E. L. *Uilkema, een historisch boerderij-onderzoek, Boerderij-onderzoek in Nederland 1914-1934* (2 vols.), Stichting Historisch Boerderij-onderzoek, 1991, Arnhem

Van Schendel, A. F. E. *Art Treasures of the Rijksmuseun, Amsterdam*, Harry N. Abrams, Inc. 1966, New York.

Vedder, J. V. V. *Historic Catskill* , n.d., n.p. (early 1920s tour and history booklet).

Versteeg, Dingman, trans. *New York Historical Manuscripts: Dutch: Kingston Papers* (2 vols., The Holland Society, Genealogical Publishing Company, Inc., 1976, Baltimore.

Walford, E. John. *Jacob van Ruisdael: and the Perception of Landscape*, Yale University Press, 1991, New Haven.

Walker, Lester. *American Shelter*, The Overlook Press, 1981, Woodstock, N.Y.

Wallace, Philip. *Colonial Houses*, Bonanza Books, 1931, New York.

Walshe, Paul and Joyn Miller. *French Farmhouses and Cottages*, Weidenfeld & Nicolson,1992, London.

Waterman, Thomas T. *The Dwellings of Colonial America*, University of North Carolina, 1950, Chapel Hill, N. C.

Whitehead, Russell F. *Early Homes of New York and the Mid-Atlantic States*, Arno Press Inc. 1977, New York.

Williams, Henry Lionel. *Old American Houses: 1700-1850*, Coward-McCann, Inc, 1957, New York.

_____. *Old American Houses: And How to Restore Them*, Doubleday & Company 1946, Garden City, New York.

Williams, Hugh. *The Preservationist's Progress*, Farrar, Straus and Giroux, 1991.

Wilson, Eva. *Ornament: 8,000 Years*, Harry N. Abrams, Inc. 1994, New York.

Wright, Christopher. *Frans Hals*, Phaidon Press Limited, 1977, Oxford.

Wright, Louis B. *The Arts in America: The Colonial Period*, Charles Scribner's Sons, 1966, New York.

Yerbury, F. R. *Old Domestic Architecture of Holland*, The Architectual Press, 1924, London.

Zink, C. W. *Dutch Frame Houses in New York and New Jersey*, Unpublished Masters Thesis MMS, Columbia University, School of Architecture, Planning, and Preservation, 1985, Princeton, N.J.

Zook, Nicholas. *Houses of New England Open to the Public*, Barre Publishers, 1968, Barre, Mass.

Index

Purple Mountain Press, established 1973, is a publishing company committed to producing the best original books of regional and maritime interest as well as bringing back into print significant older works. It has published several other titles dealing with the colonial period in the Hudson, Mohawk, and Champlain Valleys.

For a free catalog listing more than 300 hard-to-find books about New York State, write Purple Mountain Press, Ltd., P.O. Box 309, Fleischmanns, NY 12430-0309, or call 845-254-4062, or fax 845-254-4476, or email purple@catskill.net. Visit the website at http://www.catskill.net/purple.